THE SHORT PROSE READER

THE SHORT PROSE READER

NINTH EDITION

Gilbert H. Muller
The City University of New York
LaGuardia

Harvey S. Wiener
Marymount Manhattan College

Boston Burr Ridge, IL Dubuque, IA Madison, WI
New York San Francisco St. Louis Bangkok Bogotá
Caracas Lisbon London Madrid Mexico City Milan
New Delhi Seoul Singapore Sydney Taipei Toronto

McGraw-Hill Higher Education

*A Division of The **McGraw-Hill** Companies*

THE SHORT PROSE READER

This book is printed on acid-free paper.

2 3 4 5 6 7 8 9 0 DOC/DOC 9 0 9 8 7 6 5 4 3 2 1 0

ISBN 0–07–229263–6 (student ed.)
ISBN 0–07–229264–4 (annotated instructor's ed.)

Vice President/Editor-in-chief: *Thalia Dorwick*
Editorial director: *Phillip A. Butcher*
Senior sponsoring editor: *Lisa Moore*
Developmental editor: *Alexis Walker*
Project manager: *Jim Labeots*
Senior production supervisor: *Heather D. Burbridge*
Designer: *Kiera Cunningham*
Supplement coordinator: *Marc Mattson*
Compositor: *Shepherd, Incorporated*
Typeface: *10.5/12 Times*
Printer: *R. R. Donnelley & Sons Company*
Cover image: Hopper, Edward. *People in the Sun.* 1960. National Museum of American Art, Washington DC/Art Resource, NY.

Library of Congress Cataloging-in-Publication Data

The short prose reader / [compiled by] Gilbert H. Muller, Harvey S. Wiener — 9th ed.
p. cm.
Includes bibliographical references and indexes.
ISBN 0–07–229263–6 (student ed. : acid-free paper). — ISBN 0–07–229264–4 (annotated instructor's ed. : acid-free paper)
1. College readers. 2. English language—Rhetoric Problems, exercises, etc. I. Muller, Gilbert H., 1941– . II. Wiener, Harvey S.
PE1417.S446 2000 99–29905
808'.0427—dc21

http://www.mhhe.com

ABOUT THE AUTHORS

Gilbert H. Muller, who received a Ph.D. in English and American literature from Stanford University, is currently professor of English and Special Assistant to the President at LaGuardia Community College of the City University of New York. He has also taught at Stanford, Vassar, and several universities overseas. Dr. Muller is the author of the award-winning study *Nightmares and Visions: Flannery O'Connor and the Catholic Grotesque, Chester Himes,* and other critical texts. His essays and reviews have appeared in *The New York Times, The New Republic, The Nation, The Sewanee Review, The Georgia Review,* and elsewhere. He is also a noted author and editor of textbooks in English and composition, including *The McGraw-Hill Reader* and, with John Williams, *The McGraw-Hill Introduction to Literature.* Among Dr. Muller's awards are National Endowment for the Humanities Fellowships, a Fulbright Fellowship, and a Mellon Fellowship.

Harvey S. Wiener is Vice President of Adult Programs and Community Outreach at Marymount Manhattan College. Previously University Dean for Academic Affairs at the City University of New York, he was founding president of the Council of Writing Program Administrators. Dr. Wiener is the author of many books on reading and writing for college students and their teachers, including *The Writing Room* (Oxford, 1981). He is coauthor of *The McGraw-Hill College Handbook,* a reference grammar and rhetoric text. Dr. Wiener has chaired the Teaching of Writing Division of the Modern Language Association (1987). He has taught writing at every level of education from elementary school to graduate school. A Phi Beta Kappa graduate of Brooklyn College, he holds a Ph.D. in Renaissance literature. Dr. Wiener has won grants from the National Endowment for the Humanities, the Fund for the Improvement of Postsecondary Education, and the Exxon Education Foundation.

To the memory of George Groman

CONTENTS

THEMATIC CONTENTS xvii
PREFACE xxiii

CHAPTER **1**

On Writing 1

Kurt Vonnegut, Jr. ***How to Write with Style*** 12
One of America's most imaginative authors offers young writers the secrets of his success.

Walter W. Benjamin ***When an "A" Meant Something*** 20
An emeritus professor recalls how, when fresh out of the Navy, his toughest instructor, four-foot-ten Miss Garey, taught him how to write.

Amy Tan ***Mother Tongue*** 27
Chinese-American novelist Amy Tan explains how her writing style achieved both passion and simplicity when she learned to value the criticism of her mother, who said after reading her daughter's novel, "So easy to read."

William Zinsser ***Simplicity*** 38
According to this writer-teacher, "clutter is the disease of American writing." We must simplify. In this essay, Zinsser connects clear writing to clear thinking, which, he declares, doesn't appear nearly enough these days.

Summing Up: Chapter 1 **48**

CHAPTER 2

CHAPTER 3

CHAPTER 4

CHAPTER 5

CHAPTER 8

CHAPTER 9

CHAPTER 10

CHAPTER 11

CHAPTER 12

Modern Essays

THEMATIC CONTENTS

Childhood and Family

Social Problems and Issues

Men and Women Today

The Minority Experience

City and Country

Sports, Travel, and Leisure

Psychology and Behavior

Science, Technology, and Medicine

Language and Thought

Humor and Satire

PREFACE

The ninth edition of *The Short Prose Reader* maintains the best features of the earlier editions: lively reading selections supported by helpful apparatus to integrate reading and writing in college composition and reading courses. Each of the twelve chapters presents an essential pattern of writing. In working through the text, the student progresses from key aspects of the writing and reading processes to basic description and narrative, and then to the more rigorous forms of analysis and argument by means of diverse and lively prose models suited for discussion, analysis, and imitation.

New features of the ninth edition include

- greatly expanded treatment of the **writing process** in Chapter 1, including a **sample student essay** that evolves from brainstorming activities to the final product;
- added material on **critical reading** in Chapter 2, with an **annotated professional essay** for analysis and discussion;
- **sample student paragraphs** at the end of all rhetorically-focused chapter introductions;
- a new **annotated instructor's edition.** The complete text of the student edition appears in this enlarged teacher's edition, along with answers to the many questions posed in the apparatus following each essay. Moreover, in the margins of this annotated teacher's edition, we provide approaches to teaching each essay along with background information and numerous suggestions for guiding class discussion. The annotated edition offers carefully structured commentary on each essay, presenting a variety of strategies that should stimulate classroom dynamics and result in solid student writing;

- **two new sections in Chapter 12, "Short Classics" and "Modern Essays,"** which offer prose for further reading. "Short Classics" includes essays by Samuel Langhorne Clemens (Mark Twain), Martin Luther King, Jr., Plato, and Virginia Woolf, while "Modern Essays" includes selections by Annie Dillard, Yolanda Cruz, Tama Janowitz, Jamaica Kincaid, Scott Russell Sanders, and Anna Quindlen;
- **many new reading selections,** including essays by Walter Benjamin, Mary Cantwell, Barbara Ehrenreich, Molly Ivins, William Golding, Vivian Gornick, Kirk Johnson, Robert Ritchie, Jerrold Simon, and Nancy Shute. We balance these readings with favorites from the earlier editions of *The Short Prose Reader:* Langston Hughes's "Salvation," Malcolm X's "Prison Studies," Jonathon Kozol's "Are The Homeless Crazy?" and Judy Brady's "I Want a Wife" continue to offer timely and controversial subjects for reading and writing.

These new features enhance the key elements of *The Short Prose Reader* that have made the previous eight editions such a enduringly popular text.

ORGANIZATION

The organization of *The Short Prose Reader* is one of its major strengths. Chapter 1, "On Writing," is followed by "On Reading," a chapter offering four unique views on the craft of reading by well-known writers. Each of the following nine chapters contains four short essays that illustrate clearly a specific pattern or technique—description, narration, illustration, comparison and contrast, definition, classification, process analysis, causal analysis, or argumentation. Students learn to build upon earlier techniques and patterns as they progress through the book. The last chapter, consisting of ten essays, offers students the opportunity to read and discuss short prose pieces that reflect the various rhetorical strategies.

READABILITY

This is a readable text, and one that has ample representation by many different types of writers. Moreover, the essays, which range typically between 300 and 1200 words, achieve their goals succinctly and clearly and are easy to read and to understand.

The essays will alert students both to the types of college writing expected of them and to the length of an essay required frequently by teachers. The detailed questions that follow each essay can be used in reading as well as writing classes, since they ask the student to analyze both the content and the form of the prose selections.

APPARATUS

Finally, the exercises we have included for each piece are comprehensive and integrated—designed to develop and reinforce the key skills required in college writing. Before each essay, students encounter an activity called "Prereading: Thinking about the Essay in Advance" which encourages students to think and talk about the topic before reading what the writer says about it. Studies show that such prior discussion arouses interest and holds the reader's attention. Each selection includes two vocabulary exercises. "Words to Watch" alerts students to words they will read in context, and "Building Vocabulary" uses other effective methods (prefix/suffix, context clues, synonym/antonym, abstract/concrete) of teaching vocabulary.

To emphasize critical thinking as the main reason for questioning and discussion, we have grouped our conversational prods and probes under the heading "Thinking Critically About the Essay." A section called "Understanding the Writer's Ideas" reinforces reading comprehension. Sections entitled "Understanding the Writer's Techniques" and "Exploring the Writer's Ideas" provide excellent bases for class discussion and independent reading and analysis.

A section called "Prewriting" helps students record informal thoughts for writing in advance of producing an essay. A key exercise for each essay involves a dynamic approach to writing projects. Guided writing activities—a novel feature of *The Short Prose Reader*—tie the writing project to the reading selections. Instead of simply being told to write an essay on a certain topic, through "Guided Writing" students will be able to move from step to step in the composition process. "Thinking and Writing Collaboratively" activities encourage students to work together in groups on essays and ideas for writing. At the end of each chapter is a "Summing Up" section, a means for students to focus their attention on linking comparative issues in the chapter's essays and on more writing topics.

Students and teachers alike can use *The Short Prose Reader* flexibly and effectively. An alternate table of contents suggests thematic groupings of readings. The text is simple yet sophisticated, inviting students to engage in a multiplicity of cultural and traditional topics through essays and exercises that are easy to follow but never condescending. Weighing the needs and expectations of today's college freshmen, we have designed a rhetoric/reader that can serve as the primary text for almost any composition course.

For this edition of *The Short Prose Reader* we enjoyed the support of both Tim Julet and his successor as English Editor, Lisa Moore, who has brought a fresh perspective and calm persistence to the project. We are also deeply grateful for the patient and extraordinary efforts of Alexis Walker, our Development Editor, to make the text even better than its predecessors. We also owe a debt of gratitude to Igor Webb, who assisted us throughout the revision process and produced the annotated instructor's edition.

We wish to thank our colleagues across the country for their support and are especially grateful to those who reviewed the manuscript for this edition:

Kathryn Abajian, Diablo Valley College; Elizabeth Adams, Temple University; Bruce Anders, West LA College; Jessica Brown, City College San Francisco; Zeeva Bukai, Brooklyn College; Daniel Davis, Victor Valley College; Sandra Dutton, New York Institute of Technology; Anthony Gargano, Long Beach City College; Heather Gordon, Clark College; Richard Hascal, Contra Costa College; Scott Hathaway, Hudson Valley Community College; Pauline Havens, California State University Long Beach; Florence Platcow, Gateway Community Technical College; Mary Lou Skarzynski, Sacred Heart University; Jacqueline Stark, Los Angeles Valley College; Karen Tepfer, Bakersfield College; Joel Tibbetts, Rockford College; Paula Bennett, Seattle Central Community College; Elaine Brown, New York Institute of Technology; Martha Childers, Delgado Community College; Ann Clark, Shepherd College; Jennifer Collins-Friedrichs, Highline Community College; Bradford Crain, College of the Ozarks; Carol Dennis, Virginia Union University; Michael Dinielli, Chabbey College; Mary Lee Donahue, Rowan University; Thomas Ernster, Kirkwood Community College; Michael Fisher, South Georgia College; Elizabeth Flores, College of

Lake County; Mary A. Gervin, Albany State University; Sharlene Gilman, Sacramento City College; Elizabeth Green, Union County College; W. Dale Hearell, Stephen F. Austin State University; Kathleen Heilman, Ashland University; Georgina Hill, Western Michigan University; Alberta Huber, College of St. Catherine; Carol Hughes, Ricks College; Barbara Jaffe, El Camino College; Frank Kofer, Cooper State College; Joan Koplow, Los Angeles Valley College; Laurence LaPointe, University of Maine–Augusta; Leonard Lardy, San Bernardino Community College; Marybeth Maldonado, Caldwell College; Patricia Menhart, Broward Community College; Marge Morian-Boyle, Dean College; Jim Mulvey, University of Wisconsin–River Falls; L. Carl Nadeau, University of St. Francis; Miller Newman, Montgomery College; Mark Niioll-Johnson, Merced College; Stephen O'Neill, Bucks County Community College; Arlene Olson, Rowan University; Christina Parsons, Ohio University; Roger Platizky, Austin College; Linda Reeves, Mesa College; Janet Schofield, University of New Hampshire; Robbie Sullivan, Flathead Valley Community College; Ann Tagge, Lasell College; Patrick Wall, Reedley College; and Carroll Wilson, Raritan Valley Community College.

Gilbert H. Muller
Harvey S. Wiener

CHAPTER 1

On Writing

WHAT IS WRITING?

Writing helps us to record and communicate ideas. It is a definitive and essential part of daily human experience. Whether we write a shopping list or a great novel, we use a tool without which we would find ourselves isolated. Without writing we cut ourselves off from vital processes like the expression of political opinions, the description of medical emergencies, and the examination of our feelings in diaries and letters.

Writing crosses many cultures. Whether we consider historic cave drawings or the transmission of fax messages during the Chinese rebellion in Tiananmen Square, we find evidence of the human instinct to communicate ideas to other people.

In the past, writing brought about change. African-American slaves were frequently forbidden to learn to read or write, but some managed to find ways to gain literacy anyway. Their narratives of slave life helped fire the abolition movement. Women in the nineteenth century used writing to advance the cause of suffrage, winning votes with passionate speeches and articles in newspapers. Immigrants struggled to learn English in order to find a better life in the New World.

Writing celebrates human achievement. In religion, in love, in wartime and in peace, in astronomy and medicine and archaeology, in the arts and humanities, writing reminds us of our shared human identity. From the Song of Solomon in the Bible to the words of Martin Luther King, Jr.'s "I Have a Dream," from the Declaration of Independence to song lyrics by Bruce Springsteen or Tracy Chapman, writing helps us to come to terms with who we are and what we want.

What is writing, exactly? For most of us, writing is so familiar that the question seems silly. We all know what writing is. Yet when we try to write ourselves, we may find that asking and answering the question are vital.

Writing is both a product and a process. Writing is, of course, *what* we write: a letter, a law brief, a term paper, an inaugural address. Since it is a product, we must think of writing as having a public as well as a private purpose. While some writing, like shopping lists or a diary, may be meant only for our own eyes, most writing is intended for an audience. In learning what writing is, we need to think about who the audience is, and what the purpose of the writing is.

Writing is also a process; it is *how* we write. In learning to write well, we examine the process of transferring ideas from head to hand. We realize that the actual, mechanical practice of writing out ideas helps us to think more carefully, to plan and arrange ideas, to analyze our vague thoughts into solid words on a page.

HOW DO WE WRITE?

The process of writing is not absolute; there is no one sure way to learn to write well. However, there are some common elements in this process that will help anyone getting started as a writer.

Warming Up: Prewriting

Like an athlete, the writer benefits from warm-up exercises. Usually called prewriting, these steps help a writer prepare gradually and thoughtfully for the event of writing a long essay. Writers stretch their intellectual muscles by thinking about a topic before they write about it. They talk to friends and colleagues. They visit a library and flip through reference books, newspapers, magazines, and books. Sometimes, they make notes and lists as a way of putting pen to paper for the first time. Some writers brainstorm: they use free association to jot down ideas as thoroughly as possible in an unedited form. Others use "timed writing": they write nonstop whatever comes to mind in a set time period—fifteen or twenty minutes, say. Freewriting like this loosens up ideas without the worry of correctness in language too early in the writing process. After these preliminary warm-ups, many writers try to group or classify ideas by making a rough outline or drawing boxes or making lists to try to bring some plan or order to their rough ideas.

Once the writer has a rough topic area outlined, he or she may return to the audience and purpose for the essay. Who will read the essay? What material would best suit this audience? What language would be most appropriate for this audience? What is the purpose of the essay? A thesis sentence is important here. The thesis is your main point, the essential idea you want to assert about your subject. It's always a good idea to write out your thesis whether or not you ultimately use it in your essay.

Often the purpose or intent becomes clearer as the writer continues to think and write. Choosing the audience and purpose carefully—and stating the thesis succinctly—make the writer's as well as the reader's task easier.

Look at the following prewriting by a student who wanted to write about her impressions of a hospital. She made a list of free associations with the intent of using her notes to prepare the draft of an essay.

Roller skating accident
Go to the hospital for tests
My mother drops me off and has to go to work in the supermarket
I'm alone, I never stayed in a hospital before
I did visit my aunt in Atlanta when she was in the hospital and I was there for the summer
Doctors and nurses whispering
Tray drops suddenly and scares me out of my wits
A nurse helps a girl but she pulls the curtain & I can't see
My third grade class wrote letters to one of the children who was in the hospital but we never saw the hospital room
I can't sleep, there's too much noise
The nurse takes my temperature, I have 102 she gives me pills
Nobody tells me anything about what's happening or what to expect they just do things to me
The nurses heels squeak on the floor and give me the shivers
A red lite goes on and off in the opposite room

As she reviewed her prewriting list, the student realized that her purpose was to write about her own short stay in the hospital after an accident. Most of the items recorded relate directly to that incident. She saw that she had included on the list a number of impressions that, although hospital related, did not suit her purpose for this essay. She wanted to write about her own particular experiences, and so she ultimately rejected the items about her aunt in Atlanta, her mother going to work, and the third-grade classmate. With a clearer sense of how to proceed, she thought about a thesis sentence. The essay needed focus: exactly what point did she want to make in her essay? Simply presenting descriptive details might give readers a picture of the hospital but would not make an assertion about the experience. In fact she intended to write about how uncomfortable she felt and how the sights and sounds of the hospital contributed to that discomfort. She developed this thesis sentence:

> I was uncomfortable in the hospital after my accident.

This thesis states an opinion, and so it helps the writer narrow her topic. Yet it is very broad, and some of the details on the list suggest a thesis that could more accurately express the writer's main point. After several more tries, she developed the thesis which includes, as you can see, an error in spelling and verb use, that you will see in the draft:

> There I layed stiff and silent in the night listening to the noises outside my room in the long corridors and watching everything that went on around me.

First Draft

Prewriting leads to the first draft. Drafts are usually meant for the writer's eyes only; they are messy with rethinking, rewriting, and revision. Drafts help the writer figure out what to write by giving him or her a place to think on paper before having to make a public presentation of the writing. Everyone develops his or her own style of draft writing, but many writers find that double-spacing, leaving wide margins, and writing on only one side of the paper are steps that make rewriting easier. If you write on a word processor, you'll find you can easily revise and produce several drafts without discarding earlier versions of the essay.

In a first draft, a writer begins to shape paragraphs, to plan where to put each piece of the essay for maximum effect. Sometimes, a first draft doesn't have an introduction. The introduction can be written after the writer has finished the draft and has a better sense of what the essay is about. The audience will see only the final draft, after all, and will never know when the writer wrote the introduction.

Having finished the first draft, the writer tries to become the audience. How will the essay sound to someone else? Does it make sense? Are the ideas and expression clear? Is there a main point? Do all the ideas in the essay relate to this main point? Is there a coherent plan to the essay? Do ideas follow logically one from the next? Would someone unfamiliar with the topic be able to follow the ideas? Should more information be added? What should be left out?

In attempting to answer these questions, writers often try to find a friendly reader to look over the draft and give advice. Whatever else they may look for at this stage, they do not pay too much attention to spelling or grammar. A helpful reader will enable the writer to see the essay as the audience will see it, and suggest ways to reorganize and clarify ideas.

Here is an early draft of the essay written from the prewriting sample you observed on page 3.

DRAFT

All Alone

There I sat all alone in my hard bed at the hospital. This was the place I most definitly did not want to be in. But because of my rollerskating accident I had no choice. I had to listen to the doctors and go for the necessary tests. There I layed stiff and silent in the night listening to the noises outside my room in the long corridors and watching everything that went on around me.

As I layed there bundled up in my white sheets and the cold, hard steel bars of the bed surrounding me. I could hear everything that was happening on my ward. Nurses would pass up and down the corridor with their white rubber heal shoes squeeking on the white freshly polished floors. The squeaking would send shrieking chills up my spin. Soft whispers were heard as doctors and nurses exchanged conversations. If they only knew how disturbing it was for me to hear these slight mutters. The most startling noise, though, was when a tray must have accidentally slipped out of a nurses hand. The clatter of the tray echoed down the long, endless white corridors setting my nerves on end, I must have sat there shaking for at least five minutes.

Watching what was going on outside and inside my room was no picnic either. In the hall a bright light shown enabling me to view the room next door. As I was peering out my door, I noticed the little red light above the opposite door light flash along with a distantly faint ringing of a bell down the hall. The nurse, in a clean white uniform, was there in an instant to help the young curly haired girl. With a sturdy thrust of her hand the nurse pulled the white cloth divider across the room concealing the two of them in the corner.

Two other nurses were making their rounds when they noticed I was awake. One was in her mid forties, had brown hair, brown eyes and was slim. The other nurse looked slightly older, taller than the first one, had white streaks throughout her dark hair and was of medium build. The first nurse said to me, "What are you doing up at this hour." I told her I could not sleep. They noticed that I was perspiring and decided to take my temperature. The first nurse left and returned with the thermometer. She placed the cold, thin piece of glass into my warm mouth and put her cool fingers around my wrist to take my pulse. They discovered I had a fever of a hundred and two. The second nurse disappeared this time and returned holding a little silver packet with two tylonal aspirins in it. I took out the two white tablets and swallowed them with water. Every so often until the following morning either one of the nurses would saunter into my room to check on me. All this happened in one night.

Hospital visits can be very frightening. Nobody realizes the trauma patients go threw.

After discussing her draft with students in the class and with her teacher, the writer of the hospital essay knew to make revisions. As she weighed her options, she knew that an even more clearly stated thesis would help her readers understand what she was trying to accomplish, and so she revised it further. The thesis from the revised draft appears below:

> I was supposed to be in the hospital to recuperate; instead of sleeping, though, I lay there all night stiff and silent, uncomfortably listening to the noises ouside my room off the long hallway and watching everything that happened around me.

Friendly readers suggested further that the writer needed to fill in more information about the reason for her hospital stay and also to provide more snapshots of the scene around her. If in fact her objective was to portray the hospital as producing further discomfort, she needed to offer more sensory details than she had presented to her readers. (See page 3.) Some readers felt that the writer should better organize these details, perhaps considering the sights and the sounds separately or pointing out first the activity in the room and then the activity in the hallway, both places apparently contributing to the writer's unhappiness. And to improve the coherence of the essay, the writer knew that in revising she should look carefully at sentence transitions, particularly from paragraph to paragraph.

Several readers felt that the conclusion was flat and that somehow the writer had to figure out a way to raise the issue of the hospital's indifference to her discomfort. It was not enough to record the unpleasantness; she also wanted to recommend some ways hospitals could avoid distressing their patients, and she decided that the conclusion might be a good place to raise those issues.

Errors distracted readers even at the draft stage. These included the sentence fragment on lines 7 and 8 and the comma splice on line 17. Some spelling, usage, and grammar errors needed attention—*layed* in line 7 (the correct verb form needed here is *lay*) and *squeeking* for *squeaking* in line 10, for example. The use of the passive voice in line 13 does not help the descriptive and narrative flow, and the writer knew to change the passive to active as she revised. Simply by revising sentences some errors vanish and others appear, and attentive writers know that a careful editing prior to producing the final draft is critical.

Additional Drafts

After getting responses from a reader, the writer begins the second draft. And the third. And maybe the fourth. No one can predict how many drafts are necessary for a final essay, but very few writers get by with fewer than two or three drafts. Revision usually involves working first on the clear expression of ideas and later on revision for spelling, grammatical correctness, and good sentence structure.

Here is a revised draft of the essay "All Alone." Note the comments in the margin.

REVISED DRAFT

All Alone

Introductory paragraph: fills in accident details; leads comfortably to the thesis.

Thesis: last sentence of the first paragraph.

I spent a long, unpleasant weekend in a bed at University Hospital, the result of a bad roller skating accident I had one Saturday afternoon last October. There might be a concussion; there might he broken bones—and so I had no choice but to listen to the doctors and go for necessary tests. I was supposed to be in the hospital to recuperate; instead of sleeping, though, I lay there all night, stiff and silent, uncomfortably listening to the noises outside my room off the long hallway and watching everything that happened around me.

Concrete sensory details ("white sheets," "cold steel bars," "rubber heels squeaking," etc.): heighten readers' awareness of hospital room scene.

Frustration at disturbing room noises now clear; readers perceive essay's unity with repeated references to sounds.

"Perhaps the most startling noise"—effective link to thesis.

Bundled up in my white sheets and surrounded by the cold steel bars of my bed I heard every little sound in my ward all night long. Nurses, their rubber heels squeaking on the freshly polished floors, passed up and down the corridor. I heard soft whispers as one doctor in a green shirt spoke to two orderlies leaning against the wall with their arms folded. Occasionally one of them would laugh and the other two would giggle and say, "Sh! Sh!" If they only knew how disturbing it was for me to hear their muttering! At one point I almost shouted "Would you all get out of here!" but I didn't have the courage, and I pulled the blanket over my head instead. Perhaps the most startling noise, though, was the sound of a tray that must have accidentally slipped out of a nurse's hand far beyond my view. I jumped up as the clatter echoed down the long, endless white corridors, setting my nerves on end.

Perspiration streaming down my face, I must have sat there in my bed shaking for at least five minutes.

All the noises aside, watching the activity outside and inside my room disturbed me, too. Across the hall a little red light above the door of the opposite room suddenly flashed on and off. A nurse in a clean white uniform was there in an instant to help a young, curly haired girl twisting and crying on her bed. A bright light in the hall enabled me to see the actions clearly. With a sturdy thrust of her hand the nurse pulled the white cloth divider across the room, concealing the two of them in the corner. However, I saw the nurse's shadow moving up and down, back and forth, until the child quieted down.

Soon after I noted all this, two other nurses making their rounds saw that I was still awake. One, a slim woman in her mid forties with brown eyes, said in a loud voice, "What are you doing up at this hour, dear? It's after two AM." When I said I couldn't sleep, they saw how clammy I was, and the one who spoke to me rushed off for a thermometer. Placing the rigid glass rod in my mouth, she took my pulse with cool fingers at my wrist. "A hundred and two," she said. "Wanda, bring this girl something for her fever." The second nurse disappeared this time and returned holding a silver packet of Tylenol, and I swallowed the pills with water from the drinking glass on my bedstand. Every so often until morning one of the nurses would saunter in, touch my brow, and make cheerful but noisy conversation. I knew they were trying to help, but all this activity did not make me feel any better. It made me feel worse.

Because hospital stays can be very frightening, hospital employees must realize

Transition from paragraph 2 to paragraph 3: "All the noises aside" links the topic of paragraph 3 to the topic of paragraph 2 and to the thesis.

"watching the activity outside and inside my room disturbed me too": words set the topic of the next part of the essay.

Concrete sensory detail holds readers' interest and brings scene to life: "red light above the door"; "clean white uniform"; curly haired girl twisting and crying on her bed"; "nurse's shadow moving up and down, back and forth."

Clear connection to previous paragraph; "Soon after I noted all this" provides transition, helping to build essay's coherence.

Nurses' spoken words add life to the essay.

Short, succinct final sentence very effective in this paragraph.

Conclusion adds depth to the essay; it places narrative and descriptive details in a larger, more profound framework.

> the trauma patients go through just lying in their beds wondering what will happen to them next. The slightest sound, the barest visible action magnifies a million times in a tense person's mind. Couldn't the admitting clerk, a floor nurse, or an intern explain to patients about what to expect at the hospital? I would have liked knowing all about the tests I'd have to go through, but also would have liked knowing not to expect much sleep. If I knew in advance of all the noise and activity I might have relaxed.

We call attention particularly to the greatly improved last paragraph in the revised draft, the writer's conclusion. This is no mere restatement of the topic. The writer has used the experience that she revealed in the rest of the essay to establish a new context for the topic. What did her unpleasant stay in University Hospital tell her? Hospitals don't realize the trauma even a short stay can produce in a patient, and if only hospital staff would explain what to expect in advance, patients might not have such a rough time. We can see how the body paragraphs lead her to reach this conclusion and feel satisfied that the writer has led us to new insights based on her experiences.

Throughout the revised essay, the writer has tightened her sentences by combining a number of them and by eliminating unnecessary words and phrases. In addition, we note a reduction of distracting errors in sentence structure and spelling. Efforts to eliminate errors and improve language and sentences will continue as the writer moves toward producing a final draft and formally edits her paper.

Final Draft

The final draft is intended for public, rather than private, reading. It must be the writer's best effort. Most editors and teachers require final drafts to be double-spaced, neatly written or typed with wide margins, and clearly identified with the writer's name, the date, and information to locate the writer (such as class code or home address). The four writers in this chapter represent a variety of approaches to both the inspiration and the craft of writing. Kurt Vonnegut, Jr., for instance, sees style as the defining essence of good writing. Walter Benjamin recalls a college English teacher who set him on the road to good writing. Amy Tan finds her writer's voice when she realizes that her mother is the ideal audience. Like William Zinsser pleading for the preciseness that comes only with simplicity, Tan advises us to aim for direct and simple language instead of academic jargon or pretentious style.

The four writers represented here also introduce expository techniques discussed in subsequent chapters. Careful examination of their sources of inspiration *and* their revelations about the nuts and bolts of how to get the writing done prepares the way for later chapters and writing assignments.

Finally, though the Internet and CD-ROMs increasingly replace the printed page, the basic medium of communication is still words. Whether we scratch them onto stone tablets, draw them on parchment with turkey feathers, or type them into a computer, we still use words. Without writing, we risk the loss of our political freedom and our personal history. With words, we pass ideas and values on from one generation to the next. The words of Henry Miller will always ring true: "Writing, like life itself, is a voyage of discovery."

This brief overview sketches in some of the important steps in the writing process. But you don't want to lose the idea that writing is a process both of inspiration and of craft. Many writers have tried to explain how the two connect in their own particular efforts to create. The novelist and short story writer Katherine Anne Porter, for example, tells how inspiration becomes communication in her writing: "Now and again thousands of memories converge, harmonize, and arrange themselves around a central idea in a coherent form, and I write. . . ." Jean Cocteau, the playwright, asserts the need to shape inspiration into language for a page of writing: "To write, to conquer ink and paper, accumulate letters and paragraphs, divide them with periods and commas, is a different matter from carrying around the dream of a play or a book." The point made by Porter and Cocteau is that writing emerges from both creativity and skill, instruction and technique, talent and effort. As we said, writing is a process *and* craft.

How to Write with Style

Kurt Vonnegut, Jr.

Kurt Vonnegut, born in 1922, is one of America's most imaginative writers. He is best known for his biting political satire in such novels as *Slaughterhouse-Five* and *Breakfast of Champions.* He has also published nearly a hundred short stories. In this selection he offers young writers some secrets of his success.

PREREADING: THINKING ABOUT THE ESSAY IN ADVANCE

What are your thoughts about "writing with style"? What does the phrase mean? What qualities of writing do you admire? What qualities of writing do you not admire?

Words to Watch

piquant (par. 10) pleasantly disturbing
galvanized (par. 10) to coat
locutions (par. 11) speaking style
higgledy-piggledy (par. 15) in disorder or confusion
egalitarian (par. 20) equal rights for all citizens
aristocrat (par. 20) member of the nobility

Newspaper reporters and technical writers are trained to reveal almost nothing about themselves in their writings. This makes them freaks in the world of writers, since almost all of the other ink-stained wretches in that world reveal a lot about themselves to readers. We call these revelations, accidental and intentional, elements of literary style. 1

These revelations are fascinating to us as readers. They tell us what sort of person it is with whom we are spending time. Does the writer sound ignorant or informed, crazy or sane, stupid or bright, crooked or honest, humorless or playful—? And on and on. 2

When you yourself put words on paper, remember that the most damning revelation you can make about yourself is that you 3 do not know what is interesting and what is not. Don't you yourself like or dislike writers mainly for what they choose to show you or make you think about? Did you ever admire an empty-headed writer for his or her mastery of the language? No.

4 So your own winning literary style must begin with interesting ideas in your head. Find a subject you care about and which you in your heart feel others should care about. It is this genuine caring, and not your games with language, which will be the most compelling and seductive element in your style.

5 I am not urging you to write a novel, by the way—although I would not be sorry if you wrote one, provided you genuinely cared about something. A petition to the mayor about a pothole in front of your house or a love letter to the girl next door will do.

6 Do not ramble, though.

7 As for your use of language: Remember that two great masters of our language, William Shakespeare and James Joyce, wrote sentences which were almost childlike when their subjects were most profound. "To be or not to be?" asks Shakespeare's Hamlet. The longest word is three letters long. Joyce, when he was frisky, could put together a sentence as intricate and glittering as a necklace for Cleopatra, but my favorite sentence in his short story "Eveline" is this one: "She was tired." At that point in the story, no other words could break the heart of a reader as those words do.

8 Simplicity of language is not only reputable, but perhaps even sacred. The Bible opens with a sentence well within the writing skills of a lively fourteen-year-old: "In the beginning God created the heavens and the earth."

9 It may be that you, too, are capable of making necklaces for Cleopatra, so to speak. But your eloquence should be the servant of the ideas in your head. Your rule might be this: If a sentence no matter how excellent, does not illuminate my subject in some new and useful way, scratch it out. Here is the same rule paraphrased to apply to storytelling, to fiction: Never include a sentence which does not either remark on character or advance the action.

10 The writing style which is most natural for you is bound to echo speech you heard when a child. English was the novelist Joseph Conrad's third language, and much that seems piquant in his use of English was no doubt colored by his first language, which was Polish. And lucky indeed is the writer who has grown up in Ireland, for the English spoken there is so amusing and musical. I myself grew up in Indianapolis, Indiana, where common

speech sounds like a band saw cutting galvanized tin, and employs a vocabulary as unornamental as a monkey wrench.

In some of the more remote hollows of Appalachia, children still grow up hearing songs and locutions of Elizabethan times. Yes, and many Americans grow up hearing a language other than English, or an English dialect a majority of Americans cannot understand. 11

All these varieties of speech are beautiful, just as the varieties of butterflies are beautiful. No matter what your first language, you should treasure it all your life. If it happens not to be standard English, and if it shows itself when you write standard English, the result is usually delightful, like a very pretty girl with one eye that is green and one that is blue. 12

I myself find that I trust my own writing most, and others seem to trust it most, too, when I sound most like a person from Indianapolis, which is what I am. What alternatives do I have? The one most vehemently recommended by teachers has no doubt been pressed on you, as well: that I write like cultivated Englishmen of a century or more ago. 13

I used to be exasperated by such teachers, but am no more. I understand now that all those antique essays and stories with which I was to compare my own work were not magnificent for their datedness or foreignness, but for saying precisely what their authors meant them to say. My teachers wished me to write accurately, always selecting the most effective words, and relating the words to one another unambiguously, rigidly, like parts of a machine. The teachers did not want to turn me into an Englishman after all. They hoped that I would become understandable—and therefore understood. 14

And there went my dream of doing with words what Pablo Picasso did with paint or what any number of jazz idols did with music. If I broke all the rules of punctuation, had words mean whatever I wanted them to mean, and strung them together higgledy-piggledy, I would simply not be understood. So you, too, had better avoid Picasso-style or jazz-style writing, if you have something worth saying and wish to be understood. 15

If it were only teachers who insisted that modern writers stay close to literary styles of the past, we might reasonably ignore them. But readers insist on the very same thing. They want our pages to look very much like pages they have seen before. 16

Why? It is because they themselves have a tough job to do, and they need all the help they can get from us. They have to 17 identify thousands of little marks on paper, and make sense of them immediately. They have to *read,* an art so difficult that most people do not really master it even after having studied it all through grade school and high school—for twelve long years.

18 So this discussion, like all discussions of literary styles, must finally acknowledge that our stylistic options as writers are neither numerous nor glamorous, since our readers are bound to be such imperfect artists. Our audience requires us to be sympathetic and patient teachers, ever willing to simplify and clarify—whereas we would rather soar high above the crowd, singing like nightingales.

19 That is the bad news. The good news is that we Americans are governed under a unique Constitution, which allows us to write whatever we please without fear of punishment. So the most meaningful aspect of our styles, which is what we choose to write about, is unlimited.

20 Also: We are members of an egalitarian society, so there is no reason for us to write, in case we are not classically educated aristocrats, as though we were classically educated aristocrats.

21 For a discussion of literary style in a narrower sense, in a more technical sense, I commend to your attention *The Elements of Style* by William Strunk, Jr., and E. B. White (Macmillan, 1979). It contains such rules as this: "A participial phrase at the beginning of a sentence must refer to the grammatical subject," and so on. E. B. White is, of course, one of the most admirable literary stylists this country has so far produced.

22 You should realize, too, that no one would care how well or badly Mr. White expressed himself, if he did not have perfectly enchanting things to say.

BUILDING VOCABULARY

Use *context clues* (see Glossary) to determine the meanings of the words below. Use a dictionary to check your definitions.

a. intentional (par. 1)
b. compelling (par. 4)
c. intricate (par. 7)
d. reputable (par. 8)
e. eloquence (par. 9)
f. illuminate (par. 9)
g. exasperated (par. 14)

THINKING CRITICALLY ABOUT THE ESSAY

Understanding the Writer's Ideas

1. What is the difference between newspaper reporters and technical writers and the "ink-stained wretches," as Vonnegut puts it?
2. According to the writer, what is the best way to begin a "winning literary style" (par. 4)?
3. Why does Vonnegut believe that simple writing is best, and how does he try to prove his point?
4. What is the writer's attitude toward standard language versus the language "you heard when a child" (par. 10)?
5. For Vonnegut, writers should avoid "jazz-style" writing. Why?
6. How does the writer come to the conclusion that reading is "an art so difficult that most people do not really master it" (par. 17)?
7. Why does Vonnegut say it is good news that writers in America are "governed under a unique Constitution" (par. 19)?
8. What is the benefit of being a writer in an "egalitarian society" as opposed to an "aristocratic" one, according to Vonnegut (par. 20)?

Understanding the Writer's Techniques

1. What is the thesis of this essay? Who is Vonnegut's audience here? How can you tell?
2. Why does Vonnegut begin his essay with references to newspaper reporters and technical writers if he does not mention them in the rest of text?
3. Why is the *transition* (see Glossary) at the beginning of paragraph 3 effective, given the title of this essay?
4. Vonnegut suggests that writers use sentences that are almost "childlike." How can you tell that he follows his own advice?
5. What purpose does using direct quotes from William Shakespeare and James Joyce serve?
6. What is the effect of Vonnegut's switching to the first person in paragraph 13, pointing to the Indianapolis speech in his own writing?
7. How does the question "Why?" (par. 17) serve as a clear shift in the idea development of the essay?

8. The word "Also" in paragraph 20 is followed by a colon to signal a transition. Check a grammar handbook. Is this the way transitions should be punctuated?
9. Why does Vonnegut recommend the book *The Elements of Style?* Hasn't he already instructed us in these matters himself?
10. Explain how and why Vonnegut's last paragraph returns the reader to the essay's main idea in paragraph 3.

Exploring the Writer's Ideas

1. Vonnegut believes that since newspaper reporters and technical writers reveal almost nothing about themselves they are less fascinating to us. Based on your experiences as a reader, do you agree? Why or why not?
2. If you care deeply about a subject, Vonnegut claims this will make your writing more interesting to others. Has this been true in your experiences as a writer? Explain.
3. Vonnegut makes the case (par. 12) that using nonstandard English can make a writer's work "beautiful." Do you agree with him? Why or why not?
4. Vonnegut says you should use the speech you heard as a child (par. 10) to achieve a successful writing style. Then he says that if he broke all the rules of language, he "would simply not be understood" (par. 15). Is Vonnegut contradicting himself? What if a person's childhood language is not understandable outside his or her community?
5. Vonnegut reminds us that we live in an "egalitarian" society. What implications does this have for the development of your writing style?
6. Given a choice, which writers would you rather read—those that reveal "nothing about themselves" or those whose "revelations are fascinating"? Explain your preferences.

IDEAS FOR WRITING

Prewriting

Make a list of the steps you take in the process of doing something you have excelled in (for example, gardening, cooking, playing sports, making friends, and so on).

Guided Writing

Write an essay called "How to __________ with Style." Fill in the blank with something you do well, such as skiing, painting a room, and so on. Instruct the reader on how and why he or she should also do this activity and what you mean by doing it with style.

1. Begin by defining the most important quality you think someone needs to be successful at this activity.
2. In the next two or three paragraphs, elaborate on how and why this quality will help ensure a person's success in this activity.
3. Describe another quality needed to be a success at this activity. Give two or three paragraphs of supporting detail to show how others have been successful at this activity because they too have had the quality you just described. Here you should make clear what doing the activity "with style" means.
4. Tell if there is any reason why this activity can or cannot be done by most people. Is a special quality needed? Is this something a child can do? Why or why not?
5. Give personal testimony of how and why being a success at this activity is simple or complicated for you. What personal traits have you relied on to be a success at this activity?
6. Warn readers about the most common mistakes made by those who do not succeed at this activity, and suggest how to avoid such mistakes.
7. End with why you think this activity might (or might not) be well suited for people living in a society where they have the constitutional right to live freely. (Consider recommending a book that might assist the reader with this activity.)

Thinking and Writing Collaboratively

Write a short letter using the words of love you would share with someone close to you. Then write out a dictionary definition of "love." Form groups of three students each and share your letters and definitions with the members of the group, asking them: Which words would most appeal to you? Why? Note the responses and write an essay on how to write a love letter.

More Writing Projects

1. In your journal, write a short entry in language that you heard as a child. Try to capture the sounds and traits that will amuse and delight readers.
2. Write two paragraphs that contrast your language use. In paragraph one, describe with examples the kind of language you use with your friends and family. In paragraph two, describe with examples the kind of language you use with your professors or strangers.
3. Write an essay on something you care strongly about, using the language you feel best reveals something personal about yourself, as Vonnegut suggests.

When an "A" Meant Something

Walter W. Benjamin

Walter W. Benjamin, professor emeritus at Hamline University in St. Paul, Minnesota, recalls how he learned to write upon entering college as a veteran of the Navy Air Corps in 1946. His freshman English teacher was no less tough than any Marine instructor, but Miss Garey was only four-foot-ten.

PREREADING: THINKING ABOUT THE ESSAY IN ADVANCE

What do you think of when you hear someone got an "A" on an exam or a paper? Does an "A" mean something special or have grading standards slipped?

Words to Watch

diminutive (par. 1) small
sojourn (par. 2) temporary stay
pedagogical (par. 3) related to teaching
envisaged (par. 6) visualized
copious (par. 7) plentiful

As I move into the autumn of life and look back at those who helped shape my character, I often think of a diminutive freshman English professor named Doris Garey. 1

What little competence in English I had gained in high school, I had lost during a two-year sojourn in the Navy Air Corps. So as I entered Hamline University in 1946, I was slated to take "dumb-dumb" English 1, 2, a remedial course without credit. "Required of all freshmen . . . whose competence is inadequate," read the course catalog. But a scheduling problem allowed me to escape and enter Freshman Composition 11, 12. "Miss Garey will be good for you," said my adviser as I walked out the door. 2

Even though she had a bachelor's degree from Mount Holyoke and a doctorate from Wisconsin, Miss Garey was the low person in the department pecking order. And physically she was a light-weight—she could not have stood more than 4-foot-10 or 3 weighed more than 100 pounds. But she had the pedagogical mass of a Sumo wrestler. Her literary expectations were stratospheric; she was the academic equivalent of my boot camp drill instructor.

4 Thirty-five of us were sardined into a 15-by-28-foot classroom at the west end of the third floor of Old Main. In spite of her Lilliputian stature, she stood over her class like the Colossus of Rhodes. She knew we had heads full of mush.

5 The late '40s was an era before DD (dumbing down) and OTG (only two grades—A and B). Miss Garey's standards were like the Marine Corps hair cut, "high and tight." Her grading followed a bell curve—if six students received B's, six got D's. She required us to master the Harbrace English Handbook, which listed the rules of the king's English. Our essays came back covered with marginal abbreviations from the handbook, where we were expected to look up our mistakes. Miss Garey had a fundamentalist's facility for citing chapter and verse.

6 She required one theme a week—16 in all—for the term. Our first assignment—"write about a childhood experience"—I thought was a piece of cake. I wrote a five-page essay, "Hunting Rabbits with Skippy, My Chesapeake Bay Retriever." My sentences were larded with beautiful word pictures—clouds, meadows, birds, the sunset, the behavior of rabbits and Skippy, even eating my lunch. When the papers were handed back, I eagerly awaited my A. I envisaged sending it home to my parents.

7 When I received a D for grammar/construction and a C minus for content/development, my heart missed a few beats. Miss Garey's copious markings reminded me of the droppings on the paper in my parakeet's cage. I felt profaned. I had the urge to drop the course and look for some easy courses, but I feared facing my counselor. It was going to be a long 16 weeks.

8 Every Friday, Miss Garey would call on the student with the best paper to read a paragraph or two to show the rest of us what good writing was. I was glad I had picked the corner chair in the back row.

9 But the Navy had taught me a version of "Ours is not to question why, ours it but to do or die." I hung in there—and eventually I began to respond to Miss Garey's regimen. Toward the middle of the second term, I was getting A's and A-minuses. Because I had started so slow, those grades meant much more. I was gaining on myself. In April, when Miss Garey asked me to recite several paragraphs of my psychological study of the brilliant detective in Dostoevsky's "Crime and Punishment," I was ecstatic.

The other day I walked past a grading chart of one of the large departments at Hamline University, where I am now a professor emeritus. Forty students, coded by number, had their machine-graded tests totaled for the term. Thirty-seven received A's, two got A-minuses, and one laggard could manage only a B-plus. I wondered if students today had the same feeling of accomplishment that I did 50 years ago. 10

In 1949 Miss Garey quietly left our campus after a five-year sojourn, to head the English department at a black college in Kentucky. Years later I realized it took at least 10 years after graduation to know who were my best teachers. The showboats had long since faded, along with their banter, jokes and easy grades. It was the no-nonsense Miss Garey whose memory endured. 11

Miss Garey demanded and received respect, if not holy fear. No student dared call her Doris; had one had done so, she probably would have responded with a fairly decent imitation of the "war face" of Gen. George S. Patton. She didn't want to be a "Welcome Back, Kotter," high-five, buddy-buddy type of teacher. She believed that teachers, like physicians, should respect the boundaries between themselves and their charges. 12

When I was at Duke University studying for my doctorate, I thought about calling Hamline to get Miss Garey's address and write her a note of appreciation. But other duties were pressing. Now she is gone and it is too late. 13

For almost forty years, as a professor of humanities, I have walked in Miss Garey's footsteps. My feet are much larger than hers were, but I am sure she left a much bigger imprint on her students. If I have had any success as a writer, I owe much of it to her. 14

Academia could use a legion of Miss Gareys today. 15

BUILDING VOCABULARY

1. Identify the following references:
   - **a.** Sumo wrestler
   - **b.** Lilliputian stature
   - **c.** Colossus of Rhodes
   - **d.** the King's English
   - **e.** Dostoevsky's "Crime and Punishment"
   - **f.** General George S. Patton
   - **g.** Academia

2. Without looking in a dictionary, write definitions for the following words or phrases on the basis of their context in the essay. Use each phrase or word in a sentence of your own.
   a. the autumn of life (par. 1)
   b. pecking order (par. 3)
   c. a bell curve (par. 5)
   d. a fundamentalists facility (par. 5)
   e. larded with (par. 6)
   f. banter (par. 11)

THINKING CRITICALLY ABOUT THE ESSAY

Understanding The Writer's Ideas

1. What does the writer's stage in life have to do with the title of his essay?
2. What were the circumstances under which the writer entered college? How was he different from the usual freshman? How did these circumstances affect his encounter with Miss Garey?
3. Why does the writer play on Miss Garey's physical size, or the size of his composition classroom?
4. What does the writer want to suggest by using the acronyms DD and OTG?
5. Contrast DD and OTG with a bell curve.
6. What is the implication of the writer's reference to "the king's English"?
7. What were the writer's expectations as he handed in his first essay? What different expectations might he have had?
8. Judging by the writer's description, what was wrong with this first essay?
9. What was the writer's reaction to Miss Garey's grading of his first paper? Why did he persevere? How did his reaction to her grading change as the term wore on?
10. What worries the writer about the "machine graded" tests of today?
11. Why does the writer go out of his way to describe Miss Garey as "severe" (par. 11 and par. 12)?
12. Why do you think the writer ended his essay with the point that "Academia could use a legion of Miss Gareys today"?

Understanding the Writer's Techniques

1. Beginning with the title, this is an essay that relies heavily on comparisons and contrasts to get its points across. In par. 4, for example, the writer says of Miss Garey: "Lilliputian in stature, she stood over her class like the Colossus of Rhodes." List similar comparisons/contrasts in the essay, and discuss how they tie the essay together and reinforce its main theme.
2. State the author's thesis in one sentence.
3. The *tone* (see Glossary) of an essay expresses the writer's attitude toward the topic. How would you describe Benjamin's tone? What features of the writing—its word choice, its allusions, its manner of address—establish that tone?
4. *Metaphors* can enliven comparisons and contrasts (see Glossary). A metaphor compares an item from one category with an item from another. A *simile* is a comparison using the words "like" or "as."
   Explain what is being compared in the instances below, and why the comparisons are effective:
   a. She had the pedagogic mass of a Sumo wrestler (par. 3).
   b. Miss Garey's standards were like the Marine Corps hair cut (par. 5).
   c. Miss Garey's copious markings reminded me of the droppings on the paper in my parakeet's cage (par. 7).
   d. My feet are much larger than hers were, but I am sure she left a much bigger imprint on her students (par. 14).
5. The writer employs personal experience to make a general argument more powerful. How do the personal and the general reinforce each other in this essay?
6. Different settings and different audiences dictate different language. (You don't write to a friend in the same way that you might write a job application letter.) In this essay, the writer employs both semiformal and highly colloquial language. Select two or three examples of each and explain why they are appropriate and effective.

Exploring the Writer's Ideas

1. Coming to college straight from the Navy, Benjamin seems to have brought with him a healthy respect for discipline. He implies that discipline is essential for learning. But was his experience in Miss Garey's class perhaps exceptional? Might

a less sturdy soul have been discouraged by Miss Garey's harsh grades? How can severe discipline stunt instead of encourage?

2. The writer suggests that not only have standards of grading fallen, but that students' sense of accomplishment has been hurt as a result. Do you think that you value a good grade less than your father or grandmother or some other older relative might have? Explain the reasons for your answer.
3. Benjamin's language ("dumbing down") implies a negative judgment of today's teachers and students. Does his language skew the argument by invoking emotion rather than reason? Explain your answer. What is your opinion about today's standards of grading? On what do you base your opinion?
4. In what ways might student achievement be assessed other than grading?

IDEAS FOR WRITING

Prewriting

Jot down some things you are proud of having achieved that seem to have gotten easier to achieve for those younger than you, such as a Boy Scout Merit Badge, or a driving license. Choose some key words to distinguish your experience from the watered down experience of the younger generation.

Guided Writing

Write an essay about someone in your past who was tough on you but got the best out of you, and contrast that experience of achievement with today's more lax standards.

1. Begin your essay with a statement about why you are looking back at your earlier achievement, indicating your pride in what you accomplished then and your concern about what's happening now.
2. Illustrate your first involvement with your mentor with a dramatic vignette.
3. Choose some telling details from your early encounters with your mentor that highlight his or her tough standards.
4. Tell about your initial responses to this "tough love."

5. Indicate how you improved over time.
6. Contrast your hard-earned achievement with the slack standards of today.
7. Explain why we could use a lot more of the motivating toughness of your mentor today.

Thinking and Writing Collaboratively

In groups of four and five discuss your experiences with grading. Explore the good and bad sides of grading, and devise some recommendations about how best to tie grading and achievement. Discuss your group's recommendations with the rest of the class.

More Writing Projects

1. Write a portrait of a teacher whose grading made your life a misery.
2. Write a letter to a former teacher, thanking him/her for the profound impact his/her rigorous demands made on your education.
3. Conduct an informal survey in your neighborhood to determine whether people believe educational standards have worsened since they were in school or college. Write a brief summary of your findings.

Mother Tongue

Amy Tan

Amy Tan is a novelist and essayist who was born in California only two and a half years after her parents emigrated to the United States. Her first novel, *The Joy Luck Club* (1989), was extremely popular, and was followed by *The Kitchen God's Wife* (1991) and *The Hundred Secret Senses* (1995). Speaking and writing in standard English is essential, Tan argues, but the diversity of cultures in America requires that we acknowledge the different "Englishes" spoken by immigrants. As you read her essay, think about your own experience in learning English, and how you respond to the other Englishes you may have heard spoken by your family or neighbors. Consider why Tan chooses to write in standard English.

PREREADING: THINKING ABOUT THE ESSAY IN ADVANCE

What varieties of English do you speak? In other words, do you speak different kinds of English in different situations and to different individuals or groups of people? Why or why not?

Words to Watch

intersection (par. 3) crossroad
wrought (par. 3) made; worked
belies (par. 7) misrepresents; disguises
wince (par. 8) cringe; shrink
empirical (par. 9) relying on observation
guise (par. 10) outward appearance
benign (par. 14) not harmful
insular (par. 15) like an island; isolated

1 I am not a scholar of English or literature. I cannot give you much more than personal opinions on the English language and its variations in this country or others.

I am a writer. And by that definition, I am someone who has always loved language. I am fascinated by language in daily life. I spend a great deal of my time thinking about the power of language—the way it can evoke an emotion, a visual image, a complex idea, or a simple truth. Language is the tool of my trade. And I use them all—all the Englishes I grew up with. 2

Recently, I was made keenly aware of the different Englishes I do use. I was giving a talk to a large group of people, the same talk I had already given to half a dozen other groups. The nature of the talk was about my writing, my life, and my book, *The Joy Luck Club.* The talk was going along well enough, until I remembered one major difference that made the whole talk sound wrong. My mother was in the room. And it was perhaps the first time she had heard me give a lengthy speech, using the kind of English I have never used with her. I was saying things like, "The intersection of memory upon imagination" and "There is an aspect of my fiction that relates to thus-and-thus"—a speech filled with carefully wrought grammatical phrases, burdened, it suddenly seemed to me, with nominalized forms, past perfect tenses, conditional phrases, all the forms of standard English that I had learned in school and through books, the forms of English I did not use at home with my mother. 3

Just last week, I was walking down the street with my mother, and I again found myself conscious of the English I was using, the English I do use with her. We were talking about the price of new and used furniture and I heard myself saying this: "Not waste money that way." My husband was with us as well, and he didn't notice any switch in my English. And then I realized why. It's because over the twenty years we've been together I've often used that same kind of English with him, and sometimes he even uses it with me. It has become our language of intimacy, a different sort of English that relates to family talk, the language I grew up with. 4

So you'll have some idea of what this family talk I heard sounds like, I'll quote what my mother said during a recent conversation which I videotaped and then transcribed. During this conversation, my mother was talking about a political gangster in Shanghai who had the same last name as her family's, Du, and how the gangster in his early years wanted to be adopted by her family, which was rich by comparison. Later, the gangster became more powerful, far richer than my mother's family, and one day showed up at my mother's wedding to pay his respects. Here's what she said in part: 5

6 "Du Yusong having business like fruit stand. Like off the street kind. He is Du like Du Zong—but not Tsung-ming Island people. The local people call putong, the river east side, he belong to that side local people. That man want to ask Du Zong father take him in like become own family. Du Zong father wasn't look down on him, but didn't take seriously, until that man big like become a mafia. Now important person, very hard to inviting him. Chinese way, came only to show respect, don't stay for dinner. Respect for making big celebration, he shows up. Mean gives lots of respect. Chinese custom. Chinese social life that way. If too important won't have to stay too long. He come to my wedding. I didn't see. I heard it. I gone to boy's side, they have YMCA dinner. Chinese age I was nineteen."

7 You should know that my mother's expressive command of English belies how much she actually understands. She reads the *Forbes* report, listens to *Wall Street Week,* converses daily with her stockbroker, reads all of Shirley MacLaine's books with ease—all kinds of things I can't begin to understand. Yet some of my friends tell me they understand 50 percent of what my mother says. Some say they understand 80 to 90 percent. Some say they understand none of it, as if she were speaking pure Chinese. But to me, my mother's English is perfectly clear, perfectly natural. It's my mother tongue. Her language, as I hear it, is vivid, direct, full of observation and imagery. That was the language that helped shape the way I saw things, expressed things, made sense of the world.

8 Lately, I've been giving more thought to the kind of English my mother speaks. Like others, I have described it to people as "broken" or "fractured" English. But I wince when I say that. It has always bothered me that I can think of no way to describe it other than "broken," as if it were damaged and needed to be fixed, as if it lacked a certain wholeness and soundness. I've heard other terms used, "limited English," for example. But they seem just as bad, as if everything is limited, including people's perceptions of the limited English speaker.

9 I know this for a fact, because when I was growing up, my mother's "limited" English limited *my* perception of her. I was ashamed of her English. I believed that her English reflected the quality of what she had to say. That is, because she expressed them imperfectly her thoughts were imperfect. And I had plenty of empirical evidence to support me: the fact that people in department

stores, at banks, and at restaurants did not take her seriously, did not give her good service, pretended not to understand her, or even acted as if they did not hear her.

My mother has long realized the limitations of her English as well. When I was fifteen, she used to have me call people on the phone to pretend I was she. In this guise, I was forced to ask for information or even to complain and yell at people who had been rude to her. One time it was a call to her stockbroker in New York. She had cashed out her small portfolio and it just so happened we were going to go to New York the next week, our very first trip outside California. I had to get on the phone and say in an adolescent voice that was not very convincing, "This is Mrs. Tan." 10

And my mother was standing in the back whispering loudly, "Why he don't send me check, already two weeks late. So mad he lie to me, losing me money." 11

And then I said in perfect English, "Yes, I'm getting rather concerned. You had agreed to send the check two weeks ago, but it hasn't arrived." 12

Then she began to talk more loudly. "What he want, I come to New York tell him front of his boss, you cheating me?" And I was trying to calm her down, make her be quiet, while telling the stockbroker, "I can't tolerate any more excuses. If I don't receive the check immediately, I am going to have to speak to your manager when I'm in New York next week." And sure enough, the following week there we were in front of this astonished stockbroker, and I was sitting there red-faced and quiet, and my mother, the real Mrs. Tan, was shouting at his boss in her impeccable broken English. 13

We used a similar routine just five days ago, for a situation that was far less humorous. My mother had gone to the hospital for an appointment, to find out about a benign brain tumor a CAT scan had revealed a month ago. She said she had spoken very good English, her best English, no mistakes. Still, she said, the hospital did not apologize when they said they had lost the CAT scan and she had come for nothing. She said they did not seem to have any sympathy when she told them she was anxious to know the exact diagnosis, since her husband and son had both died of brain tumors. She said they would not give her any more information until the next time and she would have to make another appointment for that. So she said she would not leave until the doctor called her daughter. She wouldn't budge. And when the doctor finally called her daughter, me, who spoke in perfect 14

English—lo and behold—we had assurances the CAT scan would be found, promises that a conference call on Monday would be held, and apologies for any suffering my mother had gone through for a most regrettable mistake.

15 I think my mother's English almost had an effect on limiting my possibilities in life as well. Sociologists and linguists probably will tell you that a person's developing language skills are more influenced by peers. But I do think that the language spoken in the family, especially in immigrant families which are more insular, plays a large role in shaping the language of the child. And I believe that it affected my results on achievement tests, IQ tests, and the SAT. While my English skills were never judged as poor, compared to math, English could not be considered my strong suit. In grade school I did moderately well, getting perhaps B's, sometimes B-pluses, in English and scoring perhaps in the sixtieth or seventieth percentile on achievement tests. But those scores were not good enough to override the opinion that my true abilities lay in math and science, because in those areas I achieved A's and scored in the ninetieth percentile or higher.

16 This was understandable. Math is precise; there is only one correct answer. Whereas, for me at least, the answers on English tests were always a judgment call, a matter of opinion and personal experience. Those tests were constructed around items like fill-in-the-blank sentence completion, such as, "Even though Tom was __________ , Mary thought he was __________ ." And the correct answer always seemed to be the most bland combinations of thoughts, for example, "Even though Tom was shy, Mary thought he was charming," with the grammatical structure "even though" limiting the correct answer to some sort of semantic opposites, so you wouldn't get answers like, "Even though Tom was foolish, Mary thought he was ridiculous." Well, according to my mother, there were very few limitations as to what Tom could have been and what Mary might have thought of him. So I never did well on tests like that.

17 The same was true with word analogies, pairs of words in which you were supposed to find some sort of logical, semantic relationship—for example, "*Sunset* is to *nightfall* as __________ is to __________ ." And here you would be presented with a list of four possible pairs, one of which showed the same kind of relationship: *red* is to *stoplight, bus* is to *arrival, chills* is to *fever, yawn* is to *boring.* Well, I could never think that way. I knew what the tests were asking, but I could not block out of my mind the

images already created by the first pair, *"sunset* is to *nightfall"*—and I would see a burst of colors against a darkening sky, the moon rising, the lowering of a curtain of stars. And all the other pairs of words—red, bus, stoplight, boring—just threw up a mass of confusing images, making it impossible for me to sort out something as logical as saying: "A sunset precedes nightfall" is the same as "a chill precedes a fever." The only way I would have gotten that answer right would have been to imagine an associative situation, for example, my being disobedient and staying out past sunset, catching a chill at night, which turns into feverish pneumonia as punishment, which indeed did happen to me.

I have been thinking about all this lately, about my mother's English, about achievement tests. Because lately I've been asked, as a writer, why there are not more Asian Americans represented in American literature. Why are there few Asian Americans enrolled in creative writing programs? Why do so many Chinese students go into engineering? Well, these are broad sociological questions I can't begin to answer. But I have noticed in surveys—in fact, just last week—that Asian students, as a whole, always do significantly better on math achievement tests than in English. And this makes me think that there are other Asian-American students whose English spoken in the home might also be described as "broken" or "limited." And perhaps they also have teachers who are steering them away from writing and into math and science, which is what happened to me. 18

Fortunately, I happen to be rebellious in nature and enjoy the challenge of disproving assumptions made about me. I became an English major my first year in college, after being enrolled as pre-med. I started writing nonfiction as a freelancer the week after I was told by my former boss that writing was my worst skill and I should hone my talents toward account management. 19

But it wasn't until 1985 that I finally began to write fiction. And at first I wrote using what I thought to be wittily crafted sentences, sentences that would finally prove I had mastery over the English language. Here's an example from the first draft of a story that later made its way into *The Joy Luck Club,* but without this line: "That was my mental quandary in its nascent state." A terrible line, which I can barely pronounce. 20

Fortunately, for reasons I won't get into today, I later decided I should envision a reader for the stories I would write. And the reader I decided upon was my mother, because these were 21 stories about mothers. So with this reader in mind—and in fact she did read my early drafts—I began to write stories using all the Englishes I grew up with: the English I spoke to my mother, which for lack of a better term might be described as "simple"; the English she used with me, which for lack of a better term might be described as "broken"; my translation of her Chinese, which could certainly be described as "watered down"; and what I imagined to be her translation of her Chinese if she could speak in perfect English, her internal language, and for that I sought to preserve the essence, but neither an English nor a Chinese structure. I wanted to capture what language ability tests can never reveal: her intent, her passion, her imagery, the rhythms of her speech and the nature of her thoughts.

22 Apart from what any critic had to say about my writing, I knew I had succeeded where it counted when my mother finished reading my book and gave me her verdict: "So easy to read."

BUILDING VOCABULARY

Tan uses technical words to distinguish standard English from the English her mother speaks. Investigate the meanings of the following terms, and find examples to illustrate them for your classmates.

a. scholar (par. 1)
b. nominalized forms (par. 3)
c. transcribed (par. 5)
d. imagery (par. 7)
e. linguists (par. 15)
f. semantic opposites (par. 16)
g. word analogies (par. 17)
h. freelancer (par. 19)
i. quandary (par. 20)
j. nascent (par. 20)

THINKING CRITICALLY ABOUT THE ESSAY

Understanding the Writer's Ideas

1. Why does Tan start her essay by identifying who she is *not?* What does she see as the difference between a scholar and a writer?

2. What does Tan mean when she says, "Language is the tool of my trade"? What are the four ways she says language can work?
3. Tan speaks of "all the Englishes I grew up with" in paragraph 2, and later of the "different Englishes" she uses. Why does her mother's presence in the lecture room help her recall these Englishes? Why does she give us examples of what was "wrong" with her talk in paragraph 3?
4. In paragraph 4, Tan recognizes that she herself shifts from one English to another. Which English is "our language of intimacy"? Why?
5. Tan describes how she recorded her mother's words. Why does she give us her technique in paragraph 5 before presenting her mother's exact words in paragraph 6?
6. What do we know about Tan's mother when we learn she reads the *Forbes* report and various books? Why is it important for Tan to understand the way her mother sees the world? What connection does Tan make between the way we use language and the way we see the world?
7. In paragraph 8, Tan tries to find a suitable label for her mother's language. Why is she unwilling to use a description like "broken" or "limited" English? What does her mother's English sound like to you?
8. In what ways did outsiders (like bankers and waiters) make judgments of Tan's mother because of her language? Were the judgments deliberate or unconscious on their part?
9. How does Tan use humor as she contrasts the two Englishes in the telephone conversations she records? How does the tone change when Tan shifts to the hospital scene? Why do the authorities provide different service and different information when the daughter speaks than they do when the mother speaks?
10. How does Tan connect her math test scores with her mother's language? Why does she think she never did well on language tests? Why does she think the tests do not measure a student's language use very well? Why does Tan ultimately become an English major (par. 19)?
11. In paragraph 20, why does Tan show us the sentence: "That was my mental quandary in its nascent state"? How does it compare with the other sentences in her essay? What is wrong with this "terrible" sentence? What does it mean?

12. In her two final paragraphs, Tan returns to her mother. Why does selecting her mother as her reader help Tan learn to become a better writer? What are the elements of good writing her mother recognizes, even if she herself cannot write standard English?

Understanding the Writer's Techniques

1. What is the thesis statement in Tan's essay? Where does it appear?
2. Throughout her essay, Tan uses *dialogue,* the written reproduction of speech or conversation. Why does she do this? What is the effect of dialogue? Which sentences of dialogue do you find especially effective, and why?
3. In paragraph 3, Tan writes fairly long sentences until she writes, "My mother was in the room." Why is this sentence shorter? What is the effect of the short sentence on the reader?
4. *Narration* (see Chapter 4) is the telling of a story or series of events. *Anecdotes* are very short narrations, usually of an amusing or autobiographical nature. Point out uses of narration and anecdote in Tan's essay.
5. How does identifying her mother as her intended audience help Tan make her own language more effective? Does Tan suggest that all writing should be "simple"? Is her writing always "simple"? Why does her mother find it "easy" to read?
6. Why does Tan put quotation marks around "broken" and "limited"? What other words can describe this different English?

Exploring the Writer's Ideas

1. Why is an awareness of different kinds of English necessary for a writer? Why are writers so interested in "different Englishes"? Should all Americans speak and write the same English?
2. What is the role of parents in setting language standards for their children? How did your parents or other relatives influence your language use?
3. Reread Tan's essay, and look more carefully at her *point of view* (see Glossary) about other Englishes. How do we know what her point of view is? Does she state it directly or indirectly? Where?

4. Listen to someone who speaks a "different" English. Try to record a full paragraph of the speech, as Tan does in paragraph 6. Use a tape recorder and (or) a video camera so that you can replay the speech several times. Explain what the difficulties were in capturing the sound of the speech exactly. Write a "translation" of the paragraph into standard English.
5. Tan explores the special relation between mothers and daughters. How would you describe the author's relation with her mother?

IDEAS FOR WRITING

Prewriting

Free-associate on a sheet of paper about the language you use in daily communication, its delights, difficulties, problems, confusions, humor—in short, anything that comes to mind about the language you use in your daily life.

Guided Writing

Write a narrative essay using first-person point of view in which you contrast your language with the language of someone who speaks differently from you.

1. Begin by making some notes on your own language and by deciding whom you will choose as your other subject. It should be someone you can spend time with so that you can record his or her speech.
2. Following Tan's model, create a narrative to frame your subject's language. Tell who you are and why you speak the way you do. Introduce the other speaker, and tell why his or her speech is different.
3. Use dialogue to provide examples of both Englishes.
4. Analyze how listeners other than yourself respond to both types of speech. What are the social implications of speech differences?
5. Show how listening to the other speaker and to yourself has helped you shape your own language and write your essay. What can you learn about good writing from this project?
6. Be sure the essay has a clear thesis in the introduction. Add a strong conclusion that returns to the idea of the thesis.

Thinking and Writing Collaboratively

Exchange a draft version of your Guided Writing essay with another writer in the class. As you read each other's work, think about the suggestions you might make to help the writer produce the next draft. Is the thesis clear? Is the introduction focused? Is the conclusion linked to the thesis idea? Is the dialogue realistic?

More Writing Projects

1. In your journal, record examples of new words you have heard recently. Divide the list into columns according to whether the words are standard English or a different English. How many different Englishes can you find in your community and in college?
2. Reread question 1 in Exploring the Writer's Ideas, and write a one-paragraph response to it.
3. Tan's experience as a daughter of recent immigrants has clearly shaped her life in fundamental ways. She writes about the "shame" she once felt for her mother's speech. Write about a personal experience in which you were once embarrassed by someone close to you who was "different." Tell how you would feel about the same encounter if it happened today.

Simplicity

William Zinsser

In this chapter from *On Writing Well,* William Zinsser begins with a fairly pessimistic analysis of the clutter that pervades and degrades American writing, and he offers many examples to prove his point. Zinsser deals with almost all major aspects of the writing process—thinking, composing, awareness of the reader, self-discipline, rewriting, and editing—and concludes that simplicity is the key to them all.

PREREADING: THINKING ABOUT THE ESSAY IN ADVANCE

Do you find writing difficult or easy? Why? What is there about the act of writing that annoys, frustrates, or satisfies you?

Words to Watch

decipher (par. 2) to make out the meaning of something obscure
adulterants (par. 3) added substances which make something impure or inferior
mollify (par. 4) to appease; to soothe
spell (par. 4) a short period of time
assailed (par. 8) attacked with words or physical violence
spruce (par. 8) neat or smart in appearance
tenacious (par. 10) stubborn; persistent
rune (par. 10) character in an ancient alphabet
bearded (par. 12) approached or confronted boldly

Clutter is the disease of American writing. We are a society strangling in unnecessary words, circular constructions, pompous frills and meaningless jargon. 1

Who can understand the clotted language of everyday American commerce: the memo, the corporation report, the business letter, the notice from the bank explaining its latest "simplified" statement? What member of an insurance or medical plan can decipher the brochure explaining his costs and 2 benefits? What father or mother can put together a child's toy from the instructions on the box? Our national tendency is to inflate and thereby sound important. The airline pilot who announces that he is presently anticipating experiencing considerable precipitation wouldn't think of saying it may rain. The sentence is too simple—there must be something wrong with it.

3 But the secret of good writing is to strip every sentence to its cleanest components. Every word that serves no function, every long word that could be a short word, every adverb that carries the same meaning that's already in the verb, every passive construction that leaves the reader unsure of who is doing what—these are the thousand and one adulterants that weaken the strength of a sentence. And they usually occur in proportion to education and rank.

4 During the 1960s the president of my university wrote a letter to mollify the alumni after a spell of campus unrest. "You are probably aware," he began, "that we have been experiencing very considerable potentially explosive expressions of dissatisfaction on issues only partially related." He meant the students had been hassling them about different things. I was far more upset by the president's English than by the students' potentially explosive expressions of dissatisfaction. I would have preferred the presidential approach taken by Franklin D. Roosevelt when he tried to convert into English his own government's memos, such as this blackout order of 1942:

> Such preparations shall be made as will completely obscure all Federal buildings and non-Federal buildings occupied by the Federal government during an air raid for any period of time from visibility by reason of internal or external illumination.

5 "Tell them," Roosevelt said, "that in buildings where they have to keep the work going to put something across the windows."

6 Simplify, simplify. Thoreau said it, as we are so often reminded, and no American writer more consistently practiced what he preached. Open *Walden* to any page and you will find a man saying in a plain and orderly way what is on his mind:

> I went to the woods because I wished to live deliberately, to front only the essential facts of life, and see if I could not learn what it had to teach, and not, when I came to die, discover that I had not lived.

7 How can the rest of us achieve such enviable freedom from clutter? The answer is to clear our heads of clutter. Clear thinking

becomes clear writing; one can't exist without the other. It's impossible for a muddy thinker to write good English. He may get away with it for a paragraph or two, but soon the reader will be lost, and there's no sin so grave, for the reader will not easily be lured back.

Who is this elusive creature, the reader? The reader is some- 8
one with an attention span of about 30 seconds—a person assailed by many forces competing for attention. At one time those forces were relatively few: newspapers, magazines, radio, spouse, children, pets. Today they also include a "home entertainment center" (television, VCR, tapes, CDs), e-mail, the Internet, the cellular phone, the fax machine, a fitness program, a pool, a lawn, and that most potent of competitors, sleep. The man or woman snoozing in a chair with a magazine or a book is a person who was being given too much unnecessary trouble by the writer.

It won't do to say that the reader is too dumb or too lazy to 9
keep pace with the train of thought. If the reader is lost, it's usually because the writer hasn't been careful enough. The carelessness can take any number of forms. Perhaps a sentence is so excessively cluttered that the reader, hacking through the verbiage, simply doesn't know what it means. Perhaps a sentence has been so shoddily constructed that the reader could read it in several ways. Perhaps the writer has switched pronouns in midsentence, or has switched tenses, so the reader loses track of who is talking or when the action took place. Perhaps Sentence B is not a logical sequel to Sentence A; the writer, in whose head the connection is clear, hasn't bothered to provide the missing link. Perhaps the writer has used a word incorrectly by not taking the trouble to look it up. He or she may think "sanguine" and "sanguinary" mean the same thing, but the difference is a bloody big one. The reader can only infer (speaking of big differences) what the writer is trying to imply.

Faced with such obstacles, readers are at first tenacious. 10
They blame themselves—they obviously missed something, and they go back over the mystifying sentence, or over the whole paragraph, piecing it out like an ancient rune, making guesses and moving on. But they won't do this for long. The writer is making them work too hard, and they will look for one who is better at the craft.

Writers must therefore constantly ask: What am I trying to 11
say? Surprisingly often they don't know. Then they must look at what they have written and ask: have I said it? Is it clear to

someone encountering the subject for the first time? If it's not, some fuzz has worked its way into the machinery. The clear writer is someone clearheaded enough to see this stuff for what it is: fuzz.

12 I don't mean that some people are born clearheaded and are therefore natural writers, whereas others are naturally fuzzy and will never write well. Thinking clearly is a conscious act that writers must force upon themselves, as if they were working on any other project that requires logic: making a shopping list or doing an algebra problem. Good writing doesn't come naturally, though most people seem to think it does. Professional writers are constantly bearded by strangers who say they'd like to "try a little writing sometime"—meaning when they retire from their real profession, like insurance or real estate, which is hard. Or they say, "I could write a book about that." I doubt it.

13 Writing is hard work. A clear sentence is no accident. Very few sentences come out right the first time, or even the third time. Remember this in moments of despair. If you find that writing is hard, it's because it *is* hard.

Two pages of the final manuscript of this chapter from the First Edition of On Writing Well. Although they look like a first draft, they had already been rewritten and retyped—like almost every other page—four or five times. With each rewrite I try to make what I have written tighter, stronger and more precise, eliminating every element that is not doing useful work. Then I go over it once more, reading it aloud, and am always amazed at how much clutter can still be cut. (In later editions I eliminated the sexist pronoun "he" denoting "the writer" and "the reader.")

---

is too dumb or too lazy to keep pace with the ~~writer's~~ train of thought. My sympathies are ~~entirely~~ with him. ~~He's not so dumb~~. If the reader is lost, it is generally because the writer ~~of the article~~ has not been careful enough to keep him on the ~~proper~~ path.

This carelessness can take any number of ~~different~~ forms. Perhaps a sentence is so excessively ~~long and~~ cluttered that the reader, hacking his way through ~~all~~ the verbiage, simply doesn't know what *it* ~~the writer~~ means. Perhaps a sentence has been so shoddily constructed that the reader could read it in any of *several* ~~two or three different~~ ways. ~~He thinks he knows what the writer is trying to say, but he's not sure.~~ Perhaps the writer has switched pronouns in mid-sentence, or ~~perhaps he~~ has switched tenses, so the reader loses track of who is talking ~~to whom,~~ or ~~exactly~~ when the action took place. Perhaps Sentence B is not a logical sequel to Sentence A -- the writer, in whose head the connection is ~~perfectly~~ clear, has not *bothered to provide* ~~given enough thought to providing~~ the missing link. Perhaps the writer has used an important word incorrectly by not taking the trouble to look it up. ~~and make sure.~~ He may think that "sanguine" and "sanguinary" mean the same thing, but ~~I can assure you that~~ the difference is a bloody big one. ~~to the reader.~~ *The reader* ~~He~~ can only ~~try to~~ infer ~~what~~ (speaking of big differences) what the writer is trying to imply.

Faced with *these* ~~such a variety of~~ obstacles, the reader is at first a remarkably tenacious bird. He ~~tends to~~ blame*s* himself. He obviously missed something, ~~he thinks,~~ and he goes back over the mystifying sentence, or over the whole paragraph, piecing it out like an ancient rune, making guesses and moving on. But he won't do this for long. ~~He will soon run out of patience.~~ The writer is making him work too hard, ~~-- harder than he should have to work --~~ and the reader will look for ~~a writer~~ *one* who is better at his craft.

The writer must therefore constantly ask himself: What am I trying to say? ~~in this sentence?~~ Surprisingly often, he doesn't know. ~~And~~ Then he must look at what he has ~~just~~ written and ask: Have I said it? Is it clear to someone *encountering* ~~who is coming upon~~ the subject for the first time? If it's not, ~~clear,~~ it is because some fuzz has worked its way into the machinery. The clear writer is a person ~~who is~~ clear-headed enough to see this stuff for what it is: fuzz.

I don't mean ~~to suggest~~ that some people are born
clear-headed and are therefore natural writers, whereas
others ~~other people~~ are naturally fuzzy and will ~~therefore~~ never write
well. Thinking clearly is a ~~an entirely~~ conscious act that the
writer must force ~~keep forcing~~ upon himself, just as if he were
embarking ~~starting out~~ on any other ~~kind of~~ project that requires ~~calls for~~ logic:
adding up a laundry list or doing an algebra problem. ~~or playing
chess~~. Good writing doeesn't ~~just~~ come naturally, though most
people obviously think it does. ~~it's as easy as walking~~. The professional

---

BUILDING VOCABULARY

1. Zinsser uses a number of words and expressions drawn from areas other than writing; he uses them to make interesting combinations or comparisons in such expressions as *elusive creature* (par. 8) and *hacking through the verbiage* (par. 9). Find other such expressions in this essay. Write simple explanations for the two above and the others that you find.
2. List words or phrases in this essay that pertain to writing—the process, the results, the faults, the successes. Explain any with which you were unfamiliar.

THINKING CRITICALLY ABOUT THE ESSAY

Understanding the Writer's Ideas

1. State simply Zinsser's meaning in the opening paragraph. What faults of "bad writing" does he mention in this paragraph?
2. To what is Zinsser objecting in paragraph 2?
3. What, according to the author, is the "secret of good writing" (par. 3)? Explain this "secret" in a few simple words of your own. What does Zinsser say detracts from good writing? Why does Zinsser write that these writing faults "usually occur, in proportion to education and rank"?

4. What was the "message" in the letter from the university president to the alumni (par. 4)? Why does the writer object to it? Was it more objectionable in form or in content?
5. Who was Thoreau? What is *Walden?* Why are references to the two especially appropriate to Zinsser's essay?
6. What, according to Zinsser, is the relation between clear thinking and good writing? Can you have one without the other? What is meant by a "muddy thinker" (par. 7)? Why is it "impossible for a muddy thinker to write good English"?
7. Why does the author think most people fall asleep while reading? What is his attitude toward such people?
8. Look up and explain the "big differences" between the words *sanguine* and *sanguinary; infer* and *imply.* What is the writer's point in calling attention to these differences?
9. In paragraph 11, Zinsser calls attention to a writer's necessary awareness of the composing process. What elements of the *process* of writing does the author include in that paragraph? In that discussion, Zinsser speaks of *fuzz* in writing. What does he mean by the word as it relates to the writing process? To what does Zinsser compare the writer's thinking process? Why does he use such simple comparisons?
10. Explain the meaning of the last sentence. What does it indicate about the writer's attitude toward his work?

Understanding the Writer's Techniques

1. What is the writer's thesis? Is it stated or implied?
2. Explain the use of the words *disease* and *strangling* in paragraph 1. Why does Zinsser use these words in an essay about writing?
3. For what purpose does Zinsser use a series of questions in paragraph 2?
4. Throughout this essay, the writer makes extensive use of examples to support general opinions and attitudes. What attitude or opinion is he supporting in paragraphs 2, 4, 5, 6, and 9? How does he use examples in each of those paragraphs?
5. Analyze the specific structure and organization of paragraph 3:
   a. What general ideas about writing does he propose?
   b. Where does he place that idea in the paragraph?
   c. What examples does he offer to support his general idea?
   d. With what new idea does he conclude the paragraph? How is it related to the beginning idea?

6. Why does Zinsser reproduce exactly portions of the writings of a past president of a major university, President Franklin D. Roosevelt, and Henry David Thoreau? How do these sections make Zinsser's writing clearer, more understandable, or more important?
7. What is the effect on the reader of the words "Simplify, simplify," which begin paragraph 6? Why does the writer use them at that particular point in the essay? What do they indicate about his attitude toward his subject? Explain.
8. Why does the author begin so many sentences in paragraph 9 with the word "Perhaps"? How does that technique help to *unify* (see Glossary) the paragraph?
9. For what reasons does the writer include the two pages of "rough" manuscript as a part of the finished essay? What is he trying to show the reader in this way? How does seeing these pages help you to understand better what he is writing about in the completed essay?
10. Overall, how would you describe the writer's attitude toward the process and craft of writing? What would you say is his overall attitude toward the future of American writing? Is he generally optimistic or pessimistic? On what does his attitude depend? Refer to specifics in the essay to support your answer.
11. Do you think Zinsser expected other writers, or budding writers, to be the main readers of this essay? Why or why not? If so, with what main ideas do you think he would like them to come away from the essay? Do you think readers who were not somehow involved in the writing process would benefit equally from this essay? Why?

Exploring the Writer's Ideas

1. Do you think that Zinsser is ever guilty in this essay of the very "sins" against writing about which he is upset? Could he have simplified any of his points? Select one of Zinsser's paragraphs in the finished essay and explain how you might rewrite it more simply.
2. In the reading that you do most often, have you noticed overly cluttered writing? Or, do you feel that the writing is at its clearest level of presentation and understanding for its audience? Bring to class some examples of this writing, and be prepared to discuss it. In general, what do you consider the relation between the simplicity or complexity of a piece of writing and its intended readership?

3. In the note to the two rough manuscript pages included with this essay, the writer implies that the process of rewriting and simplifying may be endless. How do you know when to stop trying to rewrite an essay, story, or poem? Do you ever really feel satisfied that you've reached the end of the rewriting process?
4. Choose one of the rough manuscript paragraphs, and compare it with the finished essay. Which do you feel is better? Why? Is there anything Zinsser deleted from the rough copy that you feel he should have retained? Why?
5. Comment on the writer's assertion that "Thinking clearly is a conscious act that writers must force upon themselves" (par. 12). How does this opinion compare with the opinions of the three other writers in this chapter?
6. Reread Kurt Vonnegut, Jr.'s essay "How to Write with Style" (pages 12–15). What similarities and differences do you note in Zinsser's and Vonnegut's approaches to writing and language?

IDEAS FOR WRITING

Prewriting

For the most part, teachers have called upon you to put your thoughts in writing from your elementary school days onward. Make a list of your writing "problems"—the elements of writing or the elements of your personality that create problems for you whenever you try to produce something on paper.

Guided Writing

In a 500- to 750-word essay, write about what you feel are some of the problems that you face as a writer.

1. In the first paragraph, identify the problems that you plan to discuss.
2. In the course of your essay, relate your problems more generally to society at large.
3. Identify what, in your opinion, is the "secret" of good writing. Give specific examples of what measures to take to achieve that secret process and thereby to eliminate some of your problems.

4. Try to include one or two accurate reproductions of your writing to illustrate your composing techniques.
5. Point out what you believe were the major causes of your difficulties as a writer.
6. Toward the end of your essay, explain the type of writer that you would like to be in order to succeed in college.

Thinking and Writing Collaboratively

Form groups of two and exchange drafts of your Guided Writing essay. Do for your partner's draft what Zinsser did for his own: edit it in an effort to make it "stronger and more precise, eliminating every element that is not doing useful work." Return the papers and discuss whether or not your partner made useful recommendations for cutting clutter.

More Writing Projects

1. Over the next few days, listen to the same news reporter or talk-show host on television or radio. Record in your journal at least ten examples that indicate the use of "unnecessary words, circular constructions, pompous frills, and meaningless jargon." Or compile such a list from an article in a newspaper or magazine you read regularly. Then write an essay presenting and commenting on these examples.
2. Respond in a paragraph to Zinsser's observation, "Good writing doesn't come naturally."
3. In preparation for a writing assignment, collect with other class members various samples of junk mail and business correspondence that confirm Zinsser's statement that these tend to be poorly written. Write an essay describing your findings. Be certain to provide specific examples from the documents you have assembled.

SUMMING UP: CHAPTER 1

1. It sounds simple enough. Many writers, famous and unknown, have tried it at one time or another. Now, it's your turn. Write an essay simply titled "On Writing." Develop the essay in any way you please: you may deal with abstract or concrete ideas, philosophical or practical issues, emotional or intellectual processes, and so forth. Just use this essay to focus your own thoughts and to give your reader a clear idea of what writing means to you.
2. William Zinsser ("Simplicity") tells writers to simplify their writing. Select any writer from this section, and write an essay about whether you think the writer achieved (or did not achieve) simplicity. How did the writer achieve it? Where in the selection would you have preferred even more simplicity? Make specific references to the text.
3. Think about the message implicit in Amy Tan's essay on using her mother as an ideal audience. Find your own ideal listener. Then write a letter to that person in which you discuss your reactions to becoming a writer. Include observations you think your listener or reader will enjoy, such as your everyday life as a student, daydreams, descriptions of teachers, or cafeteria food, or of interesting people you have met.
4. Write a letter from Kurt Vonnegut, Jr., to Amy Tan on how style affects good writing. Draw on what you understand of Vonnegut's philosophy of writing from his essay "How to Write with Style," and what Amy Tan says in "Mother Tongue."
5. The writers in this chapter all give some sense of *why* they write. For the most part, their reasons are very personal. For example, Kurt Vonnegut, Jr., writes about trusting his writing when he sounds "most like a person from Indianapolis." However, many writers (including many represented in this book) feel that writing entails a certain social responsibility. For example, when Albert Camus received the 1957 Nobel Prize for Literature, he was cited for "illuminating the problems of the human conscience of our time." And, in his acceptance speech, he stated, "[T]he writer's function is not without arduous duties. By definition, he cannot serve today those who make history; he must serve those who are subject to it."

What do you feel are writers' responsibilities to themselves and to others? Do you agree with Camus? Do you prefer writing that deals primarily with an individual's experience or with more general social issues?

Write an essay concerning the social responsibilities of writers. As you consider the issue, refer to points made by writers in this section.

CHAPTER 2

On Reading

WHAT IS READING?

"Reading had changed forever the course of my life," writes Malcolm X in one of the essays in this chapter. For many of us, the acquisition of reading skills may not have been quite as dramatic as it was for the author of "Prison Studies," but if we are to understand the value of literacy in today's society, Malcolm X's analysis of the power of the written word is vital. Reading allows us actively to engage the minds of many writers who have much to tell us and to hear a variety of viewpoints not always available on the cable, video, and other forms of media that vie for our attention. Even the ever present computer and its brainchild, the World Wide Web, demand active reading for maximum benefit. Learning to read well opens new universes, challenges your opinions, enhances your understanding of yourself and others and of your past, present, and future. Knowledge of books is the mark of a literate person.

But how do we learn this complex skill? Ellen Tashie Frisina's essay on teaching her grandmother to read may remind you of your own early experiences with printed words. Or, if you are a parent, you may be reading stories to your own children to help them learn to read. As we become mature readers, we read not just as we once did, for the story and its magical pleasures, but also for information and for pleasure in the *style* of writing. We learn not to be passive readers but active ones.

That early love of stories, and the self-esteem that came with mastery of a once impossible task, is, however, only the first step in understanding the power of reading. Malcolm X's "Prison Studies" extends our understanding of what reading is beyond the personal into the cultural sphere. He explores not only the power of reading to excite and inspire, but also the ways in which language connects to social identity. Malcolm X uses reading, and later writing, to challenge existing assumptions and find a place as an alert and engaged member of society. He argues that his reading outside of school made him better educated than most formally educated citizens in America.

Reading gives us access to many printed stories and documents, old and new. Through reading we can see beyond the highly edited sound bites and trendy images that tempt us from the video screen. With print, we can read what we want when we want to read it. We can reread difficult passages to be sure we understand them. We have time to question the author's point; and we have time to absorb and analyze ideas not only from contemporary life but also from ancient cultures and distant places. The diverse materials in libraries allow us to select what we read rather than be channeled into one TV director's point of view. On the Web we can access stories, poems, essays, even books, and can create a home library for use on a computer monitor.

Reading lets us share ideas. Reading can teach us practical skills that we need for survival in our complex world, such as how to repair a computer or how to become a biology teacher or a certified public accountant. Good reading can inspire us, educate us, or entertain us. It can enrich our fantasy lives. Reading critically also helps us analyze how society operates, how power is distributed, how we can improve our local community or the global environment. As Eudora Welty writes, reading can lead to a life-long love affair with books and stories. The beauty of the written word and the stirrings of imagination and vision that the printed page can produce are all part of what reading is.

HOW DO WE READ?

To become a good reader, we need to think about what we read just as we think about what and how we write. In other words, we need to read *critically,* asking ourselves a series of questions about the material in order to arrive at a fair assessment of its significance.

- What is it that we're reading? (In other words, what *genre,* or type of writing, does it belong to?) What is the writer's primary purpose in writing it?

We should first examine what we are about to read to determine what it is: Is it a romance? a history book? a religious tract? Why was it written? How do the answers to these questions shape our attitude toward the material? As readers of novels, for instance, we soon learn that a gothic romance with a cover featuring a heroine snatched from a fiery castle belongs to a particular genre of literature. As potential readers, we might prepare ourselves to be skeptical about the happy ending we know awaits us, but at the same time we are prepared for a romantic tale. In contrast, if we face a hard-covered glossy textbook entitled *Economics,* we prepare ourselves to read with far more concentration. We might enjoy the love story, but if we skip whole chapters it may not matter much. If, however, we skip chapters of the textbook, we may find ourselves confused. The first book *entertains* us, while the second *informs* us. Only if we understand the *purpose* of a reading assignment are we ready to begin reading.

- Who is the writer? For whom is he or she writing? When did he or she write it?

Clues to a writer's identity can often help us establish whether the material we are reading is reliable. Would we read a slave owner's account of life in slave quarters the same way we would read a slave's diary, for instance? If a Sioux writes about the effects of a treaty on Native-American family life, we might read the essay with a different eye than if the writer were General Custer. The *audience* is also important. If we are reading a handbook on immigration policies in the United States, we might read it differently if we knew it was written for officials at Ellis Island in 1990 than we would if it were written for Chinese men arriving to work on the railroads in the nineteenth century.

- What is the precise issue or problem that the writer treats?

Reading is often a process of analyzing and synthesizing. We read an entire chapter, and then we go back and look for the key points. We try to summarize the main idea. We look for subtopics that support the main idea. We identify the writer's *exact* topic. A writer's general topic might be the Battle of Gettysburg, for instance, but if she is writing about the women at Gettysburg, then her precise topic is narrower. What is she saying, we next ask, about these women?

- What information, conclusions, and recommendations does the writer present?

The reader may find that note taking is helpful in improving understanding of a text. Creating an outline of materials after reading can help identify the writer's aims.

- How does the writer substantiate, or "prove," his or her case?

The reader must learn the difference between a writer who merely *asserts* an idea and one who effectively *substantiates* an idea. The writer who only asserts that the Holocaust never happened will be read differently from the writer who substantiates his or her claims that the Holocaust did exist with photographs of Germany in the 1940s, interviews with concentration camp survivors, military records of medical experiments, and eyewitness accounts of gas chambers.

- Is the total message successful, objective, valid, or persuasive?

Once you have answered all of the above questions, you are ready to *assess* the work you have read. As you make your evaluation, find specific evidence in the text to back up your position.

By reading critically—by reading to understand, analyze, and evaluate—you respond to an author's ideas, opinions, and arguments in an informed way. In a sense you enter into a conversation with the author. You agree or disagree with the author, "talk back," and try to understand the author's perspective on the subject. To become a critical reader, you may wish to employ a strategy called annotation in which you literally mark up the essay. Here are the basic elements of this method:

- Underline important ideas in an essay. A related strategy is to use an asterisk, star, or vertical lines in the margins next to the most important information or statements.
- Pose questions in the margins. Place question marks next to the points that you find confusing.
- Take notes in the margins.
- Use numbers in the margins to highlight the sequence of major ideas that the author presents.
- Circle key words and phrases.

Examine the annotating strategies by one student as she read an essay by Leonid Fridman titled "America Needs Its Nerds."

Nice title! Is he serious or being funny?

America Needs Its Nerds

Leonid Fridman

**Thesis (or is this the main proposition?)*

* There is something very wrong with the 1
system of values in a society that has only derogatory terms like nerd and geek for the intellectually curious and academically serious.

Key definition

A geek, according to "Webster's New 2
World Dictionary," is a street performer who shocks the public by biting off heads of live chickens. It is a telling fact about our language and our culture that someone dedicated to pursuit of knowledge is compared to a freak biting the head off a live chicken.

Is this true? Where is the evidence?

Meaning?

He mentions athletes several times. Must they be separated from intellectuals?

Even at a prestigious academic 3
institution like Harvard, anti-intellectualism ?? is rampant: Many students are ashamed to admit, even to their friends, how much they study. Although most students try to keep up their grades, there is but a minority of undergraduates for whom pursuing knowledge is the top priority during their years at Harvard. Nerds are ostracized while athletes are idolized.

Note comparison and contrast throughout essay

The same thing happens in U.S. 4
elementary and high schools. Children who prefer to read books rather than play football, prefer to build model airplanes rather than get wasted at parties with their classmates, become social outcasts. Ostracized for their intelligence and refusal to conform to society's anti-intellectual values, many are deprived of a chance to learn adequate social skills and acquire good communication tools.

**Call to action?*

Why this fragment?

* Enough is enough. 5

Nerds and geeks must stop being 6
ashamed of who they are. It is high time to face the persecutors who haunt the bright kid with thick glasses from kindergarten to the grave. For America's sake, the anti-intellectual values that pervade our society must be fought.

Geeks must rebel!

7 There are very few countries in the world where anti-intellectualism runs as high in popular culture as it does in the U.S. In most industrialized nations, not least of all our economic rivals in East Asia, a kid who studies hard is lauded and held up as an example to other students.

U.S. vs. rest of world

8 In many parts of the world, university professorships are the most prestigious and materially rewarding positions. But not in America, where average professional ballplayers are much more respected and better paid than faculty members of the best universities.

9 How can a country where typical parents are ashamed of their daughter studying mathematics instead of going dancing, or of their son reading Weber while his friends play baseball, be expected to compete in the technology race with Japan or remain a leading political and cultural force in Europe? How long can America remain a world-class power if we constantly emphasize social skills and physical prowess over academic achievement and intellectual ability?

Look up

Anti-intellectualism has negative impact on America's political and economic future. Does he prove his point?

Note series of questions. Are answers self-evident?

10 Do we really expect to stay afloat largely by importing our scientists and intellectuals from abroad, as we have done for a major portion of this century, without making an effort to also cultivate a pro-intellectual culture at home? Even if we have the political will to spend substantially more money on education than we do now, do we think we can improve our schools if we deride our studious pupils and debase their impoverished teachers?

11 Our fault lies not so much with our economy or with our politics as within ourselves, our values and our image of a good life. America's culture has not adapted to the demands of our times, to the economic realities that demand a highly

educated workforce and innovative intelligent leadership.

If we are to succeed as a society in the 21st century, we had better shed our anti-intellectualism and imbue in our children the vision that a good life is impossible without stretching one's mind and pursuing knowledge to the full extent of one's abilities. 12

Essay comes full circle—reread intro ¶

**Idea for essay: "My Favorite Nerd"*

And until the words "nerd" and "geek" become terms of approbation and not derision, we do not stand a chance. 13

The process that this student follows reflects the sort of active, critical reading expected of you in college courses. Through annotation, you actually bring the acts of reading and writing together in a mutually advantageous way. Reading critically and responding to texts through annotation prepares you for more sustained writing assignments presented in this anthology.

These steps will help you engage in an active conversation, or dialogue, with the writer, sharing ideas and debating issues. At the same time, becoming a better reader will help you become a better writer. Eudora Welty and Malcolm X became readers as part of their apprenticeship to becoming world-renowned writers. For Ellen Tashie Frisina, reading remains, as it does for most of us, a personal achievement. For Welty, words came to her "as though fed . . . out of a silver spoon." Malcolm X tells us how reading was so powerful for him that it allowed him to break down prison walls. Vivian Gornick, a well-known writer, tells of her initiation into the "faith" that books matter, and her discovery that this faith remains vigorous in the New York Public Library today. Frisina reminds us that literacy is not a birthright, but a skill that can be painstakingly learned, and taught, at any age.

One Writer's Beginnings

Eudora Welty

Eudora Welty, born in 1909, is among America's foremost writers, often focusing on the ways of life in rural Mississippi. Her novel *The Optimist's Daughter* won the 1972 Pulitzer Prize, and her *Collected Series* (1980) has been widely acclaimed. In this selection from her autobiography, *One Writer's Beginnings* (1984), Welty uses delightful descriptions and narrations of her childhood to tell how she developed her love for reading.

PREREADING: THINKING ABOUT THE ESSAY IN ADVANCE

What attitudes did your family have toward reading when you were a child? Did books surround you? Which books did your parents or other relatives read to you or suggest that you read? How did you feel about books as a child growing up?

Words to Watch

disposed (par. 4) inclined; receptive
vignettes (par. 5) charming literary sketch
roué (par. 7) lecherous, wasted man
interlocutor (par. 9) partner in a dialogue
quoth (par. 9) archaic form of word *quoted*
wizardry (par. 15) magic
sensory (par. 18) pertaining to the senses
reel (par. 19) fast chance
constellations (par. 20) positions of star groups in sky, considered to look like (and named for) mythological characters

1 I learned from the age of two or three that any room in our house, at any time of day, was there to read in, or to be read to. My mother read to me. She'd read to me in the big bedroom in the mornings, when we were in her rocker together, which ticked in rhythm as we rocked, as though we had a cricket accompanying the story. She'd read to me in the diningroom on

winter afternoons in front of the coal fire, with our cuckoo clock ending the story with "Cuckoo," and at night when I'd got in my own bed. I must have given her no peace. Sometimes she read to me in the kitchen while she sat churning, and the churning sobbed along with *any* story. It was my ambition to have her read to me while *I* churned; once she granted my wish, but she read off my story before I brought her butter. She was an expressive reader. When she was reading "Puss in Boots," for instance, it was impossible not to know that she distrusted *all* cats.

It had been startling and disappointing to me to find out 2
that story books had been written by *people,* that books were not natural wonders, coming up of themselves like grass. Yet regardless of where they came from, I cannot remember a time when I was not in love with them—with the books themselves, cover and binding and the paper they were printed on, with their smell and their weight and with their possession in my arms, captured and carried off to myself. Still illiterate, I was ready for them, committed to all the reading I could give them.

Neither of my parents had come from homes that could af- 3
ford to buy many books, but though it must have been something of a strain on his salary, as the youngest officer in a young insurance company, my father was all the while carefully selecting and ordering away for what he and Mother thought we children should grow up with. They bought first for the future.

Besides the bookcase in the livingroom, which was always 4
called "the library," there were the encyclopedia tables and dictionary stand under windows in our diningroom. Here to help us grow up arguing around the diningroom table were the Unabridged Webster, the Columbia Encyclopedia, Compton's Pictured Encyclopedia, the Lincoln Library of Information, and later the Book of Knowledge. And the year we moved into our new house, there was room to celebrate it with the new 1925 edition of the Britannica, which my father, his face always deliberately turned toward the future, was of course disposed to think better than any previous edition.

In "the library," inside the mission-style bookcase with its 5
three diamond-latticed glass doors, with my father's Morris chair and the glass-shaded lamp on its table beside it, were books I could soon begin on—and I did, reading them all alike and as they came, straight down their rows, top shelf to bottom. There was the set of Stoddard's Lectures, in all its late nineteenth-century vocabulary and vignettes of peasant life and quaint beliefs

and customs, with matching halftone illustrations: Vesuvius erupting, Venice by moonlight, gypsies glimpsed by their campfires. I didn't know then the clue they were to my father's longing to see the rest of the world. I read straight through his other love-from-afar: the Victrola Book of the Opera, with opera after opera in synopsis, with portraits in costume of Melba, Caruso, Galli-Curci, and Geraldine Farrar, some of whose voices we could listen to on our Red Seal records.

6 My mother read secondarily for information; she sank as a hedonist into novels. She read Dickens in the spirit in which she would have eloped with him. The novels of her girlhood that had stayed on in her imagination, besides those of Dickens and Scott and Robert Louis Stevenson, were *Jane Eyre, Trilby, The Woman in White, Green Mansions, King Solomon's Mines.* Marie Corelli's name would crop up but I understood she had gone out of favor with my mother, who had only kept *Ardath* out of loyalty. In time she absorbed herself in Galsworthy, Edith Wharton, above all in Thomas Mann of the *Joseph* volumes.

7 *St. Elmo* was not in our house; I saw it often in other houses. This wildly popular Southern novel is where all the Edna Earles in our population started coming from. They're all named for the heroine, who succeeded in bringing a dissolute, sinning roué and atheist of a lover (St. Elmo) to his knees. My mother was able to forgo it. But she remembered the classic advice given to rose growers on how to water their bushes long enough: "Take a chair and *St. Elmo.*"

8 To both my parents I owe my early acquaintance with a beloved Mark Twain. There was a full set of Mark Twain and a short set of Ring Lardner in our bookcase, and those were the volumes that in time united us all, parents and children.

9 Reading everything that stood before me was how I came upon a worn old book without a back that had belonged to my father as a child. It was called *Sanford and Merton.* Is there anyone left who recognizes it, I wonder? It is the famous moral tale written by Thomas Day in the 1780s, but of him no mention is made on the title page of *this* book; here it is *Sanford and Merton in Words of One Syllable* by Mary Godolphin. Here are the rich boy and the poor boy and Mr. Barlow, their teacher and interlocutor, in long discourses alternating with dramatic scenes—anger and rescue allotted to the rich and the poor respectively. It may have only words of one syllable, but one of them is "quoth." It ends with not one but two morals, both engraved on rings:

"Do what you ought, come what may," and "If we would be great, we must first learn to be good."

This book was lacking its front cover, the back held on by 10
strips of pasted paper, now turned golden, in several layers, and the pages stained, flecked, and tattered around the edges; its garish illustrations had come unattached but were preserved, laid in. I had the feeling even in my heedless childhood that this was the only book my father as a little boy had had of his own. He had held onto it, and might have gone to sleep on its coverless face: he had lost his mother when he was seven. My father had never made any mention to his own children of the book, but he had brought it along with him from Ohio to our house and shelved it in our bookcase.

My mother had brought from West Virginia that set of 11
Dickens; those books looked sad, too—they had been through fire and water before I was born, she told me, and there they were, lined up—as I later realized, waiting for *me*.

I was presented, from as early as I can remember, with 12
books of my own, which appeared on my birthday and Christmas morning. Indeed, my parents could not give me books enough. They must have sacrificed to give me on my sixth or seventh birthday—it was after I became a reader for myself—the ten-volume set of Our Wonder World. These were beautifully made, heavy books I would lie down with on the floor in front of the diningroom hearth, and more often than the rest volume 5, *Every Child's Story Book,* was under my eyes. There were the fairy tales—Grimm, Andersen, the English, the French, "Ali Baba and the Forty Thieves"; and there was Aesop and Reynard the Fox; there were the myths and legends, Robin Hood, King Arthur, and St. George and the Dragon, even the history of Joan of Arc; a whack of *Pilgrim's Progress* and a long piece of *Gulliver.* They all carried their classic illustrations. I located myself in these pages and could go straight to the stories and pictures I loved; very often "The Yellow Dwarf" was first choice, with Walter Crane's Yellow Dwarf in full color making his terrifying appearance flanked by turkeys. Now that volume is as worn and backless and hanging apart as my father's poor *Sanford and Merton.* The precious page with Edward Lear's "Jumblies" on it has been in danger of slipping out for all these years. One measure of my love for Our Wonder World was that for a long time I wondered if I would go through fire and water for it as my mother had done for Charles Dickens; and the only comfort was to think I could ask my mother to do it for me.

13 I believe I'm the only child I know of who grew up with this treasure in the house. I used to ask others, "Did you have Our Wonder World?" I'd have to tell them The Book of Knowledge could not hold a candle to it.

14 I live in gratitude to my parents for initiating me—as early as I begged for it, without keeping me waiting—into knowledge of the word, into reading and spelling, by way of the alphabet. They taught it to me at home in time for me to begin to read before starting to school. I believe the alphabet is no longer considered an essential piece of equipment for traveling through life. In my day it was the keystone to knowledge. You learned the alphabet as you learned to count to ten, as you learned "Now I lay me" and the Lord's Prayer and your father's and mother's name and address and telephone number, all in case you were lost.

15 My love for the alphabet, which endures, grew out of reciting it but, before that, out of seeing the letters on the page. In my own story books, before I could read them for myself, I fell in love with various winding, enchanted-looking initials drawn by Walter Crane at the heads of fairy tales. In "Once upon a time," an "O" had a rabbit running it as a treadmill, his feet upon flowers. When the day came, years later, for me to see the Book of Kells, all the wizardry of letter, initial, and word swept over me a thousand times over, and the illumination, the gold, seemed a part of the word's beauty and holiness that had been there from the start.

16 Learning stamps you with its moments. Childhood's learning is made up of moments. It isn't steady. It's a pulse.

17 In a children's art class, we sat in a ring on kindergarten chairs and drew three daffodils that had just been picked out of the yard; and while I was drawing, my sharpened yellow pencil and the cup of the yellow daffodil gave off whiffs just alike. That the pencil doing the drawing should give off the same smell as the flower it drew seemed part of the art lesson—as shouldn't it be? Children, like animals, use all their senses to discover the world. Then artists come along and discover it the same way, all over again. Here and there, it's the same world. Or now and then we'll hear from an artist who's never lost it.

18 In my sensory education I include my physical awareness of the *word.* Of a certain word, that is; the connection it has with what it stands for. At around age six, perhaps, I was standing by myself in out front yard waiting for supper, just at that hour in a late summer day when the sun is already below the horizon and

the risen full moon in the visible sky stops being chalky and begins to take on light. There comes the moment, and I saw it then, when the moon goes from flat to round. For the first time it met my eyes as a globe. The word "moon" came into my mouth as though fed to me out of a silver spoon. Held in my mouth the moon became a word. It had the roundness of a Concord grape Grandpa took off his vine and gave me to suck out of its skin and swallow whole, in Ohio.

This love did not prevent me from living for years in fool- 19 ish error about the moon. The new moon just appearing in the west was the rising moon to me. The new should be rising. And in early childhood the sun and moon, those opposite reigning powers, I just as easily assumed rose in east and west respectively in their opposite sides of the sky, and like partners in a reel they advanced, sun from the east, moon from the west, crossed over (when I wasn't looking) and went down on the other side. My father couldn't have known I believed that when, bending behind me and guiding my shoulder, he positioned me at our telescope in the front yard and, with careful adjustment of the focus, brought the moon close to me.

The night sky over my childhood Jackson was velvety black. 20
I could see the full constellations in it and call their names; when I could read, I knew their myths. Though I was always waked for eclipses, and indeed carried to the window as an infant in arms and shown Halley's Comet in my sleep, and though I'd been taught at our diningroom table about the solar system and knew the earth revolved around the sun, and our moon around us, I never found out the moon didn't come up in the west until I was a writer and Herschel Brickell, the literary critic, told me after I misplaced it in a story. He said valuable words to me about my new profession: "Always be sure you get your moon in the right part of the sky."

BUILDING VOCABULARY

1. Identify the following references to authors, books, and stories from Welty's essay:
   a. Charles Dickens
   b. Robert Louis Stevenson
   c. *Jane Eyre*
   d. *The Woman in White*
   e. Edith Wharton

- **f.** Thomas Mann
- **g.** Mark Twain
- **h.** Ring Lardner
- **i** *Pilgrim's Progress*
- **j.** *Gulliver*

2. Write definitions and your own sentences for the following words:

- **a.** quaint (par. 5)
- **b.** hedonist (par. 6)
- **c.** dissolute (par. 7)
- **d.** allotted (par. 9)
- **e.** garish (par. 10)
- **f.** heedless (par. 10)
- **g.** gratitude (par. 14)
- **h.** essential (par. 14)
- **i.** keystone (par. 14)
- **j.** reigning (par. 19)

THINKING CRITICALLY ABOUT THE ESSAY

Understanding the Writer's Ideas

1. Why does the writer say of her mother, "I must have given her no peace" (par. 1)?
2. Why was it "startling and disappointing" for Welty to find out that storybooks were written by *people?* Where did she think they came from? Aside from the stories themselves, what is it that the author loves so much about books?
3. How did the way Welty's mother felt toward books affect her child's attitude toward reading? In what ways did the conditions in Welty's home contribute to her attitude toward books?
4. What is it, exactly, that Welty loved about books as a child?
5. Why did Welty's parents make sacrifices to buy books for the household? What were their hopes for their children? What kinds of books did the parents choose to buy and to read? What, if anything, do these choices tell us about the parents' characters?
6. For what reasons does the writer feel that learning the alphabet is so important? To what other learning processes does she compare it? Before she learned to recite her alphabet, why was it so important to her?

7. Explain in your own words what the writer considers to be the relation between physical sensations and learning words. According to the author why is it important for parents to read to their children?
8. What does Welty mean when she says a child's learning "Isn't steady. It's a pulse"?
9. Explain the significance of Welty's description of her experience of the moon at age 6.
10. What, if anything, do we learn from Herschel Brickell's advice?

Understanding the Writer's Techniques

1. What is the main idea of Welty's essay? Is there any point at which she directly states that main idea? Explain.
2. A *reminiscence* is a narrative account of a special memory. How does the writer use reminiscence in this essay?
3. The *tone* (see Glossary) of an essay is the expression of the writer's attitude toward the topic. State the tone of this essay. What specifically about the writing contributes to that tone?
4. *Description* helps the reader to "see" objects and scenes and to feel their importance through the author's eyes. *Narration*—the telling of a story—helps the reader follow a sequence of events. (See Chapters 3 and 4.) Both techniques rely on the writer's skill in choosing and presenting details. In what way does Welty make use of description and narration in this essay? How would you evaluate her use of details?
5. Placing words in italics emphasizes them. Where does the author use italics in this essay? Why does she use them?
6. What does the writer mean by stating that the set of Dickens books "had been *through fire and water* before I was born" (par. 11)? How does the image contribute to the point she's making?
7. In paragraph 1, Welty employs a technique called *personification* (see Glossary) in stating that "the churning sobbed along with any story." Consider the effect of this technique, along with her description of her mother's reading style ("it was impossible not to know that she distrusted all cats") in the same paragraph. What does Welty seem to suggest about the connection between emotion (or expressiveness) and reading?
8. Why does Welty make a point of vividly describing books' physical characteristics, as in paragraphs 2, 10, and 15? What

do her descriptions contribute to our understanding of her relationship to reading?

9. *Similes* (see Glossary) are imaginative comparisons using the word "like" or "as." Use of similes often enlivens the writing and makes it memorable.

In your own words, explain what is being compared in the following similes (in italics) drawn from Welty's essay, and tell how they contribute to the essay:

a. . . . we were in her rocker together, which ticked in rhythm as we rocked, *as though we had a cricket accompanying the story.* (par. 1)

b. . . . books were not natural wonders, coming up of themselves like grass. (par. 2)

c. The word "moon" came into my mouth *as though fed to me out of a silver spoon.* (par. 18)

10. Welty makes a number of references to other writers, artists, and books, in addition to those listed in the "Building Vocabulary" section: for example, Nellie Melba, Enrico Caruso, Amelita Galli-Curci, and Geraldine Farrar, Sir Walter Scott, *Green Mansions,* and John Galsworthy; Walter Crane and Edward Lear—there are many others too.

a. See if you can find some information on each of these references. When did the writers and artists live? When were the books written?

b. Why do you think Welty makes these references? Do you think she expects her readers to recognize them? (Keep in mind that *One Writer's Beginnings* was first published in book form in 1984.) Do the references in any way contribute to your understanding of her piece, even if they were unfamiliar to you?

Exploring the Writer's Ideas

1. The writer believes that it is very important for parents to read to their children. Some specialists in child development even advocate reading to infants still in the womb and to babies before they've spoken their first words. For what reasons might such activities be important? Do you personally feel they are important or useful? Would you read to an unborn infant? Why or why not? If you would, *what* would you read?

2. Welty was born in 1909 and obviously belongs to a different generation from the vast majority of college students today. Do you feel that her type of love and advocacy of reading are as valid for the current generation, raised on television, video, CDs, cable, and MTV? Explain.
3. Welty describes her love of books as going beyond the words and stories they contain to their physical and visual attributes. What objects—not other people—do you love or respect with that intensity? Tell a little about why and how you have developed this feeling.

IDEAS FOR WRITING

Prewriting

In the visual and auditory age in which we live—we watch and listen to television, tune in the radio, see movies regularly—what is the proper role for reading? Talk to friends, teachers, and fellow students about the matter. Record their observations and try to classify their responses.

Guided Writing

Write an essay that describes your own attitude toward reading.

1. In order to set the stage for the discussion of your attitude, begin by recalling details about a moment with a parent or other adult.
2. Use dialogue as part of this scene.
3. Go as far back in your childhood as you can possibly remember, and narrate two or three incidents that help explain the formation of your current attitude toward reading.
4. Use sensory language (color, sound, smell, touch, and taste) to show how the environment of the home where you grew up helped shape your attitude.
5. Tell about a particular, special childhood fascination with something you *saw*—not read—in a book.
6. Try to describe the first time you were conscious of the *meaning* of a particular word.
7. Use at least one *simile* in your essay.
8. Create and keep a consistent *tone* throughout the essay.

9. End your essay with an explanation of how a particular book has been continually influential to you as well as to others of your generation.
10. Give your essay an unusual title that derives from some description in your essay.

Thinking and Writing Collaboratively

Form groups of three to five students, and read the essays you each prepared for the Guided Writing assignment. Together, make a list of the various attitudes expressed about reading by group members. Report to the class as a whole on the reading attitudes of your group.

More Writing Projects

1. Enter in your journal early memories of people who read to you or of books that you read on your own. Try to capture the sensation and importance of these early reading experiences.
2. Return to question 2 in Exploring the Writer's Ideas, and write a one-paragraph response to it.
3. Write an essay on the person who most influenced your childhood education. Did this person read to you, give you books, make you do your homework? Assess the impact of this person on your life.

Prison Studies

Malcolm X

Born Malcolm Little in Omaha, Nebraska, Malcolm X (1925–1965) was a charismatic leader of the black power movement and founded the Organization of Afro-American Unity. In prison, he became a Black Muslim. (He split with this faith in 1963 to convert to orthodox Islam.) "Prison Studies" is excerpted from the popular and fascinating *Autobiography of Malcolm X,* which he cowrote with *Roots* author Alex Haley. The essay describes the writer's struggle to learn to read as well as the joy and power he felt when he won that struggle.

PREREADING: THINKING ABOUT THE ESSAY IN ADVANCE

Reflect on what you know about prison life. Could someone interested in reading and learning find a way to pursue his or her interests in such a setting? Why or why not?

Words to Watch

emulate (par. 2) imitate, especially from respect
motivation (par. 2) reason to do something
tablets (par. 3) writing notebooks
bunk (par. 9) small bed
rehabilitation (par. 10) the process of restoring to a state of usefulness or constructiveness
inmate (par. 10) prisoner
corridor (par. 13) hallway; walkway
vistas (par. 15) mental overviews
confers (par. 15) bestows; gives ceremoniously
alma mater (par. 15) the college that one has attended

Many who today hear me somewhere in person, or on television, or those who read something I've said, will think I went to school far beyond the eighth grade. This impression is due entirely to my prison studies. 1

2 It had really begun back in the Charlestown Prison, when Bimbi first made me feel envy of his stock of knowledge. Bimbi had always taken charge of any conversation he was in, and I had tried to emulate him. But every book I picked up had few sentences which didn't contain anywhere from one to nearly all of the words that might as well have been in Chinese. When I just skipped those words, of course, I really ended up with little idea of what the book said. So I had come to the Norfolk Prison Colony still going through only book-reading motions. Pretty soon, I would have quit even these motions, unless I had received the motivation that I did.

3 I saw that the best thing I could do was get hold of a dictionary—to study, to learn some words. I was lucky enough to reason also that I should try to improve my penmanship. It was sad. I couldn't even write in a straight line. It was both ideas together that moved me to request a dictionary along with some tablets and pencils from the Norfolk Prison Colony school.

4 I spent two days just riffling uncertainly through the dictionary's pages. I'd never realized so many words existed! I didn't know which words I needed to learn. Finally, to start some kind of action, I began copying.

5 In my slow, painstaking, ragged handwriting, I copied into my tablet everything printed on that first page, down to the punctuation marks.

6 I believe it took me a day. Then, aloud, I read back, to myself, everything I'd written on the tablet. Over and over, aloud, to myself, I read my own handwriting.

7 I woke up the next morning, thinking about those words—immensely proud to realize that not only had I written so much at one time, but I'd written words that I never knew were in the world. Moreover, with a little effort, I also could remember what many of these words meant. I reviewed the words whose meanings I didn't remember. Funny thing, from the dictionary first page right now, that "aardvark" springs to my mind. The dictionary had a picture of it, a long-tailed, long-eared, burrowing African mammal, which lives off termites caught by sticking out its tongue as an anteater does for ants.

8 I was so fascinated that I went on—I copied the dictionary's next page. And the same experience came when I studied that. With every succeeding page, I also learned of people and places and events from history. Actually the dictionary is like a miniature encyclopedia. Finally the dictionary's A section had

filled a whole tablet—and I went on into the B's. That was the way I started copying what eventually became the entire dictionary. It went a lot faster after so much practice helped me to pick up handwriting speed. Between what I wrote in my tablet, and writing letters, during the rest of my time in prison I would guess I wrote a million words.

I suppose it was inevitable that as my word-base broadened, I could for the first time pick up a book and read and now begin to understand what the book was saying. Anyone who has read a great deal can imagine the new world that opened. Let me tell you something; from then until I left that prison, in every free moment I had, if I was not reading in the library, I was reading on my bunk. You couldn't have gotten me out of books with a wedge. Between Mr. Muhammad's teachings, my correspondence, my visitors—usually Ella and Reginald—and my reading of books, months passed without my even thinking about being imprisoned. In fact, up to then, I never had been so truly free in my life. . . . 9

As you can imagine, especially in a prison where there was heavy emphasis on rehabilitation, an inmate was smiled upon if he demonstrated an unusually intense interest in books. There was a sizable number of well-read inmates, especially the popular debaters. Some were said by many to be practically walking encyclopedias. They were almost celebrities. No university would ask any student to devour literature as I did when this new world opened to me, of being able to read and *understand.* 10

I read more in my room than in the library itself. An inmate who was known to read a lot could check out more than the permitted maximum number of books. I preferred reading in the total isolation of my own room. 11

When I had progressed to really serious reading, every night at about ten P.M. I would be outraged with the "lights out." It always seemed to catch me right in the middle of something engrossing. 12

Fortunately, right outside my door was a corridor light that cast a glow into my room. The glow was enough to read by, once my eyes adjusted to it. So when "lights out" came, I would sit on the floor where I could continue reading in that glow. 13

At one-hour intervals the night guards paced past every room. Each time I heard the approaching footsteps, I jumped into bed and feigned sleep. And as soon as the guard passed, I got 14 back out of bed onto the floor area of that light-glow, where I would read for another fifty-eight minutes—until the guard approached again. That went on until three or four every morning. Three or four hours of sleep a night was enough for me. Often in the years in the streets I had slept less than that.

15 I have often reflected upon the new vistas that reading opened to me. I knew right there in prison that reading had changed forever the course of my life. As I see it today, the ability to read awoke inside me some long dormant craving to be mentally alive. I certainly wasn't seeking any degree, the way a college confers a status symbol upon its students. My homemade education gave me, with every additional book that I read, a little bit more sensitivity to the deafness, dumbness, and blindness that was afflicting the black race in America. Not long ago, an English writer telephoned me from London, asking questions. One was, "What's your alma mater?" I told him, "Books." You will never catch me with a free fifteen minutes in which I'm not studying something I feel might be able to help the black man. . . .

16 Every time I catch a plane, I have with me a book that I want to read—and that's a lot of books these days. If I weren't out here every day battling the white man, I could spend the rest of my life reading, just satisfying my curiosity—because you can hardly mention anything I'm not curious about. I don't think anybody ever got more out of going to prison than I did. In fact, prison enabled me to study far more intensively than I would have if my life had gone differently and I had attended some college. I imagine that one of the biggest troubles with colleges is there are too many distractions, too much panty-raiding, fraternities, and boola-boola and all of that. Where else but in prison could I have attacked my ignorance by being able to study intensely sometimes as much as fifteen hours a day?

BUILDING VOCABULARY

1. Throughout the selection, the writer uses *figurative* and *colloquial language* (see Glossary). As you know, figurative language involves imaginative comparisons, which go beyond plain or ordinary statements. Colloquial language involves informal or conversational phrases and expressions.

The following are examples of some of the figurative and colloquial usages in this essay. Explain each italicized word group in your own words.

a. *going through only book-reading motions* (par. 2)
b. I was *lucky enough* (par. 3)
c. *Funny thing* (par. 7)
d. can imagine *the new world that opened* (par. 9)
e. *You couldn't have gotten me out of books with a wedge* (par. 9)
f. an inmate was *smiled upon* (par. 10)
g. to be practically *walking encyclopedias* (par. 10)
h. ask any student *to devour literature* (par. 10)
i. changed forever *the course of my life* (par. 15)
j. *some long dormant craving to be mentally alive* (par. 15)
k. *the deafness, dumbness, and blindness that was afflicting* the black race in America (par. 15)
l. Every time I *catch a plane* (par. 16)
m. every day *battling the white man* (par. 16)
n. just *satisfying my curiosity* (par. 16)
o. *boola-boola and all of that* (par. 16)
p. I have *attacked my ignorance* (par. 16)

2. Find the following words in the essay. Write brief definitions for them without using a dictionary. If they are unfamiliar to you, try to determine their meaning based on the context in which they appear.

a. riffling (par. 4)
b. painstaking (par. 5)
c. ragged (par. 5)
d. burrowing (par. 7)
e. inevitable (par. 9)
f. emphasis (par. 10)
g. distractions (par. 16)

THINKING CRITICALLY ABOUT THE ESSAY

Understanding the Writer's Ideas

1. What was the highest level of formal education that the writer achieved? How is this different from the impression most people got from him? Why?

2. Who was Bimbi? Where did Malcolm X meet him? How was Bimbi important to the writer?

3. What does the writer mean by stating that when he tried to read, most of the words "might as well have been in Chinese"? What happened when he skipped over such words? What motivated him to change his way of reading?
4. Why did Malcolm X start trying to improve his handwriting? How was it connected to his desire to improve his reading ability? Briefly describe how he went about this dual process. How did he feel after the first day of this process? Why?
5. How is the dictionary "like a miniature encyclopedia"?
6. Judging from this essay and his description of his "homemade education," how much time did Malcolm X spend in prison? Does the fact that he was in prison affect your appreciation of his learning process? How?
7. What is a "word-base" (par. 9)? What happened once the author's word-base expanded? How did this give him a sense of freedom?
8. Who is "Mr. Muhammad"?
9. Why did the prison officials like Malcolm X? What special privileges came to him as a result of this favorable opinion?
10. Why was Malcolm X angered with the "lights out" procedure? How did he overcome it?
11. What does the following sentence tell you about Malcolm X's life: "Often in the years in the streets I had slept less than that" (par. 14)?
12. Characterize the writer's opinion of a college education. How does he compare his education to a college degree? How did his education influence his understanding of his place and role in American society?
13. In your own words, describe the writer's attitude toward American blacks. Toward the relation between blacks and whites?
14. To what main purpose in life does the writer refer? What was the relation between this purpose and his feelings about reading? Use one word to describe Malcolm X's attitude toward reading.
15. What does the conclusion mean?

Understanding the Writer's Techniques

1. What is the thesis? Where does the writer place it?
2. In Chapters 9 and 10, you will learn about the techniques of *process analysis* and *cause-and-effect analysis*. Briefly,

process analysis tells the reader *how* something is done; cause-and-effect analysis explains *why* one thing leads to or affects another.

For this essay, outline step by step the process whereby Malcolm X developed his ability to read and enthusiasm for reading. Next, for each step in your outline, explain why one step led to the next.

3. *Narration* (see Chapter 4) is the telling of a story or the orderly relating of a series of events. How does Malcolm X use narration in this essay? How does he order the events of his narration?
4. What is the effect of the words "Let me tell you something" in paragraph 9?
5. How is the writer's memory of the first page of the dictionary like a dictionary entry itself? What does this say about the importance of this memory to the author?
6. *Tone* (see Glossary) is a writer's attitude toward his or her subject. Characterize the tone of this essay. What elements of the writing contribute to that tone? Be specific.
7. Which paragraphs make up the conclusion of this essay? How does the author develop his conclusion? How does he relate it to the main body of the essay? Do you feel that there is a change in tone (see question 6) in the conclusion? Explain, using specific examples.
8. What is Malcolm X's main purpose in writing this essay? For whom is it intended? How do you know?

Exploring the Writer's Ideas

1. Malcolm X writes about his newly found love of reading and ability to read: "In fact, up to then, I never had been so truly free in my life." Has learning any particular skill or activity ever given you such a feeling of freedom or joy? Explain.
2. What do you feel was the source of Malcolm X's attitude toward a college education? Do you think any of his points here are valid? Why? What are your opinions about the quality of the college education you are receiving?
3. The writer also implies that, in some ways, the educational opportunities of prison were superior to those he would have had at college. What is his basis for this attitude? Have you ever experienced a circumstance in which being restricted actually benefited you? Explain.

4. Malcolm X held very strong opinions about the relations between blacks and whites in America. Do some library research on him to try to understand his opinions. You might begin by reading *The Autobiography of Malcolm X,* from which this essay was excerpted. Do you agree or disagree with his feelings? Why?
5. Following Malcolm X's example, handwrite a page from a dictionary (a pocket dictionary will be fine), copying everything—including punctuation—exactly!

   How long did it take you? How did it make you feel? Did you learn anything from the experience?

IDEAS FOR WRITING

Prewriting

Brainstorm on a difficult activity that you learned how to perform. What problems did the activity present? Why did you want to learn how to do it?

Guided Writing

Write an essay in which you tell about an activity that you can now perform but that once seemed impossible to you.

1. Open your essay with an example in which you compare what most people assume about your skill or background in the activity to what the reality is.
2. Mention someone who especially influenced you in your desire to master this activity.
3. Tell what kept you from giving up on learning this activity.
4. Explain, step by step, the *process* by which you learned more and more about the activity. Explain how and why one step led to the next.
5. Use *figurative* and *colloquial* language where you think it appropriate in your essay.
6. Describe in some detail how you overcame an obstacle, imposed by others, which could have impeded your learning process.
7. Use your conclusion to express a deeply felt personal opinion and to generalize your learning of this skill to the population at large.

Thinking and Writing Collaboratively

Exchange a draft version of your Guided Writing essay with another writer in the class. After you read your partner's essay, make recommendations for helping the writer produce the next draft. Use the items numbered 1–7 above to guide your discussion.

More Writing Projects

1. Select any page of a standard dictionary and copy in your journal at least ten words, with definitions, that are new or somewhat unfamiliar to you. Then jot down some thoughts on the process.
2. Ask yourself formal, journalistic questions about Malcolm X's essay: *What* happened? *Who* was involved? *How* was it done? *Where* did it occur? *When* did it occur? *Why* did it happen? Write out answers to these questions, and then assemble them in a unified, coherent paragraph.
3. Form a group with three other classmates. Focus on the context of Malcolm X's essay and on his comment on "the deafness, dumbness, and blindness that was afflicting the black race in America" (par. 15). Discuss this issue and its connection to education. Then prepare a collaborative essay on the topic.

"See Spot Run": Teaching My Grandmother to Read

Ellen Tashie Frisina

Ellen Tashie Frisina writes about her "secret" project to teach her 70-year-old grandmother, who came to the United States from Greece in 1916, to read English. Frisina's narrative reveals the pleasures of reading and illustrates the importance of reading no matter what age the reader.

PREREADING: THINKING ABOUT THE ESSAY IN ADVANCE

What do you think it would be like to be an adult who, living in America today, cannot read or write English? What problems would such a person face? Do you know or have you read about anyone who cannot read?

Words to Watch

differentiated (par. 1) separated from; distinguished from
stealthily (par. 2) secretly
monosyllabic (par. 3) one syllable; short in length
vehemently (par. 8) severely; intensely; angrily
phonetically (par. 14) pronounced by sound
afghan (par. 15) a blanket or shawl
crocheting (par. 15) a type of needlework

1 When I was 14 years old, and very impressed with my teenage status (looking forward to all the rewards it would bring), I set for myself a very special goal—a goal that so differentiated me from my friends that I don't believe I told a single one. As a teenager, I was expected to have deep, dark secrets, but I was not supposed to keep them from my friends.

2 My secret was a project that I undertook every day after school for several months. It began when I stealthily made my way into the local elementary school—horror of horrors should I be seen; I was now in junior high. I identified myself as a

graduate of the elementary school, and being taken under wing by a favorite fifth grade teacher, I was given a small bundle from a locked storeroom—a bundle that I quickly dropped into a bag, lest anyone see me walking home with something from the "little kids" school.

I brought the bundle home—proudly now, for within the confines of my home, I was proud of my project. I walked into the living room, and one by one, emptied the bag of basic reading books. They were thin books with colorful covers and large print. The words were monosyllabic and repetitive. I sat down to the secret task at hand. 3

"All right," I said authoritatively to my 70-year-old grandmother, "today we begin our first reading lesson." 4

For weeks afterward, my grandmother and I sat patiently side by side—roles reversed as she, with a bit of difficulty, sounded out every word, then read them again, piece by piece, until she understood the short sentences. When she slowly repeated the full sentence, we both would smile and clap our hands—I felt so proud, so grown up. 5

My grandmother was born in Kalamata, Greece, in a rocky little farming village where nothing much grew. She never had the time to go to school. As the oldest child, she was expected to take care of her brother and sister, as well as the house and meals, while her mother tended to the gardens, and her father scratched out what little he could from the soil. 6

So, for my grandmother, schooling was out. But she had big plans for herself. She had heard about America. About how rich you could be. How people on the streets would offer you a dollar just to smell the flower you were carrying. About how everyone lived in nice houses—not stone huts on the sides of mountains—and had nice clothes and time for school. 7

So my grandmother made a decision at 14—just a child, I realize now—to take a long and sickening 30-day sea voyage alone to the United States. After lying about her age to the passport officials, who would shake their heads vehemently at anyone under 16 leaving her family, and after giving her favorite gold earrings to her cousin, saying "In America, I will have all the gold I want," my young grandmother put herself on a ship. She landed in New York in 1916. 8

No need to repeat the story of how it went for years. The streets were not made of gold. People weren't interested in smelling flowers held by strangers. My grandmother was a for- 9 eigner. Alone. A young girl who worked hard doing piecework to earn enough money for meals. No leisure time, no new gold earrings—and no school.

10 She learned only enough English to help her in her daily business as she traveled about Brooklyn. Socially, the "foreigners" stayed in neighborhoods where they didn't feel like foreigners. English came slowly.

11 My grandmother had never learned to read. She could make out a menu, but not a newspaper. She could read a street sign, but not a shop directory. She could read only what she needed to read as, through the years, she married, had five daughters, and helped my grandfather with his restaurant.

12 So when I was 14—the same age that my grandmother was when she left her family, her country, and everything she knew—I took it upon myself to teach my grandmother something, something I already knew how to do. Something with which I could give back to her some of the things she had taught me.

13 And it was slight repayment for all she taught me. How to cover the fig tree in tar paper so it could survive the winter. How to cultivate rose bushes and magnolia trees that thrived on her little piece of property. How to make baklava, and other Greek delights, working from her memory. ("Now we add some milk." "How much?" "Until we have enough.") Best of all, she had taught me my ethnic heritage.

14 First, we phonetically sounded out the alphabet. Then, we talked about vowels—English is such a difficult language to learn. I hadn't even begun to explain the different sounds "gh" could make. We were still at the basics.

15 Every afternoon, we would sit in the living room, my grandmother with an afghan covering her knees, giving up her crocheting for her reading lesson. I, with the patience that can come only from love, slowly coached her from the basic reader to the second-grade reader, giving up my telephone gossiping.

16 Years later, my grandmother still hadn't learned quite enough to sit comfortably with a newspaper or magazine, but it felt awfully good to see her try. How we used to laugh at her pronunciation mistakes. She laughed more heartily than I. I never knew whether I should laugh. Here was this old woman slowly and carefully sounding out each word, moving her lips, not saying anything aloud until she was absolutely sure, and then, loudly, proudly, happily saying, "Look at Spot. See Spot run."

When my grandmother died and we faced the sad task of emptying her home, I was going through her night-table drawer and came upon the basic readers. I turned the pages slowly, remembering. I put them in a paper bag, and the next day returned them to the "little kids" school. Maybe someday, some teenager will request them again, for the same task. It will make for a lifetime of memories. 17

BUILDING VOCABULARY

Put the following phrases into your own words and explain what the writer means in the context of the essay.

a. "very impressed with my teenage status" (par. 1)
b. "No need to repeat the story of how it went for years." (par. 9) Why not? What is the implication of this sentence?
c. "doing piecework to earn enough money for meals." (par. 9) What was piecework?
d. "Best of all, she had taught me my ethnic heritage." (par. 13)
e. "First, we phonetically sounded out the alphabet." (par. 14)

THINKING CRITICALLY ABOUT THE ESSAY

Understanding the Writer's Ideas

1. The author begins by saying that her project was a secret from her junior high school peers. Explain why a 14-year-old would not want to be seen carrying basic readers. What further reasons might the author have had for keeping her project a secret?
2. In paragraph 3, the author uses the words "proudly" and "proud." Why has her attitude changed?
3. How does teaching her grandmother to read change the relation between the two? How does Frisina speak to her grandmother in paragraph 4?
4. What are the myths about America that cause the grandmother to make her difficult decision to leave her family in Greece? How does the real America live up to the stories the grandmother had heard before she arrived? How common are experiences like the grandmother's for other immigrants?

5. What does Frisina imply in paragraph 10 about the daily life of immigrants in the early twentieth century? How is language usually acquired? What limits the grandmother's ability to learn English?
6. The author provides details of what her grandmother taught her for which the author is grateful. How do the specific details help the reader understand the kind of woman the grandmother was? What kind of life did the grandmother lead?
7. In paragraph 14, the author describes how hard it is to learn English. What in particular makes English a hard language to read? What can you tell from paragraph 17 about how the grandmother felt about her reading? Why does the grandmother keep the schoolbooks in her night-table drawer? What does this tell you about how she felt about learning to read?

Understanding the Writer's Techniques

1. Where does the author place her thesis statement? Why does she put it where she does? Explain the thesis in your own words.
2. *Diction* (see Glossary) refers to a writer's choice and use of words. We classify *levels of diction*—"informal," "academic," "low-class," "snobbish," "conversational," and so forth. How would you describe the general level of diction in this essay? Does the level suit the subject matter? Why?
3. Why does the author rely on short paragraphs throughout her narrative? What does the paragraph length and diction tell you about the intended audience for this piece?
4. The writer assumes that the reader is familiar with the history of immigration in America in the early twentieth century. How do we know that she makes this assumption? Should she provide readers with more historical detail? Why or why not?
5. Describe the method the author uses to teach her grandmother to read. Is this the way you remember learning to read? Describe the first book you remember reading. How did your experience compare with the grandmother's?

Exploring the Writer's Ideas

1. The author uses the story of her grandmother's life to illustrate the experiences of many immigrants who came to

America in the early twentieth century. How do those experiences compare with the arrival of immigrants to America today? Is it easier or more difficult to immigrate here now? What evidence can you provide to support your position?

2. Though the grandmother could barely read a newspaper, even her limited literacy seemed to give her pleasure. Why should learning to read be so important to an adult who cannot read? In a world of television, movies, and other visual sources of information, is learning to read truly important for illiterate adults? Why or why not?
3. The effort to teach and learn reading helps bridge the gap between generations. Do you see any practical applications here for bringing old and young people together for more harmonious relations? How else can young people and old people be united?

IDEAS FOR WRITING

Prewriting

Teaching someone to do something—anything—is fraught with problems and, at the same time, alive with possibilities and rewards. What do you see as the positive and negative aspects of teaching someone to do something? Use free association to indicate as many pluses and minuses as you can.

Guided Writing

Write an essay titled "Teaching __________ to __________." Fill in the blanks after considering your own experience with teaching someone something. You might choose one of these topics:

Teaching my daughter/son to read
Reading English as a second language (about your own experience or someone else's)
Working as a volunteer in a neighborhood literacy program

1. Begin your essay with a general discussion about the expectations you had when you started this learning project and the feelings you had when you accomplished it.

2. Define yourself as a reader. What age were you when you started the project? What kind of reading did you do? How did you feel about reading? Why?
3. Explain why you started the project of teaching someone to read or of changing the level of your own reading skill. What situation encouraged or required you to change or act?
4. Use examples and illustrations to show how you began the task. Give examples of words and sentences you worked with. Give the steps you used to carry out your project.
5. Describe the moment when a change happened—the first time your son or daughter read to you or the first time a difficult English sentence became clear. Use dialogue to capture the moment.
6. Analyze how you changed as a result of this moment, and why you remember it so vividly.
7. Conclude by describing your present status as a reader, or the skills level of the person you taught to read. Was the project worthwhile?

Thinking and Writing Collaboratively

Form groups of three students each, and read aloud drafts of each other's essays for the Guided Writing activity. Then discuss the essays. Was the writer's experience clear to you? Do you know why the writer started his or her teaching project? Do the illustrations show how the task was performed? Did the writer make clear the moment of change?

More Writing Projects

1. In your journal, write down your ideas about what the difference is between reading "See Spot Run" and reading a science textbook or a technical manual or a play by Shakespeare. Give steps by which a reader can increase his or her reading skills.
2. Write a paragraph in which you consider whether or not it is important to be a "good" reader to succeed in life.
3. Can teaching someone else, like a son or daughter, to read teach you to read better as well? Write an essay in which you discuss a parent's role in teaching his or her child to read. Consider what the child learns at school and what he or she learns at home about reading.

Apostles of the Faith That Books Matter

Vivian Gornick

The author Vivian Gornick remembers the first book she took out from a public library as a child, and the silent, forbidding librarian who lent it to her. She finds the librarians in the New York Public Library system remain fiercely committed to "bringing along the reader" in the diverse population of two million children and adults whom they serve in the city's 85 branch libraries.

PREREADING: THINKING ABOUT THE ESSAY IN ADVANCE

What, in your view, is the importance of books today compared to the time before radio and television? How important are books to you?

Words to Watch

paramount (par. 3) most important
domain (par. 14) estate, area of influence
voracious (par. 16) constantly wanting more
ephemera (par. 17) anything short lived
autocratically (par. 17) dictatorially
immutable (par. 23) unchanging

1 When I was 8 years old, my mother took me by the hand and marched me four blocks up the street to a storefront branch of the public library. We opened the door and crossed over into a rectangular room lined from floor to ceiling with books. At a desk in the center of the room sat a large woman with gray hair piled up on her head and rimless glasses secured to the bridge of her nose. My mother approached the desk, pointed at my head and said, "She likes to read."

2 I was directed to a set of shelves near the door marked "Children." I chose four books from these shelves and walked back to the desk. The librarian took the books from my hands, stamped them, and handed them to me along with the card she

had made out in my name. As she returned the books, with her fingers on one end of the stack and mine on the other, our eyes met. She didn't smile and she didn't speak. The moment felt solemn. I understand it to mean: "We are keepers of the culture, you and I. The book is everything. We're here to respect it."

3 That was 50 years ago in the Bronx. In time, I read my way around the room (I used the storefront library until I entered City College) with that same librarian sitting at that same desk for most of those years. We never became chummy. We continued as we had begun, our bargain over the book, silent and mutual, remaining paramount. It was only recently that I realized the librarian had looked something like Edith Wharton and I, of course, had looked to her like a Jewish immigrant's daughter. Keepers of the culture, indeed. But what exactly was the culture that we were keeping?

4 Not too long ago I was visiting the Aguilar branch of the library; at the time it, too, was a tiny storefront, on Third Avenue at 107th Street, making do while its permanent home on 110th Street was being renovated. The room was crowded and noisy, filled with black and brown children among whom the librarian—tall, blond, in her mid-20's—was a vivid presence.

5 A boy of 10 or 12—slight, with fragile eyes behind rimless glasses—came up to the desk where we sat talking. The librarian broke off in mid-sentence. "Yes?" she said.

6 The boy hesitated. "I need to look up rattlesnakes," he announced.

7 She told him that he could find what he was looking for under reptiles, or in the geography section under Southwest. Still, he hesitated. The librarian got up, excused herself and took him out to the shelves.

8 When she came back she said, "In this neighborhood, if a kid walks in the door and he can't find what he's looking for, I've lost him. And that hurts." She paused, and then she said: "I love helping someone find that book they need. I really love it. I bring along the reader in them. And then," she spread her hands in the air palms up and laughed, "some of them turn out to be readers! It's always a thrill."

9 I found myself thinking back to Edith Wharton in the Bronx. That was the culture we'd been keeping: the librarian providing herself with the thrill of bringing along the reader in me, and me turning out to be a reader.

10 It's one of the largest public library systems in the world: the neighborhood branches of the New York Public Library.

There are 85 of them in the Bronx, Manhattan and Staten Island (Brooklyn and Queens have their own systems). Through the branches pass more than 10 million books, magazines, pictures and records a year, circulating among more than two million cardholders, living in every grade of neighborhood from the self-assured Upper East Side to wasted stretches of the South Bronx.

Everywhere, they contain the first books that countless New York City children will read, and the librarian who will lead them into a reading life. 11

Librarians come up in the ranks; they move from assistant to head to regional head, and they work where they are assigned to work; many of them put in years in neighborhoods some would think of as undesirable. I was struck when I was wandering around talking to branch librarians by how little interested they seemed in the obvious: an assignment in a safer neighborhood. 12

The children's librarian at the Jefferson Market branch in the West Village had worked some years at the overcrowded Fort Washington branch in densely Dominican Washington Heights. Looking around the spacious children's room at Jefferson Market, I remarked on how nice it must be to work here. The librarian replied with some intensity in her voice, "I loved Fort Washington." 13

Across town, at the Ottendorfer branch on Second Avenue at Eighth Street (the oldest operating branch in the city), the rooms were shabby, worn, dingy; a wallful of paperbacks (mystery, romance, science fiction) lined the entry way. The librarian, crisp and neat, led me upstairs to a thriving children's room that shared its space with a great collection of leather-bound German language books—the branches house collections in 17 foreign languages—and gazed with pleasure on the goodness of her small domain. "People love reading up here," she said. 14

On the Upper West Side, a staff librarian described the people who use her branch as among the most literate library users in New York: "They walk in on Monday morning armed with the Times Book Review and want to know when the book they've circled will be in. Here a kid does not walk out never to return if he can't get what he wants on first request." 15

When asked if that meant there were more voracious readers up here, the librarian, who had put in years in the Bronx and on the Lower East Side, said: "No. It does not. It only means a higher level of uniformity on the shelves." 16

"Serving the needs of the community" is a commonly heard phrase among librarians. Inevitably, the question such a phrase 17 raises is, "Do you give them what they want, or do you give them what they need?" Everywhere in the branches, the shelves hold a goodly amount of the ephemera of popular culture. Today, I am told, the library, like all other institutions, can no longer pick and choose autocratically; it has, somehow, to strike a participating balance.

18 I cannot help thinking, 50 years ago in the Bronx, if the library had responded to my needs instead of shaping my needs, what sort of a reader would I have become?

19 Chatham Square was a fine place to pursue the question "Do you give them what they want, or do you give them what they need?" This Chinatown branch is a model of immigrant love for the public library (a woman from China stood in the doorway one day last year, with a child in each hand, staring at the room. "Free?" she said softly. "All this is free?").

20 The four floors at Chatham Square are, at all times, in fullest use; downstairs, in the basement reference room, there was someone at the computer 10 minutes after it was installed; upstairs, two floors of books, games, art materials—and a constant swarm of children; on the main floor, students of all ages, as well as a good sprinkling of the middle-aged and the old, everyone reading newspapers and magazines or sitting with reference books spread out on the tables before them. Nevertheless, the shelves are dominated by books on computers, on travel and on China; self-help and how-to; mysteries and best-selling fiction; fantasy and pop psychology.

21 The retiring librarian said she didn't care what was on the shelves as long as people were in here reading, forming, as she said, a lifelong habit. She had spent 47 years in the system, 30 of them here at Chatham Square. "I've had a remarkable working life," she told me, 71 years old and eyes glowing. "It's been absolutely wonderful, turning people into readers."

22 And that, she said, you did by providing the atmosphere in which to help people form the habit.

23 The single most repeated phrase among the librarians is, "bringing out the reader in them." The phrase is powerful. It speaks to a central belief about the nature of human need—of the need, timeless and immutable, for narrative; the compelling hunger to make sense of experience through the words spun out in a story; the thing that nothing but a book can deliver. The branch librarians know that those who respond to narrative are to be found everywhere, often in the most unexpected quarters.

The Columbia branch, on 113th Street, is a small, beautiful room with dark shelving all around, cozy, crowded, silent. The people who come to this branch are among the most devoted of library users. The librarian followed my brooding eyes as I scanned the room appreciatively. Then he told me that he had worked for years in the Tremont branch, a library in the Bronx that sits in the middle of blasted streets, in a seemingly deserted neighborhood. 24

"Nevertheless," the librarian said, "in 1975, when the city was threatening to slash the library system, parents sat down in only two of the branches slated for closure." He points at the floor. "Here at Columbia, and at Tremont." 25

He looked around the room and his own eyes began to brood. I knew it wasn't either Columbia or Tremont he was loving at that moment. It was both. It was the two of them together. 26

BUILDING VOCABULARY

Use the following words in sentences of your own. Check their meanings in a dictionary.

a. solemn (par. 2)
b. vivid (par. 4)
c. dingy (par. 14)
d. dominated (par. 20)
e. atmosphere (par. 22)
f. scanned (par. 24)
g. slated (par. 25)

THINKING CRITICALLY ABOUT THE ESSAY

1. Why does the writer open her essay with a personal recollection?
2. What picture of the writer as a child do we get from the first two paragraphs? What key words or phrases convey this picture?
3. Why is it so important that the librarian whom Gornick encountered at her branch library as a child "didn't smile and didn't speak" when the writer took her first books out?
4. What is the purpose of linking the major American author Edith Wharton, who wrote of high society, and a Jewish immigrant?

5. Write a list of the names and locations of the libraries the writer discusses. What do these names and locations tell you? Why did the writer select these particular branch libraries to talk about?
6. We learn in the essay that librarians in the New York public library system have no choice about which branch they are assigned to. What, according to Gornick, is the attitude of the librarians to their assignments in radically different neighborhoods?
7. The writer reports that two phrases are repeated most often by the librarians she visited. What are they? What do these phrases tell you about how the librarians see their work?
8. Explain the implied differences in philosophy in the question "Do you give them what they want, or do you give them what they need?" (par. 19). How do the librarians whom Gornick visits answer this question?
9. What is Gornick's purpose, at the close of her essay (par. 26), in associating the Columbia and Tremont branches?

Understanding the Writer's Techniques

1. Where in the essay does the writer state her purpose for writing most clearly? Is there an explicit thesis statement? If yes, quote it. If not, can you compose a thesis statement on behalf of the writer?
2. How does the writer's personal experience as a child serve as a kind of anchor for the essay? How would the essay be different if it were written without reference to the writer's childhood experience?
3. Explain the reason for the apparently abrupt transition between paragraphs 9 and 10.
4. This essay develops its argument by the use of numerous examples to flesh out its core ideas (see *illustration* in Glossary). Discuss how the writer integrates these illustrations into the flow of her essay.
5. The writer employs both "deductive" and "inductive" reasoning in this essay. That is, she moves from the general to the specific (deductive) and from specific examples to general points (induction). Identify at least one example of each mode of reasoning.
6. Toward the end of the essay (par. 23), the writer seems to shift into a different mode and *tone* (see Glossary) of writing,

becoming more direct, more judgmental, and more eloquent. How does the wealth of supporting detail in the essay give this bold expression of the writer's views authority and legitimacy? Why is her language in this paragraph more formal and elevated than elsewhere?

Exploring the Writer's Ideas

1. The writer's portrait of librarians is of noble, dedicated "apostles" who serve the cause of reading selflessly, and without exception. Might the writer be offering us an unrepresentative group of librarians? Or is the stereotype of the librarian as a severe disciplinarian standing guard over pedantry just that, a nasty and unfair portrait?
2. The writer asserts that "the reader" in each of us represents a fundamental "human need," the need for narrative. Do you think the essay provides sufficient evidence to support that assertion? Explain.
3. Is it true that "nothing but a book can deliver" the kind of illumination that the writer admires? Is the writer making too much of books?

IDEAS FOR WRITING

Prewriting

Insert a different faith in the writer's title "Apostles of the Faith That __________ Matters," and write a sentence or two as a first attempt at a thesis statement for an essay on that title.

Guided Writing

Write an essay about something you value deeply enough to call a "faith," and explain why you (or someone you know) are an "apostle" of that faith. Perhaps you have faith that *exercise* matters or *leisure* or *volunteerism* or *computers*.

1. Begin by describing an incident that initiated you into the faith.
2. Explain how that initial experience triggered a lifelong passion for the faith and nevertheless made you wonder just what your "faith" really was about.

3. Explain how you discovered the full answer to the meaning of your faith.
4. Offer two illustrations of how you (or someone you know) now act as an apostle of your faith.
5. In more general terms, state why your faith matters.

Thinking and Writing Collaboratively

In groups of four or five, discuss you first experiences of taking a book out of the library. Decide together on an illustration that the writer could add to her essay either in support of her thesis or in departure from it.

More Writing Projects

1. In your journal, list the titles of some books that were or are especially meaningful to you. Write a sentence or two to explain your selections.
2. Jot down some thoughts on the difference between what people "want" and what they "need."
3. Write an essay supporting the view that more money should be spent on libraries and less on the police.

SUMMING UP: CHAPTER 2

1. In one way or another, all the writers in this chapter explain how reading has provided them with emotional ease or intellectual stimulation at some point in their lives. Which of these writers, alone or in combination, best reflects your own view of reading? Write an essay in which you address this question.
2. On the average, Americans are said to read less than one book per person annually. Take a survey of several people who are not students to find out how often and what kind of books they read. In an essay, analyze the results. Indicate the types of people you interviewed, and explain why your results either conformed to or differed from the norm. Indicate the types of books each person read.
3. List all the books you have read in the past six months. For each, write a brief two- or three-sentence reaction. Compare your list with those of your classmates. What reading trends do you notice? From these lists, what generalizations can you draw about college students' reading habits?
4. The United States ranks forty-ninth among nations in literacy. People often ask, "Why is there such a low rate of literacy in such an advanced nation?" What is your answer to this question? How do you think the writers in this chapter would respond to the question? Write an essay that explains your response by drawing on Welty, Malcolm X, Frisina, and Gornick. Suggest some ways to improve the rate of literacy in this country. You might want to consider this fact: By the time the average American finishes high school, he or she has spent 18,000 hours in front of a television set as compared to 12,000 hours in the classroom.
5. Using Welty or Gornick as an example, write an essay in which you reflect on your early memories of reading. Describe when you learned to read, when you experienced pleasure at being read to, or when you started appreciating a particular kind of reading. Call your essay "Reading When I Was Young."

CHAPTER 3

Description

WHAT IS DESCRIPTION?

Description is a technique for showing readers what the writer sees: objects, scenes, characters, ideas, and even emotions and moods. Good description relies on the use of *sensory language*—that is, language that evokes our five senses of sight, touch, taste, smell, and sound. In writing, description uses specific *nouns* and *adjectives* to create carefully selected vivid details. The word "vehicle" is neutral, but a "rusty, green 1959 Pontiac convertible" creates a picture. Description is frequently used to make abstract ideas more *concrete.* While the abstract word "liberty" may have a definition for each reader, a description of the Statue of Liberty gleaming in New York's harbor at twilight creates an emotional description of liberty. Description, then, is used by writers who want their readers to *see* what they are writing about. A writer like Louise Erdrich uses description of the natural world to reflect on being a parent. A physician, like Richard Selzer, uses description to re-create the experience of a dying patient. Maxine Hong Kingston uses vivid description of her mother's collection of turtles, catfish, pigeons, skunks, and other unexpected food sources to re-create for her readers a culture different from their own. Mary Cantwell relies on description to capture the concrete details of an all-too-happy childhood. Each writer, then, uses description to help us, as readers, *see* the material about which he or she is writing. As writers, we can study their techniques to improve our own essays.

HOW DO WE READ DESCRIPTION?

Reading a descriptive essay requires us to

- Identify what the writer is describing, and ask why he or she is describing it.
- Look for the concrete nouns, supportive adjectives, or other sensory words that the writer uses to create vivid pictures.
- Find the perspective or angle from which the writer describes: Is it top to bottom, left to right, front to back? Or is it a mood description that relies on feelings? How has the writer *selected* details to create the mood?
- Determine how the writer has organized the description. Here we must look for a "dominant impression." This arises from the writer's focus on a single subject and the feelings that the writer brings to that subject. Each one should be identified.
- Identify the purpose of the description. What is the *thesis* of the writing?
- Determine what audience the writer is aiming toward. How do we know?

HOW DO WE WRITE DESCRIPTION?

After reading some of the selections of descriptive writing in this chapter, you should be ready to write your own description. Don't just read about Kingston's animals, though, or Erdrich's blue jay. Think critically about how you can adapt their methods to your needs.

Select a topic and begin to write a thesis statement, keeping in mind that you will want to give the reader information about what you are describing and what angle you are taking on the topic.

Sample thesis sentence:

> For a first-time tourist in New York City, the subway trains can seem confusing and threatening, but the long-time resident finds the train system a clever, speedy network for traveling around the city.

Here, we see the thesis statement sets out a purpose and an audience. The purpose is to demonstrate the virtues of the New York transit system, and the audience is not the well-traveled New Yorker, but a visitor.

Collect a list of sensory words.

New York City's subway trains are noisy and crowded, labeled with brightly colored letters, made of shiny corrugated stainless steel, travel at 90 miles per hour, display colorful graffiti and advertising signs, run on electricity.

Use the five senses:

What are subway sounds? Music by street musicians, the screech of brakes, conductors giving directions over scratchy loudspeakers, people talking in different languages.

What are subway smells? Pretzels roasting, the sweaty odor of human bodies crowded together on a hot summer day.

What are subway textures? Colored metal straps and poles for balance, the crisp corner of a newspaper you're reading.

What are subway tastes? A candy bar or chewing gum you buy at the newsstand.

What are subway sights? Crowds of people rushing to work; the colorful pillars freshly painted in each station; the drunk asleep on a bench; the police officer in a blue uniform; the litter on the ground; the subway system maps near each token booth; the advertising posters on the walls and trains.

Plan a dominant impression and an order for arranging details. You might look at the subway from a passenger's point of view and describe the travel process from getting onto the train to arriving at the destination. Your impression might be that to the uninitiated, the subway system seems confusing, but to the experienced New Yorker, trains are the fastest and safest way to get around town.

Express a *purpose* for the description. The purpose might be to prepare a visitor from out of town for her first subway ride by writing a letter to her before she arrives in New York.

Identify the audience: Who will read the essay?

If you were writing to the Commissioner of Transportation in New York, or to a cousin from Iowa whom you know well, you would write differently in each case. Awareness of audience can help you choose a level of diction and formality. Knowing your audience can also help you decide which details to include and which your readers might know. It is always best to assume that the audience knows less than you do and to include details even if they seem obvious to you.

For example, even if you, as a native New Yorker, know that subway trains run twenty-four hours a day, your cousin from Iowa would not be expected to know this, so you should include it as part of your description of how efficient the system is.

Writing the Draft

Use the thesis statement to set up an introductory paragraph. Then plan the body paragraphs so that they follow the order you decided on—from beginning the journey to arriving, from the top of a subway car to the bottom, or from the outside of the train to the inside. Include as many details in the first draft as possible; it is easier to take them out in a second or third draft than to add them later. Then plan the conclusion to help the reader understand what the purpose of the description has been.

Reading and Revising the Draft

Read your first draft, circling each description word. Then go back and add *another* description word after the ones already in the essay. If you can't think of any more words, use a *thesaurus* to find new words.

If possible, read your essay aloud to a classmate. Ask him or her to tell you if the details are vivid. Have your classmate suggest where more details are needed. Check to see that you have included some description in each sensory category: sight, sound, taste, touch, and smell.

Proofread your essay for correctness.
Make a clean, neat final copy.

A STUDENT PARAGRAPH: DESCRIPTION

Read the student paragraph below about the New York City subway. Look for descriptive elements that can help you write your own paper on description. Comments in the margin highlight important features of descriptive writing.

Topic sentence announces purpose

A first-time visitor to the New York City subway system will probably find the noise overwhelming, at least at first. The variety of sounds, and their sheer volume, can send most unprepared tourists running for the exit; those who remain tend to slip into a state of deep shock. As I wait for the Number 4 train at the Lexington Avenue station, the passing express cars explode from the tunnel in a blur of red and gray. Sometimes as many as three trains roar by at the same time. A high-pitched squeal of brakes adds powerfully to the din. A few passengers heave sighs or mutter under their breath as the crackle and hiss of an unintelligible announcement coming over the public address system adds to the uproar. As I continue to wait for the local, I can hear fragments of the shouted exchanges between weary booth attendants and impatient customers trying to communicate through the bulletproof glass. Irritably, I watch one of the many subway musicians, an old bald man who sings "O Solo Mio" off-key as a battered tape recorder behind him plays warped-sounding violin music. Once in a while some goodhearted passenger tosses a crumpled dollar bill into an old straw hat at the singer's feet. Why are they encouraging these horrible sounds, I wonder to myself? I obviously haven't been here long enough to tune them out.

Supporting detail

Supporting detail

Supporting detail

Supporting detail

Concluding sentence returns to topic, providing coherence

The Blue Jay's Dance

Louise Erdrich

Louise Erdrich, the daughter of a German immigrant and a Chippewa Indian, is best known for her novels *Love Medicine* (1984) and *Beet Queen* (1986). Note in this descriptive essay how she uses images of a hawk and a blue jay to reflect on parents' responsibilities in protecting their children.

PREREADING: THINKING ABOUT THE ESSAY IN ADVANCE

What are a parent's responsibilities to a child? What struggles do you see a parent enduring to keep a child safe from harm? When does the parent's obligation to protect the child stop? Does it ever stop?

Words to Watch

raucous (par. 2) rough-sounding and harsh

feints (par. 3) attacks in a manner designed to draw defensive action away from an intended target

manic (par. 4) excessively intense or enthusiastic

clench (par. 4) close tightly

differentiating (par. 4) to show the difference in or between

1 The hawk sweeps over, light shining through her rust red tail. She makes an immaculate cross in flight, her shadow running along the ground behind her as I'm walking below. Our shadows join, momentarily, and then separate, both to our appointed rounds. Always, she hunts flying into the cast of the sun, making a pass east to west. Once inside, I settle baby, resettle baby, settle and resettle myself, and have just lowered my head into my hands to proofread a page when a blur outside my vision causes me to look up.

2 The hawk drops headfirst out of a cloud. She folds her wings hard against her and plunges into the low branches of the apple tree, moving at such dazzling speed I can barely follow.

She strikes at one of the seven blue jays who make up the raucous gang and it tumbles before her, head over feet, end over end. She plunges after it from the branches, flops in the sun. They both light on the ground and square off, about a foot apart in the snow.

3 The struck jay thrusts out its head, screams, raises its wings, and dances *toward* the gray hawk. The plain of snow must seem endless, an arena without shelter, and the bird gets no help from the other six jays except loud encouragement at a safe distance. I hardly breathe. The hawk, on the ground, its wings clattering against the packed crust, is so much larger than its shadow, which has long brushed in and out of mine. It screams back, eyes filled with yellow light. Its hooked beak opens and it feints with its neck. Yet the jay, ridiculous, continues to dance, hopping forward, hornpiping up and down with tiny leaps, all of its feathers on end to increase its size. Its crest is sharp, its beak open in a continual shriek, its eye-mask fierce. It pedals its feet in the air. The hawk steps backward. She seems confused, cocks her head, and does not snap the blue jay's neck. She watches. Although I know nothing of the hawk and cannot imagine what moves her, it does seem to me that she is fascinated, that she puzzles at the absurd display before she raises her wings and lifts off.

4 Past the gray moralizing and the fierce Roman Catholic embrace of suffering and fate that so often clouds the subject of suicide, there is the blue jay's dance. Beyond the impossible corners, stark cliffs, dark wells of trapped longing, there is that manic, successful jig—cocky, exuberant, entirely a bluff, a joke. That dance makes me clench down hard on life. But it is also a dance that in other circumstances might lead me, you, anyone, to choose a voluntary death. I see in that small bird's crazy courage some of what it took for my grandparents to live out the tough times. I peer around me, stroke my own skin, look into this baby's eyes that register me as a blurred self-extension, as a function of her will. I have made a pact with life: if I were to die now it would be a form of suicide for her. Since the two of us are still in the process of differentiating, since my acts are hers and I do not even think, yet, where I stop for her or where her needs, exactly, begin, I must dance for her. I must be the one to dip and twirl in the cold glare and I must teach her, as she grows, the unlikely steps.

BUILDING VOCABULARY

Denotation refers to the dictionary definition of a word; *connotation* refers to the various shades of meaning and feelings readers bring to a word or phrase (see Glossary). Look up and write the dictionary definition for each of the words in italics. Then explain in your own words the connotative meaning of each sentence or phrase.

a. She makes an *immaculate* cross in flight (par. 1)
b. They both *light* on the ground and square off (par. 2)
c. The *struck* jay . . . dances toward the gray hawk. (par. 3)
d. Past the gray *moralizing* . . . there is the blue jay's dance. (par. 4)
e. *twirl* in the cold glare (par. 4)

THINKING CRITICALLY ABOUT THE ESSAY

Understanding the Writer's Ideas

1. What was the writer doing when she first looked up at the hawk? What does this tell us about the observer?
2. Why does the writer say the blue jay is "ridiculous" in paragraph 3?
3. What is Erdrich referring to in paragraph 4—the "Roman Catholic embrace of suffering and fate that so often clouds the subject of suicide"?
4. What tough times might Erdrich's grandparents have had to endure?
5. What does Erdrich mean when she says "I must dance for her"? To whom does she refer? To what dance? What is the dance's connection to the hawk?
6. What are the "unlikely steps" Erdrich concludes that she needs to teach her child? Explain.

Understanding the Writer's Techniques

1. What is the essay's thesis? How is it implied in the descriptive details of the hawk?
2. For the first three paragraphs Erdrich focuses purely on descriptive detail, but in paragraph 4 she shifts to first person narration. What impact does this have on the reader?

3. In the first sentence of paragraph 4, Erdrich writes about "gray moralizing." Can moralizing be gray or any color? (Look up the word *moralizing* in a dictionary.) Why is Erdrich using color in this way?
4. How does the essay's conclusion actually refer back to the beginning?

Exploring the Writer's Ideas

1. This essay begins with a powerful predator, the hawk, flying over a mother (the writer) settling her baby. Do you think the writer wants the reader to get the idea that the hawk might actually swoop down on this woman's child and not just the blue jay? Why or why not?
2. When the blue jay confronts the more powerful hawk, Erdrich says the jay is "ridiculous." Do you agree?
3. How would you explain the hawk's quick retreat after confronting the weaker blue jay, who "dances"?
4. Where does Erdrich get the idea that Roman Catholics embrace "suffering and fate"? What does she mean? Is she accurate?
5. Erdrich takes the position that if a mother chooses death (when confronting a stronger foe), this would be a form of suicide, and it would leave the child without protection. Is Erdrich overstating this situation? What do you think?
6. If you were to create a different title for the essay, what would it be? Explain.

IDEAS FOR WRITING

Prewriting

Make a list of the various ways that you think parents or guardians must protect children under their care.

Guided Writing

Write an essay on what you think is the single greatest threat to children today and what parents can do about it.

1. As an image to start your essay, choose a creature (the threat) that preys on smaller creatures (the child) and explore the image in at least two descriptive paragraphs. Follow Erdrich's

lead and do not make the link until later in the essay between these creatures and the idea of protecting the child.

2. Rely on concrete sensory detail to paint vivid pictures of the creatures you are describing. Use verbs that indicate precise actions; use specific nouns as opposed to too many adjectives.
3. Use a transition to bring together your view of how the creature's attack is similar to or different from the threat to children that you are writing about.
4. Explain why a caregiver should (or should not) intervene to protect a child from this threat.
5. Take a final position on how far you think a parent or guardian should go to protect his or her child. Should parents or guardians sacrifice their own lives to protect their children?

Thinking and Writing Collaboratively

Form groups of three or four students, and read your essays aloud. As a group, write a summary review of the main threats your group thinks face children today. Was there agreement on the dangers? How would the group rank these threats by importance?

More Writing Projects

1. Use your journal to record your worst or best dreams.
2. Write a descriptive paragraph that uses sensory detail to recreate one of your best or worst dreams.
3. Do the following: Imagine you are standing on the edge of the universe. You look over the edge and what you see is the ideal place to raise a child. Write an essay that describes that place.

Catfish in the Bathtub

Maxine Hong Kingston

In this selection from her best-selling *The Woman Warrior* (1976), Chinese-American author Maxine Hong Kingston describes various strange eating habits of her childhood. The author skillfully blends techniques of personal narration and rich sensory detailing to create a fascinating impression of another culture's daily lifestyle.

PREREADING: THINKING ABOUT THE ESSAY IN ADVANCE

What unusual foods have you eaten? What unusual dish can you remember one of your relatives preparing when you were a child? How did you feel about eating this food?

Words to Watch

dromedaries (par. 1) one-humped camels
sensibility (par. 1) ability to receive sensations
perched (par. 1) resting on a bird's roost
scowls (par. 1) expressions of displeasure
dismembering (par. 1) taking apart bodily limbs and innards
sprains (par. 2) sudden twists of joints such as ankles or wrists
unsettle (par. 3) make uneasy or uncomfortable
tufts (par. 4) forms into small patches of hair
awobble (par. 6) unsteady; teetering
toadstools (par. 7) mushrooms
revulsion (par. 8) a strong reaction away from something

1 My mother has cooked for us: raccoons, skunks, hawks, city pigeons, wild ducks, wild geese, black-skinned bantams, snakes, garden snails, turtles that crawled about the pantry floor and sometimes escaped under refrigerator or stove, catfish that swam in the bathtub. "The emperors used to eat the peaked hump of purple dromedaries," she would say. "They used chopsticks made from rhinoceros horn, and they ate ducks' tongues and monkeys'

lips." She boiled the weeds we pulled up in the yard. There was a tender plant with flowers like white stars hiding under the leaves, which were like the flower petals but green. I've not been able to find it since growing up. It had no taste. When I was as tall as the washing machine, I stepped out on the back porch one night, and some heavy, ruffling, windy, clawed thing dived at me. Even after getting chanted back to sensibility, I shook when I recalled that perched everywhere there were owls with great hunched shoulders and yellow scowls. They were a surprise for my mother from my father. We children used to hide under the beds with our fingers in our ears to shut out the bird screams and the thud, thud of the turtles swimming in the boiling water, their shells hitting the sides of the pot. Once the third aunt who worked at the laundry ran out and bought us bags of candy to hold over our noses; my mother was dismembering skunk on thc chopping block. I could smell the rubbery odor through the candy.

In a glass jar on a shelf my mother kept a big brown hand 2
with pointed claws stewing in alcohol and herbs. She must have brought it from China because I do not remember a time when I did not have the hand to look at. She said it was a bear's claw, and for many years I thought bears were hairless. My mother used the tobacco, leeks, and grasses swimming about the hand to rub our sprains and bruises.

Just as I would climb up to the shelf to take one look after 3
another at the hand, I would hear my mother's monkey story. I'd take my fingers out of my ears and let her monkey words enter my brain. I did not always listen voluntarily, though. She would begin telling the story, perhaps repeating it to a homesick villager, and I'd overhear before I had a chance to protect myself. Then the monkey words would unsettle me; a curtain flapped loose inside my brain. I have wanted to say, "Stop it. Stop it," but not once did I say, "Stop it."

"Do you know what people in China eat when they have 4
the money?" my mother began. "They buy into a monkey feast. The eaters sit around a thick wood table with a hole in the middle. Boys bring in the monkey at the end of a pole. Its neck is in a collar at the end of the pole, and it is screaming. Its hands are tied behind it. They clamp the monkey into the table; the whole table fits like another collar around its neck. Using a surgeon's saw, the cooks cut a clean line in a circle at the top of its head. To loosen the bone, they tap with a tiny hammer and wedge here and there with a silver pick. Then an old woman reaches out her hand to

the monkey's face and up to its scalp, where she tufts some hairs and lifts off the lid of the skull. The eaters spoon out the brains."

5 Did she say, "You should have seen the faces the monkey made"? Did she say, "The people laughed at the monkey screaming"? It was alive? The curtain flaps closed like merciful black wings.

6 "Eat! Eat!" my mother would shout at our heads bent over bowls, the blood pudding awobble in the middle of the table.

7 She had one rule to keep us safe from toadstools and such: "If it tastes good, it's bad for you," she said. "If it tastes bad, it's good for you."

8 We'd have to face four- and five-day-old leftovers until we ate it all. The squid eye would keep appearing at breakfast and dinner until eaten. Sometimes brown masses sat on every dish. I have seen revulsion on the faces of visitors who've caught us at meals.

9 "Have you eaten yet?" the Chinese greet one another.

10 "Yes, I have," they answer whether they have or not. "And you?"

11 I would live on plastic.

BUILDING VOCABULARY

1. Go through this essay again and list every animal mentioned. Then, write a short description of each, using the dictionary or encyclopedia if necessary.
2. Use any five of the Words to Watch in sentences of your own.

THINKING CRITICALLY ABOUT THE ESSAY

Understanding the Writer's Ideas

1. What is Kingston saying about her childhood? How does her opening catalogue of foods that her mother prepared, combined with further descriptions of foods, support this point? What are some of the "strange" foods that she ate but that are not mentioned in this first paragraph?
2. Who are "the emperors" mentioned in paragraph 1? What were some of their more unusual dishes?
3. What attacks and frightens the young Kingston on her back porch? Where did they come from? How do we know that

she was a young girl at the time? Explain the meaning of "even after getting chanted back to sensibility."

4. At the end of the first paragraph, the author mentions methods she and her siblings used to shut out unpleasant sensory input. What were they?
5. For what purpose did her mother keep a bear's claw in a glass jar? Where did Kingston think it came from? Why?
6. What are the "monkey words"? Summarize the "monkey words" in your own language. Kingston says that she wanted to say "Stop it" to the monkey words, but didn't. Why didn't she?
7. What was Kingston's mother's attitude toward the taste of things in relation to their healthfulness?
8. Why would there sometimes be "revulsion on the faces of visitors" who watched the author's family eating?
9. What is the traditional Chinese greeting?
10. What is the author's overall attitude toward her mother? Explain.

Understanding the Writer's Techniques

1. Does Kingston ever make a direct *thesis statement?* Why or why not?
2. In this essay, Kingston seems to shift in and out of various tenses deliberately. For example, in paragraph 3, she writes: ". . . a curtain *flapped* loose inside my brain. I *have wanted* to say. . . ." Why do you think that Kingston uses such a technique? List three other examples of such tense shifts.
3. Comment on Kingston's use of transitions. How do they contribute to the overall *coherence* (see Glossary) of the essay?
4. How does Kingston use the five senses to create descriptive imagery? Give examples of her use of sounds, tastes, smells, sights, and feelings. Which are the most effective?
5. Eliminating the specific references to China, how do we know that the author is of Chinese background? Which details or references contribute to this understanding?
6. Evaluate the use of *dialogue* (records of spoken words or conversations) in this essay. What effect does it have on the flow of the writing? On our understanding of Kingston's main point?

7. In paragraph 1, why does the author give so much attention to the white flower stars with no taste? Is she merely describing yet another thing she ate, or does she have some other purpose? Explain.
8. Although other incidents or ideas are described rather briefly, Kingston devotes a full, detailed paragraph to a description of the monkey feast. Why?
9. Throughout the essay, Kingston combines very realistic description (the bear's claw, the turtles thudding against the cook pot, the monkey feast) with various *similes* and *metaphors* (see Glossary). Explain the meaning of the following uses of *figurative language* (see Glossary):
   a. a curtain flapped loose inside my brain (par. 3)
   b. The curtain flaps closed like merciful black wings. (par. 5)
   c. Sometimes brown masses sat on every dish. (par. 8)
10. What is the effect of the series of questions in paragraph 5? Why are some in quotations and others not?
11. Explain the meaning of the last sentence. How does it relate to Kingston's *purpose* (see Glossary) in this essay?

Exploring the Writer's Ideas

1. Kingston certainly describes some "strange" foods and eating habits in this essay. But what makes particular foods "strange"? What are some of the strangest foods you have ever eaten? Where did they come from? Why did you eat them? How did you react to them? What foods or eating habits that are common to your everyday life might be considered strange by people from other cultures?
2. In this essay, Kingston concentrates on her mother, mentioning her father only once. Speculate on why she excludes her father in this way, but base your speculation on the material of the essay.
3. As we all know, different cultures have very different customs. In this essay, for example, the author describes the Chinese way of greeting one another as well as the monkey feast, both of which are quite foreign to American culture. Describe different cultural customs that you have observed in your school, among your friends, in places around your city or town. How do you feel when you observe customs

different from the ones you are familiar with? Do you believe that any particular custom is "right" or "wrong"? Why? Which custom among your own culture's would you most like to see changed? Why?

4. Describe your reaction to the monkey feast description.
5. For what reason do you think the Chinese greet each other with the words "Have you eaten yet?" Attempt to do further research on this custom. List as many different ways as you know of people greeting one another.

IDEAS FOR WRITING

Prewriting

Write the words *Family Food* on top of a sheet of paper and write everything that comes to mind about the topic. Give yourself about five minutes or so. Do not edit your writing: put as many of your ideas as you can on paper.

Guided Writing

Write an essay entitled "Food" in which you describe its importance to you, your family, and your cultural background.

1. Begin with a list of important foods related to your family's lifestyle.
2. Show the role of your parents or other relatives in relation to these foods.
3. Briefly tell about an incident involving food that affected you deeply.
4. Create strong sensory imagery. Attempt to use at least one image for each of the five senses.
5. If possible, relate food customs to your family's ethnic or cultural background.
6. Use dialogue in your essay, including some of the dialogue of your "inner voice."
7. Use transitions to make the parts of your essay cohere.
8. Mention how outsiders experienced this custom.
9. End your essay with a direct statement to summarize your current attitude toward the food you have described and those times in your life.

Thinking and Writing Collaboratively

Read a draft of the Guided Writing essay by one of your classmates. Then, write a paragraph to indicate what you learned about the importance of food to the writer and to his or her family and cultural background. What parts of the essay stand out most in your mind? Where do you think the writer might have included further details?

More Writing Projects

1. In your journal, write a description of an interesting custom or activity that you witnessed, a custom coming from outside your own cultural or social background. Include vivid sensory details.
2. Describe in detail the most wonderful meal you have ever eaten.
3. Research and write a short report about the food and eating customs of a culture other than your own.

The Discus Thrower

Richard Selzer

Richard Selzer, a surgeon, gives his readers vivid insights into the excitement as well as the pathos of the world of medicine. His books include *Rituals of Surgery* (1974) and *Mortal Lessons* (1977). His essays are widely published in magazines, including *Esquire, Harper's,* and *Redbook.* In this essay, Selzer dramatically describes a patient's final day.

PREREADING: THINKING ABOUT THE ESSAY IN ADVANCE

What experiences have you had with hospital patients? Have you ever visited anyone in a hospital? What was the experience like? What did the patient look like?

Words to Watch

furtive (par. 1) sly
pruned (par. 2) cut back; trimmed
facsimile (par. 2) an exact copy
forceps (par. 19) an instrument used in operations for holding or pulling
shard (par. 19) a broken piece; fragment
athwart (par. 20) across
probes (par. 32) investigates thoroughly
hefts (par. 32) tests the weight of by lifting; heaves

I spy on my patients. Ought not a doctor to observe his patients by any means and from any stance, that he might the more fully assemble evidence? So I stand in the doorways of hospital rooms and gaze. Oh, it is not all that furtive an act. Those in bed need only look up to discover me. But they never do. 1

From the doorway of Room 542 the man in the bed seems deeply tanned. Blue eyes and close-cropped white hair give him the appearance of vigor and good health. But I know that his skin is not brown from the sun. It is rusted, rather, in the last stage of 2 containing the vile repose within. And the blue eyes are frosted, looking inward like the windows of a snowbound cottage. This man is blind. This man is also legless—the right leg missing from midthigh down, the left from just below the knee. It gives him the look of a bonsai, roots and branches pruned into the dwarfed facsimile of a great tree.

3 Propped on pillows, he cups his right thigh in both hands. Now and then he shakes his head as though acknowledging the intensity of his suffering. In all of this he makes no sound. Is he mute as well as blind?

4 The room in which he dwells is empty of all possessions—no get-well cards, small, private caches of food, day-old flowers, slippers, all the usual kick-shaws of the sickroom. There is only the bed, a chair, a nightstand, and a tray on wheels that can be swung across his lap for meals.

5 "What time is it?" he asks.

6 "Three o'clock."

7 "Morning or afternoon?"

8 "Afternoon."

9 He is silent. There is nothing else he wants to know.

10 "How are you?" I say.

11 "Who is it?" he asks.

12 "It's the doctor. How do you feel?"

13 He does not answer right away.

14 "Feel?" he says.

15 "I hope you feel better," I say.

16 I press the button at the side of the bed.

17 "Down you go," I say.

18 "Yes, down," he says.

19 He falls back upon the bed awkwardly. His stumps, unweighted by legs and feet, rise in the air, presenting themselves. I unwrap the bandages from the stumps, and begin to cut away the black scabs and the dead, glazed fat with scissors and forceps. A shard of white bone comes loose. I pick it away. I wash the wounds with disinfectant and redress the stumps. All this while, he does not speak. What is he thinking behind those lids that do not blink? Is he remembering a time when he was whole? Does he dream of feet? Of when his body was not a rotting log?

20 He lies solid and inert. In spite of everything, he remains impressive, as though he were a sailor standing athwart a slanting deck.

21 "Anything more I can do for you?" I ask.

22 For a long moment he is silent.

23 "Yes," he says at last and without the least irony. "You can bring me a pair of shoes."

24 In the corridor, the head nurse is waiting for me.

25 "We have to do something about him," she says. "Every morning he orders scrambled eggs for breakfast, and, instead of eating them, he picks up the plate and throws it against the wall."

26 "Throws his plate?"

27 "Nasty. That's what he is. No wonder his family doesn't come to visit. They probably can't stand him any more than we can."

28 She is waiting for me to do something.

29 "Well?"

30 "We'll see," I say.

31 The next morning I am waiting in the corridor when the kitchen delivers his breakfast. I watch the aide place the tray on thc stand and swing it across his lap. She presses the button to raise the head of the bed. Then she leaves.

32 In time the man reaches to find the rim of the tray, then on to find the dome of the covered dish. He lifts off the cover and places it on the stand. He fingers across the plate until he probes the eggs. He lifts the plate in both hands, sets it on the palm of his right hand, centers it, balances it. He hefts it up and down slightly, getting the feel of it. Abruptly, he draws back his right arm as far as he can.

33 There is the crack of the plate breaking against the wall at the foot of his bed and the small wet sound of the scrambled eggs dropping to the floor.

34 And then he laughs. It is a sound you have never heard. It is something new under the sun. It could cure cancer.

35 Out in the corridor, the eyes of the head nurse narrow.

36 "Laughed, did he?"

37 She writes something down on her clipboard.

38 A second aide arrives, brings a second breakfast tray, puts it on the nightstand, out of his reach. She looks over at me shaking her head and making her mouth go. I see that we are to be accomplices.

39 "I've got to feed you," she says to the man.

40 "Oh, no you don't," the man says.

41 "Oh, yes I do," the aide says, "after the way you just did. Nurse says so."

42 "Get me my shoes," the man says.

43 "Here's oatmeal," the aide says. "Open." And she touches the spoon to his lower lip.

44 "I ordered scrambled eggs," says the man.

45 "That's right," the aide says.

46 I step forward.

47 "Is there anything I can do?" I say.

48 "Who are you?" the man asks.

49 In the evening I go once more to that ward to make my rounds. The head nurse reports to me that Room 542 is deceased. She has discovered this quite by accident, she says. No, there had been no sound. Nothing. It's a blessing, she says.

50 I go into his room, a spy looking for secrets. He is still there in his bed. His face is relaxed, grave, dignified. After a while, I turn to leave. My gaze sweeps the wall at the foot of the bed, and I see the place where it has been repeatedly washed, where the wall looks very clean and very white.

BUILDING VOCABULARY

1. In this essay, Selzer uses a few words that derive from languages other than English. Look up the following words and tell what language they come from. Then, write a definition for each.
   - **a.** bonsai (par. 2)
   - **b.** caches (par. 4)
   - **c.** kick-shaws (par. 4)
2. Use these words from the essay in complete sentences of your own.
   - **a.** vile (par. 2)
   - **b.** repose (par. 2)
   - **c.** dwarfed (par. 2)
   - **d.** glazed (par. 19)
   - **e.** inert (par. 20)
   - **f.** accomplices (par. 38)

THINKING CRITICALLY ABOUT THE ESSAY

Understanding the Writer's Ideas

1. What reason does Selzer give for a doctor's spying on his patients?

2. What does the man in Room 542 look like? Why is his skin brown? How does Selzer know he is blind? Why does Selzer think the patient may be mute? When do we know that he is not mute?
3. What is the author's meaning of the phrase "vile repose" (par. 2)?
4. How do we know that this patient does not receive many visitors?
5. Aside from wanting to know the time of day, what is the patient's one request? Do you think he is serious about his request? Why?
6. Why does the patient hurl his food tray against the wall?
7. For what reason does the head nurse complain about the patient?
8. What does Selzer feel and think about the patient? How do you know?

Understanding the Writer's Techniques

1. What is the author's thesis? Where is it stated?
2. Throughout the essay, Selzer asks a number of questions. Locate at least three of these questions that are not a part of the dialogue. To whom do you think they are addressed? What is their effect on the reader?
3. Selzer heightens the description by making vivid and unusual comparisons. Locate and explain in your own words three comparisons that you feel are especially descriptive and intriguing.
4. Selzer uses some very short sentences interspersed among longer ones. Locate at least four very short sentences. How do they draw your attention to the description?
5. Locate in Selzer's essay at least five examples of vivid description (imagery) relating to illness. What is their emotional effect on the reader?
6. How does Selzer use *dialogue* to reveal the personality of the patient? of the doctor? of the head nurse?
7. In paragraph 23, Selzer states that the patient delivers his request "without the least irony." *Irony* (see Glossary) is saying what is opposite to what one means. Why might Selzer have expected irony from the patient? Why might someone in the sick man's condition use irony? What do you think the man

means by his request "You can bring me a pair of shoes"—if, in fact, the remark is not an ironical one?

8. What does the title of the essay mean? What is a discus thrower? Why has Selzer chosen an ancient image of an athlete as the title of this essay? In what way is the title ironic?
9. Why does Selzer use such an unusual word as *kick-shaws* (par. 4)?
10. *Double entendre* is a French expression that indicates that something has a double meaning, each equally valid. What might be the two meanings of the nurse's words "It's a blessing"?
11. In this essay, the author uses a *framing* device: that is, he opens and closes the essay with a similar image or idea. What is that idea? Why is it effective? What are the differences in the use of this idea in the opening and closing paragraphs?
12. The heart of this essay is the patient's insistence upon throwing his breakfast plate at the wall, and yet Selzer does not attempt to explain the man's reasons for such an act. Why do you think the man hurls his breakfast across the room each morning—and why does he laugh? Why does Selzer not provide an analysis of the action? How does the title help us see Selzer's attitude toward the man's act?

Exploring the Writer's Ideas

1. In the beginning of the essay Selzer asks, "Ought not a doctor to observe his patients by any means from any stance, that he might the more fully assemble evidence?" Do you feel that a doctor should have this right? Why? What rights do you believe patients should have in a hospital?
2. The head nurse in Selzer's description seems fed up with the patient in Room 542. Why do you think she feels this way? Do you think that a person in her position has the right to express this feeling on his or her job? Why or why not?
3. The patient's attitude is influenced by his physical state and his nearness to death. How have physical ailments or handicaps changed the attitudes of people you have known? Has an illness influenced your thoughts at any time?

IDEAS FOR WRITING

Prewriting

How can you tell when a person is ill or under stress? Make a list of the behavioral qualities that tell you that the person is not him- or herself.

Guided Writing

Describe a person you have observed who was seriously ill, in danger, or under great stress.

1. Base your description on close observation of the person during a short but concentrated span of time: a morning or afternoon, an hour or two, even a few minutes.
2. Begin with a short, direct paragraph in which you introduce the person and the critical situation he or she faces.
3. Include yourself ("I") in the description.
4. Describe the vantage point from which you are "spying" or observing, and focus on the particular subject of the scene.
5. Throughout your essay, ask key questions.
6. Use imagery and original comparisons to highlight the description of your subject.
7. Include some dialogue with either the subject or another person.
8. Describe at least one very intense action performed by your subject.
9. Tell how the subject and scene had changed when you next saw them.

Thinking and Writing Collaboratively

Assisted suicide for terminally ill patients has received a great deal of attention in the national press recently. Form discussion groups of about five students and consider the issue. Then, have the group write a paragraph summarizing its views on a patient's "right to die."

More Writing Projects

1. In your journal, describe a hospital room in which you stayed or visited some other person. Focus on your sensory perceptions of the place.

2. Describe in an extended paragraph an interaction you had with a person who was blind or deaf or was disabled in some other way. In your description, focus closely on the person's features. Write about your reactions during and after the interaction.
3. Using both description and commentary, analyze the people you observe in one of the following situations: a bus or train during rush hour; breakfast at a diner or restaurant; a sports event or concert. Incorporate the description and observation into a five-paragraph essay.

The Burden of a Happy Childhood

Mary Cantwell

Mary Cantwell, author of *Manhattan, When I was Young,* writes with affection and relief about the sale of the rambling, memory-laden house that was her family's home for 77 years. Relief? Yes, because before the house was sold she was imprisoned in her all-too-happy childhood.

PREREADING: THINKING ABOUT THE ESSAY IN ADVANCE

How can a happy childhood be too much of a good thing? How can our happiest times also become a burden?

Words to Watch

Victorian (par. 2) dating from around 1840 to 1900
sluiced (par 5.) sprayed with water
immured (par. 6) walled in

Every time I described the house to friends—the two porches, the bay windows, the balcony over the front door, the stone tubs on either side of the front steps that, before they crumbled, always held geraniums—they said, "It sounds wonderful." 1

"No, it's not wonderful," I'd protest. "It's too narrow, even if it runs deep, and why in a town of beautiful houses my grandfather had to buy that one. . . ." Then I'd stop, partly because no amount of words could disabuse my listeners of the notion that all big Victorian houses resembled the charmer in "Meet Me in St. Louis," and partly out of guilt. How could I say such things about three tall stories of white clapboard that had housed my grandparents, a widowed great-aunt, an aunt, the husband she acquired at 56, my parents, my sister, myself and, on occasion, whatever distant relatives were passing through. 2

Oh, yes, I forgot. Until I was 19, there was a cocker spaniel named Judy and in my earliest childhood a series of canaries, all of which were named Dickie and all of which flew away because 3 my aunt trusted them to stay on their perches when she cleaned their cages out of doors.

4 My grandfather bought the house in 1920. My mother's wedding reception was in the backyard; my aunt's, when she finally married, on the first floor; my sister's, on the second. I remember coffins in the first-floor bay window (there is nothing like an old-fashioned New England upbringing to acquaint you with life's realities) and, in the same place, the narrow bed in which my father died. It was there so he could have a view of the main street. My grandmother and I loved that view. When I was little we would sit in the window, she in her rocker, I in a hard cut-velvet-upholstered chair, and monitor the passersby.

5 The house was across the street from a little beach, and after our morning dip our grandfather sluiced my sister and me with the garden hose. Years later my aunt's husband sluiced my daughters and, eventually, my niece after their dips. In my grandfather's day the garden was beautiful. After his death my grandmother, who was not one for gardening, said there was nothing nicer than a nice green lawn. Perhaps there isn't, but I have always missed his rosebushes and peonies and his patches of sweet william and pansies.

6 Recently, after 77 years as one family's residence, the house was sold. "How dreadful for you!" friends said. Not at all. What in my childhood had been not only my home but also my fortress, because outside of it lurked every grade-school classmate who didn't like me, had become my prison. As long as it was the place to which I fled whenever my life as an adult became too hard to bear, I was immured in childhood. I was also incapable of calling the apartments in which I lived with my husband and, later, my children "home." Home was where members of my family, some of whom were long gone, were forever baking apple pies, smoking pipes while patting the dog, reading *The Providence Evening Bulletin* and crocheting elaborate bedspreads.

7 An unhappy childhood can cripple, but so can one as blessed as mine. You go through life with the sense that something has been mislaid, something you think that, with luck, you can find again. Only you can't, because what you're looking for is unconditional love. My family was too strict to spoil a child, but I knew, even before I knew the words, that they would betray me only by dying. As long as they lived, my cradle would never fall.

If you're smart you give up the search early on, but that is hard when the house in which you lived your joy is still yours for the wandering. Furthermore, the ghost I met in every room was not that of a grandparent or the father who died when I was 20 but of my past self. In most particulars she was pretty much the person I am today. But I have lost forever, and mourn, the innocence that had her greeting every morning as if it were the world's first. 8

Today, though, the house is gone and with it a sadness I wore as a turtle wears its shell. The old radiators are in the side yard and a big hose is hanging out the third-floor window. Its buyers are updating the heating system, gutting the attic. The door on which I had painted "Artist's Den, Keep Out" has disappeared, and once the painters move in, my family's fingerprints will disappear too. But when its new occupants first toured the house, the real-estate agent reported that they said it had "good vibes." So the family that once owned it is still there, not only in my memory but in its laths and beams and solid—oh, so solid—foundation. 9

BUILDING VOCABULARY

Use the following words in a sentence of your own:

- **a.** clapboard (par. 2)
- **b.** peonies, pansies (par. 5)
- **c.** lurked (par. 6)
- **d.** crocheting (par. 6)
- **e.** unconditional (par. 7)

THINKING CRITICALLY ABOUT THE ESSAY

1. What qualities in the writer's description of her family house make her friends say, "It sounds wonderful"?
2. Why does the writer protest at such a reaction? And why does she stop short in her protestation?
3. What would you say is the picture the writer paints through the details she provides in paragraphs 2–5?
4. Why does the writer think it is not dreadful that, after 77 years as her family's residence, the house was sold?
5. How did the continued residence of someone from her family in the family house cripple the writer's adulthood?

6. What is it about childhood that the writer mistakenly believed she could retrieve while her family's house still stood?
7. In addition to dead relatives, whom else did the writer miss from her life in the family house?
8. What is the sadness from which the writer is freed now that the house is sold?
9. What is the writer's intention in the emphasis of the last paragraph on "foundation"?

Understanding the Writer's Techniques

1. The very phrase "Victorian house" suggests meandering houses and bustling families. How does the writer convey the size of her family through her recollections about her family's house?
2. How do the writer's references to her relatives suggest a rich family life?
3. What else in the account suggests a vivid childhood?
4. What is the *tone* (see Glossary) of this essay? How is this tone established?
5. How do the opening and closing paragraphs mirror and reinforce one another?

Exploring the Writer's Ideas

1. Are you persuaded that the writer is pleased and relieved that her old family house is being sold at last? Indicate why you are or are not persuaded.
2. Why does the writer fail to mention family quarrels or bad times? How could the essay have incorporated less comforting examples of family life?
3. A happy, secure childhood, we are told, is the best basis for adult independence. But Cantwell's happy childhood seems to have become a prison. What do we learn from the essay to suggest how this might have come about?

IDEAS FOR WRITING

Prewriting

Jot down the details that evoke the touch and feel of a place you associate with deep happiness in the past, such as a summer home.

Guided Writing

Write an essay describing a place you loved as a child. For the purposes of the essay, imagine that the place is gone—sold, destroyed by fire or flood—and suggest that actually you are relieved about its passing.

1. Begin by recounting the shocked reaction of your friends when they learned your old summer house, say, was destroyed by fire.
2. Explain why actually you are not disturbed.
3. Recount your happy times there. Be specific, be careful to use rich, evocative details or examples.
4. Write a paragraph telling why one of the prices of maturity is the loss of childhood, and thus of the places we most associate with childhood.
5. End with a sad but accepting farewell to the place you have described.

Thinking and Writing Collaboratively

In groups of four or five discuss your attachments to childhood—such as pictures of your old pets in your wallet, stuffed animals you still keep on the pillow, baseball gloves you still keep on the shelf, etc. Explore how you would feel to have to give these up.

More Writing Projects

1. Write an essay titled "Goodbye to Childhood—and Good Riddance!"
2. Describe your room at different stages of your life, concentrating on what you kept in the room and what you changed as you moved from stage to stage.
3. Write two paragraphs about your first car (or bicycle or . . .), in each case describing it in detail but with one paragraph mourning its loss in somber tones; and one delighted to be rid of the old piece of junk.

SUMMING UP: CHAPTER 3

1. As you have discovered in this chapter, one of the keys to writing effective description is the selection and creation of vivid and relevant images. How do the writers in this chapter use imagery? Which writer's images do you find most concrete, original, vivid, and creative? For each of the four essays of description in this chapter, write a paragraph in which you evaluate the writer's use of imagery.
2. Cantwell and Selzer provide vivid descriptions of people. What general guidelines for describing people do you derive from these writers? Write a short essay called "How to Describe People," basing your observations on Cantwell's and Selzer's techniques.
3. Maxine Hong Kingston and Louise Erdrich both write from their experience as members of a multicultural society. Is there any evidence that their ethnic backgrounds shape their choice of subject or method of description? Write a short essay on the relation between the writers' backgrounds and the nature of their descriptions.
4. The essays by Erdrich and Selzer are, each in its own way, meditations on life and death. What did you learn about life and death from these two writers?

CHAPTER 4

Narration

WHAT IS NARRATION?

Narration is the telling of a story. As a technique in essay writing, it normally involves a discussion of events that are "true" or real, events that take place over a period of time. Narration helps a writer explain things and, as such, it is an important skill for the kind of writing often required of you.

Narration often includes the use of *description* in order to make the *purpose* of the story clear. A good narrative, then, must have a *thesis*. The thesis tells the reader that the narrative goes beyond just telling a story for entertainment. Like description, the narrative has a purpose, and an audience. The writer puts forth a main idea through the events and details of the story. For example, a writer might decide to *narrate* the events that led her to leave her native country and come to the United States as an immigrant. She would establish her thesis—her main point—quickly, and then use the body of the essay to tell about the event itself. She would use narration as the means to an end—to make a significant statement about the important decision that changed her life.

Writer Elizabeth Wong uses narrative to explore the pitfalls of divorcing herself from her cultural heritage as she tells about events in her youth with the purpose of pointing out the dangers of becoming "All-American." In his comic narrative "Salvation," Langston Hughes reveals his disillusionment as he cannot find Jesus as his family expects him to. The renowned writer George Orwell narrates events at a hanging he witnessed in Burma to call attention to how all too often we can take the value of life for granted. The novelist Grace Paley uses the narrative of two trips to the American South to raise questions about both race relations and memory. Each writer, then, whose work you will read in this chapter, uses narrative to tell a story of events that take place over a period of time, but also to put forward a thesis or main idea that comes directly out of events in the story.

HOW DO WE READ NARRATIVE?

Reading narrative requires us to look for more than the story, but not to overlook the story. So, as we read, we should ask ourselves:

- What are the main events in the narrative or story?
- What is the writer's purpose in telling us about these events, as stated in the thesis?
- How is the story organized? Is it chronological? Does the writer use *flashback* (see Glossary)? How much time is covered in the narrative?
- Does the author use description to make the narrative more vivid for a reader?
- What point of view does the author use? Are events told through his or her own eyes, or from a detached and objective point of view? Why did the writer make this choice about point of view? How would altering the point of view alter the purpose of the narrative?
- What transitions of time does the writer use to connect events? Look for expressions that link events: *next, soon after, a day later, suddenly, after two years.* These expressions act like bridges to connect the various moments in the narrative pattern.
- Does the writer use dialogue? What is the effect of dialogue in the narrative?
- What audience is the author aiming at? How do we know?

HOW DO WE WRITE NARRATIVE?

After reading the selections of narrative writing in this chapter, you should be ready to try narrative writing on your own. Fortunately, most individuals have a basic storytelling ability and know how to develop stories that make a point. Once you master narration as a writing pattern, you will be able to use it in a variety of situations.

Select the event you want to tell a story about. Begin with a thesis statement that gives the reader the purpose of the narrative.

Sample thesis statement:

> My year studying abroad in Paris was an adventure that taught me not only skills in a foreign language but also a new respect for people with cultural values different from my own.

Decide which point of view you will use: first person? third person? Think about who your audience is, and choose the point of view best suited for that audience. If you are writing to a friend, first person may be more informal. If you are writing to address a wider public audience, as Orwell is, third person might be more effective.

First person: I saw a man hanged, and the experience changed my views on capital punishment.

Third person: Spending a day at a Planned Parenthood clinic would help opponents of abortion understand the other side's fervent commitment to choice.

Determine the purpose of the narrative in relation to your audience. If you were writing for a Roman Catholic newspaper, for instance, your audience would be different from the audience you'd address in a feminist magazine like *Ms.*: the purpose would be different as well. In one case, you might be trying to get readers to change their views through your description. In another case, you might be showing how weak the opposition was by the way you described them.

Plan the scope of the piece: How much time will events cover? Can you describe all the events within the required length of the essay?

Plan to include dialogue. For example, you might include a few fragments of conversation between lost or confused freshmen to give a "first day at school" story real-life flavor:

"Did you buy your books yet?"

"No, I couldn't find the bookstore!"

"Well, I already spent $125, and that was only for two courses. I'm going to have to ask my Mom for more money."

"Yeah, I'm thinking maybe I'm going to need a part-time job."

"Yeah, maybe we can work in the bookstore and get a discount."

Make a list of *transitions* that show the passage of time and use as many as you need to help your reader follow the sequence of events in the narrative. Check that there are transitions between events: *after that, a few hours later, by the time the day ended.*

State your *thesis.* Write out the thesis statement so that you know the *subject* and the *purpose* of the essay. Then make a list of the major events in the story. You might begin with why you chose the college you did, and how you felt when you got accepted. Or you might begin with your arrival on the first day of classes, and go through the main events of the day—going to class, buying books, meeting other new students, evaluating teachers, having lunch, and so forth.

Plan an arrangement of events. Most narratives benefit from a clear chronological sequence. All the writers here pay careful attention to the march of events over time, and you should follow their lead. As in Orwell's focused narrative, integrate commentary, analysis, or assessment, but keep your eye on the order of events.

Writing the Draft

Once you have structured your essay, build your ideas by including descriptive details. Insert as many descriptive words as possible to help a reader *see* the campus, the students, the cafeteria, and so on:

the bright-colored sofas in the student lounge, filled with cigarette burns
the smells of french fries from the cafeteria, with its long rows of orange tables
the conversations of the biology majors at the next table, who were talking about cutting up frogs
the large, imposing library, with its rows of blue computer terminals and its hushed whispered noises

Discuss how these events made you feel about your decision. Did you choose the right college?

Write a conclusion that reinforces the purpose of the essay. Make a direct statement of the way the events in the narrative changed you, or how your expectations for the day compare with what really happened.

Reading and Revising the Draft

Read the essay aloud to a classmate who is also a new freshman. Ask your listener if his or her day was the same as yours. Did you put the events in a logical sequence? Can your listener suggest more ideas to add? Have you included enough details so that a reader who was not a member of the college community could see the events as you saw them?

Proofread carefully for correctness and make a neat final copy.

A STUDENT PARAGRAPH: NARRATION

In preparation for the essay on narration, one student wrote a narrative paragraph to tell part of the story of his first day on campus. Look at the selection and the annotations, which highlight important elements of narrative writing.

Topic sentence	It was my first official day as a student here at
Statement of time and place helps set narrative scene	State; the September morning had hardly begun, and I was already in a sweat. The crisp, colorful map I'd picked up shortly after passing
"I" sets narrative point of view (first-person)	through the wrought iron gates had collapsed into a moist crumpled ball in my clenched fist.
Supporting detail	Now I was flushed, panting, and miserable, as I
Transitions ("now," "next") promote chronological sequence	tried to decide which seemingly endless line of students I needed to join next in order to fix the financial mess the university's computers had put me in. Standing in the middle of the
Supporting detail	quad, hemmed in on all sides by towering brick and marble buildings, I gazed helplessly around me. Suddenly, I caught a glimpse of a familiar
Supporting detail	face: Dan Merritt, a tall, skinny kid with bright red hair who had quit the Westmont High football team in his sophomore year, a few weeks before I did. Springing into action, I virtually tackled the poor guy, frantic lest he should escape and leave me alone with my rapidly disappearing self-confidence. I felt a real jolt of pleasure, though, when I saw relief
Dialogue adds real-life flavor	flood his face. "Boy, am I glad to see you," Dan said. "I was beginning to think I wouldn't get out of here alive."

The Struggle to Be an All-American Girl

Elizabeth Wong

In this poignant remembrance, Elizabeth Wong tells of the hurts and sorrows of her bicultural upbringing. Wong effectively blends concrete description and imaginative comparisons to give a vivid look into the life of a child who felt she had a Chinese exterior but an American interior.

PREREADING: THINKING ABOUT THE ESSAY IN ADVANCE

America prides itself on its ability to assimilate cultures, yet the process of assimilation is not without difficulties, particularly for children. What problems do you foresee for a child of one cultural background growing up in the midst of another culture?

Words to Watch

stoically (par. 1) without showing emotion

dissuade (par. 2) to talk out of doing something

ideographs (par. 7) Chinese picture symbols used to form words

disassociate (par. 8) to detach from association

vendors (par. 8) sellers of goods

gibberish (par. 9) confused, unintelligible speech or language

pidgin (par. 10) simplified speech that is usually a mixture of two or more languages

1 It's still there, the Chinese school on Yale Street where my brother and I used to go. Despite the new coat of paint and the high wire fence, the school I knew 10 years ago remains remarkably, stoically the same.

2 Every day at 5 P.M., instead of playing with our fourth- and fifth-grade friends or sneaking out to the empty lot to hunt ghosts and animal bones, my brother and I had to go to Chinese school. No amount of kicking, screaming, or pleading could dissuade my mother, who was solidly determined to have us learn the language of our heritage.

Forcibly, she walked us the seven long, hilly blocks from our home to school, depositing our defiant tearful faces before the stern principal. My only memory of him is that he swayed on his heels like a palm tree, and he always clasped his impatient twitching hands behind his back. I recognized him as a repressed maniacal child killer, and knew that if we ever saw his hands we'd be in big trouble. 3

We all sat in little chairs in an empty auditorium. The room smelled like Chinese medicine, an imported faraway mustiness. Like ancient mothballs or dirty closets. I hated that smell. I favored crisp new scents. Like the soft French perfume that my American teacher wore in public school. 4

There was a stage far to the right, flanked by an American flag and the flag of the Nationalist Republic of China, which was also red, white and blue but not as pretty. 5

Although the emphasis at the school was mainly language—speaking, reading, writing—the lessons always began with an exercise in politeness. With the entrance of the teacher, the best student would tap a bell and everyone would get up, kowtow, and chant, "Sing san ho," the phonetic for "How are you, teacher?" 6

Being ten years old, I had better things to learn than ideographs copied painstakingly in lines that ran right to left from the tip of a *moc but,* a real ink pen that had to be held in an awkward way if blotches were to be avoided. After all, I could do the multiplication tables, name the satellites of Mars, and write reports on "Little Women" and "Black Beauty." Nancy Drew, my favorite book heroine, never spoke Chinese. 7

The language was a source of embarrassment. More times than not, I had tried to disassociate myself from the nagging loud voice that followed me wherever I wandered in the nearby American supermarket outside Chinatown. The voice belonged to my grandmother, a fragile woman in her seventies who could outshout the best of the street vendors. Her humor was raunchy, her Chinese rhythmless, patternless. It was quick, it was loud, it was unbeautiful. It was not like the quiet, lilting romance of French or the gentle refinement of the American South. Chinese sounded pedestrian. Public. 8

In Chinatown, the comings and goings of hundreds of Chinese on their daily tasks sounded chaotic and frenzied. I did not 9 want to be thought of as mad, as talking gibberish. When I spoke English, people nodded at me, smiled sweetly, said encouraging words. Even the people in my culture would cluck and say that I'd do well in life. "My, doesn't she move her lips fast," they would say, meaning that I'd be able to keep up with the world outside Chinatown.

10 My brother was even more fanatical than I about speaking English. He was especially hard on my mother, criticizing her, often cruelly, for her pidgin speech—smatterings of Chinese scattered like chop suey in her conversation. "It's not 'What it is,' Mom," he'd say in exasperation. "It's 'What *is* it, what *is* it, what *is* it!'" Sometimes Mom might leave out an occasional "the" or "a," or perhaps a verb of being. He would stop her in mid-sentence: "Say it again, Mom. Say it right." When he tripped over his own tongue, he'd blame it on her: "See, Mom, it's all your fault. You set a bad example."

11 What infuriated my mother most was when my brother cornered her on her consonants, especially "r." My father had played a cruel joke on Mom by assigning her an American name that her tongue wouldn't allow her to say. No matter how hard she tried, "Ruth" always ended up "Luth" or "Roof."

12 After two years of writing with a *moc but* and reciting words with multiples of meanings, I finally was granted a cultural divorce. I was permitted to stop Chinese school.

13 I thought of myself as multicultural. I preferred tacos to egg rolls; I enjoyed Cinco de Mayo more than Chinese New Year.

14 At last, I was one of you; I wasn't one of them.

15 Sadly, I still am.

BUILDING VOCABULARY

For each of the words in italics, choose the letter of the word or expression that most closely matches its meaning.

1. the *stern* principal (par. 3)
   a. military **b.** very old **c.** immoral **d.** strict
2. *repressed* maniacal child killer (par. 3)
   a. quiet **b.** ugly **c.** held back **d.** retired

3. an imported faraway *mustiness* (par. 4)
   a. country **b.** moth balls **c.** chair **d.** staleness
4. a *fragile* woman (par. 8)
   a. elderly **b.** frail **c.** tall **d.** inconsistent
5. her humor was *raunchy* (par. 8)
   a. obscene **b.** unclear **c.** childish **d.** very funny
6. quiet *lilting* romance of French (par. 8)
   a. musical **b.** tilting **c.** loving **d.** complicated
7. thought of as *mad* (par. 9)
   a. foreign **b.** angry **c.** stupid **d.** crazy
8. what *infuriated* my mother most (par. 11)
   a. angered **b.** humiliated **c.** made laugh **d.** typified

THINKING CRITICALLY ABOUT THE ESSAY

Understanding the Writer's Ideas

1. What did Elizabeth Wong and her brother do every day after school? How did that make them different from their friends? What was their attitude toward what they did? How do you know?
2. What does Wong mean when she says of the principal "I recognized him as a repressed maniacal child killer"? Why were she and her brother afraid to see his hands?
3. What was the main purpose of going to Chinese school? What did Wong feel she had learned at "regular" American school? Which did she feel was more important? What are *Little Women, Black Beauty,* and Nancy Drew?
4. In the first sentence of paragraph 8, what language is "the language"?
5. What was Wong's grandmother like? What was Wong's attitude toward her? Why?
6. When Wong spoke English in Chinatown, why did the others think it was good that she moved her lips quickly?
7. What was her brother's attitude toward speaking English? How did he treat their mother when she tried to speak English? Why was it unfortunate that the mother had the American name *Ruth?* Who gave her that name? Why?
8. Explain the expression "he tripped over his own tongue" (par. 10).

9. In paragraph 13, Wong states, "I thought of myself as multicultural." What does that mean? What are tacos, egg rolls, and Cinco de Mayo? Why is it surprising that Wong includes those items as examples of her multiculturalism?
10. Who are the "you" and "them" of paragraph 14? Explain the significance of the last sentence. What does it indicate about Wong's attitude toward Chinese school from the vantage point of being an adult?

Understanding the Writer's Techniques

1. Wong does not state a thesis directly in a thesis sentence. How does her title imply a thesis? If you were writing a thesis sentence of your own for this essay, what would it be?
2. What is Wong's purpose in writing this narrative? Is the technique of narration an appropriate one to her purpose? Why or why not?
3. This narrative contains several stories. The first one ends after paragraph 7 and tells about Wong's routine after 5 P.M. on school days. Paragraphs 8 and 9, 10 and 11, and 12 and 13 offer other related narratives. Summarize each of these briefly. How does Wong help the reader shift from story to story?
4. The writer of narration will present *time* in a way that best fulfills the purpose of the narration. This presentation may take many forms: a single, personal event; a series of related events; a historical occurrence; an aging process. Obviously Wong chose a series of related events. Why does she use such a narrative structure to make her point? Could she have chosen an alternative plan, do you think? Why or why not?
5. Writers of narration often rely upon descriptive details to flesh out their stories. Find examples of sensory language here that makes the scene come alive for the reader.
6. Writers often use figurative comparisons to enliven their writing and to make it more distinctive. A *simile* is an imaginative form of figurative comparison using "like" or "as" to connect two items. One thing is similar to another in this figure. A *metaphor* is a figure of speech in which the writer compares two items not normally thought of as similar, but unlike in a simile, the comparison is direct—that is, it does

not use "like" or "as." In other words, one thing is said to be the other thing, not merely to be like it. For example, if you wanted to compare love to a rose, you might use these two comparisons:

Simile:
  My love is *like* a red, red rose.
Metaphor:
  My love *is* a red, red rose.

In Wong's essay, find the similes and metaphors in paragraphs 2, 3, 4, 10, and 12. For each, name the two items compared and explain the comparison in your own words.

7. Narratives often include lines of spoken language—that is, one person in the narrative talking alone or to another. Wong uses quoted detail sparsely here. Why did she choose to limit the dialogue? How effective is the dialogue that appears here? Where do you think she might have used more dialogue to advance the narrative?
8. The last two paragraphs are only one sentence each. Why do you think the author chose this technique?
9. What is the *irony* (see Glossary) in the last sentence of the essay? How would the meaning of the last sentence change if you eliminated the word "sadly"? What is the irony in the title of the essay?
10. What is the *tone* (see Glossary) of this essay? How does Wong create that tone?

Exploring the Writer's Ideas

1. Wong and her brother deeply resented being forced to attend Chinese school. When children very clearly express displeasure or unhappiness, should parents force them to do things anyway? Why or why not?
2. On one level this essay is about a clash of cultures, here the ancient Chinese culture of Wong's ancestry and the culture of twentieth-century United States. Is it possible for someone to maintain connections to his or her ethnic or cultural background and at the same time to become an All-American girl or boy? What do people of foreign backgrounds gain when they become completely Americanized? What do they lose?

3. Because of their foreign ways, the mother and grandmother clearly embarrassed the Wong children. Under what other conditions that you can think of do parents embarrass children? Children, parents?

IDEAS FOR WRITING

Prewriting

Do timed writing—that is, write nonstop for fifteen or twenty minutes without editing or correcting your work—on the topic of your grade school or high school. What experience stands out most in your mind? What moment taught you most about yourself?

Guided Writing

Write a narration in which you tell about some difficult moment that took place in grade school or high school, a moment that taught you something about yourself, your needs, or your cultural background.

1. Provide a concrete description of the school.
2. Tell in correct sequence about the event.
3. Identify people who play a part in this moment.
4. Use concrete, sensory description throughout your essay.
5. Use original similes and metaphors to make your narrative clearer and more dramatic.
6. Use dialogue (or spoken conversation) appropriately in order to advance the narrative.
7. In your conclusion, indicate what your attitude toward this moment is now that you are an adult.
8. Write a title that implies your thesis.

Thinking and Writing Collaboratively

In groups of two or three, read aloud drafts of each other's essays, looking particularly at the use of concrete sensory detail and figures of speech—metaphors and similes. Which images strike you as most clear, original, and easy to visualize?

More Writing Projects

1. Did you have any problems in grade school or high school because of your background or ancestry? Did you know someone who had such problems? Record a specific incident in your journal.
2. Write a narrative paragraph explaining some basic insights about your heritage or culture.
3. Get together with other classmates in a small group and brainstorm or bounce ideas off one another on troubling ethnic, racial, or cultural issues on campus. Write down all the incidents. Then write a narrative essay tracing one episode or connecting a series of them.

Salvation

Langston Hughes

For more than forty years, Langston Hughes (1902–1967) was a major figure in American literature. In poetry, essays, drama, and fiction he attempted, as he said himself, "to explain and illuminate the Negro condition in America." This selection from his autobiography, *The Big Sea* (1940), tells the story of his "conversion" to Christ. Salvation was a key event in the life of his community, but Hughes tells comically how he bowed to pressure by permitting himself to be "saved from sin."

PREREADING: THINKING ABOUT THE ESSAY IN ADVANCE

What is the role of religion today in the lives of most Americans? What role does religion play in your life? In what ways do the religious values of your family compare and contrast with your own?

Words to Watch

dire (par. 3) terrible; disastrous

gnarled (par. 4) knotty; twisted

rounder (par. 6) watchman; policeman

deacons (par. 6) members of the clergy or laypersons who are appointed to help the minister

serenely (par. 7) calmly; tranquilly

knickerbockered (par. 11) dressed in short, loose trousers that are gathered below the knees

1 I was saved from sin when I was going on thirteen. But not really saved. It happened like this. There was a big revival at my Auntie Reed's church. Every night for weeks there had been much preaching, singing, praying, and shouting, and some very hardened sinners had been brought to Christ, and the membership of the church had grown by leaps and bounds. Then just before the revival ended, they held a special meeting for children, "to bring the young lambs to the fold." My aunt spoke of it for days ahead.

That night I was escorted to the front row and placed on the mourners' bench with all the other young sinners, who had not yet been brought to Jesus.

My aunt told me that when you were saved you saw a light, and something happened to you inside! And Jesus came into your life! And God was with you from then on! She said you could see and hear and feel Jesus in your soul. I believed her. I had heard a great many old people say the same thing and it seemed to me they ought to know. So I sat there calmly in the hot, crowded church, waiting for Jesus to come to me. 2

The preacher preached a wonderful rhythmical sermon, all moans and shouts and lonely cries and dire pictures of hell, and then he sang a song about the ninety and nine safe in the fold, but one little lamb was left out in the cold. Then he said: "Won't you come? Won't you come to Jesus? Young lambs, won't you come?" And he held out his arms to all us young sinners there on the mourners' bench. And the little girls cried. And some of them jumped up and went to Jesus right away. But most of us just sat there. 3

A great many old people came and knelt around us and prayed, old women with jet-black faces and braided hair, old men with work-gnarled hands. And the church sang a song about the lower lights are burning, some poor sinners to be saved. And the whole building rocked with prayer and song. 4

Still I kept waiting to *see* Jesus. 5

Finally all the young people had gone to the altar and were saved, but one boy and me. He was a rounder's son named Westley. Westley and I were surrounded by sisters and deacons praying. It was very hot in the church, and getting late now. Finally Westley said to me in a whisper: "God damn! I'm tired o' sitting here. Let's get up and be saved." So he got up and was saved. 6

Then I was left all alone on the mourners' bench. My aunt came and knelt at my knees and cried, while prayers and songs swirled all around me in the little church. The whole congregation prayed for me alone, in a mighty wail of moans and voices. And I kept waiting serenely for Jesus, waiting, waiting—but he didn't come. I wanted to see him, but nothing happened to me. Nothing! I wanted something to happen to me, but nothing happened. 7

I heard the songs and the minister saying: "Why don't you come? My dear child, why don't you come to Jesus? Jesus is waiting for you. He wants you. Why don't you come? Sister Reed, what is this child's name?" 8

9 "Langston," my aunt sobbed.

10 "Langston, why don't you come? Why don't you come and be saved? Oh, Lamb of God! Why don't you come?"

11 Now it was really getting late. I began to be ashamed of myself, holding everything up so long. I began to wonder what God thought about Westley, who certainly hadn't seen Jesus either, but who was now sitting proudly on the platform, swinging his knickerbockered legs and grinning down at me, surrounded by deacons and old women on their knees praying. God had not struck Westley dead for taking his name in vain or for lying in the temple. So I decided that maybe to save further trouble, I'd better lie, too, and say that Jesus had come, and get up and be saved.

12 So I got up.

13 Suddenly the whole room broke into a sea of shouting, as they saw me rise. Waves of rejoicing swept the place. Women leaped in the air. My aunt threw her arms around me. The minister took me by the hand and led me to the platform.

14 When things quieted down, in a hushed silence, punctuated by a few ecstatic "Amens," all the new young lambs were blessed in the name of God. Then joyous singing filled the room.

15 That night, for the last time in my life but one—for I was a big boy twelve years old—I cried. I cried, in bed alone, and couldn't stop. I buried my head under the quilts, but my aunt heard me. She woke up and told my uncle I was crying because the Holy Ghost had come into my life, and because I had seen Jesus. But I was really crying because I couldn't bear to tell her that I had lied, that I had deceived everybody in the church, that I hadn't seen Jesus, and that now I didn't believe there was a Jesus any more, since he didn't come to help me.

BUILDING VOCABULARY

1. Throughout this essay, Hughes selects words dealing with religion to emphasize his ideas. Look the following words up in a dictionary. Then tell what *connotations* (see Glossary) the words have for you.

  a. sin (par. 1)
  b. mourner (par. 1)
  c. lamb (par. 3)
  d. salvation (title)

2. Locate additional words that deal with religion.
3. When Hughes talks about lambs in the fold—and lambs in general—he is using a figure of speech, a comparison (see Chapter 6). What is being compared? How does religion enter into the comparison? Why is it useful as a figure of speech?

THINKING CRITICALLY ABOUT THE ESSAY

Understanding the Writer's Ideas

1. According to Hughes's description, what is a revival meeting like? What is the effect of the "preaching, singing, praying, and shouting" on the "sinners" and the "young lambs"?
2. Why does Westley "see" Jesus? Why does Langston Hughes come to Jesus?
3. How does the author feel after his salvation? Does Hughes finally believe in Christ after his experience? How do you know?

Understanding the Writer's Techniques

1. Is there a thesis statement in the essay? Where is it located?
2. How does the first paragraph serve as an introduction to the narrative?
3. What is the value of description in this essay? List several instances of vivid description that contribute to the narrative.
4. Where does the main narration begin? How much time passes in the course of the action?
5. In narration, it is especially important to have effective *transitions*—or word bridges—from stage to stage in the action. Transitions help the reader shift easily from idea to idea, event to event. List several transition words that Hughes uses.
6. A piece of writing has *coherence* if all its parts relate clearly and logically to one another. Each sentence grows naturally from the sentence before it; each paragraph grows naturally from the paragraph before it. Is Hughes's essay coherent? Which transitions help advance the action and relate the parts of a single paragraph to one another? Which transitions help connect paragraphs together? How does the way Hughes organized this essay help establish coherence?

7. A story (whether it is true or fiction) has to be told from the first-person ("I, we"), second-person ("you"), or third-person ("he, she, it, they") *point of view.* Point of view in narration sets up the author's position in regard to the action, making the author either a part of the action or an observer of it.
   a. What is the point of view in "Salvation"—is it first, second, or third person?
   b. Why has Hughes chosen this point of view instead of any other? Can you think of any advantages to this point of view?
8. What is your opinion about the last paragraph, the conclusion of this selection? What does it suggest about the mind of a twelve-year-old boy? What does it say about adults' misunderstanding of the activities of children?
9. What does the word "conversion" mean? What conversion really takes place in this piece? How does that compare with what people usually mean when they use "conversion" in a religious sense?

Exploring the Writer's Ideas

1. Hughes seems to suggest that we are forced to do things because of social pressures. Do you agree with his suggestion? Do people do things because their friends or families expect them to? To what extent are we part of the "herd"? Is it possible for a person to retain individuality under pressure from a group? When did you bow to group pressures? When did you resist?
2. Do you find the religious experience in Hughes's essay unusual or extreme? Why or why not? How do *you* define religion?
3. Under what circumstances might a person lie in order to satisfy others? Try to recall a specific episode in which you or someone you know was forced to lie in order to please others.

IDEAS FOR WRITING

Prewriting

Write a few sentences to define *group pressure.* Then give an example or two of a time when you gave in to group pressure or were forced to lie in order to impress others.

Guided Writing

Narrate an event in your life where you (or someone you know) gave in to group pressure or were forced to lie in order to please those around you.

1. Start with a thesis statement.
2. Set the stage for your narrative in the opening paragraph by telling where and when the incident took place. Use specific names for places.
3. Try to keep the action within as brief a time period as possible. If you can write about an event that took no more than a few minutes, so much the better.
4. Use description to sketch in the characters around you. Use colors, actions, sounds, smells, sensations of touch to fill in details of the scene.
5. Use effective transitions of time to link sentences and paragraphs.
6. Use the last paragraph to explain how you felt immediately after the incident.

Thinking and Writing Collaboratively

Exchange drafts of your Guided Writing essay with one other person in the class. Then, write out a brief outline of the events the writer has presented in the narrative. Is the sequence clear? Do the introduction and thesis set the stage appropriately for the sequence of events? Do the transitions link paragraphs and sentences effectively? Return the paper with your written response.

More Writing Projects

1. Explain in a journal entry an abstract word like "salvation," "sin," "love," or "hatred" by narrating an event that reveals the meaning of the word to you.
2. Write an extended paragraph on an important event that affected your relationship with family, friends, or your community during your childhood.
3. Make a list of all the important details that you associate with some religious occasion in your life. Then write a narrative essay on the experience.

A Hanging

George Orwell

One of the masters of English prose, George Orwell (1903–1950) often used narration of personal events to explore important social issues. Notice here how he involves the reader in a simple yet fascinating and tragic story, almost as if he were writing fiction. Orwell takes a brief time span and expands that moment with specific language. At one point, as you will see, the purpose of the narrative comes into sharp focus.

PREREADING: THINKING ABOUT THE ESSAY IN ADVANCE

The number of people executed through the system of justice in the United States has increased dramatically over the past few years. How do you explain the growth of executions by hanging, lethal injection, and the electric chair? Why does U.S. society provide for capital punishment? Under what circumstances is a person sentenced to capital punishment?

Words to Watch

sodden (par. 1) heavy with water

absurdly (par. 2) ridiculously

desolately (par. 3) gloomily; lifelessly; cheerlessly

prodding (par. 3) poking or thrusting at something

Dravidian (par. 4) any member of a group of intermixed races of southern India and Burma

pariah (par. 6) outcast; a member of a low caste of southern India and Burma

servile (par. 11) slavelike; lacking spirit or independence

reiterated (par. 12) repeated

abominable (par. 13) hateful; disagreeable; unpleasant

timorously (par. 15) fearfully

oscillated (par. 16) moved back and forth between two points

garrulously (par. 20) in a talkative manner

refractory (par. 22) stubborn

amicably (par. 24) in a friendly way; peaceably

It was in Burma, a sodden morning of the rains. A sickly light, like yellow tinfoil, was slanting over the high walls into the jail yard. We were waiting outside the condemned cells, a row of sheds fronted with double bars, like small animal cages. Each cell measured about ten feet by ten and was quite bare within except for a plank bed and a pot of drinking water. In some of them brown silent men were squatting at the inner bars, with their blankets draped round them. These were the condemned men, due to be hanged within the next week or two. 1

One prisoner had been brought out of his cell. He was a Hindu, a puny wisp of a man, with a shaven head and vague liquid eyes. He had a thick, sprouting moustache, absurdly too big for his body, rather like the moustache of a comic man on the films. Six tall Indian warders were guarding him and getting him ready for the gallows. Two of them stood by with rifles with fixed bayonets, while the others handcuffed him, passed a chain through his handcuffs and fixed it to their belts, and lashed his arms tight to his sides. They crowded very close about him, with their hands always on him in a careful, caressing grip, as though all the while feeling him to make sure he was there. It was like men handling a fish which is still alive and may jump back into the water. But he stood quite unresisting, yielding his arms limply to the ropes, as though he hardly noticed what was happening. 2

Eight o'clock struck and a bugle call, desolately thin in the wet air, floated from the distant barracks. The superintendent of the jail, who was standing apart from the rest of us, moodily prodding the gravel with his stick, raised his head at the sound. He was an army doctor, with a grey toothbrush moustache and a gruff voice. "For God's sake hurry up, Francis," he said irritably. "The man ought to have been dead by this time. Aren't you ready yet?" 3

Francis, the head jailer, a fat Dravidian in a white drill suit and gold spectacles, waved his black hand. "Yes sir, yes sir," he bubbled. "All iss satisfactorily prepared. The hangman iss waiting. We shall proceed." 4

"Well, quick march, then. The prisoners can't get their breakfast till this job's over." 5

We set out for the gallows. Two warders marched on either side of the prisoner, with their files at the slope; two others marched close against him, gripping him by arm and shoulder, as though at once pushing and supporting him. The rest of us, magistrates and the like, followed behind. Suddenly, when we had gone ten yards, the procession stopped short without any order or 6 warning. A dreadful thing had happened—a dog, come goodness knows whence, had appeared in the yard. It came bounding among us with a loud volley of barks, and leapt round us wagging its whole body, wild with glee at finding so many human beings together. It was a large woolly dog, half Airedale, half pariah. For a moment it pranced round us, and then, before anyone could stop it, it had made a dash for the prisoner, and jumping up tried to lick his face. Everyone stood aghast, too taken aback even to grab at the dog.

7 "Who let that bloody brute in here?" said the superintendent angrily. "Catch it, someone!"

8 A warder, detached from the escort, charged clumsily after the dog, but it danced and gambolled just out of his reach, taking everything as part of the game. A young Eurasian jailer picked up a handful of gravel and tried to stone the dog away, but it dodged the stones and came after us again. Its yaps echoed from the jail walls. The prisoner, in the grasp of the two warders, looked on incuriously, as though this was another formality of the hanging. It was several minutes before someone managed to catch the dog. Then we put my handkerchief through its collar and moved off once more, with the dog still straining and whimpering.

9 It was about forty yards to the gallows. I watched the bare brown back of the prisoner marching in front of me. He walked clumsily with his bound arms, but quite steadily, with that bobbing gait of the Indian who never straightens his knees. At each step his muscles slid neatly into place, the lock of hair on his scalp danced up and down, his feet printed themselves on the wet gravel. And once, in spite of the men who gripped him by each shoulder, he stepped slightly aside to avoid a puddle on the path.

10 It is curious, but till that moment I had never realised what it means to destroy a healthy, conscious man. When I saw the prisoner step aside to avoid the puddle, I saw the mystery, the unspeakable wrongness, of cutting a life short when it is in full tide. This man was not dying, he was alive just as we were alive. All the organs of his body were working—bowels digesting food, skin renewing itself, nails growing, tissues forming—all toiling away in solemn foolery. His nails would still be growing when he stood on the drop, when he was falling through the air with a tenth of a second to live. His eyes saw the yellow gravel and the grey walls, and his brain still remembered, foresaw, reasoned—reasoned even about puddles. He and we were a party of men walking together, seeing, hearing, feeling, understanding the

same world; and in two minutes, with a sudden snap, one of us would be gone—one mind less, one world less.

The gallows stood in a small yard, separate from the main grounds of the prison, and overgrown with tall prickly weeds. It was a brick erection like three sides of a shed, with planking on top, and above that two beams and a crossbar with the rope dangling. The hangman, a grey-haired convict in the white uniform of the prison, was waiting beside his machine. He greeted us with a servile crouch as we entered. At a word from Francis the two warders, gripping the prisoner more closely than ever, half led, half pushed him to the gallows and helped him clumsily up the ladder. Then the hangman climbed up and fixed the rope round the prisoner's neck. 11

We stood waiting, five yards away. The warders had formed in a rough circle round the gallows. And then, when the noose was fixed, the prisoner began crying out on his god. It was a high, reiterated cry of "Ram! Ram! Ram! Ram!", not urgent and fearful like a prayer or a cry for help, but steady, rhythmical, almost like the tolling of a bell. The dog answered the sound with a whine. The hangman, still standing on the gallows, produced a small cotton bag like a flour bag and drew it down over the prisoner's face. But the sound, muffled by the cloth, still persisted, over and over again: "Ram! Ram! Ram! Ram! Ram!" 12

The hangman climbed down and stood ready, holding the lever. Minutes seemed to pass. The steady, muffled crying from the prisoner went on and on, "Ram! Ram! Ram!" never faltering for an instant. The superintendent, his head on his chest, was slowly poking the ground with his stick; perhaps he was counting the cries, allowing the prisoner a fixed number—fifty, perhaps, or a hundred. Everyone had changed colour. The Indians had gone grey like bad coffee, and one or two of the bayonets were wavering. We looked at the lashed, hooded man on the drop, and listened to his cries—each cry another second of life; the same thought was in all our minds: oh, kill him quickly, get it over, stop that abominable noise! 13

Suddenly the superintendent made up his mind. Throwing up his head he made a swift motion with his stick. "Chalo!" he shouted almost fiercely. 14

There was a clanking noise, and then dead silence. The prisoner had vanished, and the rope was twisting on itself. I let go of the dog, and it galloped immediately to the back of the gallows; but when it got there it stopped short, barked, and then retreated into a corner of the yard, where it stood among the weeds, 15 looking timorously out at us. We went round the gallows to inspect the prisoner's body. He was dangling with his toes pointed straight downwards, very slowly revolving, as dead as a stone.

16 The superintendent reached out with his stick and poked the bare body; it oscillated, slightly. "*He's* all right," said the superintendent. He backed out from under the gallows, and blew out a deep breath. The moody look had gone out of his face quite suddenly. He glanced at his wristwatch. "Eight minutes past eight. Well, that's all for this morning, thank God."

17 The warders unfixed bayonets and marched away. The dog, sobered and conscious of having misbehaved itself, slipped after them. We walked out of the gallows yard, past the condemned cells with their waiting prisoners, into the big central yard of the prison. The convicts, under the command of warders armed with lathis, were already receiving their breakfast. They squatted in long rows, each man holding a tin pannikin, while two warders with buckets marched round ladling out rice; it seemed quite a homely, jolly scene, after the hanging. An enormous relief had come upon us now that the job was done. One felt an impulse to sing, to break into a run, to snigger. All at once everyone began chattering gaily.

18 The Eurasian boy walking beside me nodded towards the way we had come, with a knowing smile: "Do you know, sir, our friend (he meant the dead man), when he heard his appeal had been dismissed, he pissed on the floor of his cell. From fright—Kindly take one of my cigarettes, sir. Do you not admire my new silver case, sir? From the boxwallah, two rupees eight annas. Classy European style."

19 Several people laughed—at what, nobody seemed certain.

20 Francis was walking by the superintendent, talking garrulously: "Well, sir, all hass passed off with the utmost satisfactoriness. It wass all finished—flick! like that. It iss not always so—oah, no! I have known cases where the doctor wass obliged to go beneath the gallows and pull the prisoner's legs to ensure decease. Most disagreeable!"

21 "Wriggling about, eh? That's bad," said the superintendent.

22 "Ach, sir, it iss worse when they become refractory! One man, I recall, clung to the bars of hiss cage when we went to take him out. You will scarcely credit, sir, that it took six warders to dislodge him, three pulling at each leg. We reasoned with him. 'My dear fellow,' we said, 'think of all the pain and trouble you are causing to us!' But no, he would not listen! Ach, he wass very troublesome!"

I found that I was laughing quite loudly. Everyone was laughing. Even the superintendent grinned in a tolerant way. "You'd better all come out and have a drink," he said quite genially. "I've got a bottle of whisky in the car. We could do with it." 23

We went through the big double gates of the prison, into the road. "Pulling at his legs!" exclaimed a Burmese magistrate suddenly, and burst into a loud chuckling. We all began laughing again. At that moment Francis's anecdote seemed extraordinarily funny. We all had a drink together, native and European alike, quite amicably. The dead man was a hundred yards away. 24

BUILDING VOCABULARY

1. Use *context clues* (see Glossary) to make an "educated guess" about the definitions of the following words in italics. Before you guess, look back to the paragraph for clues. Afterward, check your guess in a dictionary.
   a. *condemned* men (par. 1)
   b. puny *wisp* of a man (par. 2)
   c. Indian *warders* (par. 2)
   d. careful, *caressing* grip (par. 2)
   e. stood *aghast* (par. 6)
   f. it danced and *gambolled* (par. 8)
   g. *solemn* foolery (par. 10)
   h. armed with *lathis* (par. 17)
   i. a tin *pannikin* (par. 17)
   j. quite *genially* (par. 23)
2. What are definitions for the words below? Look at words within them, which you may be able to recognize.
   a. moodily
   b. dreadful
   c. Eurasian
   d. incuriously
   e. formality

THINKING CRITICALLY ABOUT THE ESSAY

Understanding the Writer's Ideas

1. The events in the essay occur in Burma, a country in Asia. Describe in your own words the specific details of the action.

2. Who are the major characters in this essay? Why might you include the dog as a major character?
3. In a narrative essay the writer often tells the events in chronological order. Examine the following events from "A Hanging." Arrange them in the order in which they occurred.
   a. A large woolly dog tries to lick the prisoner's face.
   b. A Eurasian boy talks about his silver case.
   c. The superintendent signals "Chalo!" to the hangman.
   d. One prisoner, a Hindu, is brought from his cell.
   e. Francis discusses with the superintendent a prisoner who had to be pulled off the bars of his cage.
   f. The prisoner steps aside to avoid a puddle as he marches to the gallows.
4. What is the author's opinion of *capital punishment* (legally killing someone who has disobeyed the laws of society)? How does the incident with the puddle suggest that opinion, even indirectly?

Understanding the Writer's Techniques

1. What is the main point that the writer wishes to make in this essay? Which paragraph tells the author's thesis most clearly? Which sentence in that paragraph best states the main idea of the essay?
2. In the first paragraph of the essay, we see clear images such as "brown silent men were squatting at the inner bars, with their blankets draped around them." The use of color and action makes an instant appeal to our sense of sight.
   a. What images in the rest of the essay do you find most vivid?
   b. Which sentence gives the best details of sound?
   c. What word pictures suggest action and color?
   d. Where do you find words that describe a sensation of touch?
3. In order to make their images clearer, writers use *figurative language* (see Glossary). "A Hanging" is especially rich in *similes,* which are comparisons using the word "like" or "as."
   a. What simile does Orwell use in the first paragraph in order to let us see how the light slants over the jail yard walls? How does the simile make the scene clearer?
   b. What other simile does Orwell use in the first paragraph?

c. Discuss the similes in the paragraphs listed below. What are the things being compared? Are the similes, in your opinion, original? How do they contribute to the image the author intends to create?

(1) It was like men handling a fish (par. 2)

(2) a thick sprouting moustache . . . rather like the moustache of a comic man on the films (par. 2)

(3) It was a high, reiterated cry . . . like the tolling of a bell. (par. 12)

(4) The Indians had gone grey like bad coffee (par. 13)

(5) He was dangling with his toes pointed straight downwards, slowly revolving, as dead as a stone. (par. 15)

4. You know that an important feature of narration is the writer's ability to look at a brief span of time and to expand that moment with specific language.

a. How has Orwell limited the events in "A Hanging" to a specific moment in time and place?

b. How does the image "a sodden morning of the rains" in paragraph 1 set the mood for the main event portrayed in the essay? What is the effect of the image "brown silent men"? Why does Orwell describe the prisoner as "a puny wisp of a man, with a shaven head and vague liquid eyes" (par. 2)? Why does the author present him in almost a comic way?

c. What is the effect of the image about the bugle call in paragraph 3? Why does Orwell create the image of the dog trying to lick the prisoner's face (par. 6)? How does it contribute to his main point? In paragraph 12, Orwell tells us that the dog whines. Why does he give that detail? Discuss the value of the images about the dog in paragraphs 15 and 17.

d. Why does Orwell offer the image of the prisoner stepping aside "to avoid a puddle on the path"? How does it advance the point of the essay? What is the effect of the image of the superintendent poking the ground with his stick (par. 13)?

e. What is the importance of the superintendent's words in paragraph 3? What is the value of the Eurasian boy's conversation in paragraph 18? How does the dialogue in paragraphs 20 to 24 contribute to Orwell's main point?

f. Why has Orwell left out information about the crime the prisoner committed? How would you feel about the prisoner if you knew he were, say, a rapist, a murderer, a molester of children, or a heroin supplier?

5. Analyze the point of view in the essay. Is the "I" narrator an observer, a participant, or both? Is he neutral or involved? Support your opinion.
6. In "A Hanging," Orwell skillfully uses several forms of *irony* to support his main ideas. Irony, in general, is the use of language to suggest the opposite of what is said. First, there is *verbal irony,* which involves a contrast between what is said and what is actually meant. Second, there is *irony of situation,* where there is a contrast between what is expected or thought appropriate and what actually happens. Then, there is *dramatic irony,* in which there is a contrast between what a character says and what the reader (or the audience) actually knows or understands.
   a. In paragraph 2, why does Orwell describe the prisoner as a *comic* type? Why does he emphasize the prisoner's *smallness?* Why does Orwell write that the prisoner "hardly noticed what was happening"? Why might this be called ironic?
   b. When the dog appears in paragraph 6, how is its behavior described? How do the dog's actions contrast with the situation?
   c. What is the major irony that Orwell analyzes in paragraph 10?
   d. In paragraph 11, how does the fact that one prisoner is being used to execute another prisoner strike you?
   e. Why is the superintendent's remark in paragraph 16—"*He's* all right"—a good example of verbal irony?
   f. After the hanging, the men engage in seemingly normal actions. However, Orwell undercuts these actions through the use of irony. Find at least two examples of irony in paragraphs 17 to 24.

Exploring the Writer's Ideas

1. Orwell is clearly against capital punishment. Why might you agree or disagree with him? Are there any crimes for which capital punishment is acceptable to you? If not, what should society do with those convicted of serious crimes?

2. Do you think the method used to perform capital punishment has anything to do with the way we view it? Is death by hanging or firing squad worse than death by gas or by the electric chair? Or are they all the same? Socrates—a Greek philosopher convicted of conspiracy—was forced to drink *hemlock,* a fast-acting poison. Can you accept that?
3. Orwell shows a variety of reactions people have to an act of execution. Can you believe the way the people behave here? Why? How do you explain the large crowds that gathered to watch public executions in Europe in the sixteenth and seventeenth centuries?

IDEAS FOR WRITING

Prewriting

Make two columns on a sheet of paper that you have headed *Capital Punishment.* In one column, jot down all the reasons you can think of in favor of capital punishment. In the other column, indicate all the reasons you can think of against it.

Guided Writing

Write a narrative essay in which you tell about a punishment you either saw or received. Use sensory language, selecting your details carefully. At one point in your paper—as Orwell does in paragraph 10—state your opinion or interpretation of the punishment clearly.

1. Use a number of images that name colors, sounds, smells, and actions.
2. Try to write at least three original similes. Think through your comparisons carefully. Make sure they are logical. Avoid overused comparisons like "He was white as a ghost."
3. Set your narrative in time and place. Tell the season of the year and the place in which the event occurred.
4. Fill in details of the setting. Show what the surroundings look like.
5. Name people by name. Show details of their actions. Quote some of their spoken dialogue.
6. Use the first-person point of view.

Thinking and Writing Collaboratively

In small groups, read drafts of each other's essays for the Guided Writing activity. Look especially at the point at which the writer states an opinion about or interprets the punishment received. Does the writer adequately explain the event? What insights has the writer brought to the moment by analyzing it? How could either the narrative itself or the interpretation be made clearer or more powerful?

More Writing Projects

1. Narrate in your journal an event that turned out differently from what you expected—a blind date, a picnic, a holiday. Try to stress the irony of the situation.
2. Write a narrative paragraph that describes a vivid event in which you hid your true feelings about the event, such as a postelection party, the wedding of someone you disliked, a job interview, a visit to the doctor.
3. Write an editorial for your college newspaper supporting or attacking the idea of capital punishment. Communicate your position through the use of real or hypothetical narration of a relevant event.

Travelling

Grace Paley

The author Grace Paley tells two stories about traveling into the American South by bus during the time of racial segregation. In recounting journeys by her mother and herself, she also asks: Why do we remember some things and not others?

PREREADING: THINKING ABOUT THE ESSAY IN ADVANCE

What stories in your family make up the family saga, the tales that identify you as a family group? How do you know that these stories are "true"? Are there stories in your family about the days of racial segregation?

Words to Watch

fatigues (par. 10) clothing worn by soldiers in training
ebbed (par. 12) flowing of tide back to the sea
Gentile (par. 16) any person not a Jew
anti-Semitism (par. 16) prejudice against Jews
adamant (par. 20) unyielding

My mother and sister were travelling South. The year was 1927. 1
They had begun their journey in New York. They were going to visit my brother, who was studying at the Medical College of Virginia, in Richmond. Their bus was an express and had stopped only in Philadelphia, Wilmington, and now Washington. Here the darker people who had got on in Philadelphia or New York rose from their seats, put their bags and boxes together, and moved to the back of the bus. People who boarded in Washington knew where to seat themselves. My mother had heard that something like this would happen. My sister had heard of it, too. They had not lived in it. This reorganization of passengers by color happened in silence. My mother and sister remained in their seats, which were about three-quarters of the way back.

2 When everyone was settled, the bus driver began to collect tickets. My sister saw him coming. She pinched my mother—"Ma! Look!" Of course, my mother saw him, too. What frightened my sister was the quietness. The white people in front, the black people in back—silent.

3 The driver sighed, said, "You can't sit here, ma'am. It's for them—waving over his shoulder at the Negroes, among whom they were now sitting. "Move, please."

4 My mother said, "No."

5 He said, "You don't understand, ma'am. It's against the law. You have to move to the front."

6 My mother said, "No."

7 When I first tried to write this scene, I imagined my mother saying, "That's all right, mister. We're comfortable. I can't change my seat every minute." I read this invention to my sister. She said it was nothing like that. My mother did not try to be friendly or pretend innocence. While my sister trembled in the silence, my mother said for the third time—quietly—"No."

8 Somehow, finally, they were in Richmond. There was my brother, in school among so many American boys. After hugs and my mother's anxious looks at her young son, my sister said, "Vic, you know what Mama did?"

9 My brother remembers thinking, What? Oh! She wouldn't move? He had a classmate, a Jewish boy like him, but from Virginia, who had had a public confrontation with a Negro man. He had punched that man hard, knocked him down. My brother couldn't believe it. He was stunned. He couldn't imagine a Jewish boy wanting to knock anyone down. He had never wanted to. But he thought, looking back, that he had been set down to work and study in a nearly foreign place, and had had to get used to it. Then he told me about the Second World War, when the disgrace of black soldiers forced to sit behind white German P.O.W.s shook him. Shamed him.

10 About fifteen years later, in 1943, in early summer, I rode the bus for about three days from New York to Miami Beach, where my husband and hundreds of other boys in sweaty fatigues were trudging up and down the streets and beaches to prepare themselves for war.

11 By late afternoon of the second long day, we were well into the South, beyond Richmond, maybe in South Carolina or Georgia. My excitement about travel in the wide world was damaged

a little by a sudden fear that I might not recognize Jess, or he me. We hadn't seen each other for two months. I took a photograph out of my pocket; yes, I would know him.

I had been sleeping, waking, reading, writing, dozing, waking. So many hours, the movement of the passengers was like a tide that sometimes ebbed and now seemed to be noisily rising. I opened my eyes to the sound of people brushing past my aisle seat. And looked up to see a colored woman holding a large sleeping baby, who, with the heaviness of sleep, his arms tight around her neck, seemed to be pulling her head down. I looked around and noticed that I was in the last white row. The press of new travellers had made it impossible for her to move farther back. She seemed so tired, and I had been sitting and sitting for a day and a half at least. Not thinking, or maybe refusing to think, I offered her my seat. 12

She looked to the right and left as well as she could. Softly, she said, "Oh, no." I became fully awake. A white man was standing right beside her, but on the other side of the invisible absolute racial border. Of course, she couldn't accept my seat. Her sleeping child hung mercilessly from her neck. She shifted a little to balance the burden. She whispered to herself, "Oh, I just don't know." So I said, "Well, at least give me the baby." First, she turned, barely looking at the man beside her. He made no move. Then, to my surprise, but obviously out of sheer exhaustion, she disengaged the child from her body and placed him on my lap. He was deep in child-sleep. He stirred, but not enough to bother himself or me. I liked holding him, aligning him along my twenty-year-old young woman's shape. I thought ahead to that holding, that breathing together that would happen in my life if this war would ever end. I was so comfortable under his nice weight. I closed my eyes for a couple of minutes, but suddenly opened them to look up into the face of a white man talking. In a loud voice, he addressed me: "Lady, I wouldn't of touched that thing with a meat hook." 13

I thought, Oh, this world will end in ice. I could do nothing but look straight into his eyes. I did not look away from him. Then I held that little boy a little tighter, kissed his curly head, pressed him even closer, so that he began to squirm. So sleepy, he re-shaped himself inside my arms. His mother tried to narrow herself away from that dangerous border, too frightened at first to move at all. After a couple of minutes, she 14 leaned forward a little, placed her hand on the baby's head, and held it there until the next stop. I couldn't look up into her mother face.

15 I write this remembrance more than fifty years later. I look back at that mother and child. I see how young she is. Her hand on his head is quite small, though she tries by spreading her fingers wide to hide him from the white man. But the child I'm holding, his little face as he turns toward me, is the dark-brown face of my *own* grandson, my daughter's boy, the open mouth of the sleeper, the full lips, the thick little body of a child who runs wildly from one end of the yard to the other, leaps from dangerous heights with experienced caution, muscling his body, his mind, for coming realities.

16 Of course, when my mother and sister returned from Charlottesville the family at home wanted to know: How was Vic doing in school among all those Gentiles? Was the long bus ride hard? Was the anti-Semitism really bad or just normal? What happened on the bus? I was probably present at that supper, the attentive listener and total forgetter of information that immediately started to form me.

17 Then, last year, my sister, casting the net of old age (through which recent experience easily slips), brought up that old story. First, I was angry. How come you never told me about your bus ride with Mama? I mean, really, so many years ago.

18 I don't know, she said. Anyway, you were only about four years old and, besides, maybe I did.

19 I asked my brother why we'd never talked about that day. He said he thought now that it had had a great effect on him; he had tried unravelling its meaning for years—then life, family, work happened. So I imagined him, a youngster, really, a kid from the Bronx in Virginia in 1927—why, he was a stranger there himself.

20 In the next couple of weeks, we continued to talk about our mother, the way she was principled, adamant, and at the same time so shy. What else could we remember . . . Well, I said, I have a story about those buses, too. Then I told them: how it happened on just such a journey, when I was still quite young, that I first knew my grandson, first held him close but could protect him for only about twenty minutes fifty years ago.

BUILDING VOCABULARY

Use the following words in sentences of your own:

a. confrontation (par. 9)
b. absolute (par. 13)
c. remembrance (par. 15)
d. principled (par. 20)

THINKING CRITICALLY ABOUT THE ESSAY

Understanding the Writer's Ideas

1. What is the effect of the writer's reference to some of the passengers as "the darker people"?
2. After the writer's mother utters her dramatic "No" the essay seems to shift (par. 7) to a new subject. What is that subject? What is the connection between this subject and the apparent subject of the first six paragraphs? Why does the writer connect these two subjects?
3. What do we learn from her brother's recollection of her mother's trip?
4. Compare and contrast the writer's experience riding a bus into the South in 1943 and her mother's experience fifteen years earlier.
5. What does the writer mean by "Oh, this world will end in ice" (par. 14)?
6. Why does the writer say, at the end of par. 14, "I couldn't look up into her mother face"?
7. What do we learn in the concluding paragraphs of the essay, paragraphs located in the present?

Understanding the Writer's Techniques

1. An essay in the form of *narrative* may not follow the conventions of a more argumentative essay. For instance, the essay does not have an explicit thesis statement but rather is written to answer two related questions. What are these questions?
2. A narrative by its nature is likely to make its points differently from a less literary kind of essay. A narrative, for example, may stress emotion more than reason. Give some

examples of techniques the writer employs to build an *emotional* argument.

3. This essay has four main sections (par. 1–par. 6; par. 7–par. 14; par. 15; and par. 16–par. 20). Indicate briefly the purpose of each section and note how the writer connects these sections.
4. This essay has at least two focuses—one on specific incidents in the context of racism, one on recollection. How does the writer keep the time frame of the various incidents of the story clearly before the reader? How does the writer weave the process of recollecting into the narrating of the actual incidents?
5. Narration allows a writer to suggest or evoke meanings rather than to specify or to hone in for greater precision. Can you find examples in the essay where instead of clear-cut statements meaning is suggested or evoked?
6. Why are the details of the essay's last section (par. 16 on) left to the end?

Exploring the Writer's Ideas

1. The writer emphasizes the process of remembering as perilous, incomplete, open to reverie. Do you agree? Can you give examples from your own experience that confirm or refute Paley's view of memory?
2. The stories the writer tells about her mother and herself portray them both as principled people doing the right thing. What evidence does the essay provide to support the view of Paley and her mother as people of rectitude? Or do you find evidence that in fact Paley has exaggerated what happened?
3. Do you think the experience of "seeing before the fact" that Paley narrates (see par. 15) is true to life, or colored for the purposes of storytelling? Defend your view.

IDEAS FOR WRITING

Prewriting

Write a few sentences telling something about an especially "principled, adamant" member of your family.

Guided Writing

Narrate an incident or related incidents that (a) show you or a member of your family doing something "principled"; and (b) make the process of remembering a part of your essay.

1. Begin with the account of an incident—without indicating that you are writing out of second-hand knowledge or recollection.
2. Then suggest an alternative way you may have narrated the incident.
3. Indicate how you concluded what was true to the incident and belonged in your narration.
4. Write a paragraph that reflects on the incident(s) and ties its meaning to the process of recollection.
5. End by offering some matter-of-fact details about the process of remembering that fill in some of the blanks of "what actually happened."

Thinking and Writing Collaboratively

In a small group of four or five students, share your Guided Writing essays with each other. Then attempt alternative narrative lines for each essay, suggesting different possible openings, sequences of events, emphases, and endings. Ask each other which versions you prefer, and why. Discuss the problems of trying to recapture "what really happened" in the past in an essay.

More Writing Projects

1. Write a paragraph or more about your personal experience of relations among white and African-American people.
2. Talk with two or three members of your family about an important incident in the family's history. Write an account that weighs these different recollections, and what each person thinks to be most important.
3. In a few paragraphs, explore the narrative possibilities of an incident in your life that could be interpreted as "foreseeing" a future event, just as Paley's encounter with the black baby on the bus "foretold" her acquaintance with her grandchild.

SUMMING UP: CHAPTER 4

1. Orwell's essay has remained one of the outstanding essays of the century, widely anthologized and frequently taught in English writing classes. How do you account for its popularity? Would you consider it the best essay in this chapter or in the four chapters you have read so far? Why or why not? Write an essay in which you analyze and evaluate "A Hanging."
2. Elizabeth Wong and Grace Paley both challenge cultural assumptions. Use their narratives as a starting point, and write an essay about a particular time in your childhood when you tried to accept, ignore, or defy a given cultural or social expectation.
3. You are Richard Selzer (author of "The Discus Thrower," pages 110–113) and you have been asked by a local newspaper to write a short review of George Orwell's "A Hanging." Basing your insights on the philosophy of "The Discus Thrower," write the review. Or, if you choose, be George Orwell and write a review of Selzer's "The Discus Thrower."
4. What have you learned about writing strong narratives from the writers in this chapter? What generalizations can you draw? What "rules" can you derive? Write an essay called "How to Write Narratives" based on what you have learned from Wong, Hughes, Orwell and (or) Paley. Make specific references to the writer(s) of your choice.
5. Hughes's essay highlights the role of religion in life. Write an essay in which you narrate an important religious experience that you remember. You might want to narrate the story of your own "conversion."

CHAPTER 5

Illustration

WHAT IS ILLUSTRATION?

One convenient way for writers to present and to support a point is through *illustration*—that is, by means of several examples to back up an idea. Illustration (or *exemplification*) helps a writer put general or abstract thoughts into specific examples. As readers, we often find that we are able to understand a writer's point more effectively because we respond to the concrete examples. We are familiar with illustration in everyday life. If a police officer is called a racist, the review board will want *illustrations* of the racist behavior. The accuser will have to provide concrete examples of racist language, or present arrest statistics that show the officer was more likely to arrest Koreans, for instance, than white Americans.

Writing that uses illustration is most effective if it uses *several* examples to support the thesis. A single, isolated example might not convince anyone easily, but a series of examples builds up a stronger case. Writers can also use an *extended example,* which is one example that is developed at length.

For instance, you might want to illustrate your thesis that American patchwork quilts are an important record of women's history. Since your reader might not be familiar with quilts, you would have to illustrate your argument with examples such as these:

- Baltimore album quilts were given to eastern women heading west in the nineteenth century, and contain signatures and dates stitched in the squares to mark the event.

- Women used blue and white in quilt patterns to show their support for the temperance movement that opposed sale of alcohol.
- Women named patterns after geographic and historical events, creating such quilts as Rocky Road to Kansas and Abe Lincoln's Platform.
- African-American quilters adapted techniques from West Africa to make blankets for slave quarters.
- One quilter from Kentucky recorded all the deaths in her family in her work. The unusual quilt contains a pattern of a cemetery and coffins with names for each family member!

If you visited a museum and there was only one painting on the wall, you would probably feel that you hadn't gotten your money's worth. You expect a museum to be a *collection* of paintings, so that you can study a variety of types of art or several paintings by the same painter in order to understand the whole field of art. In the same way, through the accumulation of illustrations, the writer builds a case for the thesis.

In this chapter, writers use illustration forcefully to make their points. Brent Staples, an African-American journalist, shows how some people perceive his mere presence on a street at night as a threat. Barbara Ehrenreich uses irony to illustrate, from a feminist perspective, what women can learn from men. James Popkin with Katia Hetter looks at America's gambling craze. Finally, Lewis Thomas uses examples from his experience as a surgeon to illustrate how death is a natural part of the life cycle. Each writer knows that one example is insufficient to create a case, but that multiple examples yield a convincing essay.

HOW DO WE READ ILLUSTRATION?

Reading illustration requires us to ask ourselves these questions:

- What is the writer's thesis? What is the *purpose* of the examples?
- What audience is the writer addressing? How do we know?
- What other techniques is the writer using? Is there narration? description? How are these used to help the illustration?
- In what order has the writer arranged the examples? Where is the most important example placed?
- How does the writer use *transitions?* Often, transitions in illustration essays enumerate: *first, second, third; one, another.*

HOW DO WE WRITE WITH ILLUSTRATIONS?

Read the selections critically to see the many ways in which writers can use illustrations to support an idea. Notice how many illustrations each writer provides, and plan to do the same in your essay.

Select your topic and write a thesis sentence that tells the reader what you are going to illustrate and what your main idea is about the subject.

Sample thesis statement:

> Many people have long cherished quilts for their beautiful colors and patterns, but few collectors recognize the history stitched into the squares.

Make a list of *examples* to support the thesis.

Examples by quilt types: Baltimore album quilts, political quilts, suffrage quilts, slave quilts, graveyard quilts

Examples by quilt pattern names: Radical Rose; Drunkard's Path; Memory Blocks; Old Maid's Puzzle; Wheel of Mystery; Log Cabin; Rocky Road to Kansas; Slave Chain; Underground Railroad; Delectable Mountains; Union Star; Jackson Star; Old Indian Trail; Trip around the World

Determine who the audience will be: a group of experienced quilters? museum curators? a PTA group? Each is a different audience with different interests and needs.

Plan an arrangement of the examples. Begin with the least important and build up to the most important. Or arrange the examples in chronological order.

Plan to use other techniques (such as description), especially if your audience is unfamiliar with your subject. If you are writing the quilt paper and using the example of the Baltimore album quilt, you would then have to *describe* it for readers who do not know what such a quilt looks like.

Be sure that the *purpose* of the illustrations is clearly stated, especially in the conclusion. In the quilt essay, for instance, different quilt patterns might be illustrated in order to encourage readers to preserve and study quilts.

Writing and Revising the Draft

Use the first paragraph to introduce the subject and to set up a clear thesis. You might introduce an *abstract* idea, such as forgotten history, that will be *illustrated* in the examples.

Plan the body to give the reader lots of examples, and to develop the examples if necessary. Use narration, description, and dialogue to enhance the illustrations. Write a conclusion that returns to the abstract idea you began with in the introduction.

Write a second draft for reading aloud.

Revise, based on your listener's comments. Proofread the essay carefully. Check spelling and grammar. Make a final copy.

A STUDENT PARAGRAPH: ILLUSTRATION

This paragraph from a student's illustration paper on quiltmaking shows how the use of examples advances the thesis of the essay. The thesis, which you examined on page 164, asserts that, the colors and patterns of quilts aside, "few collectors recognize the history stitched into the squares."

We can find one of the most significant examples of the historical, recordkeeping function of quiltmaking in the needlework of Mary Kinsale. Kinsale lived and worked in the state of Kentucky in the mid-nineteenth century. Unlike the political quilts discussed earlier, and the various quilts that document "official" history, Kinsale's quilts deal only with the private sphere—the history of her own family. Specifically, Kinsale set out to document the precise dates of death of all her family members, illustrating the squares with coffins, open graves, and other symbols of death. What we might call morbid or tasteless today probably struck members of Kinsale's community as natural and proper; the American culture had not yet restricted images of gaunt, grinning skulls, mossy tombstones, and other symbols of death to horror movies. In fact, Kinsale's images served an important religious and social purpose by reminding family and friends to reform their lives while there was still time. Kinsale decided to record the vital dates of her dearly departed, and remind the living of their duty in life, by stitching a quilt, rather

Reference to essay thesis, "history stitched into squares"

Transition ("one of the most significant examples") asserts order according to significance

Reference to other points in essay provides <u>unity</u>

Kinsale's work is main <u>illustration</u> developed in the paragraph

Supporting detail

Supporting detail

than simply writing an entry in the family Bible, or leaving the task to government bureaucrats. Her quiltmaking illustrates nineteenth-century society's distinctly old-fashioned attitude towards death, as well as their different understanding of the role ordinary individuals could play in recording history.

Closing sentence connects to essay's thesis

Night Walker

Brent Staples

Brent Staples is an editorial writer for *The New York Times* and holds a Ph.D. in psychology from the University of Chicago. Yet, since his youth, he has instilled fear and suspicion in many just by taking nighttime walks to combat his insomnia. In this essay, which appeared in the *Los Angeles Times* in 1986, Staples explains how others perceive themselves as his potential victim simply because he is a black man in "urban America."

PREREADING: THINKING ABOUT THE ESSAY IN ADVANCE

Imagine this scene: you are walking alone at night in a relatively wealthy neighborhood and you hear footsteps behind you that you believe are the footsteps of someone of a different race from yours. How do you feel? What do you do? Why?

Words to Watch

affluent (par. 1) wealthy
discreet (par. 1) showing good judgment; careful
quarry (par. 2) prey; object of a hunt
dismayed (par. 2) discouraged
taut (par. 4) tight; tense
warrenlike (par. 5) like a crowded tenement district
bandolier (par. 5) gun belt worn across the chest
solace (par. 5) relief; consolation; comfort
retrospect (par. 6) review of past event
ad hoc (par. 7) unplanned; for the particular case at hand
labyrinthine (par. 7) like a maze
skittish (par. 9) nervous; jumpy
constitutionals (par. 10) regular walks

1 My first victim was a woman—white, well dressed, probably in her early 20s. I came upon her late one evening on a deserted street in Hyde Park, a relatively affluent neighborhood in an

otherwise mean, impoverished section of Chicago. As I swung onto the avenue behind her, there seemed to be a discreet, uninflammatory distance between us. Not so. She cast back a worried glance. To her, the youngish black man—a broad six feet two inches with a beard and billowing hair, both hands shoved into the pockets of a bulky military jacket—seemed menacingly close. She picked up her pace and was soon running in earnest. Within seconds she disappeared into a cross street.

That was more than a decade ago. I was 22 years old, a graduate student newly arrived at the University of Chicago. It was in the echo of that terrified woman's footfalls that I first began to know the unwieldy inheritance I'd come into—the ability to alter public space in ugly ways. It was clear that she thought herself the quarry of a mugger, a rapist, or worse. Suffering a bout of insomnia, however, I was stalking sleep, not defenseless wayfarers. As a softy who is scarcely able to take a knife to a raw chicken—let alone hold one to a person's throat—I was surprised, embarrassed, and dismayed all at once. Her flight made me feel like an accomplice in tyranny. It also made it clear that I was indistinguishable from the muggers who occasionally seeped into the area from the surrounding ghetto. I soon gathered that being perceived as dangerous is a hazard in itself: Where fear and weapons meet—and they often do in urban America—there is always the possibility of death. 2

In that first year, my first away from my hometown, I was to become thoroughly familiar with the language of fear. At dark, shadowy intersections, I could cross in front of a car stopped at a traffic light and elicit the *thunk, thunk, thunk, thunk* of the driver—black, white, male, female—hammering down the door locks. On less traveled streets after dark, I grew accustomed to but never comfortable with people crossing to the other side of the street rather than pass me. Then there were the standard unpleasantries with policemen, doormen, bouncers, cabdrivers, and others whose business it is to screen out troublesome individuals *before* there is any nastiness. 3

I moved to New York nearly two years ago and I have remained an avid night walker. In central Manhattan, the near-constant crowd covers the tense one-on-one street encounters. Elsewhere, things can get very taut indeed. 4

After dark, on the warrenlike streets of Brooklyn where I live, I often see women who fear the worst from me. They seem to have set their faces on neutral, and with their purse straps 5 strung across their chests bandolier-style, they forge ahead as though bracing themselves against being tackled. I understand, of course, that the danger they perceive is not a hallucination. Women are particularly vulnerable to street violence, and young black males are drastically overrepresented among the perpetrators of that violence. Yet these truths are no solace against the alienation that comes of being ever the suspect, an entity with whom pedestrians avoid making eye contact.

6 It is not altogether clear to me how I reached the ripe old age of 22 without being conscious of the lethality nighttime pedestrians attributed to me. Perhaps it was because in Chester, Pa., the small, angry industrial town where I came of age in the 1960s, I was scarcely noticeable against a backdrop of gang warfare, street knifings, and murders. I grew up one of the good boys, had perhaps a half-dozen fistfights. In retrospect, my shyness of combat has clear sources. As a boy, I saw countless tough guys locked away; I have since buried several, too. They were babies, really—a teen-age cousin, a brother of 22, a childhood friend in his mid-20s—all gone down in episodes of bravado played out in the streets. I chose, perhaps unconsciously, to remain a shadow—timid, but a survivor.

7 The fearsomeness mistakenly attributed to me in public places often has a perilous flavor. The most frightening of these confusions occurred in the late 1970s and early 1980s, when I worked as a journalist in Chicago. One day, rushing into the office of a magazine I was writing for with a deadline story in hand, I was mistaken for a burglar. The office manager called security and, with an ad hoc posse, pursued me through the labyrinthine halls, nearly to my editor's door. I had no way of proving who I was. I could only move briskly toward the company of someone who knew me.

8 Relatively speaking, however, I never fared as badly as another black male journalist. He went to nearby Waukegan, Ill., a couple of summers ago to work on a story about a murderer who was born there. Mistaking the reporter for the killer, police officers hauled him from his car at gunpoint and but for his press credentials would probably have tried to book him. Such episodes are not uncommon. Black men trade tales like this all the time.

9 Over the years, I learned to smother the rage I felt at so often being mistaken for a criminal. Not to do so would surely have led to madness. I now take precautions to make myself less

threatening. I move about with care, particularly late in the evening. I give a wide berth to nervous people on subway platforms during the wee hours. If I happen to be entering a building behind some people who appear skittish, I may walk by, letting them clear the lobby before I return, so as not to seem to be following them. I have been calm and extremely congenial on those rare occasions when I've been pulled over by the police.

And on late-evening constitutionals I employ what has proved to be an excellent tension-reducing measure: I whistle melodies from Beethoven and Vivaldi and the more popular classical composers. Even steely New Yorkers hunching toward nighttime destinations seem to relax, and occasionally they even join in the tune. Virtually everybody seems to sense that a mugger wouldn't be warbling bright, sunny selections from Vivaldi's "Four Seasons." It is my equivalent of the cowbell that hikers wear when they are in bear country. 10

BUILDING VOCABULARY

1. Use context clues to determine the meaning of each word in italics. Return to the appropriate paragraph in the essay for more clues. Then, if necessary, check your definitions in a dictionary and compare the dictionary meaning with the meaning you derived from the context.
   - **a.** seemed *menacingly* close (par. 1)
   - **b.** I was *indistinguishable* from the muggers who occasionally *seeped* into the area (par. 2)
   - **c.** I have remained an *avid* night walker (par. 4)
   - **d.** they *forge* ahead (par. 5)
   - **e.** Women are particularly *vulnerable* to street violence (par. 5)
   - **f.** the *lethality* nighttime pedestrians attributed to me (par. 6)
   - **g.** episodes of *bravado* played out in the streets (par. 6)
   - **h.** I learned to *smother* the rage I felt . . . so often (par. 9)
   - **i.** I now take *precautions* to make myself less threatening (par. 9)
   - **j.** Even *steely* New Yorkers *hunching* toward nighttime destinations (par. 10)
2. Reread paragraph 1. List all the words suggesting action and all the words involving emotion. What is the cumulative effect?

THINKING CRITICALLY ABOUT THE ESSAY

Understanding the Writer's Ideas

1. How does Staples describe himself in paragraph 1? What point is he making by such a description?
2. Explain in your own words the incident Staples narrates in paragraph 1. Where does it take place? When? How old was the author at the time? What was he doing? During the incident, why did the woman "cast back a worried glance"? Was she really his "victim"? Explain. What was Staples's reaction to the incident?
3. What is the "unwieldy inheritance" mentioned in paragraph 2? What is Staples's definition of it? What is the implied meaning?
4. How would you describe Staples's personality? What does he mean when he describes himself as "a softy"? How does he illustrate the fact that he is "a softy"? Why did he develop this personality?
5. Explain the meaning of the statement, "I soon gathered that being perceived as dangerous is a hazard in itself" (par. 2).
6. What is "the language of fear" (par. 3)? What examples does Staples provide to illustrate this "language"?
7. Why did car drivers lock their doors when the author walked in front of their cars? How did Staples feel about that?
8. Where did Staples grow up? Did he experience the same reactions there to his nighttime walks as he did in Chicago? Why? How was Manhattan different from Chicago for the author? How was Brooklyn different from Manhattan?
9. What has been Staples's reaction to the numerous incidents of mistaken identity? How has he dealt with that reaction? What "precautions" does he take to make himself "less threatening"?
10. Summarize the example Staples narrates about the black journalist in Waukegan.
11. What has been the author's experiences with the police? Explain.
12. Does the author feel that all the danger people attribute to him when he takes night walks is unfair or unwarranted? Explain.
13. Why does his whistling selections from Beethoven and Vivaldi seem to make people less afraid of the author?

Understanding the Writer's Techniques

1. What is Staples's thesis in this essay?
2. How do the title and opening statement of this essay grasp and hold the reader's interest?
3. Reread the first paragraph. What *mood* or *tone* does Staples establish here? How? Does he sustain that mood? Is there a shift in tone? Explain.
4. How does the author use *narration* in paragraph 1 as a way to illustrate a point? What point is illustrated? Where else does he use narration?
5. What is the effect of the two-word sentence "Not so" in paragraph 1?
6. Staples uses *description* in this essay. Which descriptions serve as illustrations? Explain what ideas they support.
7. *Onomatopoeia* is the use of words whose sounds suggest their sense or action. Where in the essay does Staples use this technique? What action does the sound represent? Why does the author use this technique instead of simply describing the action?
8. What examples from Staples's childhood illustrate why he developed his particular adult personality?
9. Explain the meaning of the final sentence in the essay.
10. *Stereotypes* are oversimplified, uncritical judgments about people, races, issues, events, and so forth. Where in this essay does the author present stereotypes? For what purpose?
11. For whom was this article intended? Why do you think so? Is it written primarily for a white or black audience? Explain.

Exploring the Writer's Ideas

1. In this essay, Staples gives not only examples of his own experiences but also those of other black men. It is interesting, however, that he does not include examples of the experiences of black women. Why do you think he omitted these references? How do you feel about the omission? Are there any recent news stories, either in your city or in others, which might be included as such illustrations?
2. What prejudices and stereotypes about different racial and cultural groups do people in your community hold? Where do these prejudices and stereotypes come from? Do you think any are justified?

3. What everyday situations do you perceive as most dangerous? Why do you perceive them as such? How do you react to protect yourself? Do you feel your perceptions and reactions are realistic? Explain.

IDEAS FOR WRITING

Prewriting

Write down a few of your personality traits, and then jot down ways in which people identify those traits. Also, indicate how people misperceive you—that is, how they reach wrong conclusions about your personality.

Guided Writing

Write an essay that illustrates how something about your personality has been incorrectly perceived at some time or over a period of time.

1. Begin your essay by narrating a single incident that vividly illustrates the misperception. Begin this illustration with a statement.
2. Explain the time context of this incident as it fits into your life or into a continuing misperception.
3. Describe and illustrate "who you really are" in relation to this misperception.
4. Explain how this misperception fits into a larger context outside your immediate, personal experience of it.
5. Write a series of descriptive illustrations to explain how this misperception has continued to affect you over time.
6. Explain how you first became aware of the misperception.
7. If possible, offer illustrations of others who have suffered the same or similar misperceptions of themselves.
8. Write about your emotional reaction to this overall situation.
9. Illustrate how you have learned to cope with the situation.
10. Give your essay a "catchy" title.

Thinking and Writing Collaboratively

Form groups of four or five, and recommend productive ways to solve the key problems raised by Staples in his essay. Take notes, and then as a group write down the problems and their possible solutions. Share the group's writing with the rest of the class.

More Writing Projects

1. Usually stereotypes are thought of as negative. Illustrate at least three *positive* stereotypes in your latest journal entry.
2. Write a paragraph in which you illustrate your family's or friends' misconceptions about your girlfriend/boyfriend, wife/husband, or best friend.
3. What tension reducing measures do you use in situations that might frighten you or in which you might frighten others? Write an essay to address the issue.

What I've Learned From Men

Barbara Ehrenreich

The feminist writer and historian Barbara Ehrenreich, Fellow of the Institute for Policy Studies in Washington, D.C., illustrates that sometimes you can learn the most important things from your enemies, in this case, men. Aside from being able to catch the eye of a waiter, a not inconsiderable attribute, men have one wrongly maligned quality that women would do well to learn from, Ehrenreich argues: how to be tough.

PREREADING: THINKING ABOUT THE ESSAY IN ADVANCE

What have you learned from the opposite sex? What expectations are raised by a woman saying she has learned something from men?

Words to Watch

euthanasia (par. 1) mercy killing
lecherous (par. 3) lewd
unconscionable (par. 3) beyond reasonable bounds
servility (par. 4) attitude appropriate to servants
AWOL (par. 4) used in military for Absent Without Leave
veneer (par. 4) mere outside show
rueful (par. 4) regretful
aura (par. 6) distinctive air
self-deprecation (par. 6) putting oneself down
brazenly (par. 6) shamelessly
taciturn (par. 9) silent
purveyors (par. 10) providers
emulating (par. 11) imitating
basso profundo (par. 11) deep bass voice
blandishments (par. 12) allurements

1 For many years I believed that women had only one thing to learn from men: how to get the attention of a waiter by some

means short of kicking over the table and shrieking. Never in my life have I gotten the attention of a waiter, unless it was an off-duty waiter whose car I'd accidentally scraped in a parking lot somewhere. Men, however, can summon a maître d' just by thinking the word "coffee," and this is a power women would be well advised to study. What else would we possibly want to learn from them? How to interrupt someone in mid-sentence as if you were performing an act of conversational euthanasia? How to drop a pair of socks three feet from an open hamper and keep right on walking? How to make those weird guttural gargling sounds in the bathroom?

But now, at mid-life, I am willing to admit that there are some real and useful things to learn from men. Not from all men—in fact, we may have the most to learn from some of the men we like the least. This realization does not mean that my feminist principles have gone soft with age: what I think women could learn from men is how to get *tough.* After more than a decade of consciousness-raising, assertiveness training, and hand-to-hand combat in the battle of the sexes, we're still too ladylike. Let me try that again—we're just too *damn* ladylike. 2

Here is an example from my own experience, a story that I blush to recount. A few years ago, at an international conference held in an exotic and luxurious setting, a prestigious professor invited me to his room for what he said would be an intellectual discussion on matters of theoretical importance. So far, so good. I showed up promptly. But only minutes into the conversation—held in all-too-adjacent chairs—it emerged that he was interested in something more substantial than a meeting of minds. I was disgusted, but not enough to overcome 30-odd years of programming in ladylikeness. Every time his comments took a lecherous turn, I chattered distractingly; every time his hand found its way to my knee, I returned it as if it were something he had misplaced. This went on for an unconscionable period (as much as 20 minutes); then there was a minor scuffle, a dash for the door, and I was out—with nothing violated but my self-esteem. I, a full-grown feminist, conversant with such matters as rape crisis counseling and sexual harassment at the workplace, had behaved like a ninny—or, as I now understand it, like a lady. 3

The essence of ladylikeness is a persistent servility masked as "niceness." For example, we (women) tend to assume that it is our responsibility to keep everything "nice" even when the per- 4 son we are with is rude, aggressive, or emotionally AWOL. (In the above example, I was so busy taking responsibility for preserving the veneer of "niceness" that I almost forgot to take responsibility for myself.) In conversations with men, we do almost all the work: sociologists have observed that in male-female social interactions it's the woman who throws out leading questions and verbal encouragements ("So how did you *feel* about that?" and so on) while the man, typically, says "Hmmmm." Wherever we go, we're perpetually smiling—the on-cue smile, like the now-outmoded curtsy, being one of our culture's little rituals of submission. We're trained to feel embarrassed if we're praised, but if we see a criticism coming at us from miles down the road, we rush to acknowledge it. And when we're feeling aggressive or angry or resentful, we just tighten up our smiles or turn them into rueful little moues. In short, we spend a great deal of time acting like wimps.

5 For contrast, think of the macho stars we love to watch. Think, for example, of Mel Gibson facing down punk marauders in "The Road Warrior" . . . John Travolta swaggering his way through the early scenes of "Saturday Night Fever" . . . or Marlon Brando shrugging off the local law in "The Wild One." Would they simper their way through tight spots? Chatter aimlessly to keep the conversation going? Get all clutched up whenever they think they might—just might—have hurt someone's feelings? No, of course not, and therein, I think, lies their fascination for us.

6 The attraction of the "tough guy" is that he has—or at least seems to have—what most of us lack, and that is an aura of power and control. In an article, feminist psychiatrist Jean Baker Miller writes that "a woman's using self-determined power for herself is equivalent to selfishness [and] destructiveness"—an equation that makes us want to avoid even the appearance of power. Miller cites cases of women who get depressed just when they're on the verge of success—and of women who do succeed and then bury their achievement in self-deprecation. As an example, she describes one company's periodic meetings to recognize outstanding salespeople: when a woman is asked to say a few words about her achievement, she tends to say something like, "Well, I really don't know how it happened. I guess I was just lucky this time." In contrast, the men will cheerfully own up to the hard work, intelligence, and so on, to which they owe their success. By putting herself

down, a woman avoids feeling brazenly powerful and potentially "selfish"; she also does the traditional lady's work of trying to make everyone else feel better ("She's not really so smart, after all, just lucky").

So we might as well get a little tougher. And a good place to start is by cutting back on the small acts of deference that we've been programmed to perform since girlhood. Like unnecessary smiling. For many women—waitresses, flight attendants, receptionists—smiling is an occupational requirement, but there's no reason for anyone to go around grinning when she's not being paid for it. I'd suggest that we save our off-duty smiles for when we truly feel like sharing them, and if you're not sure what to do with your face in the meantime, study Clint Eastwood's expressions—both of them. 7

Along the same lines, I think women should stop taking responsibility for every human interaction we engage in. In a social encounter with a woman, the average man can go 25 minutes saying nothing more than "You don't say?" "Izzat so?" and, of course, "Hmmmm." Why should we do all the work? By taking so much responsibility for making conversations go well, we act as if we had much more at stake in the encounter than the other party—and that gives him (or her) the power advantage. Every now and then, we deserve to get more out of a conversation than we put into it: I'd suggest not offering information you'd rather not share ("I'm really terrified that my sales plan won't work") and not, out of sheer politeness, soliciting information you don't really want ("Wherever did you get that lovely tie?"). There will be pauses, but they don't have to be awkward for *you*. 8

It is true that some, perhaps most, men will interpret any decrease in female deference as a deliberate act of hostility. Omit the free smiles and perky conversation-boosters and someone is bound to ask, "Well, what's come over *you* today?" For most of us, the first impulse is to stare at our feet and make vague references to a terminally ill aunt in Atlanta, but we should have as much right to be taciturn as the average (male) taxi driver. If you're taking a vacation from smiles and small talk and some fellow is moved to inquire about what's "bothering" you, just stare back levelly and say, the international debt crisis, the arms race, or the death of God. 9

There are all kinds of ways to toughen up—and potentially move up—at work, and I leave the details to the purveyors of assertiveness training. But Jean Baker Miller's study underscores a 10 fundamental principle that anyone can master on her own. We can stop acting less capable than we actually are. For example, in the matter of taking credit when credit is due, there's a key difference between saying "I was just lucky" and saying "I had a plan and it worked." If you take the credit you deserve, you're letting people know that you were confident you'd succeed all along, and that you fully intend to do so again.

11 Finally, we may be able to learn something from men about what to do with anger. As a general rule, women get irritated: men get *mad.* We make tight little smiles of ladylike exasperation; they pound on desks and roar. I wouldn't recommend emulating the full basso profundo male tantrum, but women do need ways of expressing justified anger clearly, colorfully, and, when necessary, crudely. If you're not just irritated, but *pissed off,* it might help to say so.

12 I, for example, have rerun the scene with the prestigious professor many times in my mind. And in my mind, I play it like Bogart. I start by moving my chair over to where I can look the professor full in the face. I let him do the chattering, and when it becomes evident that he has nothing serious to say, I lean back and cross my arms, just to let him know that he's wasting my time. I do not smile, neither do I nod encouragement. Nor, of course, do I respond to his blandishments with apologetic shrugs and blushes. Then, at the first flicker of lechery, I stand up and announce coolly, "All right, I've had enough of this crap." Then I walk out—slowly, deliberately, confidently. Just like a man.

13 Or—now that I think of it—just like a woman.

BUILDING VOCABULARY

1. The writer uses a number of words ascribed to "ladies" for ironic effect. Try the same in sentences of your own that use the following:
   a. curtsy **b.** simper **c.** chatter
2. The writer is comfortable using a mixture of formal and informal words, as the essay requires. Use the following combinations of words in sentences or paragraphs of your own:
   a. prestigious (par. 3) *and* hand-to-hand combat (par. 2)
   b. theoretical (par. 3) *and* clutched up (par. 5)
   c. deliberate (par. 9) *and* perky (par. 9)

THINKING CRITICALLY ABOUT THE ESSAY

Understanding the Writer's Ideas

1. What does the writer's opening paragraph tell us about her attitude toward men?
2. The writer contrasts "being tough" and "being ladylike." What are the attitudes and behaviors that she associates with these opposing ways of being?
3. Why does the writer risk embarrassing herself by telling the story of her encounter with the "prestigious professor" of paragraph 3?
4. According to Ehrenreich, why are women reluctant to exert power?
5. The writer advocates two alternative strategies women should pursue "to get tough." The first is to stop doing things that are subservient; the second is to begin to act differently. What does she recommend women should stop doing, and why? What does she recommend women should start doing, and why?

Understanding the Writer's Techniques

1. *Tone* (see Glossary) expresses a writer's attitude toward his or her subject. What is the tone of the opening paragraph? What does the tone of this paragraph suggest we can expect in the rest of the essay?
2. Why does the author delay her thesis statement until close to the end of the second paragraph?
3. One key to a smooth, graceful essay is effective use of transitions. Explain how the writer establishes effective transitions between paragraphs 3 and 4, 4 and 5, and 6 and 7.
4. Writers sometimes seek to strengthen their arguments by quoting supporting views from authorities. For what reasons does the writer quote Jean Baker Miller?
5. Why does the writer mix informal and formal diction in this essay? What does this choice of diction suggest about the writer's intended audience?
6. Why does the writer "rerun" the scene with the "prestigious professor" to conclude her essay?

Exploring the Writer's Ideas

1. Perhaps it is in the nature of waiters—who are often busy and pestered by customers—to make it hard for you to catch their attention, regardless of your gender. In that case, was Ehrenreich's envy of "men's" sway over waiters another case of a feminine inferiority complex, or is Ehrenreich simply using a rhetorical ploy to grab your attention at the start of her essay? Explain.
2. Ehrenreich seems to want us to distinguish between the servile characteristics of what is ladylike and the more robust qualities of women. Do you believe her portrait of a lady is fair and accurate? Why?
3. Is it a moral failing of the essay that the writer acknowledges only one possible character for all men, and that is the unattractive character of the "macho" male? Ought the essay to have provided us with a positive example of male character too? Does the absence of positive male role models weaken the essay's argument about women? Why, or why not?
4. Ehrenreich's argument proceeds by building one generalization on another. She quotes Jean Baker Miller, for example, to make the point that *for all women* the exercise of power is associated with selfishness and destructiveness. If you can think of exceptions to her main general statements, does this undermine her argument for you, or do you remain persuaded of her generalizations despite the exceptions. Discuss in relation to one or two examples.
5. You are likely to have heard someone described as "one tough lady." How are the attributes of such a person the same as or different from those that Ehrenreich advocates for all women?

IDEAS FOR WRITING

Prewriting

Make a list of character traits generally associated with men, and another of traits generally associated with women. Then make a second list of those traits men might wish to adapt from women, and women from men.

Guided Writing

Write an essay titled "What I've Learned From . . ." Fill in the blank with a word of your choice. Your essay should illustrate how you came to realize you could learn something positive from those you had long ago given up on as sources of wisdom. Some possible titles might be "What I've Learned From Parents," "What I've Learned From Professional Wrestlers," or "What I've Learned From the Boss."

1. Begin your essay by indicating why you long ago abandoned the idea that you could learn anything from "__________."
2. But then explain why you have realized that the very thing that made "__________" so unattractive, might be instructive after all.
3. Provide an example from your own behavior where having a little more of that something undesirable you always disliked in "__________" might have been a good thing.
4. Now explain how that nice quality of your own character that is just the opposite of the undesirable "__________" might actually reflect a weakness or flaw in your character.
5. If possible, quote an authoritative source to underscore how your apparently good quality masks a serious weakness (as in the flaws of being a lady).
6. Now illustrate how adopting some of "__________" behaviors would be a good thing.
7. Conclude by showing how this quality in "__________," when adopted by you and those like you, actually brings out better what you are truly like.

Thinking and Writing Collaboratively

In small groups, discuss the lists of attributes of men and women you had drawn up in your Prewriting exercise. Do the qualities listed compose stereotypes, or do they reflect abiding truths about the differences between the sexes? Compare the lists made up by the students in your group—what can you conclude from the similarities and differences among these lists?

More Writing Projects

1. For a journal entry, write about a quality usually associated with the opposite sex that you secretly admire, or wish you could say was a quality of your own.
2. In an essay, explore a quality in yourself or in people more generally that is commonly viewed as good—such as kindness—for its possibly "weak" or self-defeating underside (in the case of kindness, for example, always doing for others and never thinking of yourself).
3. Write an essay on the dangers of stereotyping, that is, of thinking of individuals as necessarily having the characteristics of a group.

America's Gambling Craze

James Popkin with Katia Hetter

James Popkin and Katia Hetter explore the growth and history of gambling in America. They look at its impact on cities and suburbs seeking to raise tax money from gambling revenues, as well as the increasing social problems associated with gambling. They use compelling statistics and facts to illustrate their point.

PREREADING: THINKING ABOUT THE ESSAY IN ADVANCE

What are your views on gambling? Should it be legal? Why or why not? Should states use any form of gambling to raise money for services and reduce taxes? Why or why not?

Words to Watch

sanctioned (par. 3) gave approval or consent to

jai alai (par. 4) an extremely fast court game in which players use a long, hand-shaped basket strapped to the wrist to propel the ball against a wall

Prohibition (par. 5) a period in American history (1920–33) during which laws prohibited the sale, manufacture, transport, or possession of alcoholic beverages

revenue (par. 8) all the income produced by a particular source

No one howled in protest last month when H&R Block set up makeshift tax-preparation offices in four Nevada casinos and offered gamblers same-day "refund-anticipation loans." And few people cared recently when a Florida inventor won a U.S. patent that could someday enable television audiences to legally bet on game shows, football games and even beauty pageants from their homes. 1

What's the deal? Not that long ago, Americans held gambling in nearly the same esteem as heroin dealing and applauded when ax-wielding police paid a visit to the corner dice room. But moral outrage has become as outmoded as a penny slot machine. In 1955, for example, baseball commissioner Ford Frick 2 considered wagering so corrupt he prohibited major leaguers from overnighting in Las Vegas. Last year, by contrast, Americans for the first time made more trips to casinos than they did to Major League ballparks—some 92 million trips, according to one study.

3 It took six decades for gambling to become America's Pastime, from the legalization of Nevada casinos in 1931 to April Fool's Day 1991, when Davenport, Iowa, launched the Diamond Lady, the nation's first legal riverboat casino. The gradual creation of 37 state lotteries broke down the public's mistrust, conveying a clear message that the government sanctioned gambling; indeed, is even coming to depend on it as a tax-revenue source. Corporate ownership of casinos helped in its own way, too, replacing shady operators with trusted brand names like Hilton and MGM. Casinos now operate or are authorized in 23 states, and 95 percent of all Americans are expected to live within a three- or four-hour drive of one by the year 2000.

4 Today, the Bible Belt might as well be renamed the Blackjack Belt, with floating and land-based casinos throughout Mississippi and Louisiana and plans for more in Florida, Texas, Alabama and Arkansas. Meanwhile, the Midwest is overrun with slot hogs, none of the porcine variety. Iowa, Illinois, Indiana and Missouri allow riverboat gambling, and a 50,000-square-foot land-based casino is scheduled to open in mid-May just outside Detroit, in Windsor, Ontario. Low-stakes casinos attract visitors to old mining towns in Colorado and South Dakota, and Indian tribes operate 225 casinos and high-stakes bingo halls nationwide. Add church bingo, card rooms, sports wagering, dog and horse racing and jai alai to the mix and it becomes clear why Americans legally wagered $330 billion in 1992—a 1,800 percent increase over 1976.

5 **Calling for new games.** Like the first bars that opened after Prohibition, modern gambling halls are enormously successful. "It will be impossible not to make a lot of money," one executive in New Orleans bragged before his casino had even opened. "It's like spitting and missing the floor." Such boasts—and the real possibility that the boom will create 500,000 jobs nationwide this decade—have not been lost on federal, state and local lawmakers. In the first six weeks of this year alone they introduced more than 200 bills regarding gambling.

6 But casinos and lotteries may not guarantee the jackpots many politicians expect. When urban-planning professor Robert

Goodman reviewed the economic-impact studies that 14 government agencies relied upon before deciding to embrace casino gambling, he found that most were written with a pro-industry spin and only four were balanced and factored in gambling's hidden costs. Goodman's two-year study, due out next week, concludes that newly opened casinos "suck money out of the local economy," away from existing movie theaters, car dealerships, clothing shops and sports arenas. In Atlantic City, for example, about 100 of 250 local restaurants have closed since the casinos debuted in 1978, says Goodman, who teaches at the University of Massachusetts at Amherst.

"Slum by the sea." States that get hooked on gambling revenues soon suffer withdrawal symptoms when local competition kicks in. Although pioneering casinos and lotteries typically are profitable, gambling grosses decline when lotteries or casinos open in neighboring states. In Biloxi, Miss., for example, slot revenues at first topped about $207 per machine per day. A year later when competitors moved in, however, the daily win-per-machine figure dipped to $109. 7

States frequently overestimate the financial impact of gambling revenues, too. "Legalized gambling is never large enough to solve any social problems," says gambling-law professor and paid industry consultant I. Nelson Rose. In New Jersey, for example, horse racing alone accounted for about 10 percent of state revenue in the 1950s. Today, despite the addition of a lottery and 12 casinos, the state earns only 6 percent of its revenue through gambling. "Atlantic City used to be a slum by the sea," says Rose. "Now it's a slum by the sea with casinos." 8

America's love affair with dice and cards has always been a fickle romance, and some academics predict a breakup soon. Legalized gambling in America has been running on a 70-year boom-and-bust cycle since the colonists started the first lotteries. "We're now riding the third wave of legal gambling" that began with the Depression, says Rose, who has written extensively on the subject and teaches at Whittier Law School in Los Angeles. The trend self-destructs after a few decades, when the public simply gets fed up and embraces more-conservative values. Rose believes a cheating or corruption scandal will trigger the next crash in about 35 years, an idea that most casino officials think is ludicrous. 9

The sky is not falling yet. Apart from a handful of academics and the odd politician, few Americans are seriously questioning the morality of an industry that is expected to help gamblers 10 lose a record $35 billion in 1995 alone. Religious leaders have been oddly silent, perhaps because so many churches and synagogues rely on bingo revenues. "The biggest things we have to help people are churches and temples and the government," says Arnie Wexler, executive director of the Council on Compulsive Gambling of New Jersey. "And now they're all in the gambling business."

11 **Getting hooked.** The consequences can be damaging. Wexler says he got a phone call late last week from a man in his 70s who ran up $150,000 in debt just by buying lottery tickets. Although most gambling experts believe that only 1 percent to 3 percent of Americans have a serious gambling problem at any given time, a July 1993 Gallup Poll funded by Wexler's group suggests that the figure may be closer to 5 percent. Regardless, now that casinos are no longer located just in Atlantic City and Nevada it's reasonable to assume that the total number of problem gamblers will soar. "If you put a guy who wouldn't cheat on his wife in a room with a gorgeous nude woman, some guys would fall by the wayside," Wexler says. "When you make gambling legal and socially acceptable, people will try it and some of them will get hooked."

12 But try telling that to a gambler happily feeding a slot machine and waiting for a multimillion-dollar payoff. Fifty-one percent of American adults now find casino gambling "acceptable for anyone," and 35 percent describe it as "acceptable for others but not for me," according to a recent Yankelovich Inc. survey paid for by Harrah's Casinos. The attraction is simple. "The action for them is the thrill of what's going to happen in the next pull of that slot-machine handle," explains Harrah's president, Phil Satre.

BUILDING VOCABULARY

Write sentences in which you use the following words correctly. Use a dictionary.

a. spin (par. 6)
b. factored (par. 6)
c. debuted (par. 6)
d. fickle (par. 9)
e. ludicrous (par. 9)

THINKING CRITICALLY ABOUT THE ESSAY

Understanding the Writer's Ideas

1. How do Americans view gambling today as opposed to forty years ago?
2. What eventually broke down the public's mistrust of gambling?
3. Gambling enthusiasts claim that gambling has economic benefits other than tax revenues. What are they? Do you think this claim is accurate? Why or why not?
4. What do the writers mean when they refer to the "slum by the sea"? Explain.
5. Why, according to this article, are religious leaders silent about the ills of gambling?
6. What is the theory about the history of gambling?
7. According to the essay, can someone who gambles get hooked and ruin his or her life? Do you see the potential of getting hooked as a serious objection to gambling? Why or why not?
8. If most people don't get rich on gambling, why do so many do it, according to the writers?

Understanding the Writer's Techniques

1. What is unusual about the way the writers introduce the thesis? What is the thesis?
2. How does the word "howled" (par. 1) set the tone of the essay?
3. Before paragraphs 5, 7, and 11 there are subheads (the words in bold print). How are these related to topic sentences?
4. These writers use different kinds of detail to support their thesis. What kinds do they use? Give examples.
5. What is unusual about the topic sentence of the concluding paragraph 12?
6. Will this analysis of gambling find readers who are pro- or anti-gambling? Explain.
7. There are quotes that illustrate the writers' point. But what do you note about the people who are quoted? Are they people who are knowledgeable about the topic? Why? And what does this say about choosing people to quote in an essay?

Exploring the Writer's Ideas

1. Should gambling be considered as morally corrupt as the writers explain? Why or why not?
2. The writers claim that by the year 2000, 95 percent of all Americans will live within a short drive to a gambling casino. Is there any reason to slow such growth? Why or why not?
3. If gamblers wagered $330 billion in 1992, how is it possible for casinos to "suck money from the economy" as the writers suggest? Are the casinos or the gamblers at fault for the implied waste? Explain your answers.
4. Is there something unethical about or wrong with so many churches and synagogues using gambling to raise revenues? Why or why not?
5. Given that gambling is addictive and leads to serious debt problems, why is the government sponsoring it in the form of lotteries? Should governments be more responsible? Explain your position.
6. What does Harrah's Casinos president mean by the fact that the attraction to gambling is simple: "The thrill of what's going to happen . . . next"? Do you agree or disagree?
7. If, as these writers suggest, TV audiences will one day be able to bet on games from the home, should Americans rethink the future of such technology given the problems with gambling stated in this essay? Use examples to illustrate your view.

IDEAS FOR WRITING

Prewriting

Write a letter to your local political leader in which you outline reasons that gambling as a source of revenue would be good or bad for your community.

Guided Writing

Illustrate a problem in your community that could be solved with money (i.e., building repair, new schools, etc.). Look at whether or not gambling would be a good way for your community to obtain this money.

1. Begin the essay by illustrating the problem in your community.
2. Give the details of how money could solve this problem.
3. Illustrate the kinds of problems and benefits associated with gambling that might occur in your community.
4. Take a position on why gambling is or is not the best way for your community to raise money to solve its problem.
5. Offer other ways of raising money in your community without resorting to gambling.
6. In conclusion, take a final position on gambling and its place in your community.

Thinking and Writing Collaboratively

Exchange essays with another student in the class and, after you read the paper, make an outline to show the writer's thesis and the different examples provided to support the thesis. Then discuss with the writer the clarity and force of his or her essay, using the outline you prepared.

More Writing Projects

1. In your journal, reflect on your earliest experiences with some type of gambling. If you've never been exposed to gambling, why is that?
2. Write a paragraph about why you find the kind of gambling described in the above essay acceptable or against your moral code.
3. Write an essay that uses illustration to detail your own experience (or the experience of someone close to you) with gambling, highlighting your personal views on the issue.

Death in the Open

Lewis Thomas

Dr. Lewis Thomas was president of the Memorial Sloan-Kettering Cancer Center in New York City. He wrote numerous articles about science, medicine, and life structures and cycles geared for the lay reader. His observations often bring fascinating clarity to the cycles of life and death on our planet. The following essay, a brilliant inquiry into the "natural marvel" of death, appears in his book *Lives of a Cell* (1974), which won the National Book Award for Arts and Letters in 1975.

PREREADING: THINKING ABOUT THE ESSAY IN ADVANCE

A familiar phenomenon that many of us have witnessed is an animal's dead body—a squirrel, a mouse, a bird, a cat or dog—on a street or highway, dead either as roadkill or from natural causes. Reflect a moment on such a phenomenon. What do you think of and feel when you witness such a scene?

Words to Watch

voles (par. 1) the members of any one of several species of small rodents

impropriety (par. 2) an improper action or remark

progeny (par. 4) descendants or offspring

mutation (par. 4) a sudden genetic change

amebocytes (par. 4) one-celled organisms

stipulated (par. 6) made a special condition for

incongruity (par. 6) something which is not consistent with its environment

conspicuous (par. 7) very obvious

inexplicably (par. 7) unexplainably

anomalies (par. 10) irregularities

notion (par. 11) an idea

detestable (par. 11) hateful

synchrony (par. 11) simultaneous occurrence

Most of the dead animals you see on highways near the cities are dogs, a few cats. Out in the countryside, the forms and coloring of the dead are strange; these are the wild creatures. Seen from a car window they appear as fragments, evoking memories of woodchucks, badgers, skunks, voles, snakes, sometimes the mysterious wreckage of a deer. 1

It is always a queer shock, part a sudden upwelling of grief, part unaccountable amazement. It is simply astounding to see an animal dead on a highway. The outrage is more than just the location; it is the impropriety of such visible death, anywhere. You do not expect to see dead animals in the open. It is the nature of animals to die alone, off somewhere, hidden. It is wrong to see them lying out on the highway; it is wrong to see them anywhere. 2

Everything in the world dies, but we only know about it as a kind of abstraction. If you stand in a meadow, at the edge of a hillside, and look around carefully, almost everything you can catch sight of is in the process of dying, and most things will be dead long before you are. If it were not for the constant renewal and replacement going on before your eyes, the whole place would turn to stone and sand under your feet. 3

There are some creatures that do not seem to die at all; they simply vanish totally into their own progeny. Single cells do this. The cell becomes two, then four, and so on, and after a while the last trace is gone. It cannot be seen as death; barring mutation, the descendants are simply the first cell, living all over again. The cycles of the slime mold have episodes that seem as conclusive as death, but the withered slug, with its stalk and fruiting body, is plainly the transient tissue of a developing animal; the free-swimming amebocytes use this organ collectively in order to produce more of themselves. 4

There are said to be a billion billion insects on the earth at any moment, most of them with very short life expectancies by our standards. Someone has estimated that there are 25 million assorted insects hanging in the air over every temperate square mile, in a column extending upward for thousands of feet, drifting through the layers of the atmosphere like plankton. They are dying steadily, some by being eaten, some just dropping in their tracks, tons of them around the earth, disintegrating as they die, invisibly. 5

Who ever sees dead birds, in anything like the huge numbers stipulated by the certainty of the death of all birds? A dead 6 bird is an incongruity, more startling than an unexpected live bird, sure evidence to the human mind that something has gone wrong. Birds do their dying off somewhere, behind things, under things, never on the wing.

7 Animals seem to have an instinct for performing death alone, hidden. Even the largest, most conspicuous ones find ways to conceal themselves in time. If an elephant missteps and dies in an open place, the herd will not leave him there; the others will pick him up and carry the body from place to place, finally putting it down in some inexplicably suitable location. When elephants encounter the skeleton of an elephant out in the open, they methodically take up each of the bones and distribute them, in a ponderous ceremony, over neighboring acres.

8 It is a natural marvel. All of the life of the earth dies, all of the time, in the same volume as the new life that dazzles us each morning, each spring. All we see of this is the odd stump, the fly struggling on the porch floor of the summer house in October, the fragment on the highway. I have lived all my life with an embarrassment of squirrels in my backyard, they are all over the place, all year long, and I have never seen, anywhere, a dead squirrel.

9 I suppose it is just as well. If the earth were otherwise, and all the dying were done in the open, with the dead there to be looked at, we would never have it out of our minds. We can forget about it much of the time, or think of it as an accident to be avoided, somehow. But it does make the process of dying seem more exceptional than it really is, and harder to engage in at the times when we must ourselves engage.

10 In our way, we conform as best we can to the rest of nature. The obituary pages tell us of the news that we are dying away, while the birth announcements in finer print, off at the side of the page, inform us of our replacements, but we get no grasp from this of the enormity of scale. There are 3 billion of us on the earth, and all 3 billion must be dead, on a schedule, within this lifetime. The vast mortality, involving something over 50 million of us each year, takes place in relative secrecy. We can only really know of the deaths in our households, or among our friends. These, detached in our minds from all the rest, we take to be unnatural events, anomalies, outrages. We speak of our own dead in low voices; struck down, we say, as though visible death can only occur for cause, by disease or violence, avoidably. We send off for flowers, grieve, make ceremonies, scatter bones, unaware

of the rest of the 3 billion on the same schedule. All of that immense mass of flesh and bone and consciousness will disappear by absorption into the earth, without recognition by the transient survivors.

Less than a half century from now, our replacements will have more than doubled the numbers. It is hard to see how we can continue to keep the secret, with such multitudes doing the dying. We will have to give up the notion that death is catastrophe, or detestable, or avoidable, or even strange. We will need to learn more about the cycling of life in the rest of the system, and about our connection to the process. Everything that comes alive seems to be in trade for something that dies, cell for cell. There might be some comfort in the recognition of synchrony, in the information that we all go down together, in the best of company. 11

BUILDING VOCABULARY

1. Thomas makes imaginative and often unique use of adjectival expressions. Explain the meaning of each adjective in the phrases below:
   a. *queer* shock (par. 2)
   b. *unaccountable* amazement (par. 2)
   c. *visible* death (pars. 2 and 10)
   d. *transient* tissue (par. 4)
   e. *ponderous* ceremony (par. 7)
   f. *neighboring* acres (par. 7)
   g. *natural* marvel (par. 8)
   h. *vast* mortality (par. 10)
   i. *relative* secrecy (par. 10)
   j. *transient* survivors (par. 10)
2. An *idiom* is an expression that has a special meaning only when taken as a whole; taken separately, the words may not make sense. What are the meanings of the following idioms?
   a. upwelling of grief (par. 2)
   b. catch sight of (par. 3)
   c. on the wing (par. 6)
   d. in time (par. 7)
   e. no grasp . . . of (par. 10)
   f. for cause (par. 10)

THINKING CRITICALLY ABOUT THE ESSAY

Understanding the Writer's Ideas

1. Why does Thomas feel that it is strange to see dead animals in the countryside? How are dead animals more varied in the country than in the city? According to Thomas, for what reason is it a shock to see a dead animal on the road?
2. In paragraph 3, Thomas suggests that death is often an "abstraction." What does he mean by this statement? How does he suggest we can make death something more real? In your own words, for what reasons does he suggest we accept the life-death cycle as a more concrete idea?
3. Why, according to Thomas, do single cells seem not to die?
4. What is the meaning of the question at the beginning of paragraph 6? How does it relate to the theme of the essay? To what does the author compare seeing a dead bird? Why does he call it an "incongruity"? How is it "sure evidence . . . that something has gone wrong"?
5. Explain the process of death among elephants as Thomas describes it.
6. Explain the meaning of "the odd stump" in paragraph 8. What two examples of "the odd stump" does Thomas offer?
7. What example from personal experience does Thomas give to show that dead animals seem "to disappear"?
8. Explain the meaning of the first sentence of paragraph 9. In your own words, tell why Thomas feels the way he does.
9. What is the "secret" in paragraph 11?
10. In paragraph 10 Thomas says, "In our way, we conform as best we can to the rest of nature." What does he mean? What supporting examples does he offer? What is the result? What examples does Thomas give of our reactions to the death of other human beings?
11. Why does Thomas say we must change our attitude toward death? How does he suggest that we do so?

Understanding the Writer's Techniques

1. What is Thomas's thesis in this essay? In what way is it reinforced by the concluding paragraph?

2. Study the introductory paragraphs. Why does the author offer several examples? Why is "the mysterious wreckage of a deer" an especially effective example?
3. Are there any clear illustrations in paragraph 2? Why or why not? What is the effect? Explain the connection between paragraphs 2 and 3.
4. Paragraphs 4 to 8 use illustrations to support a series of generalizations or topic sentences. Put a check mark by the topic sentence in these paragraphs and identify the generalization. Then analyze the illustrations used to support each one. Which examples are the most specific? the most visual? the most personal? Are there any extended examples?
5. How does paragraph 9 serve as a transition to the topic of paragraph 10? Why does Thomas use statistics in paragraph 10? How do they drive his point home?
6. Examine the author's use of pronouns in this essay. First, trace the use of first-person pronouns ("I," "we," "my," "our"). Why does Thomas use such pronouns? Why is their use in paragraph 8 especially effective? Next, consider Thomas's frequent use of the pronoun *it.* (Beginning writers are often instructed to minimize their use of such pronouns as *it, this,* and *that* because they are not specific and may leave the reader confused.) Explain what the word *it* stands for in paragraphs 2, 4, 8, and 9. Why does Thomas use a word whose meaning may be confusing?
7. Thomas uses *figurative language* (see Glossary) in this essay, particularly *similes* and *metaphors* (see Glossary). Explain in your own words the meanings of the following similes and metaphors:
   a. *the mysterious wreckage* of a deer (par. 1)
   b. episodes that seem *as conclusive as death* (par. 4)
   c. drifting through the layers of the atmosphere *like plankton* (par. 5)
8. We may say that the expression "dropping in their tracks" in paragraph 5 is a kind of pun. (A *pun* is a humorous use of a word or an expression that suggests two meanings.) What is the popular expression using the words *dropping* and *flies* that Thomas's phrase puns on?
9. Thomas makes use of a technique called "repetition with a difference"—that is, saying *almost* the same thing for added emphasis. Explain how repetition with a difference

adds effectiveness to the sentences in which each of the following expressions is used:
   a. alone, hidden (par. 7)
   b. each morning, each spring (par. 8)
   c. unnatural events, anomalies, outrages (par. 10)
   d. catastrophe, or detestable, or avoidable, or even strange (par. 11)

10. *Parallelism* (see Glossary) is a type of sentence structure within a paragraph that creates a balance in the presentation of ideas and adds emphasis. It often uses a repeating pattern of subjects and verbs, prepositional phrases, questions, and so on. How does Thomas use parallelism in paragraph 3? paragraph 10? paragraph 11?

Exploring the Writer's Ideas

1. We might say that Thomas's title, "Death in the Open," is a double entendre (that is, has a double meaning). In what two ways may we interpret the phrase "in the open" as it relates to the contents of the essay? How do the two meanings relate to the philosophical points Thomas makes, especially in the two opening paragraphs and in the conclusion? Do you feel it is important to be more "open" about death? Why?

2. In paragraph 10, Thomas writes, "We speak of our own dead in low voices; struck down, we . . ." "Struck down" is used here as a *euphemism* (see Glossary) in place of other words that might be upsetting or distasteful. What other euphemisms do we have for death? Euphemisms for dying are often used to explain death to children. Do you think it is right, or necessary, to use such "guarded language" with youngsters? Why? For what other words or expressions do we commonly use euphemisms?

3. At the end of the essay, Thomas suggests that we might be more comfortable with death if we understood it as a natural, common occurrence. What are your feelings about this philosophy?

4. According to Thomas's views in paragraph 9, because we don't often see dead animals "in the open," we are less prepared when we do encounter death. Do you think this reasoning is correct? Why or why not?

5. In paragraph 7 Thomas explains the process of death among elephants. What is your impression of the elephant herd's behavior at the death of one of its members? Why does Thomas call it "a natural marvel"? Have you ever heard the expression "the elephant dying grounds"? What does it mean?
6. Reread Louise Erdrich's "The Blue Jay's Dance" (pages 98–99). What similarities do you find between Thomas's and Erdrich's visions of nature? Discuss them with specific references to the essays. How are the visions different? alike? Which author's ideas most closely resemble your own view of nature?

IDEAS FOR WRITING

Prewriting

Brainstorm for five to ten minutes on the phrase "in the open." What does it mean? What does it mean to you? What various ways can you apply it to elements in your life? What other acts "in the open" surprise, puzzle, stir, or shock you?

Guided Writing

Write an essay in which you illustrate "__________ in the Open." Fill in the blank with a word of your choice, a word that reflects some phenomenon, emotion, or idea whose features are often hard to understand. You might write about birth in the open, concerts in the open, love in the open, fear in the open, or war in the open, for example.

1. Develop an introduction with general examples that are relevant to your topic.
2. Add one or two paragraphs in which you speculate or philosophize on the phenomenon you are writing about.
3. Point out how the topic is most common throughout nature, society, or the world.
4. Give at least three extended examples that illustrate your topic.
5. Use the first-person pronouns "I" and "we" to add emphasis.
6. Illustrate ways in which people are generally unaware of certain features of the topic or tend to hide these features.
7. Try to include at least one statistic in your essay.

8. Use some idiomatic expressions in your essay.
9. Conclude your essay with some examples of how and why we can become more "open" about the topic.

Thinking and Writing Collaboratively

Form small groups, and read the drafts of each other's Guided Writing essays. After general comments about how to take the essay to the next draft, concentrate on the conclusions in each piece. Does the writer give appropriate examples in the conclusion? Do you see how and why the writer feels that we can become more open about the topic at hand?

More Writing Projects

1. For a journal entry, use examples to tell of your first experiences with death. You may want to write about the death of a relative, a friend, an acquaintance, a celebrity, or a pet.
2. Visit a place in the countryside (or a park) for one hour. Make a written record as you walk around detailing all evidence of natural death that you come across. Then write an illustrative paragraph on natural death as you observed it.
3. In your library, explore various burial practices among different races, religions, or ethnic groups and write an essay in which you illustrate several of these practices.

SUMMING UP: CHAPTER 5

1. Richard Selzer ("The Discus Thrower," pages 110–113), Lewis Thomas ("Death in the Open," pages 192–194), and George Orwell ("A Hanging," pages 144–148) all deal with death and dying. Write your own essay about the issue, drawing on points from these three authors to illustrate your own position.
2. From this chapter select the essay that you think best uses the mode of illustration. Write an essay in which you analyze the writer's techniques and strategies. Make specific references to the text.
3. The world of the night, the environment of Staples's "Night Walker," challenges our senses and our perceptions, simply because it is so different from the typical daytime worlds we usually inhabit. What unusual nighttime experiences have you had? How do you feel about the night? Write an essay of illustration to address these questions.
4. The sports arena draws considerable attention from gamblers. What do you think should be the appropriate relation between sports and gambling? What insights from Popkin inform your thoughts about betting on the outcomes of games or matches—baseball, football, basketball, boxing? Write an essay using illustration to make your point.

CHAPTER 6

Comparison and Contrast

WHAT IS COMPARISON AND CONTRAST?

When we compare two things, we look for similarities. When we contrast, we look for differences. The comparison-contrast writing strategy, then, is a way of analyzing likenesses and differences between two or more subjects. Usually, the purpose is to evaluate or judge which is superior. Thus we might appreciate soccer if we compare it with football; we understand Roman Catholicism better if we see it in light of Buddhism.

Writers who use the comparison-contrast technique know that careful planning is required to *organize* the likenesses and differences into logical patterns. Some authors might use only *comparison,* to look at the similarities between subjects. Others might use only *contrast.* Often, writers combine the two in a carefully structured essay that balances one with the other.

Like many of the writing and reading strategies you have learned, comparison and contrast is familiar from everyday life. If you were about to buy a new car, for instance, you would look at several models before you made a choice. You might consider price, size, horsepower, options, safety features, status, and dependability before you spent such a large amount of money. If you were deciding whether to send your daughter to a public school or a private school, you would compare and contrast the features of each type of institution: cost, teacher quality, class size, location, curriculum, and composition of the student body might all be considered. If you were an art historian, you might compare and contrast an early picture by Matisse with one he completed late in life in order to understand his development as an artist.

Writing a comparison-contrast essay requires more careful planning, however, than the everyday life application technique. Both call for common sense. You wouldn't compare parochial schools with an Oldsmobile, for instance; they simply don't relate. But you would compare The Dalton School with Public School 34, or a Cutlass Supreme with a Volvo, a Matisse with a Cezanne. Clearly, any strong pattern of comparison and contrast treats items that are in the same category or class. Moreover, there always has to be a basis for comparison; in other words, you compare or contrast two items in order to try to deal with all-important aspects of the objects being compared before arriving at a final determination. These commonsense characteristics of comparison and contrast apply to our pattern of thought as well as our pattern of writing.

Author Rachel Carson, for instance, contrasts two visions of the future for planet Earth: a flourishing environment or a devastated landscape. Thus she has a common category: the condition of the global ecology. She can use *contrast* because she has a common ground for her analysis. Ellen Goodman looks at friendships, Robert C. Ritchie at two seashores, and Michele Ingrassia at the different body images of black girls and white girls. Each author sets up a formal pattern for contrasting and comparing subjects within a related class. One side of the pattern helps us understand the other. Finally, we may establish a preference for one or the other subject.

HOW DO WE READ COMPARISON AND CONTRAST?

Reading comparison and contrast requires us to ask ourselves these questions:

- What subjects has the author selected? Are they from a similar class or category?
- What is the basis for the comparison or contrast? What is the writer's *thesis?*
- What is the arrangement of topics? How has the writer organized each paragraph? Notice where transitional expressions (*on the one hand, on the other hand, similarly, in contrast*) help the reader follow the writer's train of thought.

- Is the writer fair to each subject, devoting an equal amount of space to each side? Make an outline of one of the reading selections to see how the writer has balanced the two subjects.
- Has the writer used narration, description, or illustration to develop the comparison? What other techniques has the author used?
- Does the conclusion show a preference for one subject over the other? Is the conclusion justified by the evidence in the body?

HOW DO WE WRITE COMPARISON AND CONTRAST?

After reading the professional writers in this chapter, you will be better prepared to organize your own essay. Begin by clearly identifying the subjects of your comparison and by establishing the basis for it. The thesis sentence performs this important function for you.

Sample thesis statement:

> Living in a small town is better than living in a big city because life is safer, friendlier, and cheaper.

Plan a strategy for the comparison and contrast. Writers can use one of three main techniques: block, alternating, or combination. The *block method* requires that the writer put all the points about one side (the small town in this case) in one part of the essay, and all the points about the other side (big-city life) together in another part of the essay. In the *alternating method,* the writer explains one point about small-town life and then immediately gives the contrasting point about big-city life. The *combination* pattern allows the writer to use both alternating and block techniques.

Make a careful outline. For each point about one side, try to find a balancing point about the other. If, for instance, you write about the housing available in a small town, write about housing in the big city. Although it may be impossible to manage exact matches, try to be as fair as possible to each side.

Writing and Revising the Draft

Set up a purpose for the comparison and contrast in the thesis sentence.

Write an outline using paragraph blocks to indicate subject A and subject B. For instance, if you were going to write in the block form, your outline would look like this:

Introduction (with thesis)
Block A: Small Town
1. housing
2. jobs
3. social life
Block B: Big City
1. housing
2. jobs
3. social life
Conclusion

If you were going to use the alternating form, the outline would look as follows:

Introduction (with thesis)
Block A: Housing
1. big city
2. small town
Block B: Jobs
1. big city
2. small town
Block C: Social Life
1. big city
2. small town
Conclusion

Use transitional devices, especially with the alternating form. Each time you shift from one subject to the other, use a transition as needed: *like, unlike, on the one hand, on the other hand, in contrast, similarly.*

In the conclusion, offer your view of the two subjects.

Proofread carefully. Check the draft for clarity and correctness and make a final copy.

A STUDENT PARAGRAPH: COMPARISON AND CONTRAST

Here is a body paragraph from a student essay comparing small town life and city life. Using the alternating method described above, the student concentrates here on housing, presenting the efforts she made first to find an apartment in her home town and then to find a place to live in Chicago.

Finding an apartment back home in Quincy was easy, but Chicago was a whole different ball game.	Topic statement
In Quincy, I found an affordable one-bedroom place with the help of a friendly local real estate agent.	Alternating method of contrast: Quincy first
The apartment consisted of three huge, sunny, high-ceilinged rooms that looked out over a stretch of velvety green lawn—and it was all just for me, no roommates, since I could easily pay the rent out of my weekly paycheck.	Supporting detail
When I moved to the big city, however, my luck ran out.	Transition reminds reader of previous point and flows smoothly into next point to produce *coherence*
The phonebook's long list of realtors looked too intimidating, so I first scoured the classified ads in the Chicago Tribune.	Alternating method: Chicago second
After visiting all the places I could afford, I realized that in the language of the classifieds, "cozy" meant the size of a Quincy closet, and "fixer-upper" meant that slamming a door would bring the place tumbling down over my ears.	Supporting detail; "Quincy closet" connects to previous point
I decided to try an apartment-finding service instead. When I admitted how little I had to spend on rent, a grim-faced woman who worked there offered me a list of apartments to share.	Supporting detail
The first potential roomie I met this way opened the door flushed, sweating, and dressed in blue Spandex from head to toe. Bad 1980s dance music blared from the living room. She looked put out that I had interrupted her aerobics routine and handed me a list of rules that specified, among other things, that I could bring only fat-free food into the kitchen. Another required an oath to engage only in "healthy thoughts" while on the premises.	Supporting detail
I excused myself as politely as I could and called home to Quincy to see if I could get my old place back.	Closing sentence clinches paragraph's main point

A Fable for Tomorrow

Rachel Carson

Rachel Carson wrote a number of books and articles in the 1950s and 1960s that alerted Americans to dangers facing our natural environment. In this section from *Silent Spring* (1962), look for the ways in which Carson establishes a series of contrasts for her imaginary American town.

PREREADING: THINKING ABOUT THE ESSAY IN ADVANCE

What dangers do you see affecting our environment over the next decades? How can we as a society address these environmental problems?

Words to Watch

migrants (par. 2) people, animals, or birds that move from one place to another

blight (par. 3) a disease or condition that kills or checks growth

maladies (par. 3) illnesses

moribund (par. 4) dying

pollination (par. 5) the transfer of pollen (male sex cells) from one part of the flower to another

granular (par. 7) consisting of grains

specter (par. 9) a ghost; an object of fear or dread

stark (par. 9) bleak; barren; standing out in sharp outline

There was once a town in the heart of America where all life seemed to live in harmony with its surroundings. The town lay in the midst of a checkerboard of prosperous farms, with fields of grain and hillsides of orchards where, in spring, white clouds of bloom drifted above the green fields. In autumn, oak and maple and birch set up a blaze of color that flamed and flickered across a backdrop of pines. Then foxes barked in the hills and deer silently crossed the fields, half hidden in the mists of the fall mornings. 1

2 Along the roads, laurel, viburnum and alder, great ferns and wildflowers delighted the traveler's eye through much of the year. Even in winter the roadsides were places of beauty, where countless birds came to feed on the berries and on the seed heads of the dried weeds rising above the snow. The countryside was, in fact, famous for the abundance and variety of its bird life, and when the flood of migrants was pouring through in spring and fall people traveled from great distances to observe them. Others came to fish the streams, which flowed clear and cold out of the hills and contained shady pools where trout lay. So it had been from the days many years ago when the first settlers raised their houses, sank their wells, and built their barns.

3 Then a strange blight crept over the area and everything began to change. Some evil spell had settled on the community: mysterious maladies swept the flocks of chickens; the cattle and sheep sickened and died. Everywhere was a shadow of death. The farmers spoke of much illness among their families. In the town the doctors had become more and more puzzled by new kinds of sickness appearing among their patients. There had been several sudden and unexplained deaths not only among adults but even among children, who would be stricken suddenly while at play and die within a few hours.

4 There was a strange stillness. The birds, for example—where had they gone? Many people spoke of them, puzzled and disturbed. The feeding stations in the backyards were deserted. The few birds seen anywhere were moribund; they trembled violently and could not fly. It was a spring without voices. On the mornings that had once throbbed with the dawn chorus of robins, catbirds, doves, jays, wrens, and scores of other bird voices there was now no sound; only silence lay over the fields and woods and marsh.

5 On the farms the hens brooded, but no chicks hatched. The farmers complained that they were unable to raise any pigs—the litters were small and the young survived only a few days. The apple trees were coming into bloom but no bees droned among the blossoms, so there was no pollination and there would be no fruit.

6 The roadsides, once so attractive, were now lined with browned and withered vegetation as though swept by fire. These, too, were silent, deserted by all living things. Even the streams were now lifeless. Anglers no longer visited them, for all the fish had died.

In the gutters under the eaves and between the shingles of the roofs, a white granular powder still showed a few patches; some weeks before it had fallen like snow upon the roofs and the lawns, the fields and streams. 7

No witchcraft, no enemy action had silenced the rebirth of new life in this stricken world. The people had done it themselves. 8

This town does not actually exist, but it might easily have a thousand counterparts in America or elsewhere in the world. I know of no community that has experienced all the misfortunes I describe. Yet every one of these disasters has actually happened somewhere, and many real communities have already suffered a substantial number of them. A grim specter has crept upon us almost unnoticed, and this imagined tragedy may easily become a stark reality we all shall know. 9

BUILDING VOCABULARY

1. In the second paragraph, find at least five concrete words that relate to trees, birds, and vegetation. How many of these objects could you identify? Look in a dictionary for the meanings of those words you do not know.
2. Try to identify the italicized words through the *context clues* (see Glossary) provided by the complete sentence.
   - **a.** half-hidden in the *mists* (par. 1)
   - **b.** when the first settlers *raised* their houses (par. 2)
   - **c.** *stricken* suddenly while at play (par. 3)
   - **d.** the hens *brooded,* but no chicks hatched (par. 5)
   - **e.** *Anglers* no longer visited them, for all the fish had died. (par. 6)

THINKING CRITICALLY ABOUT THE ESSAY

Understanding the Writer's Ideas

1. What is the quality of the world that Carson describes in her opening paragraph? If you had to describe it in just one or two words, which would you use?
2. What are some of the natural objects that Carson describes in her first two paragraphs? Why does she not focus on simply one aspect of nature—like animals, trees, or flowers?

3. How does Carson describe the "evil spell" that settles over the countryside?
4. What does Carson mean when she declares, "It was a spring without voices" (par. 4)? Why does she show that the critical action takes place in the springtime?
5. What do you think is the "white granular powder" that Carson refers to in paragraph 7? Why does she not explain what it is or where it came from?
6. In paragraph 9, the author states her basic point. What is it? Does she offer a solution to the problem that she poses?

Understanding the Writer's Techniques

1. A *fable* is a story with a moral; in other words, a fable is a form of teaching narrative. How does Carson structure her narrative in this essay? What is the "moral" or thesis?
2. What is the purpose of the description in this essay? Why does the writer use such vivid and precise words?
3. Where in this essay does Carson begin to shift from an essentially optimistic tone to a negative one?
4. Does Carson rely on comparison or contrast in this essay?
5. In the *block method* of comparison and contrast, the writer presents all information about one subject, and then all information about a second subject, as in the following:

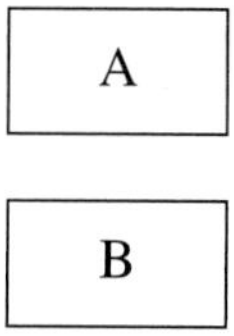

   a. How does Carson use this pattern in her essay?
   b. Are there actually two subjects in this essay, or two different aspects of one subject? How does chronology relate to the block structure?
   c. Are the two major parts of Carson's essay equally weighted? Why or why not?
   d. In the second part of the essay, does Carson ever lose sight of the objects introduced in the first part? What new terms does she introduce?

6. How can you explain paragraphs 8 and 9—which do not involve narration, description, or comparison and contrast—in relation to the rest of the essay? What is the nature of Carson's conclusion?

Exploring the Writer's Ideas

1. Today chemicals are used to destroy crop insects, to color and preserve food, and to purify our water, among other things. Would Carson term this "progress"? Would you? Do you think that there are inadequate safeguards and controls in the use of chemicals? What recent examples of chemical use have made the news?
2. Why would you agree or disagree that factories and corporations should protect the environment that they use? Should a company, for example, be forced to clean up an entire river that it polluted? What about oil spills?
3. Have there been any problems with the use of chemicals and the environment in your own area? Describe them. How do local citizens feel about these problems?
4. Do you think that it will be possible in the future for Americans to "live in harmony" with their natural surroundings? Why do you believe what you do?

IDEAS FOR WRITING

Prewriting

Define the word *fable.* List the various elements that you think contribute to successful fables.

Guided Writing

Write a fable (an imaginary story with a moral) in which you contrast one aspect of the life of a person, community, or nation with another.

1. Begin with a phrase similar to Carson's "There was once . . ." so that the reader knows you are writing a narrative fable.
2. Relate your story to an American problem.

3. Use the block method in order to establish your contrast. Write first about one aspect of the topic and then about the other.
4. Use sensory detail in order to make your narrative clear and interesting.
5. Make certain that you establish an effective transition as you move into the contrast.
6. In the second part of your essay, be sure to refer to the same points you raised in the first part.
7. Use the conclusion to establish the "moral" of your fable.

Thinking and Writing Collaboratively

Exchange Guided Writing essays with another member of the class. Has the writer produced a successful fable? Why or why not? Is the moral clear? Is the American problem well defined? Finally, discuss the structure of the essay. Has the writer used the block method of development appropriately? Does an effective transition link the contrast with the stated problem?

More Writing Projects

1. In a journal entry, describe a place you know well, one that has changed for better or worse. Contrast the place as it once was with the way it is now. Use concrete images that appeal to color, action, sound, smell, taste, and touch.
2. Examine in two block paragraphs the two sides of a specific ecological issue today—for instance, acid rain, the global warming trend, or the use of nuclear energy.
3. Using the block method, compare and contrast Carson's fable with the fable you wrote in Guided Writing.

The Coast With the Most

Robert C. Ritchie

Robert C. Ritchie, the research director of the Huntington Library in California, compares the two coasts, by which he means the Northeast and Southern California. He sees the Northeast as barely capable of claiming a desirable life by the sea. At best the Northeast has a "shore" but you have to go to California to enjoy the beach.

PREREADING: THINKING ABOUT THE ESSAY IN ADVANCE

What are your prejudices about the two coasts—cast and west? What are the main characteristics, for you, of a Southern California beach and of the Maine shore?

Words to Watch

implication (par. 1) suggestion
rustic (par. 3) countryfied
in perpetuity (par. 3) forever
prodigious (par. 6) extraordinary, immense
berms (par. 7) road shoulder
gores (par. 7) triangle of land
tsunami (par.7) tidal wave
ephemeral (par. 8) fleeting

America likes to think of itself as a bicoastal country—or at least the people on the coasts do. The implication is that the coasts are the same and that compared with the vast interior, where the tornadoes are, they share a beach culture. Nothing could be further from the truth, especially when comparing Southern California with the Northeast. 1

Californians, when asked if they have ever seen a green-headed fly, are likely to wonder if Vincent Price was in the movie, little realizing that the fly is a dreaded foe of Eastern beachgoers. 2

Along with the greenhead, the horse fly, the "no-see'um" and the deer fly are all happy grazers on the sunburned flesh of their Eastern brethren. Californians, on the other hand, can look to skies empty of the blood-sucking flying critters that can clear an Eastern beach in minutes.

3 Other contrasts are cultural. Easterners go to the shore; Californians visit the beach. Going to the shore means to visit an expensive if rustic cottage as often as possible. Middle-class folks lust to own a place, but in the meantime they rent, preferably the same shack in perpetuity. This is always a good idea because the real issue is getting near the private beaches that are off-limits to everyone except the landowners and renters.

4 That leaves the rest of the population to pay the hefty parking fees that shorefront townships charge the lowly day-tripper. The higher the fee the better, because high fees mean lower taxes for the local residents.

5 Californians, on the other hand, can visit the many state, Federal and municipal public beaches with low parking fees (via the convenient freeways). They may object to government, but they do like a public beach. Few Californians own a second house near the beach; they prefer to get a mini-ranch and pave over Montana.

6 Easterners love to remind Californians that they live with the daily threat of an earthquake. But the East Coast gets pummeled by nasty storms. Hurricanes and nor'easters may not be as willfully destructive of property as an unfriendly temblor but they are much more likely to destroy the beach. Eastern beaches are always heading out to sea regardless of the prodigious works of the Army Corps of Engineers.

7 We Westerners have to pay Federal taxes to keep the East Coast in sand. If, as predicted, the number of hurricanes increases, then Eastern beaches are likely to be good places only for geologists who go to pick up rocks and engineers who create ever longer dikes, berms, piers and gores in an effort to keep the beach close to the shore. (Or is it vice versa?) Californians can always retreat to the beach after the earthquakes roll through, although they might have to dodge the tsunami.

8 The beach season in the Northeast is ephemeral. Come September, the chill will drive sunbathers from the sand. Californians know the joys of endless summer. For them the beach is a way of life. Whoever heard of a Massachusetts beach bum, let alone a New Jersey surfer dude?

Californians can also engage in the quest to see the green flash just as the sun sets into the ocean, and they can do it year round. On a January evening, Californians can pull off their in-line skates, untangle the CD-player cord, walk past the volleyball players, and settle into the sand to await the sunset. 9

Who cares about the shore when you have a real beach? 10

BUILDING VOCABULARY

Identify the italicized words through the *context clues* (see Glossary) provided by the complete sentence.

a. the sunburned flesh of their Eastern *brethren* (par. 2)
b. to pay the *hefty* parking fees (par. 4)
c. visit the many state, Federal and *municipal* public beaches (par. 4)
d. gets *pummeled* by nasty storms (par. 6)

THINKING CRITICALLY ABOUT THE ESSAY

Understanding the Writer's Ideas

1. In his opening paragraph, Ritchie identifies a misconception he is going to clarify. What is that misconception?
2. In the second paragraph, Ritchie begins to compare and contrast the seashores of the two coasts. What is the first difference between the coasts that he brings out?
3. Aside from differences of environment, the other contrasts, the writer says, are "cultural." What does he mean by this word?
4. According to the writer, what follows from the Easterner's preference for private beaches?
5. What differences in weather conditions does writer note between the two coasts?
6. Which coast does the writer favor, and why?

Understanding the Writer's Techniques

1. In this essay, the writer compares and contrasts (mainly the latter) the beach cultures of the nation's two coasts. He does so by discussing some of the main aspects of beach life—insects,

access, weather, seasons—in successive paragraphs. In each paragraph he explores the topic from the vantage point of each coast, adapting the *alternating method* (see pages 203–204) to his purposes. Identify two techniques the writer uses to shift from one coast to the other.

2. How does the writer convey the fact that his subject is both trivial and of great interest to many people?
3. What is the thesis of this essay? Where is it stated? Chart how the writer supports his thesis in the body of the essay.
4. How does the writer exploit the connotations of "shore" and "beach" to establish his contrast?
5. At what point in the essay does the writer begin to make his preference for West over East explicit? Why does he choose to do so at this point in his essay?

Exploring the Writer's Ideas

1. Does the writer overstate a point in order to establish a premise for his essay when he says that "America likes to think of itself as a bicoastal country"? Or do you agree with him? Explain.
2. Does the comparison of Southern California and the Northeast further skew the argument? Why or why not? How do you think readers of this essay from Oregon or North Carolina would view its generalizations about the two coasts?
3. Explain why you are or are not persuaded that the dangers of earthquakes and of nasty storms are comparable.
4. Do you think the essay, with its casual "Who cares . . ." conclusion risks our passing it off as altogether inconsequential, or has the writer pitched his argument at the right level to engage your interest without getting too serious? Explain your answer by explicit reference to words, phrases, and sentences in the essay.

IDEAS FOR WRITING

Prewriting

The lifestyles of various sections of the nation are rich in topics for comparison and contrast. Select both a focus for comparison/contrast (for example, cooking) and two different regions of the country; list common and contrasting attributes.

Guided Writing

Write an essay contrasting the lifestyles of two regions of the nation. Focus on one central subject for the contrast—for example, attitude toward work, food, dress, and leisure.

1. Begin the essay with an example or anecdote to introduce the subject of the contrast.
2. In the next paragraph state your thesis.
3. Develop your contrast in the body of your essay using opposing examples characteristic of the two regions you have chosen to discuss.
4. Do not make your preference for one or another region obvious until near the end of the essay.
5. As you approach your conclusion, discuss one or two examples at greater length, now making your preference clear.
6. Conclude your essay with a generalization, based on the subject of contrast you have chosen, that highlights the differences of life style between the two regions of the country that you are discussing.

Thinking and Writing Collaboratively

In small groups of four or five, discuss each student's preconceptions about regions of the country, or different cities. Choosing two or three subjects of focus, write the first two paragraphs of an essay about the difference between common conceptions of a place and the reality. Compare the introductory paragraphs written by each student in the group. Which rouse your interest in reading more of the essay? Why?

The Tapestry of Friendships

Ellen Goodman

Syndicated columnist for the *Boston Globe, Washington Post,* and other newspapers, Ellen Goodman presents a thought-provoking comparison of two categories of human relations in this selection from her book *Close to Home.* Notice especially how she blends personal experience with a clipped, direct journalistic style to examine the ways in which "friends" and "buddies" relate to one another.

PREREADING: THINKING ABOUT THE ESSAY IN ADVANCE

How do you define "friendship"? Does this definition apply to both your female and male friends? Is there a difference between your male and female friendships, and if so, how do you explain it?

Words to Watch

slight (par. 1) not having much substance

fragility (par. 2) condition of being easily broken or harmed

resiliency (par. 2) condition of being able to recover easily from misfortune or change

binge (par. 4) spree; indulgence

atavistic (par. 5) manifesting a throwback to the past

culled (par. 5) chosen from

palpably (par. 8) in a way that can be touched or felt

loathsome (par. 10) detestable; hateful

wretched (par. 13) miserable; woeful

claustrophobic (par. 16) uncomfortable at being confined in small places

1 It was, in many ways, a slight movie. Nothing actually happened. There was no big-budget chase scene, no bloody shoot-out. The story ended without any cosmic conclusions.

2 Yet she found Claudia Weill's film *Girlfriends* gentle and affecting. Slowly, it panned across the tapestry of friendship—

showing its fragility, its resiliency, its role as the connecting tissue between the lives of two young women.

3 When it was over, she thought about the movies she'd seen this year—*Julia, The Turning Point* and now *Girlfriends.* It seemed that the peculiar eye, the social lens of the cinema, had drastically shifted its focus. Suddenly the Male Buddy movies had been replaced by the Female Friendship flicks.

4 This wasn't just another binge of trendiness, but a kind of *cinéma vérité.* For once the movies were reflecting a shift, not just from men to women but from one definition of friendship to another.

5 Across millions of miles of celluloid, the ideal of friendship had always been male—a world of sidekicks and "pardners," of Butch Cassidys and Sundance Kids. There had been something almost atavistic about these visions of attachments—as if producers culled their plots from some pop anthropology book on male bonding. Movies portrayed the idea that only men, those direct descendants of hunters and Hemingways, inherited a primal capacity for friendship. In contrast, they portrayed women picking on each other, the way they once picked berries.

6 Well, that duality must have been mortally wounded in some shoot-out at the You're OK, I'm OK Corral. Now, on the screen, they were at least aware of the subtle distinction between men and women as buddies and friends.

7 About 150 years ago, Coleridge had written, "A woman's friendship borders more closely on love than man's. Men affect each other in the reflection of noble or friendly acts, whilst women ask fewer proofs and more signs and expressions of attachment."

8 Well, she thought, on the whole, men had buddies, while women had friends. Buddies bonded, but friends loved. Buddies faced adversity together, but friends faced each other. There was something palpably different in the way they spent their time. Buddies seemed to "do" things together; friends simply "were" together.

9 Buddies came linked, like accessories, to one activity or another. People have golf buddies and business buddies, college buddies and club buddies. Men often keep their buddies in these categories, while women keep a special category for friends.

10 A man once told her that men weren't real buddies until they'd been "through the wars" together—corporate or athletic

or military. They had to soldier together, he said. Women, on the other hand, didn't count themselves as friends until they'd shared three loathsome confidences.

11 Buddies hang tough together; friends hang onto each other.

12 It probably had something to do with pride. You don't show off to a friend; you show need. Buddies try to keep the worst from each other; friends confess it.

13 A friend of hers once telephoned her lover, just to find out if he were home. She hung up without a hello when he picked up the phone. Later, wretched with embarrassment, the friend moaned, "Can you believe me? A thirty-five-year-old lawyer, making a chicken call?" Together they laughed and made it better.

14 Buddies seek approval. But friends seek acceptance.

15 She knew so many men who had been trained in restraint, afraid of each other's judgment or awkward with each other's affection. She wasn't sure which. Like buddies in the movies, they would die for each other, but never hug each other.

16 She'd reread *Babbitt* recently, that extraordinary catalogue of male grievances. The only relationship that gave meaning to the claustrophobic life of George Babbitt had been with Paul Riesling. But not once in the tragedy of their lives had one been able to say to the other: You make a difference.

17 Even now men shocked her at times with their description of friendship. Does this one have a best friend? "Why, of course, we see each other every February." Does that one call his most intimate pal long distance? "Why, certainly, whenever there's a real reason." Do those two old chums ever have dinner together? "You mean alone? Without our wives?"

18 Yet, things were changing. The ideal of intimacy wasn't this parallel playmate, this teammate, this trenchmate. Not even in Hollywood. In the double standard of friendship, for once the female version was becoming accepted as the general ideal.

19 After all, a buddy is a fine life-companion. But one's friends, as Santayana once wrote, "are that part of the race with which one can be human."

BUILDING VOCABULARY

1. The first six paragraphs of this essay use many words and expressions related to film. Explain the meaning or connotation

of each of the following words and expressions. Pay special attention to their context in Goodman's article.

a. big-budget chase scene (par. 1)
b. bloody shoot-out (par. 1)
c. it panned (par. 2)
d. the peculiar eye (par. 3)
e. the social lens of the cinema (par. 3)
f. shifted its focus (par. 3)
g. flicks (par. 3)
h. *cinéma vérité* (par. 4)
i. millions of miles of celluloid (par. 5)
j. plots (par. 5)
k. on the screen (par. 6)

2. Write an *antonym* (word with an opposite meaning) for each of the following words from the Words to Watch section. Then use each antonym in a sentence.

a. slight
b. fragility
c. resiliency
d. atavistic
e. palpably
f. loathsome
g. wretched

THINKING CRITICALLY ABOUT THE ESSAY

Understanding the Writer's Ideas

1. What does the author mean when she writes that the movie "ended without any cosmic conclusions" (par. 1)? Is she being critical or descriptive in this statement? Explain.
2. Who is the "she" first mentioned at the beginning of paragraph 2 and referred to throughout the essay?
3. What pattern of change does the author note in the same-year releases of the films *Julia, The Turning Point,* and *Girlfriends?* Does she feel this is a superficial or real change? How do you know?
4. What is the author's main complaint about the ways in which movies have traditionally portrayed friendships? What example does she offer? Explain the meaning of the sentence, "Movies portrayed the idea that only men, those direct descendants of

hunters and Hemingway, inherited a primal capacity for friendship" (par. 5). What is "male bonding"?

5. What two allusions does Goodman combine to produce the expression "the You're OK, I'm OK Corral"? Explain the full meaning of the sentence in which that expression appears.
6. According to Goodman, what is the main difference between male and female friendships? Which type do you think she prefers? Why?
7. What quality of friendships is suggested by the title?
8. What is meant by "the double standard of friendship"?
9. How does Goodman's conclusion support her preference for male or female types of friendships?

Understanding the Writer's Techniques

1. What is the main idea of this essay? Which sentence serves as the thesis statement? What two subjects form the basis for comparison in this essay?
2. Like most well-constructed essays, this one has three clear sections: introduction, body, conclusion. Specify which paragraphs make up each section. Does this seem a good balance? Explain.
3. How would you describe the effect of the writing in the opening paragraph? Does it give you a clear idea of the subject of this essay? Is that important in this essay? Why?
4. In the beginning, Goodman uses a number of *metaphors* (see Glossary), including the title. Explain the following metaphors in your own words:
   a. The Tapestry of Friendships (title and par. 2)
   b. the connecting tissue between the lives of two young women (par. 2)

   In what ways do the two metaphors convey similar ideas? Which do you prefer? Why?
5. What is the effect of the use of the pronoun "she" throughout the essay? Why do you suppose Goodman chose to use "she" rather than "I"?
6. Among the main purposes of a comparison-contrast essay are (a) *to explain* something unfamiliar in terms of something already familiar, (b) *to understand* better two things already known by comparing them point for point, (c) *to evaluate* the relative value of two things. Which of these objectives most closely describes Goodman's purpose? Explain.

7. Which of the three methods of writing comparison essays—block, alternating, or combination—dominates in this essay? Explain.
8. Who is the intended audience for this essay? Why?
9. There are four literary *allusions* (see Glossary) in this essay: (a) Hemingway, (b) Coleridge, (c) *Babbitt,* and (d) Santayana. Identify each and explain why Goodman chose to include it.
10. Throughout the essay, Goodman uses short, direct sentences and relatively short paragraphs. What is her purpose for that? Does it allow for adequate development of this subject matter? Why or why not?
11. At what points does Goodman make use of relatively *extended illustrations?*
12. Goodman chooses to point out the contrasts between her two subjects in short, directly opposing sentences or clauses, beginning with paragraph 8: ". . . men had buddies, while women had friends. Buddies bonded, but friends loved."

    Go through the essay and list all such opposing statements. How do these statements affect your reading of the essay?
13. How does Goodman use *repetition* as a transitional device in the essay?
14. What is the effect of the series of questions that comprise paragraph 17? How is it like a dialogue? Why are some of the questions in quotation marks and others not?
15. A good conclusion for an essay of comparison or contrast will either (a) restate the main idea, (b) offer a solution, or (c) set a new frame of reference by generalizing from the thesis. Which approach or combination of approaches does Goodman use? How effective is her conclusion? Why?

Exploring the Writer's Ideas

1. Do you agree with Goodman's basic distinction between female and male friendships? Why or why not? How closely does it relate to your own experiences? Do you have any friendships that don't fit into either of the two categories she describes?
2. In the beginning of this essay, Goodman refers to the "binge of trendiness" toward pop anthropology and psychology. Such periodicals, books, and syndicated columns as *Psychology Today, Men Are from Mars, Women Are from Venus,* and

Dr. Joyce Brothers—to name just a few—are widely read. What's more, radio call-in shows offering on-the-air advice are nationally syndicated and immensely popular.

What are your feelings about such media presentations? Do you think they are useful? Are there instances when they might be harmful? Why do you think they are so popular?

3. Why does Goodman avoid any discussion of friendship between men and women? Do you feel this omission in any way affects the forcefulness or completeness of her essay? Explain.

IDEAS FOR WRITING

Prewriting

Draw a line down a sheet of paper, labeling the left side *Women* and the right side *Men.* Then identify a topic—for example, dating—that you think men and women approach differently. Next, jot down a few points of contrast that help to explain the precise nature of the differences you plan to investigate.

Guided Writing

Write an essay that contrasts the ways in which men and women perceive or approach some aspect of interpersonal relationships. You might choose, for example, dating, parenting, expressing affection, or divorce.

1. Begin with a description of some depiction of the subject in the contemporary media (for example, a film, TV program, book, video, commercial).
2. Staying with the same medium, give other examples that illustrate how the medium is shifting away from the old, established ways of viewing the subject. Use language specific to that medium.
3. In the rest of your introductory section, use a few metaphors.
4. As a transitional device, cite a statement from a well-known authority (not necessarily on the particular subject).
5. State the main idea of your essay at the beginning of the body section.
6. Develop your contrast using short, direct, opposing statements that summarize the different approaches of men and women.

7. Develop at least two of these opposing statements through extended personal examples.
8. Make your preference for either approach *implicit* (subtle) rather than *explicit* (obvious) throughout.
9. Make the last paragraph of the body of your essay a series of questions that form an internal dialogue.
10. Conclude with a statement that generalizes the main differences and your evaluation of the two approaches.

Thinking and Writing Collaboratively

Working in groups of four, examine the opening paragraphs of your Guided Writing essays. Which of the four introductory paragraphs encourage you to read more of the essay? Which, if any, need revision for stronger effect? Suggest specific ways to improve each introductory paragraph. Revise your own introduction based on readers' responses.

More Writing Projects

1. Compare and contrast in a journal entry two films or books, plays, or television programs that portray contrasting views of friendship, love, or marriage.
2. Compare in one or two paragraphs the ways you relate to two close friends.
3. Write an essay that compares and/or contrasts what was considered physically attractive in two different time periods in America. You may either focus your essay on one sex or attempt to discuss both.

The Body of the Beholder

Michele Ingrassia

Newsweek writer Michele Ingrassia takes a look at a study that shows why white girls dislike their bodies, but black girls are proud of theirs. Why do some find that being fat can also mean being fit?

PREREADING: THINKING ABOUT THE ESSAY IN ADVANCE

Look in the mirror. What do you see? How do you feel about your body? Why do you feel that way?

Words to Watch

dissect (par. 1) to cut apart or separate (tissue), especially for anatomical study

anthropologist (par. 3) a scientist who studies the origin, behavior, and physical, social, and cultural development of human beings

superwaif (par. 4) a slang phrase meaning a model who makes a lot of money because she looks gaunt, like an orphaned child (waif)

magnetism (par. 5) unusual power to attract, fascinate, or influence

1 When you're a teenage girl, there's no place to hide. Certainly not in gym class, where the shorts are short, the T shirts revealing and the adolescent critics eager to dissect every flaw. Yet out on the hardwood gym floors at Morgan Park High, a largely African-American school on Chicago's Southwest Side, the girls aren't talking about how bad their bodies are, but how good. Sure, all of them compete to see how many sit-ups they can do—Janet Jackson's washboard stomach is their model. But ask Diane Howard about weight, and the African-American senior, who carries 133 pounds on her 5-foot 7½-inch frame, says she'd happily add 15 pounds—if she could ensure they'd land on her hips. Or La'Taria Stokes, a stoutly built junior who takes it as high praise when boys remark, "Your hips are screaming for twins!" "I know I'm fat," La'Taria says. "I don't care."

In a society that worships at the altar of supermodels like Claudia, Christy and Kate, white teenagers are obsessed with staying thin. But there's growing evidence that black and white girls view their bodies in dramatically different ways. The latest findings come in a study to be published in the journal *Human Organization* this spring by a team of black and white researchers at the University of Arizona. While 90 percent of the white junior-high and high-school girls studied voiced dissatisfaction with their weight, 70 percent of African-American teens were satisfied with their bodies. 2

In fact, even significantly overweight black teens described themselves as happy. That confidence may not carry over to other areas of black teens' lives, but the study suggests that, at least here, it's a lifelong source of pride. Asked to describe women as they age, two thirds of thc black teens said they get more beautiful, and many cited their mothers as examples. White girls responded that their mothers may have been beautiful—back in their youth. Says anthropologist Mimi Nichter, one of the study's coauthors, "In white culture, the window of beauty is so small." 3

What is beauty? White teens defined perfection as 5 feet 7 and 100 to 110 pounds—superwaif Kate Moss's vital stats. African-American girls described the perfect size in more attainable terms—full hips, thick thighs, the sort of proportions about which Hammer ("Pumps and a Bump") and Sir Mix-Alot ("Baby Got Back") rap poetic. But they said that true beauty—"looking good"—is about more than size. Almost two thirds of the black teens defined beauty as "the right attitude." 4

The disparity in body images isn't just in kids' heads. It's reflected in fashion magazines, in ads, and it's out there, on TV, every Thursday night. On NBC, the sitcom "Friends" stars Courteney Cox, Jennifer Aniston and Lisa Kudrow, all of them white and twentysomething, classically beautiful and reed thin. Meanwhile, Fox Television's "Living Single," aimed at an African-American audience, projects a less Hollywood ideal—its stars are four twentysomething black women whose bodies are, well, *real.* Especially the big-boned, bronze-haired rapper Queen Latifah, whose size only adds to her magnetism. During a break at the Lite Nites program at the Harlem YMCA, over the squeal of sneakers on the basketball court, Brandy Wood, 5

14, describes Queen Latifah's appeal: "What I like about her is the way she wears her hair and the color in it and the clothes she wears."

6 Underlying the beauty gap are 200 years of cultural differences. "In white, middle-class America, part of the great American Dream of making it is to be able to make yourself over," says Nichter. "In the black community, there is the reality that you might not move up the ladder as easily. As one girl put it, you have to be realistic—if you think negatively about yourself, you won't get anywhere." It's no accident that Barbie has long embodied a white-adolescent ideal—in the early days, she came with her own scale (set at 110) and her own diet guide ("How to Lose Weight: Don't Eat"). Even in this postfeminist era, Barbie's tight-is-right message is stronger than ever. Before kindergarten, researchers say, white girls know that Daddy eats and Mommy diets. By high school, many have split the world into physical haves and have-nots, rivals across the beauty line. "It's not that you hate them [perfect girls]," says Sarah Immel, a junior at Evanston Township High School north of Chicago. "It's that you're kind of jealous that they have it so easy, that they're so perfect-looking."

7 In the black community, size isn't debated, it's taken for granted—a sign, some say, that after decades of preaching black-is-beautiful, black parents and educators have gotten across the message of self-respect. Indeed, black teens grow up equating a full figure with health and fertility. Black women's magazines tend to tout NOT TRYING TO BE SIZE 8, not TEN TIPS FOR THIN THIGHS. And even girls who fit the white ideal aren't necessarily comfortable there. Supermodel Tyra Banks recalls how, in high school in Los Angeles, she was the envy of her white girlfriends. "They would tell me, 'Oh, Tyra, you look so good'," says Banks. "But I was like, 'I want a booty and thighs like my black girlfriends'."

8 Men send some of the strongest signals. What's fat? "You got to be *real* fat for me to notice," says Muhammad Latif, a Harlem 15-year-old. White girls follow what they *think* guys want, whether guys want it or not. Sprawled across the well-worn sofas and hard-back chairs of the student lounge, boys at Evanston High scoff at the girls' idealization of Kate Moss. "Sickly," they say, "gross." Sixteen-year-old Trevis Milton, a

blond swimmer, has no interest in dating Kate wanna-bes. "I don't want to feel like I'm going to break them." Here, perfection is a hardbody, like Linda Hamilton in "Terminator II." "It's not so much about eating broccoli and water as running," says senior Kevin Mack.

And if hardbodies are hot, girls often need to diet to 9
achieve them, too. According to the Arizona study, which was funded by the National Institute of Child Health and Human Development, 62 percent of the white girls reported dieting at least once in the past year. Even those who say they'd rather be fit than thin get caught up. Sarah Martin, 16, a junior at Evanston, confesses she's tried forcing herself to throw up but couldn't. She's still frustrated: ". . . have a big appetite, and I feel so guilty when I eat."

Black teens don't usually go to such extremes. Anorexia 10
and bulimia are relatively minor problems among African-American girls. And though 51 percent of the black teens in the study said they'd dieted in the last year, follow-up interviews showed that far fewer were on sustained weight-and-exercise programs. Indeed, 64 percent of the black girls thought it was better to be "a little" overweight than underweight. And while they agreed that "very overweight" girls should diet, they defined that as someone who "takes up two seats on the bus."

The black image of beauty may seem saner, but it's not 11
necessarily healthy. Black women don't obsess on size, but they do worry about other white cultural ideals that black men value. "We look at Heather Locklear and see the long hair and the fair, pure skin," says *Essence* magazine senior editor Pamela Johnson. More troubling, the acceptance of fat means many girls ignore the real dangers of obesity. Dieting costs money—even if it's not a fancy commercial program; fruits, vegetables and lean meats are pricier than high-fat foods. Exercise? Only one state—Illinois—requires daily physical education for every kid. Anyway, as black teenagers complain, exercise can ruin your hair—and, if you're plunking down $35 a week at the hairdresser, you don't want to sweat out your 'do in the gym. "I don't think we should obsess about weight and fitness, but there is a middle ground," says the well-toned black actress Jada Pinkett. Maybe that's where Queen Latifah meets Kate Moss.

BUILDING VOCABULARY

These words have medical denotations. What are they? Check a medical dictionary.

a. anorexia (par. 10)
b. bulimia (par. 10)
c. obsess (par. 11)

THINKING CRITICALLY ABOUT THE ESSAY

Understanding the Writer's Ideas

1. What does the writer mean when she says teenage girls generally have "no place to hide" (par. 1)?
2. What did the findings of a study by the journal *Human Organization* reveal about the way young girls see their bodies?
3. How did black and white teens view the bodies of their mothers?
4. How does superwaif Kate Moss serve as a role model for teenage girls?
5. Television seems to reflect the different attitudes about body image of black and white teenage girls. How?
6. What may account for the differing views of beauty for black and white girls?
7. How are full-figured black women viewed in their community? Why?
8. Dieting is an American obsession. But is this true for black teens? Explain.
9. Are attitudes about black women's bodies potentially harmful, leading to an increase in obesity in black girls?

Understanding the Writer's Techniques

1. Where does the writer state her thesis? How does the statement make the essay's plan clear?
2. How are the essay's paragraphs ordered around the comparison-contrast structure?
3. How does the writer use statistics to support the comparison-contrast paragraph technique?

4. What audience does the writer have in mind? Do you think this essay is written for men or women? Explain.
5. What makes the transition sentences in paragraph 4 different from the others?
6. Do all the paragraphs (including par. 4) have a topic sentence? Give examples.
7. In the concluding paragraph of the comparison-contrast essay, it is common to bring the two subjects together for a final observation. How does this writer follow that strategy?

Exploring the Writer's Ideas

1. Do you agree with the writer's premise that white girls are mostly obsessed with being thin? Explain.
2. Given the reported differences in the way black and white girls see their bodies, whose view do you prefer and why?
3. Is there a connection between how girls see their mothers' bodies and how they see their own, as the essay suggests? What is your feeling?
4. Television is blamed for many of society's ills. Should television be more responsible for the body types it chooses if it influences the way young girls see their own bodies? Explain.
5. In the black community, "there is the reality that you might not move up the ladder as easily." How do you feel about this statement? What does it mean and how does it relate to body image?
6. If the "black-is-beautiful" movement helped black women avoid negative body images, do white women need a similar movement? Give examples in your response.
7. How do men in your community communicate what they think constitutes a beautiful body? What is a beautiful man's body?
8. Despite the positive aspects of liking yourself (even if you are heavy), can an acceptance of weight lead to ill health? Why or why not? What do you propose?

IDEAS FOR WRITING

Prewriting

Make a list of your body features, explaining what you like or dislike about yourself (and/or others).

Guided Writing

Compare your attitudes about your body to those examined in Ingrassia's essay.

1. Begin with a description that shows how your attitudes about your body are shared (or not) by your community.
2. Make sure your thesis reflects the comparison your essay plans to make between your body image and those discussed in the above essay.
3. Focus on how your ideas of beauty differ from (or are the same as) the ideas in the essay. Try to make at least three comparisons (paragraphs).
4. Tell how your culture has historically looked at beauty.
5. How (and what) do men make clear about feminine (or masculine) beauty in your community?
6. Conclude by evaluating what the ideal body type should be for you (and/or men and women).

Thinking and Writing Collaboratively

Working in a group of four, use what you know about body image and the ways it can hurt some people, and research ways society can change to make people of all body types feel more comfortable with themselves. Then write an essay using what the group has gathered to compare ways society can change to help all people develop a positive body image.

More Writing Projects

1. Watch television commercials for women's and men's products. Reflect in your journal on what beauty messages the television commercials are communicating.
2. Look at the body images of men and women in magazine ads. Then write a paragraph that compares the beauty messages you find in television commercials and magazine ads.
3. Write an essay that compares the images of men and women in television commercials and magazine ads. Take a position on which ones are acceptable or not acceptable. Consider which ones have the most harmful effects on young people or society in general.

SUMMING UP: CHAPTER 6

1. In the essays you have read thus far in this book, you have learned much about the personal lives of many of the authors. Select two whose lives seem very different, and write an essay in which you contrast their lives. In your essay, use only illustrations that you can cite or derive from the selections; that is, do not do research or use other outside information about the authors.
2. In this chapter, Rachel Carson deals with a very old fictional form: the fable. Check the definition of this term. Then, write an essay in which you explore the author's use of the word.
3. Which author in this chapter do you think most successfully uses the comparison-contrast form? Write an essay in which you analyze the best comparison-contrast essay as you see it. Indicate the techniques and strategies that you feel work best. Make specific references to the essay that you have chosen as a model.
4. In the manner of Rachel Carson, write your own "Fable for Tomorrow," in which you show how today's indifference to the environment will affect the future. Remember: *Silent Spring* was written in 1962, and many scholars believe that the way people abuse the environment today is even more serious than it was then.
5. Examine the essays by Ellen Goodman ("The Tapestry of Friendships") and Michele Ingrassia ("The Body of the Beholder"). Compare and contrast the ways in which they discuss men and women, and white and black Americans, respectively.
6. Obtain a copy of Alice Walker's essay, "Beauty: When the Other Dancer Is the Self." Then compare her views on beauty with Michele Ingrassia's presentation of the subject in "The Body of the Beholder."

CHAPTER 7

Definition

WHAT IS DEFINITION?

We are used to opening a dictionary when we want to *define* a word. Often, however, the dictionary definition is brief, and does not fully explain the meaning of a word as an individual writer sees it. An *extended definition* is necessary when a writer wishes to convey the full meaning of a word that is central to the writer's or a culture's thought. When an entire essay focuses on the meaning of a key word or group of related words, extended definition becomes the primary method of organization.

Definition can look at the *denotation* of a word, which is its literal meaning, or at the *connotations,* which are the variety of meanings associated with the word through common use (see Glossary). Denotation is generally available in the dictionary. Connotation, on the other hand, requires that the writer examine not only the denotation but also the way the word is used. In defining, a writer can also explore levels of *diction* (see Glossary), such as standard English, colloquial expressions, and slang. The word "red," for example, denotes a primary color. The connotations, however, are varied: In the early twentieth century Communists were called "Reds" because of the color of the Russian flag. We also associate red with the color of Valentine's cards, with passion and romance. "Redneck" derives from the sunburned skin of a white person who works outdoors and connotes a lifestyle associated with outdoor living and conservative political views. "Redskin" was a pejorative term used by European settlers to describe Native Americans.

We need extended definition to help us fully understand the complexity of our language. Most often, we use definition when words are abstract, controversial, or complex. Terms like "freedom," "pornography," "affirmative action," "bisexual," and "feminism" demand extended definition because they are often confused with some other word or term; because they are so easily misunderstood; or because they are of special importance to the writer, who chooses to redefine the term for his or her own purposes.

Although we can, of course, offer an extended definition just for the sake of definition, we usually go through the trouble of defining because we have strong opinions about complex and controversial words; consequently, we try to provide an extended definition for the purpose of illuminating a thesis for readers. Writer Alice Walker, for instance, once wrote an essay about feminism and African-American women. In her extended definition, she said that the meaning of "feminism" was restricted to white, upper- and middle-class women. As a result, the word did not apply to black women. She created the term "womanist," and wrote her essay to define it. Because of the controversial nature of her definition of "feminist," Walker relied on extended definition to support her thesis that the women's movement needed to pay more attention to women of color.

It *is* possible to give an objective definition of "feminism," with the writer tracing its history, explaining its historic applications, and describing its various subdivisions, such as "radical feminism." However, most of the time, writers have strong opinions. They would want to develop a thesis about the term, perhaps covering much of the same ground as the objective account but taking care that the reader understands the word as they do. It is normal for us to have our own opinions about any word, but in all instances we must make the reader understand fully what we mean by it.

In this chapter Gloria Naylor, an African-American woman, uses extended definition to confront the hate word "nigger." Her many *illustrations* of how and where the word is used show how definition is often determined by context. Janice Castro, with Dan Cook and Cristina Garcia, tackle the issue of what is English as they define a new American language, "Spanglish." Suzanne Britt Jordan has fun defining "fun," and, in a light but serious vein, Kirk Johnson shows how teenage usage has changed the definitions of certain words and phrases for the better.

HOW DO WE READ DEFINITION?

Reading definition requires us to ask ourselves these questions:

- What is the writer's thesis? Determine if the definition is *objective* or *subjective* (see Glossary).
- Does the writer state the definition directly, or expect the reader to understand it from the information the writer gives? When you finish reading the essay, write out a one-sentence definition of the term the writer has defined.
- What are the various techniques the writer uses, such as illustration with examples, description, narration, comparison and contrast? The writer may also use *negation,* a technique of defining a word by what it does *not* mean. In addition, a writer may use a strategy of defining some general group to which the subject belongs (for instance, an orange is a member of the larger group of citrus), and to show how the word differs from all other words in the general group (by its color, acid content, size, and so forth).
- What is the writer's tone? Is the definition comic or serious? Does it rely on *irony* (see Glossary)?

HOW DO WE WRITE A DEFINITION?

Reading the variety of *definitions* in this chapter will prepare you to write your own. The skill required in good definition writing is to make abstract ideas concrete. Writing good definitions allows you to practice many of the other writing strategies you already know, including narration, description, and illustration.

The thesis for your definition does not have to appear in the introduction, but it is helpful to write it out for yourself before you begin.

- Select the word: for example, *multiculturalism.*
- Place it in a class: Multiculturalism is a *belief,* or *system of values,* or *philosophy.*
- Distinguish it from other members of that class: Multiculturalists favor recognition and celebration of differences among various social groups instead of seeking similarities.
- Use negation: Multiculturalism is not the "melting pot" metaphor of how American society is constituted.

By arranging these pieces, and revising the language, you can create a working thesis.

Sample thesis statement:

> Multiculturalism supports the preservation and celebration of differences among people of diverse cultures rather than urging them to replace their ethnic identities with one single "American" identity.

Select support to illustrate, narrate, and describe the term. The selection of evidence can demonstrate the writer's *point of view* on the term. Is multiculturalism splitting the nation into separate groups, or is it affirming the identity of both minority and majority citizens? Look at how the term is used in a variety of settings, such as education, government, social services agencies, and religious institutions.

You might want to visit the library to see how a reference book's definition compares with your own. Libraries have a variety of dictionaries. Depending on the kind of word you are researching, you might want to look at a dictionary of slang, or even a dictionary of quotations to read some famous opinions about abstract words like "love," "hope," and "truth."

What is the *purpose* of the definition? Decide whether you want to show support for the policy or argue against its effectiveness.

Who is the audience? The writer would choose different language for addressing a PTA meeting than for writing to Congress.

Plan an arrangement of the supporting evidence. Unlike comparison and contrast, for instance, definition does not require a formal method of outlining. Examples can be arranged to suit the kind of word being defined, and the mood of the writer. Because so many methods can be applied effectively in an essay of extended definition, you should be able to organize and develop this type of composition easily.

Review the *transitions* you have used in other essays and see which ones apply here. You might want to focus on transitions that show addition: *another, in addition, furthermore.*

Writing and Revising the Draft

Think about where to put the thesis. What is the effect of placing it at the end rather than at the beginning?

Plan your strategy. Arrange the examples so that they most effectively create the extended definition you want. Your essay should have *coherence.* Avoid an unrelated collection of definitions.

Read your essay to a classmate who has defined a similar word. Decide whose definition is more successful, and why.

Revise. Revision may require that you reorganize, moving the examples and other supporting evidence to different sentences and paragraphs to make your argument more effective for a reader.

Proofread for correctness and make a final copy of your work.

A STUDENT PARAGRAPH: DEFINITION

Look at this introductory paragraph of a student's definition essay on multiculturalism and examine the comments in the margin to help you see the various elements of writing definitions.

Some people these days use the term "multiculturalism" as a kind of insult, as if the idea of the American "melting pot" is the only valid way to define a culture of different peoples. The American Heritage Dictionary defines "melting pot" as "a place where immigrants of different cultures or races form an integrated society." "Melting pot," of course is a metaphor. The image suggests that different cultures are like different kinds of metals that meld to form a new alloy—an alloy that is stronger and more versatile than the original metals. This "alloy," of course, is the integrated society, in which everybody gives up his or her own distinctive cultural heritage to make a new (and, by implication, "better," "stronger") culture. "Multiculturalism," on the other hand, makes a very different point. Without rejecting the idea of an integrated society, it rejects the idea of a homogenous one. The idea is more along the lines of different vegetables in a big cauldron, imparting their various flavors to make the perfect soup, while still retaining much of their distinctive shape and color. Those who criticize the term

Introduction of word to be defined

Comparison-contrast to aid definition: *melting pot* and *multiculturalism*

Supporting detail: dictionary citation

Detail helps reader see "melting pot" metaphor

Transition "on the other hand" signals shift to topic *multiculturalism* "multicultural" are actually criticizing the diversity that enriches our American culture. Multiculturalism celebrates the differences among people of diverse cultures rather than urging them to replace their ethnic identities with an "American" identity.

Essay thesis; body paragraphs will offer support

Spanglish

Janice Castro with Dan Cook and Cristina Garcia

Janice Castro and her co-authors Dan Cook and Cristina Garcia are staff writers for *Time* magazine. This essay explores hybrid languages, such as the free-form blend of English and Spanish known as "Spanglish." They survey this hybrid language's growing influence on American English.

PREREADING: THINKING ABOUT THE ESSAY IN ADVANCE

Some people think America should be an English-only country. For example, they object to government tax forms or road signs in languages like Spanish or Chinese. What do you think?

Words to Watch

bemused (par. 1) caused to be bewildered; confused

melting pot (par. 3) a place where immigrants of different cultures or races form an integrated society

transplanted (par. 5) transferred from one place or residence to another; resettled or relocated

luxuriant (par. 10) excessively elaborate

mangled (par. 10) butchered; deformed

1 In Manhattan a first-grader greets her visiting grandparents, happily exclaiming, "Come here, *siéntate!*" Her bemused grandfather, who does not speak Spanish, nevertheless knows she is asking him to sit down. A Miami personnel officer understands what a job applicant means when he says, "*Quiero un* part time." Nor do drivers miss a beat reading a billboard alongside a Los Angeles street advertising CERVEZA—SIX-PACK!

2 This free-form blend of Spanish and English, known as Spanglish, is common linguistic currency wherever concentrations of Hispanic Americans are found in the U.S. In Los Angeles, where 55% of the city's 3 million inhabitants speak Spanish, Spanglish is as much a part of daily life as sunglasses. Unlike the broken-English efforts of earlier immigrants from Europe, Asia

and other regions, Spanglish has become a widely accepted conversational mode used casually—even playfully—by Spanish-speaking immigrants and native-born Americans alike.

Consisting of one part Hispanicized English, one part Americanized Spanish and more than a little fractured syntax, Spanglish is a bit like a Robin Williams comedy routine: a crackling line of cross-cultural patter straight from the melting pot. Often it enters Anglo homes and families through the children, who pick it up at school or at play with their young Hispanic contemporaries. In other cases, it comes from watching TV; many an Anglo child watching *Sesame Street* has learned *uno dos tres* almost as quickly as one two three. 3

Spanglish takes a variety of forms, from the Southern California Anglos who bid farewell with the utterly silly "*hasta la* bye-bye" to the Cuban-American drivers in Miami who *parquean* their *carros*. Some Spanglish sentences are mostly Spanish, with a quick detour for an English word or two. A Latino friend may cut short a conversation by glancing at his watch and excusing himself with the explanation that he must "*ir al* supermarket." 4

Many of the English words transplanted in this way are simply handier than their Spanish counterparts. No matter how distasteful the subject, for example, it is still easier to say "income tax" than *impuesto sobre la renta.* At the same time, many Spanish-speaking immigrants have adopted such terms as VCR, microwave and dishwasher for what they view as largely American phenomena. Still other English words convey a cultural context that is not implicit in the Spanish. A friend who invites you to *lonche* most likely has in mind the brisk American custom of "doing lunch" rather than the languorous afternoon break traditionally implied by *almuerzo.* 5

Mainstream Americans exposed to similar hybrids of German, Chinese or Hindi might be mystified. But even Anglos who speak little or no Spanish are somewhat familiar with Spanglish. Living among them, for one thing, are 19 million Hispanics. In addition, more American high school and university students sign up for Spanish than for any other foreign language. 6

Only in the past ten years, though, has Spanglish begun to turn into a national slang. Its popularity has grown with the explosive increases in U.S. immigration from Latin American countries. English has increasingly collided with Spanish in retail stores, offices and classrooms, in pop music and on street 7 corners. Anglos whose ancestors picked up such Spanish words as *rancho, bronco, tornado* and *incommunicado,* for instance, now freely use such Spanish words as *gracias, bueno, amigo* and *por favor.*

8 Among Latinos, Spanglish conversations often flow easily from Spanish into several sentences of English and back.

9 Spanglish is a sort of code for Latinos: the speakers know Spanish, but their hybrid language reflects the American culture in which they live. Many lean to shorter, clipped phrases in place of the longer, more graceful expressions their parents used. Says Leonel de la Cuesta, an assistant professor of modern languages at Florida International University in Miami: "In the U.S., time is money, and that is showing up in Spanglish as an economy of language." Conversational examples: *taipiar* (type) and *winshi-wiper* (windshield wiper) replace *escribir a máquina* and *limpia-parabrisas.*

10 Major advertisers, eager to tap the estimated $134 billion in spending power wielded by Spanish-speaking Americans, have ventured into Spanglish to promote their products. In some cases, attempts to sprinkle Spanish through commercials have produced embarrassing gaffes. A Braniff airlines ad that sought to tell Spanish-speaking audiences they could settle back *en* (in) luxuriant *cuero* (leather) seats, for example, inadvertently said they could fly without clothes (*encuero*). A fractured translation of the Miller Lite slogan told readers the beer was "Filling, and less delicious." Similar blunders are often made by Anglos trying to impress Spanish-speaking pals. But if Latinos are amused by mangled Spanglish, they also recognize these goofs as a sort of friendly acceptance. As they might put it, *no problema.*

BUILDING VOCABULARY

The words below all refer to language use. Write definitions for the words. Then use each word in a sentence.

a. linguistic (par. 2)
b. syntax (par. 3)
c. patter (par. 3)
d. implicit (par. 5)
e. hybrids (par. 6)
f. gaffes (par. 10)

THINKING CRITICALLY ABOUT THE ESSAY

Understanding the Writer's Ideas

1. A street advertisement "CERVEZA—SIX PACK," is an example of what type of language?
2. How do many youngsters (Hispanics and Anglos) pick up cross-cultural speech?
3. What are the different forms of Spanglish?
4. Why is Spanglish sometimes handier for Hispanics than their Spanish language?
5. What makes Spanglish easier to understand for most Americans than, say, a hybrid of English and Hindi?
6. For Anglos, Spanglish can result in some embarrassing gaffes. Why and how? Give an example.

Understanding the Writer's Techniques

1. What is the thesis of the essay?
2. How does the title reflect the essay's thesis?
3. These writers give a clear definition of Spanglish. Where and what is it, precisely?
4. What statistics do the writers present to help inform readers about Spanglish? What effect does the use of statistics have on the essay? Would this essay be as instructive without them? Explain.
5. In the essay the writer makes use of many of the other expository techniques. Explain where the writer uses these techniques: illustration; process; comparison and contrast.
6. Some information in this essay is highlighted by the use of italics. Why is the material set off from the main text of the essay? Explain.
7. Is this essay written for English or Spanish speakers? Why?

Exploring the Writer's Ideas

1. What attitudes do Americans have about those who speak "broken" English?
2. Do you believe Spanglish, as this essay suggests, is more accepted by Americans who studied a foreign language in school, especially Spanish?

3. What in your high school experience was the language most studied? Was it Spanish? Why or why not?
4. What is your experience with a hybrid language? Describe. What is your feeling about hybrid languages? Are they a threat to the purity of our national language—English? Explain.
5. Teachers often tell students to learn proper English in order to get a job. According to this essay, advertisers and people in business have found it worthwhile to use Spanglish to sell their products. Why do schools emphasize proper language when businesses are trying to learn and use hybrid languages? What is going on?

IDEAS FOR WRITING

Prewriting

Freewrite for fifteen minutes about whatever comes to mind when you think of the word "language." Consider social, political, and cultural elements as well as the obvious linguistic elements.

Guided Writing

Write an extended definition of the term "language," focusing on the key element or elements that you think are most important for someone to understand about the word. Address social, political, or cultural features that help explain the importance of language as a human phenomenon.

1. Begin with a short anecdote from personal experience to introduce the concept of language.
2. Write a thesis sentence to link language with the concept you are addressing. For example, you might write, "Because the idea of language is so connected to cultural identity, understanding a culture can help us understand why certain groups resist learning the language of a new country." Or you might write, "Teenagers have a distinct language all their own."
3. Define "language" from your particular perspective, drawing on the element you have chosen for your focus.
4. Give some examples of the language element that you are focusing on.

5. Explain how people understand or do not understand the element you are exploring. What problems are created because people do not understand or appreciate that element?
6. Propose the results if, in fact, people did come to understand the language feature you are dealing with.
7. Give your essay a lively title that blends the elements you are considering in the way that Castro has blended them in her title "Spanglish."

Thinking and Writing Collaboratively

In groups of three, read drafts of each other's essays and write a one-paragraph critique for each of the two papers you have read. What language element does the writer focus on? Does the thesis sentence explain the writer's position clearly? Do the examples illustrate the point effectively? Then, read the critiques of your own essay, and use them to help you think your essay through before you do your next revision.

More Writing Projects

1. In your journal, reflect on the possible advantages and problems that result when cultures come in close contact with each other.
2. Write a paragraph to define the word "slang."
3. Select any cultural group that you think has had a major impact on American culture, and write an essay to examine that impact. Consider linguistic, social, and economic contributions.

Fun, Oh Boy. Fun. You Could Die from It.

Suzanne Britt Jordan

Most of us never really consider exactly what it means to have a good time. Suzanne Britt Jordan, a writer who claims she "tries to have fun, but often fails," offers an extended definition of the word "fun" by pointing out what it is *not.*

PREREADING: THINKING ABOUT THE ESSAY IN ADVANCE

What expectations do you bring to an article entitled "Fun, Oh Boy. Fun. You Could Die from It"? Can "fun" actually harm or kill you? In what ways? Do you think that we are too much of a "fun" culture? Why or why not?

Words to Watch

puritan (par. 3) one who practices or preaches a stricter moral code than that which most people now follow

selfless (par. 4) unselfish; having no concern for oneself

fetish (par. 5) something regarded with extravagant trust or respect

licentiousness (par. 9) a lack of moral restraints

consumption (par. 9) act of taking in or using up a substance; eating or drinking

epitome (par. 11) an ideal; a typical representation

capacity (par. 12) the ability to hold something

damper (par. 13) something that regulates or that stops something from flowing

reverently (par. 13) respectfully; worshipfully

blaspheme (par. 13) to speak of without reverence

weary (par. 14) tired; worn-out

horizon (par. 14) the apparent line where the earth meets the sky

scan (par. 14) to examine something carefully

1 Fun is hard to have.

2 Fun is a rare jewel.

Somewhere along the line people got the modern idea that fun was there for the asking, that people deserved fun, that if we didn't have a little fun every day we would turn into (sakes alive!) puritans. 3

"Was it fun?" became the question that overshadowed all other questions: good questions like: Was it moral? Was it kind? Was it honest? Was it beneficial? Was it generous? Was it necessary? And (my favorite) was it selfless? 4

When the pleasure got to be the main thing, the fun fetish was sure to follow. Everything was supposed to be fun. If it wasn't fun, then by Jove, we were going to make it fun, or else. 5

Think of all the things that got the reputation of being fun. Family outings were supposed to be fun. Sex was supposed to be fun. Education was supposed to be fun. Work was supposed to be fun. Walt Disney was supposed to be fun. Church was supposed to be fun. Staying fit was supposed to be fun. 6

Just to make sure that everybody knew how much fun we were having, we put happy faces on flunking test papers, dirty bumpers, sticky refrigerator doors, bathroom mirrors. 7

If a kid, looking at his very happy parents traipsing through that very happy Disney World, said, "This ain't fun, ma," his ma's heart sank. She wondered where she had gone wrong. Everybody told her what fun family outings to Disney World would be. Golly gee, what was the matter? 8

Fun got to be such a big thing that everybody started to look for more and more thrilling ways to supply it. One way was to step up the level of danger or licentiousness or alcohol or drug consumption so that you could be sure that, no matter what, you would manage to have a little fun. 9

Television commercials brought a lot of fun and fun-loving folks into the picture. Everything that people in those commercials did looked like fun: taking Polaroid snapshots, swilling beer, buying insurance, mopping the floor, bowling, taking aspirin. We all wished, I'm sure, that we could have half as much fun as those rough-and-ready guys around the locker room, flicking each other with towels and pouring champagne. The more commercials people watched, the more they wondered when the fun would start in their own lives. It was pretty depressing. 10

Big occasions were supposed to be fun. Christmas, Thanksgiving and Easter were obviously supposed to be fun. Your wedding day was supposed to be fun. Your wedding night 11 was supposed to be a whole lot of fun. Your honeymoon was supposed to be the epitome of fundom. And so we ended up going through every Big Event we ever celebrated, waiting for the fun to start.

12 It occurred to me, while I was sitting around waiting for the fun to start, that not much is, and that I should tell you just in case you're worried about your fun capacity.

13 I don't mean to put a damper on things. I just mean we ought to treat fun reverently. It is a mystery. It cannot be caught like a virus. It cannot be trapped like an animal. The god of mirth is paying us back for all those years of thinking fun was everywhere by refusing to come to our party. I don't want to blaspheme fun anymore. When fun comes in on little dancing feet, you probably won't be expecting it. In fact, I bet it comes when you're doing your duty, your job, or your work. It may even come on a Tuesday.

14 I remember one day, long ago, on which I had an especially good time. Pam Davis and I walked to the College Village drug store one Saturday morning to buy some candy. We were about 12 years old (fun ages). She got her Bit-O-Honey. I got my malted milk balls, chocolate stars, Chunkys, and a small bag of M & M's. We started back to her house. I was going to spend the night. We had the whole day to look forward to. We had plenty of candy. It was a long way to Pam's house but every time we got weary Pam would put her hand over her eyes, scan the horizon like a sailor and say, "Oughta reach home by nightfall," at which point the two of us would laugh until we thought we couldn't stand it another minute. Then after we got calm, she'd say it again. You should have been there. It was the kind of day and friendship and occasion that made me deeply regretful that I had to grow up.

15 It was fun.

BUILDING VOCABULARY

1. *Trite language* refers to words and expressions that have been overused and, consequently, have lost much of their effectiveness. People do rely on trite language in their conversations, but writers usually avoid overused expressions. However, a good writer will be able to introduce such

vocabulary at strategic points. Examples of trite language in Jordan's essay appear below. Explain in your own words what they mean.

   a. a rare jewel (par. 2)
   b. by Jove (par. 5)
   c. his ma's heart sank (par. 8)
   d. golly gee (par. 8)

2. For each of the following words drawn from Jordan's essay, write a denotative definition. Then list four *connotations* (see Glossary) that each word has for you.

   a. overshadowed (par. 4)
   b. flunking (par. 7)
   c. traipsing (par. 8)
   d. swilling (par. 10)
   e. mirth (par. 13)

3. Select five words from the Words to Watch section and use them in sentences of your own.

THINKING CRITICALLY ABOUT THE ESSAY

Understanding the Writer's Ideas

1. What are some of the things Jordan says fun is not?
2. What does Jordan suggest we did to something if it wasn't already fun? Identify some of the things she says are "supposed" to be fun.
3. In paragraph 6, Jordan lists some familiar things that seem empty of fun. How does she say people made them fun anyway?
4. What are some of the ways people make fun even more thrilling?
5. What does Jordan list as looking like fun on television commercials?
6. Discuss the relationship between big occasions and the experience of fun. Explain the meaning of the statement, "It may even come on a Tuesday" (par. 13).
7. Describe Jordan's attitude concerning how much in life really is fun. According to Jordan, how should we treat fun? Why? Is it something she says can be experienced only at special times?

8. How old was Jordan at the time she remembers having an especially good time with her friend Pam? Describe in your own words why she had such a good time that day. What are some of the candies she remembers buying? Why was it especially funny when Pam would say, "Oughta reach home by nightfall"?
9. For what reason does Jordan feel regretful at the end of the essay? Although she is regretful, do you think she is actually sad? Why?

Understanding the Writer's Techniques

1. What is the author's thesis? Where is it in the essay?
2. Does Jordan ever offer a single-sentence definition of "fun"? Where? Is that sentence sufficient to define the concept? Why?
3. Jordan employs the technique of *negation*—defining a term through showing what it is *not*—so strongly in this essay that the writing verges on *irony.* Irony is using language to suggest the opposite of what is said (see Glossary). Explain the irony in paragraphs 9, 10, and 11.
4. Why does the author continually point out things that are supposed to be fun? What is she trying to tell us about these things?
5. Writers usually avoid vague language such as "everything" and "everybody" in their writing, yet Jordan uses these words frequently in her essay. Explain her purpose in deliberately avoiding concrete terms.
6. What is the *tone* (see Glossary) of this essay? Is it fun? How does Jordan create the tone? Much of the writing in this essay has a very conversational quality to it, as though the author were speaking directly to the reader. Locate five words or phrases that have this quality.
7. Why does Jordan use so many examples and illustrations in this essay? Which paragraphs use multiple illustrations with special effectiveness?
8. There is a definite turning point in this essay where Jordan switches from an ironic to an affirmative point of view and begins to explain what fun *can be* rather than what it *is not.* One paragraph in particular serves as the transition between the two attitudes. Which one is it? Which is the first paragraph to be mostly affirmative? What is the result of this switch?

9. Jordan uses specific brand names in the essay. Locate at least four of them. Why do you think she uses these brand names instead of names that simply identify the object?
10. What is the function of narration in the development of this essay? Where does the author *narrate* an imagined incident? Where does she use a real incident? Why does Jordan use narration in this paper?
11. Compare the effects of the two simple, direct statements that begin and end the essay. Why does Jordan not develop a more elaborate introduction and conclusion?

Exploring the Writer's Ideas

1. Jordan begins her essay by stating, "Fun is hard to have." At one point she indicates, "Fun got to be such a big thing that everybody started looking for more and more thrilling ways to supply it" (par. 9). Do you think that fun is hard to have? Why or why not? What relationship does the epidemic use of drugs and alcohol have to our difficulties in having fun today?
2. The author raises the question of how at big events we are sometimes left "waiting for the fun to start" (par. 11). What functions do events or occasions such as holidays, weddings, or birthdays play in our society? Why is there an emphasis placed on having fun at those events? Do you think there should be such an emphasis? Why?
3. This essay appeared as a guest editorial in the *New York Times*. We do not usually think of the *New York Times* as a "fun" newspaper, but rather as one that deals with serious issues of international significance. Jordan's article might be considered popular writing or light reading. Do you feel there is a place in the media—newspapers, magazines, radio, television—for a mixture of "heavy" and "light" attitudes? What well-respected newspapers or magazines that you know include articles on popular topics? What subjects do you think would currently be most appealing to popular audiences?
4. At the end of the essay, Jordan seems to imply that it is easier for children to have fun than it is for grownups. Do you agree? Is the basic experience of fun any different for kids or for adults? Do you feel it was any easier for people to have fun in days past than it is now? Why?

IDEAS FOR WRITING

Prewriting

Words like "fun," "love," and "prejudice" have strong connotations—many shades of meaning—associated with them. Select your own highly connotative word, and then make a list of words and phrases that help to define it.

Guided Writing

Select one of the following highly connotative terms for various types of experiences and write an extended definition about it: love, creativity, alienation, prejudice, fidelity.

1. Prepare for your essay by consulting a good dictionary for the lexical definition (denotation) of the term. However, instead of beginning with this definition, start with some catchy, interesting opening statements related to the definition.
2. Write a thesis sentence that names the word you will define and that tells the special opinion, attitude, or point of view you have about the word.
3. Attempt to establish the importance of your subject by considering it in terms of our current understanding of fun.
4. Use the technique of negation (see page 235) by providing various examples and illustrations of what your topic *is not* in order to establish your own viewpoint of what it *is*.
5. Use other strategies—description, narration, comparison and contrast, and so forth—to aid in clearly establishing an extended definition of your topic.
6. At the end of your essay dramatize through narration at least one personal experience that relates the importance of the topic to your life.

Thinking and Writing Collaboratively

Exchange a draft version of your Guided Writing definition essay with another class member, and review your partner's paper carefully. Does it follow the recommendations in the Guided Writing exercise? Which strategies for writing an extended definition have been used? Does the essay incorporate personal experience? Write a one-paragraph evaluation of your classmate's essay.

More Writing Projects

1. Sit someplace on campus and observe people having fun. Record in your journal their behavior—actions, gestures, noises, and so forth. Then turn these notes into a definition of "campus fun."
2. Write a brief one-paragraph definition of a "funny person." Use vivid details to create this portrait.
3. From a book of popular quotations (*Bartlett's Familiar Quotations,* the *Oxford Dictionary of Quotations*) check under the heading "fun" and select a number of statements about fun by professional writers. Then write an essay in which you expand one of those definitions. Draw upon your own experiences or readings to support the definition you choose to expand.

A Word's Meaning

Gloria Naylor

Gloria Naylor is best known for her novel *The Women of Brewster Place* (1982). She has also published *Mama Day* (1986) and *Bailley's Cafe* (1992) to critical acclaim. As an African-American woman and a writer, Naylor has found that words can change their meaning, depending on who defines them. Telling of a confrontation with an angry classmate who called her a "nigger" in the third grade, Naylor develops an extended definition of the word and its multiple meanings. As you read, think about other words that depend on context for their meaning.

PREREADING: THINKING ABOUT THE ESSAY IN ADVANCE

Naylor suggests that different words—even offensive words—mean different things to different people. Would you agree or disagree, and why? Can you think of a word that you personally find very offensive but others might find acceptable?

Words to Watch

transcendent (par. 1) rising above
fleeting (par. 1) moving quickly
intermittent (par. 2) alternate; repeated
consensus (par. 2) agreement
verified (par. 3) confirmed
gravitated (par. 4) moved toward
inflections (par. 5) pitch or tone of voice
endearment (par. 9) expression of affection
disembodied (par. 9) separated from the body
unkempt (par. 10) messy
social stratum (par. 14) status

1 Language is the subject. It is the written form with which I've managed to keep the wolf away from the door and, in diaries, to keep my sanity. In spite of this, I consider the written word

inferior to the spoken, and much of the frustration experienced by novelists is the awareness that whatever we manage to capture in even the most transcendent passages falls far short of the richness of life. Dialogue achieves its power in the dynamics of a fleeting moment of sight, sound, smell and touch.

I'm not going to enter the debate here about whether it is language that shapes reality or vice versa. That battle is doomed to be waged whenever we seek intermittent reprieve from the chicken and egg dispute. I will simply take the position that the spoken word, like the written word, amounts to a nonsensical arrangement of sounds or letters without a consensus that assigns "meaning." And building from the meanings of what we hear, we order reality. Words themselves are innocuous; it is the consensus that gives them true power. 2

I remember the first time I heard the word nigger. In my third-grade class, our math tests were being passed down the rows, and as I handed the papers to a little boy in back of me, I remarked that once again he had received a much lower mark than I did. He snatched his test from me and spit out that word. Had he called me a nymphomaniac or a necrophiliac, I couldn't have been more puzzled. I didn't know what a nigger was, but I knew that whatever it meant, it was something he shouldn't have called me. This was verified when I raised my hand, and in a loud voice repeated what he had said and watched the teacher scold him for using a "bad" word. I was later to go home and ask the inevitable questions that every black parent must face—"Mommy, what does 'nigger' mean?" 3

And what exactly did it mean? Thinking back, I realize that this could not have been the first time the word was used in my presence. I was part of a large extended family that had migrated from the rural South after World War II and formed a close-knit network that gravitated around my maternal grandparents. Their ground-floor apartment in one of the buildings they owned in Harlem was a weekend mecca for my immediate family, along with countless aunts, uncles and cousins who brought along assorted friends. It was a bustling and open house with assorted neighbors and tenants popping in and out to exchange bits of gossip, pick up an old quarrel or referee the ongoing checkers game in which my grandmother cheated shamelessly. They were all there to let down their hair and put up their feet after a week of labor in the factories, laundries and shipyards of New York. 4

Amid the clamor, which could reach deafening proportions—two or three conversations going on simultaneously, punctuated 5 by the sound of a baby's crying somewhere in the back rooms or out on the street—there was still a rigid set of rules about what was said and how. Older children were sent out of the living room when it was time to get into the juicy details about "you-know-who" up on the third floor who had gone and gotten herself "p-r-e-g-n-a-n-t!" But my parents, knowing that I could spell well beyond my years, always demanded that I follow the others out to play. Beyond sexual misconduct and death, everything else was considered harmless for our young ears. And so among the anecdotes of the triumphs and disappointments in the various workings of their lives, the word nigger was used in my presence, but it was set within contexts and inflections that caused it to register in my mind as something else.

6 In the singular, the word was always applied to a man who had distinguished himself in some situation that brought their approval for his strength, intelligence or drive:

7 "Did Johnny *really* do that?"

8 "I'm telling you, that nigger pulled in $6,000 of overtime last year. Said he got enough for a down payment on a house."

9 When used with a possessive adjective by a woman—"my nigger"—it became a term of endearment for husband or boyfriend. But it could be more than just a term applied to a man. In their mouths it became the pure essence of manhood—a disembodied force that channeled their past history of struggle and present survival against the odds into a victorious statement of being: "Yeah, that old foreman found out quick enough—you don't mess with a nigger."

10 In the plural, it became a description of some group within the community that had overstepped the bounds of decency as my family defined it: Parents who neglected their children, a drunken couple who fought in public, people who simply refused to look for work, those with excessively dirty mouths or unkempt households were all "trifling niggers." This particular circle could forgive hard times, unemployment, the occasional bout of depression—they had gone through all of that themselves—but the unforgivable sin was a lack of self-respect.

11 A woman could never be a "nigger" in the singular, with its connotation of confirming worth. The noun "girl" was its closest equivalent in that sense, but only when used in direct address and regardless of the gender doing the addressing. "Girl" was a token of respect for a woman. The one-syllable word was drawn out to sound like three in recognition of the

extra ounce of wit, nerve or daring that the woman had shown in the situation under discussion.

"G-i-r-l, stop. You mean you said that to his face?" 12

But if the word was used in a third-person reference or 13 shortened so that it almost snapped out of the mouth, it always involved some element of communal disapproval. And age became an important factor in these exchanges. It was only between individuals of the same generation, or from an older person to a younger (but never the other way around), that "girl" would be considered a compliment.

I don't agree with the argument that use of the word nigger 14 at this social stratum of the black community was an internalization of racism. The dynamics were the exact opposite: the people in my grandmother's living room took a word that whites used to signify worthlessness or degradation and rendered it impotent. Gathering there together, they transformed "nigger" to signify the varied and complex human beings they knew themselves to be. If the word was to disappear totally from the mouths of even the most liberal of white society, no one in that room was naïve enough to believe it would disappear from white minds. Meeting the word head-on, they proved it had absolutely nothing to do with the way they were determined to live their lives.

So there must have been dozens of times that the "nigger" 15 was spoken in front of me before I reached the third grade. But I didn't "hear" it until it was said by a small pair of lips that had already learned it could be a way to humiliate me. That was the word I went home and asked my mother about. And since she knew that I had to grow up in America, she took me in her lap and explained.

BUILDING VOCABULARY

1. In paragraph 3, Naylor says the word "nigger" is as puzzling to her as "nymphomaniac" and "necrophiliac." Using a dictionary, find both the meanings of these two terms and their etymology, or roots.
2. In paragraph 14, Naylor writes, "I don't agree with the argument that use of the word nigger at this social stratum of the black community was an internalization of racism." Put Naylor's idea into your own words. Use the context of the sentence to understand key terms such as "social stratum" and "internalization."

THINKING CRITICALLY ABOUT THE ESSAY

Understanding the Writer's Ideas

1. What is the original situation in which Naylor recognizes that "nigger" can be a hate word? What clues from outside the dictionary meaning of the word help her to recognize this meaning? What confirms her suspicion that the word is "bad"?
2. In paragraph 4, Naylor gives us information about her family and background. In your own words, what kind of family did Naylor come from? Where did she grow up? What economic and social class did her family come from? How do you know?
3. In paragraph 5, Naylor explains the values of her group. What was considered appropriate and what was inappropriate for children to hear? What kind of behavior was condemned by the group?
4. Naylor defines at least five contexts in which the word "nigger" might be used. Make a list giving the five contexts, and write a sentence putting the use of the word into your own definition.
5. Explain one context in which Naylor says "nigger" was never used (par. 11). How are age and gender important in determining how the word was used?
6. When Naylor says in paragraph 14 that blacks' use of the word "nigger" about themselves rendered the word "impotent," what does she mean? How do they "transform" the meaning of the word?
7. In the last paragraph, Naylor recalls her mother's reaction to the experience of hearing a third-grade classmate use the word to humiliate her. What do you think the mother explained?

Understanding the Writer's Techniques

1. Where is the thesis statement of Naylor's essay? How do you know?
2. Why does Naylor begin with two paragraphs about language, in a very general or theoretical way? Explain what these two paragraphs tell us about the writer's authority to define words. How does she use her introduction to make herself sound like an expert on the problem of defining words?

3. In paragraph 3, the author shifts tone. She moves from the formal language of the introduction to the personal voice as she retells her childhood experience. What is the effect of this transition on the reader? Why?
4. Look closely at the examples of usage Naylor provides in paragraphs 8, 9, 10, and 11. Why does she give dialogue to illustrate the various contexts in which she heard the word "nigger" used? In what way is this variety of speakers related to her thesis statement?
5. Naylor uses grammatical terms to clarify differences in meaning, such as "in the singular" (par. 6), "possessive adjective" (par. 9), "plural" (par. 10), and "third-person reference" (par. 13). Why does she use these technical terms? What does it reveal about the audience for whom she is writing? What does it reveal about Naylor's understanding of that audience?
6. What do you think about the last sentence of the essay? Why does the author return to the simple and direct language of her childhood experience in order to conclude rather than using the theoretical and technical language of other parts of the essay?

Exploring the Writer's Ideas

1. Naylor chooses to define a difficult and controversial word in her essay. Does she define it in a way that makes you think again about the meaning of the word "nigger"? Have you used the word in any of the ways she defines? How have contemporary rap musicians used the word in ways to suggest that Naylor's definition is accurate?
2. Naylor argues that the definition of words emerges from consensus. So, if the third-grader used "nigger" to humiliate his classmate, we must draw the conclusion that that little boy's society consented to the racism he intended by using the word. How does this idea get reinforced in the last paragraph of the essay? What attitude toward racism does the mother seem to reveal when she picks up her daughter? Does Naylor's definition essay offer any solutions to the negative meaning the word carries?
3. The classic American novel *The Adventures of Huckleberry Finn* by Mark Twain uses the word "nigger" almost 200 times. For this reason, some school libraries want to

ban the book. Does Naylor's definition essay offer any solutions to this censorship debate?

4. In what way does Naylor's discussion of language raise issues similar to those discussed by Amy Tan in "Mother Tongue" (pages 27–33)? While Tan is dealing with language among immigrants and Naylor is addressing the varieties of meaning of words to native speakers of English, both writers deal with the politics of language. How does each writer define the relationship between language and power?

IDEAS FOR WRITING

Prewriting

Select an objectionable or offensive word, and for five minutes freewrite on the subject, trying to cover as many ways in which the word is used as possible.

Guided Writing

Choose a word that you have recently heard used that offended you because it was sexist, racist, homophobic, or otherwise objectionable. Write a definition essay in which you define the word, show examples of its power to offend, and conclude by offering alternate words.

1. Use an anecdote to show whom you heard using the word, where it was used, and how you felt when you heard it used. Explain who you are, and who the other speaker was in your introduction.
2. In your thesis give the word and give an expanded definition of what the word means to you.
3. Explain the background of the word's negative use. Who uses it? What is the dictionary meaning of the word? How do you think the word got corrupted?
4. Give examples to expand your thesis that the word has negative meanings. Show who uses it, and for what purpose. Draw your examples from people at work, the media, or historical figures.
5. Use another example to show how the word can change meaning if the speaker deliberately uses it in order to mock its usual meaning or "render it impotent" as Naylor says.

6. If possible, try to define the word by negation—that is, by what it does not mean.
7. Connect your paragraphs with transitions that relate one idea thoughtfully to the next.
8. In your conclusion, place the term in a broader perspective, one that goes beyond the specific word to the power of language to shape reality or control behavior.

Thinking and Writing Collaboratively

Many colleges and universities are trying to find ways to discourage or prevent hate speech by writing codes of conduct. In groups of five or six, discuss possible approaches to this issue, and then draft a policy statement that defines what unacceptable language is and how your campus will respond to it.

More Writing Projects

1. In your journal, record an incident in which someone addressed you or someone you know with an offensive word. Explain how you reacted and why.
2. Write a one-paragraph definition of a word or phrase by which you would feel comfortable being labeled. Are you a single parent? an Italian-American? an honor student? Write a sharp thesis to define the term, and then expand the definition with examples.
3. The term "multicultural" refers to a perspective on society that values the differences among people of varying ethnic origin, religious belief, sexual preference, and social class. In an essay, write an extended definition of the term "multicultural society." Draw upon your own experiences and (or) your readings to support your definition.

Today's Kids Are, Like, Killing the English Language. Yeah, Right.

Kirk Johnson

Remember when it seemed enough to say yes or no? Well, duh, forget it. Like, if you have two pre-teen boys, as does Kirk Johnson, then you understand those days have gone the way of Kukla, Fran and Ollie. Yeah, right.

PREREADING: THINKING ABOUT THE ESSAY IN ADVANCE

Can you think of examples of new ways of saying things, or new words and phrases, that you especially enjoy using? And that you really don't like? What are your views about the impact of television or the computer on the English language?

Words to Watch

maligned (par. 1) wronged
brahmins (par. 1) snobbish aristocrats
hyperbole (par. 3) exaggeration
archaic (par. 4) obsolete
Manichean (par. 4) belief that reality is composed of opposed doubles, such as body and soul
saturation (par. 6) soaking
caustic (par. 7) sharp
auxiliary (par. 8) supporting
esthetic (par. 11) artistic
thesis, antithesis (par. 11) in logic, a proposition or argument, and its opposite
semiotics (par. 14) art of signs
hypothetical (par. 15) for the sake of example
unpalatable (par. 16) unpleasant tasting
superficiality (par. 19) shallowness
paradox (par. 21) apparent contradiction
binary (par. 21) made up of two things or parts

1 As a father of two pre-teen boys, I have in the last year or so become a huge fan of the word "duh." This is a word much maligned by educators, linguistic brahmins and purists, but they are all quite wrong.

2 Duh has elegance. Duh has shades of meaning, even sophistication. Duh and its perfectly paired linguistic partner, "yeah right," are the ideal terms to usher in the millennium and the information age, and to highlight the differences from the stolid old 20th century.

3 Even my sons might stop me at this point and quash my hyperbole with a quickly dispensed, "Yeah, right, Dad." But hear me out: I have become convinced that duh and yeah right have arisen to fill a void in the language because the world has changed. Fewer questions these days can effectively be answered with yes or no, while at the same time, a tidal surge of hype and mindless blather threatens to overwhelm old-fashioned conversation. Duh and yeah right are the cure.

4 Good old yes and no were fine for their time—the archaic, black and white era of late industrialism that I was born into in the 1950's. The yes-or-no combo was hard and fast and most of all simple: It belonged to the Manichean red-or-dead mentality of the cold war, to manufacturing, to "Father Knows Best" and "It's a Wonderful Life."

5 The information-age future that my 11-year-old twins own is more complicated than yes or no. It's more subtle and supple, more loaded with content and hype and media manipulation than my childhood—or any adult's, living or dead—ever was.

6 And duh, whatever else it may be, is drenched with content. Between them, duh and yeah-right are capable of dividing all language and thought into an exquisitely differentiated universe. Every statement and every question can be positioned on a gray scale of understatement or overstatement, stupidity or insightfulness, information saturation or yawning emptiness.

7 And in an era when plain speech has become endangered by the pressures of political correctness, duh and yeah right are matchless tools of savvy, winking sarcasm and skepticism: caustic without being confrontational, incisive without being quite specific.

8 With duh, you can convey a response, throw in a whole basket full of auxiliary commentary about the question or the statement you're responding to, and insult the speaker all at once! As in this hypothetical exchange:

9 *Parent: "Good morning, son, it's a beautiful day."*

10 *Eleven-year-old boy: "Duh."*

11 And there is a kind of esthetic balance as well. Yeah—right is the yin to duh's yang, the antithesis to duh's empathetic thesis. Where duh is assertive and edgy, a perfect tool for undercutting mindless understatement or insulting repetition, yeah right is laid back, a surfer's cool kind of response to anything overwrought or oversold.

12 New York, for example, is duh territory, while Los Angeles is yeah—right. Television commercials can be rendered harmless and inert by simply saying, "yeah, right," upon their conclusion. Local television news reports are helped out with a sprinkling of well-placed duhs, at moments of stunning obviousness. And almost any politician's speech cries out for heaping helpings of both at various moments.

13 Adolescent terms like "like," by contrast, scare me to death. While I have become convinced through observation and personal experimentation that just about any adult of even modest intelligence can figure out how to use duh and yeah right properly, like is different. Like is hard. Like is, like, dangerous.

14 Marcel Danesi, a professor of linguistics and semiotics at the University of Toronto who has studied the language of youth and who coined the term "pubilect" to describe the dialect of pubescence, said he believes like is in fact altering the structure of the English language, making it more fluid in construction, more like Italian or some other Romance language than good old hard-and-fast Anglo-Saxon. Insert like in the middle of a sentence, he said, and a statement can be turned into a question, a question into an exclamation, an exclamation into a quiet meditation.

15 Consider these hypothetical expressions: "If you're having broccoli for dinner, Mr. Johnson, I'm, like, out of here!" and "I was, like, no way!" and perhaps most startlingly, "He was, like, duh!"

16 In the broccoli case, like softens the sentence. It's less harsh and confrontational than saying flatly that the serving of an unpalatable vegetable would require a fleeing of the premises.

17 In the second instance, like functions as a kind of a verbal quotation mark, an announcement that what follows, "no way," is to be heard differently. The quote itself can then be loaded up with any variety of intonation—irony, sarcasm, even self-deprecation—all depending on the delivery.

18 In the third example—"He was, like, duh!"—like becomes a crucial helping verb for duh, a verbal springboard. (Try saying the sentence without like and it becomes almost incomprehensible.)

19 But like and duh and yeah right, aside from their purely linguistic virtues, are also in many ways the perfect words to convey

the sense of reflected reality that is part of the age we live in. Image manipulation, superficiality, and shallow media culture are, for better or worse, the backdrop of adolescent life.

Adults of the yes-or-no era could perhaps grow up firm in their knowledge of what things "are," but in the Age of Duh, with images reflected back from every angle at every waking moment, kids swim in a sea of what things are "like." Distinguishing what is from what merely seems to be is a required skill of an 11-year-old today; like reflects modern life, and duh and yeah right are the tools with which such a life can be negotiated and mastered. 20

But there is a concealed paradox in the Age of Duh. The information overload on which it is based is built around the computer, and the computer is, of course, built around—that's right—the good old yes-or-no binary code: Billions of microcircuits all blinking on or off, black or white, current in or current out. Those computers were designed by minds schooled and steeped in the world of yes or no, and perhaps it is not too much of a stretch to imagine my sons' generation, shaped by the broader view of duh, finding another path: binary code with attitude. Besides, most computers I know already seem to have an attitude. Incorporating a little duh would at least give them a sense of humor. 21

BUILDING VOCABULARY

Here is an essay that pulls in words from the street and from fairly specialized usage to achieve a kind of vigorous appreciation of how we talk.

Rewrite the passages below, substituting synonyms from the appropriate level of diction for the italicized words.

For example, you might change this sentence—"This is a word *much maligned* by *educators, linguistic brahmins and purists,* but they are all quite wrong."—as follows: This is a word *often traduced* by *teachers, snobs and the language police . . .*"

1. Fewer questions these days can effectively be answered with yes or no, while at the same time, *a tidal surge of hype and mindless blather threatens to overwhelm old-fashioned conversation.*
2. And in an era when plain speech has become endangered by the pressures of political correctness, duh and yeah right are *matchless tools of savvy, winking sarcasm and*

skepticism: caustic without being confrontational, incisive without being quite specific.

3. Where duh is *assertive* and *edgy,* a perfect tool for undercutting *mindless understatement or insulting repetition,* yeah right is *laid back, a surfer's cool* kind of response to anything *overwrought or oversold.*

THINKING CRITICALLY ABOUT THE ESSAY

Understanding the Writer's Ideas

1. Why does the writer think that duh and yeah right are "the ideal terms to usher in the millennium"?
2. What are the writer's associations with yes and no?
3. Why are yes and no inadequate today?
4. How are duh and yeah right more supple than yes or no?
5. What are the special uses of duh and yeah right?
6. In contrast to his approval of duh and yeah right, why is the writer "scared to death" by terms like "like"?
7. But the writer quotes the professor of linguistics Marcel Danesi to show the power of like. What is that power, according to Professor Danesi?
8. What other virtues, besides their purely linguistic ones, does the writer attribute to like, duh, and yeah right?
9. The writer ends his essay by identifying a "concealed paradox in the Age of Duh." What is that paradox?

Understanding the Writer's Techniques

1. What is the thesis of this essay? What evidence can you find that the writer anticipates disagreement with if not disbelief in his thesis from his readers?
2. Illustrate how the writer employs comparison and contrast (see Glossary) to show that duh and yeah right are the contemporary replacements of the outmoded yes and no.
3. The writer only once in his essay quotes from an authority to support or advance his argument. Why does he do so?
4. The writer explains the uses and impact of duh and yeah right differently from how he explains like. Why?
5. Explain how the writer's concluding paragraph aptly ties together the themes of the essay.

Exploring the Writer's Ideas

1. The basic premise of this essay is that there is a distinct and fundamental divide between the clunky old industrial age, limited to yes or no, and the complex information age, in need of the supple duh, yeah right, and like. Do you agree that the information age is drastically different from the past? If so, what are its fundamental departures from the past? If not, why not?
2. In parts of this essay, the writer seems to suggest that duh and yeah right are necessary because the information age is more subtle than its late industrial predecessor; but in other parts the writer seems to suggest something more menacing, a new reality of "image manipulation, superficiality, and [shallowness]" (par. 19). Explain why you think these two emphases are either compatible or in tension with one another.
3. Explore the question of whether the language of adolescents has not always been at variance with that of the adult world by reference to the language spoken by famous literary adolescents in previous eras, such as Holden Caulfield in *Catcher in the Rye* by J. D. Salinger or Huck in *Huckleberry Finn* by Mark Twain.
4. "Distinguishing what is from what merely seems to be is a required skill of an 11-year-old today," says Johnson (par. 20). Give some examples to support his observation.

IDEAS FOR WRITING

Prewriting

Can you think of some words commonly used by adolescents that fit experience better than the more formal words adults might use? Make a list of some words of that kind, and briefly explain how the word is used.

Guided Writing

Write an essay contrasting the way some words commonly used by adolescents *either* convey certain meanings better than the more formal diction of adults *or* less effectively than the words that would be used by adults.

1. Begin with a thesis statement that identifies the words you are going to talk about, and states why these words are better or worse than those of the past.
2. Give a brief sociological sketch differentiating the past and the present, with the intention of using this contrast to support your thesis.
3. Offer a general explanation of why the words you are discussing are well-suited to convey the new reality of the present *or* are not as good at conveying our experience than the older words.
4. Illustrate your general point by reference to one or two examples, and then briefly analyze these examples to underscore your thesis.
5. Restate your contrast between past and present in light of your examples.
6. Write a conclusion that takes your examples into account and indirectly restates your thesis.

Thinking and Writing Collaboratively

In groups of four or five create lists of words that you think are especially characteristic of the speech of your peers. Then ask people of different ages to explain the uses of these words, keeping a careful record of their explanations. Reconvene and analyze what you have discovered.

More Writing Projects

1. Choose a few "everyday" words and trace their use over time, both by reference to an etymological dictionary and through examples from newspapers or stories and novels. Write notes toward an essay about your findings.
2. Write an essay that explains why you are especially fond of certain words or expressions. Choose words or expressions that are both casual (slang) and more formal.
3. Copy one or two sentences, or certain key words or phrases from the opening pages of one great American novel of the eighteenth, nineteenth, and twentieth centuries. Write a few paragraphs that begin to compare and contrast these sentences, words, or phrases as they are used in these works, and thus in their time.

SUMMING UP: CHAPTER 7

1. In her essay on fun in this chapter, Suzanne Britt Jordan defines a term we all understand but might have difficulty explaining. One way she approaches this definition is through negation—that is, explaining what fun *is not.* Write an essay that defines by negation a similar, understood but difficult-to-explain term—for example "privacy," "the blues," "class," "happiness," or "success."
2. Both Gloria Naylor and Janice Castro define words that relate to values placed on language within an ethnic community. Think of a word that has troubled you or been used against you in your early life. It might be a word you associate, for example, with ethnicity, economic status, or personal appearance. Write an essay in which you define this word, considering both how the people who aimed it meant it to be interpreted and how an outsider might define it.
3. Gloria Naylor argues that a word is defined by "consensus." That is, a community agrees among its members on how the word will be used, despite outside definitions. On your campus find examples of current words, defined by "consensus" in the college community, whose meanings would be surprising to outsiders like your parents.
4. Is there a contradiction between Naylor's view of definition by "consensus" and Johnson's view of certain new usages that seems to go contrary to consensus? Johnson's essay aims to show how language evolves and changes constructively in response to new social realities. Is he offering a persuasive account of how definitions change or is he paying undue attention to passing fads? Write an essay that compares two words, one which was commonly used in the slang of the near past but has vanished from the language, and one that has assumed a "permanent" place in the dictionary.
5. Look back over the titles of all the essays in this chapter and previous chapters of this book. Choose one term from any title (for example, "All-American Girl," "Salvation," or "Night Walker"), and write an essay defining that term *subjectively* (from a personal viewpoint).

CHAPTER 8

Classification

WHAT IS CLASSIFICATION?

Classification is the arrangement of information into groups or categories in order to make clear the relations among members of the group. In a supermarket, the soups are together in one aisle, the frozen foods in another. In a record, tape, and disc store, all the jazz is in one section while the rap music is in a separate section. You wouldn't expect to find a can of tomato soup next to the butter pecan ice cream any more than you'd look for a CD of George Gershwin's *An American in Paris* in the same section as a CD by Ice-T.

Writers need to classify, because it helps them present a mass of material by means of some orderly system. Related bits of information seem clearer when presented together as parts of a group. Unlike writing narrative, for example, developing classification requires a different level of analysis and planning. The writer not only presents a single topic or event, but also places the subject into a complex network of relations. In a narrative, we can tell the story of a single event from start to finish, such as the time we saw a Van Gogh painting in an art museum. In classification, we have to think beyond the personal experience to try to place that Van Gogh painting in a wider context. Where does Van Gogh "fit" in the history of painting? Why is he different from other painters? How does his style relate to other work of the same period? In pursuing these questions, we seek not only to *record* our experience in looking at the painting but to *understand* it more fully.

Classification, then, begins by thinking about a body of material and trying to break it down into distinct parts, or categories.

Called *division* or *analysis,* this first task helps split an idea or object into usable components. Then, some of the parts can serve as categories into which the writer can fit individual pieces that share some common qualities.

For example, if the writer wanted to *analyze* the Van Gogh painting, she might begin with the large subject of painting. Then she could *divide,* or break the subject down, into two groups.

traditional painting
modern painting

Then, she could further *divide* the types of modern painting:

impressionist
postimpressionist
fauvist
art nouveau
cubist
art deco
abstract expressionist
op art
minimalist art

The purpose is to determine what the parts of the whole are. If we know what the components of *modern painting* are, then we can place or locate the Van Gogh painting in relation to other paintings. We would know whether it belonged in the soup aisle or the freezer section, so to speak. In this case, we would decide that it is *not* traditional painting, so that we would separate it from that group. We would place it in the modern group. Now we know which aisle it belongs in. But is it tomato or chicken soup? Now we relate it to the other modern types of painting, and place it in the postimpressionist group. Our decision is based on an analysis of the painter's use of color, his style, and the ways he differs from painters in the other groups.

Our analysis does not mean that the Van Gogh has nothing in common with traditional painting. Van Gogh, for instance, shares an interest in landscape and self-portraits with Rembrandt. But the bright, bold colors of his *Starry Night* are so dramatically different from the somber colors of the older Dutch painter's *Nightwatch* that we are inclined to emphasize their *division.* We could, for instance, set up a supermarket on the basis of what color the food labels were: all the red labels in one aisle, all the yellow labels together. But such a system would make it much harder to find what we wanted unless we were experts in package design. Similarly, our classification of painting is based on the most sensible method of division.

In this chapter, Judith Viorst classifies friends into eight groups, and even numbers them to make it is easy to follow her divisions. E. B. White analyzes three New Yorks, first separating its various strands for a close look at the city, but then weaving them back together to create the "whole" city he loved so much. James T. Baker brings together a variety of writing techniques to analyze the world of education with some humor. William Golding tells how he discovered there are three distinct grades of thinkers. Each writer has a different purpose for classification, but each uses the same basic system of organization.

HOW DO WE READ CLASSIFICATION?

Reading classification involves the following steps:

- Identify what the author is classifying. Find the thesis to determine what the purpose or basis of the classification is.
- Make an outline of the essay. Find the divisions and the classifications into which the author has sorted the subject.
- Determine whether the categories are clearly defined. Do they overlap?
- Be alert for stereotypes. Has the author used them in order to build the groups? If so, see if the groups are oversimplified and thus unreliable.
- Identify the intended audience. How do we know who the audience is?

HOW DO WE WRITE CLASSIFICATION?

The four essayists in this chapter should provide you with enough examples of how to classify to make your writing task easy. Classification resembles outlining. Whether the subject is personal, technical, simple, complex, or abstract, the writer can organize material into categories, and can move carefully from one category to another in developing an essay.

Select your topic and begin to separate it into categories. Try drawing a tree with branches or use a model from a biology book that shows the division of life into genus, species, phyla, and so on. Or make lists. Think about how your library classifies books. Arranging books by the color of the covers might look attractive, but it would presume that all library users already knew what a book looked like before they came to the library. Instead, libraries divide books by type. They generally begin with two large groups: fiction and nonfiction. Within these categories, they create small ones: English fiction, Mexican fiction, Australian fiction. Within nonfiction, they divide books into history, religion, geography, mathematics, and so on. In this way, a reader can find a book based on need, and not prior knowledge. Keeping the library in mind, make a list of categories for your topic.

Make an outline and arrange the groups to avoid overlap from one group to the next.

Decide on a system of classification. Don't force objects into arbitrary slots, though. Don't ignore differences that violate your categories. Try to create a legitimate system that avoids stereotyping or oversimplification; don't classify invalidly. Be sure your categories are legitimate.

Write a thesis that identifies the purpose of your system of classification. Think of the ways in which your system can broaden a reader's understanding of the subject rather than narrow it.

Sample thesis statement:

> At least three groups of immigrants reach the United States today—political refugees seeking asylum, economic refugees looking for a better life, and religious dissidents looking for freedom to practice their chosen beliefs.

Writing the Draft

Write a rough draft. Be sure that you explain the categories and give examples for each one.

For each category, use definition, description, illustration, or narrative to help the reader see the distinct nature of the division you have created. Use transitions between each category or group.

Proofread for correctness. Make a final copy.

A STUDENT PARAGRAPH: CLASSIFICATION

The student who wrote the following paragraph considered the sample thesis statement on immigration appearing earlier, and then modified it to suit her approach to the topic. Observe her various strategies for paragraph development, especially the way she subdivides the last of her categories.

Americans have mixed feelings about immigrants; they tend to judge different categories of immigrants—illegal aliens, poor immigrants, and political or religious refugees—very differently. Illegal aliens encounter the greatest degree of hostility, despite the fact that U.S. citizens often benefit from their work as maids, gardeners, and street vendors. The second category of immigrants, poor people who are here legally but who are looking to improve their standards of living, also tend to encounter some hostility from Americans. These immigrants, according to some Americans, compete for low-level jobs, go on welfare, and strain such social services as schools and hospitals. By contrast, Americans are usually more welcoming to political and religious refugees. For one thing, political refugees and religious dissidents are fewer in number, which automatically makes them less threatening. In addition, whether from Cuba, Iran, or the former Soviet Union, they are often better educated and wealthier than the illegal aliens and economic refugees, so they are perceived as less of a drain on resources. Undoubtedly, too, they receive a warmer welcome from many Americans because of the belief that their aims are "nobler" than those of illegal aliens or economic refugees, because they flee their homelands to maintain political and religious ideals, rather than simply to make more money.

Thesis statement announces classification scheme

First category with brief examples

Second category with greater detail.

Transition "By contrast," introduces third category, further subdivided into two subcategories

Evidence supports position

Friends, Good Friends—and Such Good Friends

Judith Viorst

In this essay Judith Viorst, who writes for numerous popular magazines, examines types of friends in her life. Her pattern of development is easy to follow, because she tends to stay on one level in the process of classification. As you read this essay, try to keep in mind the similarities and distinctions that Viorst makes among types of friends, as well as the principles of classification that she uses.

PREREADING: THINKING ABOUT THE ESSAY IN ADVANCE

Take a few moments to think about the types of friends that play various roles in your life. How many distinct varieties of friends can you identify? Do you act differently with each type or have different expectations? How does each type of friend make you feel?

Words to Watch

nonchalant (par. 3) showing an easy unconcern or disinterest
endodontist (par. 14) a dentist specializing in diseases of dental pulp and root canals
sibling (par. 16) brother or sister
dormant (par. 19) as if asleep; inactive
self-revelation (par. 22) self-discovery; self-disclosure
calibrated (par. 29) measured; fixed; checked carefully

Women are friends, I once would have said, when they totally love and support and trust each other, and bare to each other the secrets of their souls, and run—no questions asked—to help each other, and tell harsh truths to each other (no, you can't wear that dress unless you lose ten pounds first) when harsh truths must be told. 1

Women are friends, I once would have said, when they share the same affection for Ingmar Bergman, plus train rides, 2 cats, warm rain, charades, Camus, and hate with equal ardor Newark and Brussels sprouts and Lawrence Welk and camping.

3 In other words, I once would have said that a friend is a friend all the way, but now I believe that's a narrow point of view. For the friendships I have and the friendships I see are conducted at many levels of intensity, serve many different functions, meet different needs and range from those as all-the-way as the friendship of the soul sisters mentioned above to that of the most nonchalant and casual playmates.

4 Consider these varieties of friendship:

5 1. Convenience friends. These are the women with whom, if our paths weren't crossing all the time, we'd have no particular reason to be friends: a next-door neighbor, a woman in our car pool, the mother of one of our children's closest friends or maybe some mommy with whom we serve juice and cookies each week at the Glenwood Co-op Nursery.

6 Convenience friends are convenient indeed. They'll lend us their cups and silverware for a party. They'll drive our kids to soccer when we're sick. They'll take us to pick up our car when we need a lift to the garage. They'll even take our cats when we go on vacation. As we will for them.

7 But we don't, with convenience friends, ever come too close or tell too much; we maintain our public face and emotional distance. "Which means," says Elaine, "that I'll talk about being overweight but not about being depressed. Which means I'll admit being mad but not blind with rage. Which means I might say that we're pinched this month but never that I'm worried sick over money."

8 But which doesn't mean that there isn't sufficient value to be found in these friendships of mutual aid, in convenience friends.

9 2. Special-interest friends. These friendships aren't intimate, and they needn't involve kids or silverware or cats. Their value lies in some interest jointly shared. And so we may have an office friend or a yoga friend or a tennis friend or a friend from the Women's Democratic Club.

10 "I've got one woman friend," says Joyce, "who likes, as I do, to take psychology courses. Which makes it nice for me—and nice for her. It's fun to go with someone you know and it's fun to discuss what you've learned, driving back from the classes." And for the most part, she says, that's all they discuss.

11 "I'd say that what we're doing is *doing* together, not being together," Suzanne says of her Tuesday-doubles friends. "It's

mainly a tennis relationship, but we play together well. And I guess we all need to have a couple of playmates."

I agree. 12

My playmate is a shopping friend, a woman of marvelous taste, a woman who knows exactly *where* to buy *what,* and furthermore is a woman who always knows beyond a doubt what one ought to be buying. I don't have the time to keep up with what's new in eyeshadow, hemlines and shoes and whether the smock look is in or finished already. But since (oh, shame!) I care a lot about eyeshadow, hemlines and shoes, and since I don't *want* to wear smocks if the smock look is finished, I'm very glad to have a shopping friend. 13

3. Historical friends. We all have a friend who knew us when . . . maybe way back in Miss Meltzer's second grade, when our family lived in that three-room flat in Brooklyn, when our dad was out of work for seven months, when our brother Allie got in that fight where they had to call the police, when our sister married the endodontist from Yonkers and when, the morning after we lost our virginity, she was the first, the only, friend we told. 14

The years have gone by and we've gone separate ways and we've little in common now, but we're still an intimate part of each other's past. And so whenever we go to Detroit we always go to visit this friend of our girlhood. Who knows how we looked before our teeth were straightened. Who knows how we talked before our voice got unBrooklyned. Who knows what we ate before we learned about artichokes. And who, by her presence, puts us in touch with an earlier part of ourself, a part of ourself it's important never to lose. 15

"What this friend means to me and what I mean to her," says Grace, "is having a sister without sibling rivalry. We know the texture of each other's lives. She remembers my grandmother's cabbage soup. I remember the way her uncle played the piano. There's simply no other friend who remembers those things." 16

4. Crossroads friends. Like historical friends, our crossroads friends are important for *what was*—for the friendship we shared at a crucial, now past, time of life. A time, perhaps, when we roomed in college together; or worked as eager young singles in the Big City together; or went together, as my friend Elizabeth and I did through pregnancy, birth and that scary first year of new motherhood. 17

18 Crossroads friends forge powerful links, links strong enough to endure with not much more contact than once-a-year letters at Christmas. And out of respect for those crossroads years, for those dramas and dreams we once shared, we will always be friends.

19 5. Cross-generational friends. Historical friends and crossroads friends seem to maintain a special kind of intimacy—dormant but always ready to be revived—and though we may rarely meet, whenever we do connect, it's personal and intense. Another kind of intimacy exists in the friendships that form across generations in what one woman calls her daughter-mother and her mother-daughter relationships.

20 Evelyn's friend is her mother's age—"but I share so much more than I ever could with my mother"—a woman she talks to of music, of books and of life. "What I get from her is the benefit of her experience. What she gets—and enjoys—from me is a youthful perspective. It's a pleasure for both of us."

21 I have in my own life a precious friend, a woman of 65 who has lived very hard, who is wise, who listens well; who has been where I am and can help me understand it; and who represents not only an ultimate ideal mother to me but also the person I'd like to be when I grow up.

22 In our daughter role we tend to do more than our share of self-revelation; in our mother role we tend to receive what's revealed. It's another kind of pleasure—playing wise mother to a questing younger person. It's another very lovely kind of friendship.

23 6. Part-of-a-couple friends. Some of the women we call our friends we never see alone—we see them as part of a couple at couples' parties. And though we share interests in many things and respect each other's views, we aren't moved to deepen the relationship. Whatever the reason, a lack of time or—and this is more likely—a lack of chemistry, our friendship remains in the context of a group. But the fact that our feeling on seeing each other is always, "I'm *so* glad she's here" and the fact that we spend half the evening talking together says that this too, in its own way, counts as a friendship.

24 (Other part-of-a-couple friends are the friends that came with the marriage, and some of these are friends we could live without. But sometimes, alas, she married our husband's best friend; and sometimes, alas, she *is* our husband's best friend. And so we find ourself dealing with her, somewhat against our will, in a spirit of what I'll call *reluctant* friendship.)

7. Men who are friends. I wanted to write just of women friends, but the women I've talked to won't let me—they say I must mention man-woman friendships too. For these friendships can be just as close and as dear as those that we form with women. Listen to Lucy's description of one such friendship: 25

"We've found we have things to talk about that are different from what he talks about with my husband and different from what I talk about with his wife. So sometimes we call on the phone or meet for lunch. There are similar intellectual interests—we always pass on to each other the books that we love—but there's also something tender and caring too." 26

In a couple of crises, Lucy says, "he offered himself, for talking and for helping. And when someone died in his family he wanted me there. The sexual, flirty part of our friendship is very small, but *some*—just enough to make it fun and different." She thinks—and I agree—that the sexual part, though small, is always *some,* is always there when a man and a woman are friends. 27

It's only in the past few years that I've made friends with men, in the sense of a friendship that's *mine,* not just part of two couples. And achieving with them the ease and the trust I've found with women friends has value indeed. Under the dryer at home last week, putting on mascara and rouge, I comfortably sat and talked with a fellow named Peter. Peter, I finally decided, could handle the shock of me minus mascara under the dryer. Because we care for each other. Because we're friends. 28

8. There are medium friends, and pretty good friends, and very good friends indeed, and these friendships are defined by their level of intimacy. And what we'll reveal at each of these levels of intimacy is calibrated with care. We might tell a medium friend, for example, that yesterday we had a fight with our husband. And we might tell a pretty good friend that this fight with our husband made us so mad that we slept on the couch. And we might tell a very good friend that the reason we got so mad in that fight that we slept on the couch had something to do with that girl who works in his office. But it's only to our very best friends that we're willing to tell all, to tell what's going on with that girl in his office. 29

The best of friends, I still believe, totally love and support and trust each other, and bare to each other the secrets of their souls, and run—no questions asked—to help each other, and tell harsh truths to each other when they must be told. 30

But we needn't agree about everything (only 12-year-old girl friends agree about *everything*) to tolerate each other's point 31 of view. To accept without judgment. To give and to take without ever keeping score. And to *be* there, as I am for them and as they are for me, to comfort our sorrows, to celebrate our joys.

BUILDING VOCABULARY

1. Find *antonyms* (words that mean the opposite of given words) for the following entries.
   - **a.** harsh (par. 1)
   - **b.** mutual (par. 8)
   - **c.** crucial (par. 17)
   - **d.** intimacy (par. 29)
   - **e.** tolerate (par. 31)
2. The *derivation* of a word—how it originated and where it came from—can make you more aware of meanings. Your dictionary normally lists abbreviations (for instance, L. for Latin, Fr. for French) for word origins, and sometimes explains fully the way a word came into use. Look up the following words to determine their origins.
   - **a.** psychology (par. 10)
   - **b.** historical (par. 14)
   - **c.** sibling (par. 16)
   - **d.** Christmas (par. 18)
   - **e.** sexual (par. 27)

THINKING CRITICALLY ABOUT THE ESSAY

Understanding the Writer's Ideas

1. What is Viorst's definition of friendship in the first two paragraphs? Does she accept this definition? Why or why not?
2. Name and describe in your own words the types of friends that Viorst mentions in her essay.
3. In what way are "convenience friends" and "special-interest friends" alike? How are "historical friends" and "crossroads friends" alike?
4. What does Viorst mean when she writes, "In our daughter role we tend to do more than our share of self-revelation; in our mother role we tend to receive what's revealed" (par. 22)?

5. How do part-of-a-couple friends who came with the marriage differ from primary part-of-a-couple friends?
6. Does Viorst think that men can be friends for women? Why or why not? What complicates such friendships?
7. For Viorst, who are the best friends?

Understanding the Writer's Techniques

1. Which paragraphs make up the introduction in this essay? How does Viorst organize these paragraphs? Where does she place her thesis sentence?
2. How does the thesis sentence reveal the principles of classification (the questions Viorst asks to produce the various categories) that the author employs in the essay?
3. Does Viorst seem to emphasize each of her categories equally? Is she effective in handling each category? Why or why not? Do you think that men belong in the article as a category? For what reasons?
4. Analyze the importance of illustration in this essay. From what sources does Viorst tend to draw her examples?
5. How do definition and comparison and contrast operate in the essay? Cite specific examples of these techniques.
6. The level of language in this essay tends to be informal at times, reflecting patterns that are as close to conversation as to formal writing. Identify some sentences that seem to resemble informal speech. Why does Viorst try to achieve a conversational style?
7. Which main group in the essay is further broken down into categories?
8. Analyze Viorst's conclusion. How many paragraphs are involved? What strategies does she use? How does she achieve balanced sentence structure (parallelism) in her last lines?

Exploring the Writer's Ideas

1. Do you accept all of Viorst's categories of friendship? Which categories seem the most meaningful to you?
2. Try to think of people you know who fit into the various categories established by Viorst. Can you think of people who might exist in more than one category? How do you explain this fact? What are the dangers in trying to stereotype people in terms of categories, roles, backgrounds, or functions?

3. Viorst maintains that you can define friends in terms of functions and needs (see paragraph 3 and paragraphs 29 to 31). Would you agree? Why or why not? What principle or principles do you use to classify friends? In fact, *do* you classify friends? For what reasons?

IDEAS FOR WRITING

Prewriting

Select a specific category of people—for example, teachers, friends, or family members—and freewrite for fifteen minutes about the characteristics of each type within the group.

Guided Writing

Using the classification method, write an essay on a specific group of individuals—for instance, types of friends, types of enemies, types of students, types of teachers, types of politicians, types of dates.

1. Establish your subject in the first paragraph. Also indicate to the reader the principle(s) of classification that you plan to use. (For guidelines look again at the second sentence in paragraph 3 of Viorst's essay.)
2. Start the body of the essay with a single short sentence that introduces categories, as Viorst does in paragraph 4. In the body, use numbers and category headings ("Convenience friends" . . . "Special-interest friends") to separate groups.
3. Try to achieve a balance in the presentation of information on each category. Define each type and provide appropriate examples.
4. If helpful, use comparison and contrast to indicate from time to time the similarities and differences among groups. Try to avoid too much overlapping of groups, since this is harmful to the classification process.
5. Employ the personal "I" and other conversational techniques to achieve an informal style.
6. Return to your principle(s) of classification and amplify this feature in your conclusion. If you want, make a value judgment, as Viorst does, about which type of person in your classification scheme is the most significant.

Thinking and Writing Collaboratively

Form groups of three or four, and have each group member draw a diagram showing the types of teachers they have encountered in school and college. Then, discuss the various divisions and try to develop one combined diagram. Finally, present your findings to the class.

More Writing Projects

1. As journal practice, classify varieties of show business comedians, singers, talk-show hosts, star athletes, or the like.
2. In a paragraph, use division and (or) classification to explain the various roles that you must play as a friend.
3. Ask each student in your class to explain what he or she means by the term "friendship." List all responses and then divide the list into at least three categories. Using your notes, write a classification essay reporting your findings.

The Three New Yorks

E. B. White

E. B. White, whose frequently used book *The Elements of Style* is well known to college composition students, here classifies "The Three New Yorks." Although the selection is an excerpt from his book *Here Is New York* (1949), the descriptive illustrations remain remarkably fresh after more than fifty years. Look closely at the way White clearly defines his categories of classification, then skillfully blends them to create a vivid sense of the whole city.

PREREADING: THINKING ABOUT THE ESSAY IN ADVANCE

As you prepare to read White's essay, take a few minutes to think about the place where you live or, if you have lived in several locations, the place that you know best. What is the place like? Are there different classes of people in this place or different parts with specific features or functions? How would you divide the place in terms of people, sections, and functions?

Words to Watch

locusts (par. 1) migratory grasshoppers that travel in swarms, stripping vegetation as they pass over the land

disposition (par. 1) temperament; way of acting

deportment (par. 1) the way in which a person carries himself or herself

tidal (par. 1) coming in wavelike motions

continuity (par. 1) uninterrupted flow of events

slum (par. 1) a highly congested residential area marked by unsanitary buildings, poverty, and social disorder

indignity (par. 1) humiliating treatment

vitality (par. 2) lively and animated character

gloaming (par. 2) a poetic term for "twilight"

ramparts (par. 2) high, broad structures guarding a building

negligently (par. 2) nonchalantly; neglectfully

loiterer (par. 2) a person who hangs around aimlessly

spewing (par. 2) coming in a flood or gush

rover (par. 2) wanderer; roamer

1 There are roughly three New Yorks. There is, first, the New York of the man or woman who was born here, who takes the city for granted and accepts its size and its turbulence as natural and inevitable. Second, there is the New York of the commuter—the city that is devoured by locusts each day and spat out each night. Third, there is the New York of the person who was born somewhere else and came to New York in quest of something. Of these three trembling cities the greatest is the last—the city of final destination, the city that is a goal. It is this third city that accounts for New York's high-strung disposition, its poetical deportment, its dedication to the arts, and its incomparable achievements. Commuters give the city its tidal restlessness; natives give it solidity and continuity; but the settlers give it passion. And whether it is a farmer arriving from Italy to set up a small grocery store in a slum, or a young girl arriving from a small town in Mississippi to escape the indignity of being observed by her neighbors, or a boy arriving from the Corn Belt with a manuscript in his suitcase and a pain in his heart, it makes no difference; each embraces New York with the intense excitement of first love, each absorbs New York with the fresh eyes of an adventurer, each generates heat and light to dwarf the Consolidated Edison Company.

2 The commuter is the queerest bird of all. The suburb he inhabits has no essential vitality of its own and is a mere roost where he comes at day's end to go to sleep. Except in rare cases, the man who lives in Mamaroneck or Little Neck or Teaneck, and works in New York, discovers nothing much about the city except the time of arrival and departure of trains and buses, and the path to a quick lunch. He is deskbound, and has never, idly roaming in the gloaming, stumbled suddenly on Belvedere Tower in the Park, seen the ramparts rise sheer from the water of the pond, and the boys along the shore fishing for minnows, girls stretched out negligently on the shelves of the rocks; he has never come suddenly on anything at all in New York as a loiterer, because he has had no time between trains. He has fished in Manhattan's wallet and dug out coins, but has never listened to Manhattan's breathing, never awakened to its morning, never dropped off to sleep in its night. About 400,000 men and women come charging onto the Island each week-day morning, out of the mouths of tubes and tunnels. Not many among them have ever spent a drowsy afternoon in the great rustling oaken silence of the reading room of the Public Library,

with the book elevator (like an old water wheel) spewing out books onto the trays. They tend their furnaces in Westchester and in Jersey, but have never seen the furnaces of the Bowery, the fires that burn in oil drums on zero winter nights. They may work in the financial district downtown and never see the extravagant plantings of Rockefeller Center—the daffodils and grape hyacinths and birches of the flags trimmed to the wind on a fine morning in spring. Or they may work in a midtown office and may let a whole year swing round without sighting Governor's Island from the sea wall. The commuter dies with tremendous mileage to his credit, but he is no rover. His entrances and exits are more devious than those in a prairie-dog village; and he calmly plays bridge while his train is buried in the mud at the bottom of the East River. The Long Island Rail Road alone carried forty million commuters last year; but many of them were the same fellow retracing his steps.

3 The terrain of New York is such that a resident sometimes travels farther, in the end, than a commuter. The journey of the composer Irving Berlin from Cherry Street in the lower East Side to an apartment uptown was through an alley and was only three or four miles in length; but it was like going three times around the world.

BUILDING VOCABULARY

1. Underline the numerous references in this essay to buildings, people, and areas in and around New York City and identify them. If necessary, consult a guidebook, map, or history of New York City for help.
2. Write *synonyms* (words that mean the same) for each of these words in the essay. Use a dictionary if necessary.
   a. turbulence (par. 1)
   b. inevitable (par. 1)
   c. quest (par. 1)
   d. high-strung (par. 1)
   e. incomparable (par. 1)
   f. essential (par. 2)
   g. deskbound (par. 2)
   h. drowsy (par. 2)
   i. extravagant (par. 2)
   j. devious (par. 2)

THINKING CRITICALLY ABOUT THE ESSAY

Understanding the Writer's Ideas

1. What are the three New Yorks?
2. What single-word designation does E. B. White assign to each of the three types of New Yorkers? Match up each of the three New Yorks you identified in the first question with each of the three types of New Yorkers.
3. For what reasons do people born elsewhere come to New York to live? What three illustrations of such people does White describe? What is the young girl's indignity? What is the occupation or hope of the boy from the Corn Belt? Why might he have "a pain in his heart"?
4. What does each type of New Yorker give to the city?
5. What is White's attitude toward the suburbs? What key phrases reveal this attitude?
6. What are some of the things commuters miss about New York by dashing in and out of the city? What does White ironically suggest will be the commuter's final fate?
7. Are we to take literally White's conclusion that "many of them were the same fellow retracing his steps"? Why or why not?
8. Explain the sentence "The terrain of New York is such that a resident sometimes travels farther, in the end, than a commuter." Be aware that White is using language figuratively.
9. The author tells of composer Irving Berlin's journey through an alley. He is referring to "Tin Pan Alley." Identify this place.

Understanding the Writer's Techniques

1. In this essay what is the thesis? Where is it? Is it developed fully?
2. What is the purpose of classification in this essay? What is the basis of the classification White uses? What key words at the beginning of paragraph 1 direct your attention to each category discussed? How do these key words contrast in tone with the descriptions in the first few sentences? What sort of rhythm is established?
3. White vividly *personifies* (see Glossary) New York City in paragraph 1. List and explain the effects of these personifications. Where else does he personify?

4. Refer to your answers to question 2 in the Building Vocabulary section. Are the literal meanings of those words appropriate to White's three types of New Yorkers? Defend your answer. Figuratively, what does each term make you think of? How do the figurative meanings enhance the essay?
5. How does White use *illustration* in this essay? Where does he use it most effectively?
6. What is the function of *negation* (see page 235) in the first part of paragraph 2? What is the *implied contrast* in this paragraph?
7. How is White's attitude toward New York reflected in the *tone* (see Glossary) of this essay?
8. White makes widespread use of *metaphor* (see Glossary) in this essay. How does his use of metaphor affect the tone of the essay? State in your own words the meaning of each of the following metaphors.
    a. the city that is devoured by locusts each day and spat out each night (par. 1)
    b. The commuter is the queerest bird of all. (par. 2)
    c. a mere roost (par. 2)
    d. idly roaming in the gloaming (par. 2)
    e. He has fished in Manhattan's wallet and dug out coins, but has never listened to Manhattan's breathing (par. 2)
    f. the great rustling oaken silence (par. 2)
9. Among all the metaphors, White uses just one *simile* (see Glossary). What is it? What is the effect of placing it where he did?

Exploring the Writer's Ideas

1. At the beginning of the essay, E. B. White states that New York's "turbulence" is considered "natural and inevitable" by its native residents. But such a condition is true for any large city. If you live in a large city, or if you have ever visited one, what are some examples of its turbulence? Do you think it is always a good idea to accept the disorder of the place where you live? How can such acceptance be a positive attitude? How can it be negative? How do you deal with disruptions in your environment?
2. White writes of "a young girl arriving from a small town in Mississippi to escape the indignity of being observed by her neighbors." Tell in your own words what might cause her indignity. How can neighbors bring about such a condition?

3. Some people feel that the anonymity of a big city like New York makes it easier just to "be yourself" without having to worry about what others might say. Others feel such anonymity creates a terrible feeling of impersonality. Discuss the advantages and disadvantages of each attitude.
4. Do you agree that the suburbs have "no essential vitality"? Explain your response by referring to suburbs you have visited, have read about, or have inhabited.
5. White claims that those who choose to leave their homes and who come to live in New York give the place a special vitality. Do you know any people who chose to leave their places of birth to live in a large city like New York? Why did they move? How have things gone for them since they began living in the city? Have you noticed any changes? For what reasons do people leave one place to live in another? When have you moved from place to place? Why?

IDEAS FOR WRITING

Prewriting

Write "The Three __________" at the top of a sheet of paper, and fill in the blank with the name of the town or city where you live. Below the title, draw a diagram or visual presentation in which you establish and label at least three distinct types of people in your community.

Guided Writing

Organize a classification essay around the city or town in which you live.

1. Begin with a simple direct thesis statement that tells the reader how many categories of classification you will consider.
2. Briefly outline the different categories. Indicate each with a key organizational word or phrase.
3. Indicate which category is the most important. Tell why.
4. Develop this category with at least three vivid illustrations.
5. Define one of the categories through both negation and an implied contrast to another category.
6. Use figurative language (metaphors, similes, personification) throughout your essay.

7. Use specific name or place references.
8. End your essay with a brief factual narrative that gives the reader a feel for your town or city.

Thinking and Writing Collaboratively

Exchange your classification essay with a class member. Then assess the accuracy of your classmate's division of her or his subject into categories. Underline the subdivisions within the paper. Check to see that there is no overlap or omission of key categories. Recommend revisions, if any, and make any appropriate revisions suggested by your partner to your own paper.

More Writing Projects

1. Use classification in a journal entry to capture at least three ways of viewing your college.
2. Write a classification paragraph on the suburbs or the country.
3. Select a cultural group and classify in an essay various characteristics common to that group. Be careful to avoid stereotyping.

How Do We Find the Student in a World of Academic Gymnasts and Worker Ants?

James T. Baker

As you look around your classrooms, school cafeteria, lecture halls, or gymnasium, perhaps you will recognize representatives of the types of students that James Baker classifies in this witty, wry essay. The author enhances his unique categories by using description, definition, and colloquial language, which help make his deliberate stereotypes come alive.

PREREADING: THINKING ABOUT THE ESSAY IN ADVANCE

Prior to reading this essay, think about the different types of students you have encountered and the forms of behavior distinguishing one from the other. Does each type behave in a predictable way? Which category would you place yourself in? Which types do you prefer or associate with, and why?

Words to Watch

musings (par. 3) dreamy, abstract thoughts

sabbatical (par. 3) a paid leave from a job earned after a certain period of time

malaise (par. 3) uneasiness; feelings of restlessness

impaired (par. 3) made less effective

clones (par. 4) exact biological replicas, asexually produced

recuperate (par. 5) to undergo recovery from an illness

esoteric (par. 7) understood by a limited group with special knowledge

primeval (par. 7) primitive; relating to the earliest ages

mundane (par. 8) ordinary

jaded (par. 20) exhausted; bored by something from overexposure to it

Anatole France once wrote that "the whole art of teaching is only the art of awakening the natural curiosity of young minds." I fully agree, except I have to wonder if, by using the word "only," he 1 thought that the art of awakening such natural curiosity was an easy job. For me, it never has been—sometimes exciting, always challenging, but definitely not easy.

2 Robert M. Hutchins used to say that a good education prepares students to go on educating themselves throughout their lives. A fine definition, to be sure, but it has at times made me doubt that my own students, who seem only too eager to graduate so they can lay down their books forever, are receiving a good education.

3 But then maybe these are merely the pessimistic musings of someone suffering from battle fatigue. I have almost qualified for my second sabbatical leave, and I am scratching a severe case of the seven-year itch. About the only power my malaise has not impaired is my eye for spotting certain "types" of students. In fact, as the rest of me declines, my eye seems to grow more acute.

4 Has anyone else noticed that the very same students people college classrooms year after year? Has anyone else found the same bodies, faces, personalities returning semester after semester? Forgive me for violating my students' individual "personhoods," but reality makes it so tempting to see them as types. Doubtless you will recognize at least some of them. They have twins, or perhaps clones, on your campus, too.

5 There is the eternal Good Time Charlie (or Charlene), who makes every party on and off the campus, who by November of his freshman year has worked his face into a case of terminal acne, who misses every set of examinations because of "mono," who finally burns himself out physically and mentally by the age of 19 and drops out to go home and recuperate, and who returns at 20 after a long talk with Dad to major in accounting.

6 There is the Young General Patton, the one who comes to college on an R.O.T.C. scholarship and for a year twirls his rifle at basketball games while loudly sniffing out pinko professors, who at midpoint takes a sudden but predictable, radical swing from far right to far left, who grows a beard and moves in with a girl who refuses to shave her legs, who then makes the just as predictable, radical swing back to the right and ends up preaching fundamentalist sermons on the steps of the student union while the Good Time Charlies and Charlenes jeer.

7 There is the Egghead, the campus intellectual who shakes up his fellow students—and even a professor or two—with references to esoteric formulas and obscure Bulgarian poets, who is recognized by friend and foe alike as a promising young academic,

someday to be a professional scholar, who disappears every summer for six weeks ostensibly to search for primeval human remains in Colorado caves, and who at 37 is shot dead by Arab terrorists while on a mission for the C.I.A.

There is the Performer—the music or theater major, the rock or folk singer—who spends all of his or her time working up an act, who gives barely a nod to mundane subjects like history, sociology, or physics, who dreams only of the day he or she will be on stage full time, praised by critics, cheered by audiences, who ends up either pregnant or responsible for a pregnancy and at 30 is either an insurance salesman or a housewife with a very lush garden. 8

There is the Jock, of course—the every-afternoon intramural champ, smelling of liniment and Brut, with bulging calves and a blue eyed twinkle, the subject of untold numbers of female fantasies, the walking personification of he-manism—who upon graduation is granted managerial rank by a California bank because of his golden tan and low golf score, who is seen five years later buying the drinks at a San Francisco gay bar. 9

There is the Academic Gymnast—the guy or gal who sees college as an obstacle course, as so many stumbling blocks in the way of a great career or a perfect marriage—who strains every moment to finish and be done with "this place" forever, who toward the end of the junior year begins to slow down, to grow quieter and less eager to leave, who attends summer school, but never quite finishes those last six hours, who never leaves "this place," and who at 40 is still working at the campus laundry, still here, still a student. 10

There is the Medal Hound, the student who comes to college not to learn or expand any intellectual horizons but simply to win honors—medals, cups, plates, ribbons, scrolls—who is here because this is the best place to win the most the fastest, who plasticizes and mounts on his wall every certificate of excellence he wins, who at 39 will be a colonel in the U.S. Army and at 55 Secretary of something or other in a conservative Administration in Washington. 11

There is the Worker Ant, the student (loosely rendered) who takes 21 hours a semester and works 49 hours a week at the local car wash, who sleeps only on Sundays and during classes, who will somehow graduate on time and be the owner of his own vending-machine company at 30 and be dead of a heart attack at 40, and who will be remembered for the words chiseled on his tombstone: 12

13 All This Was Accomplished Without Ever Having So Much As Darkened The Door Of A Library

14 There is the Lost Soul, the sad kid who is in college only because teachers, parents, and society at large said so, who hasn't a career in mind or a dream to follow, who hasn't a clue, who heads home every Friday afternoon to spend the weekend cruising the local Dairee-Freeze, who at 50 will have done all his teachers, parents, and society said to do, still without a career in mind or a dream to follow or a clue.

15 There is also the Saved Soul—the young woman who has received, through the ministry of one Gospel freak or another, a Holy Calling to save the world, or at least some special part of it—who majors in Russian studies so that she can be caught smuggling Bibles into the Soviet Union and be sent to Siberia where she can preach to souls imprisoned by the Agents of Satan in the Gulag Archipelago.

16 Then, finally, there is the Happy Child, who comes to college to find a husband or wife—and finds one—and there is the Determined Child, who comes to get a degree—and gets one.

17 Enough said.

18 All of which, I suppose, should make me throw up my hands in despair and say that education, like youth and love, is wasted on the young. Not quite.

19 For there does come along, on occasion, that one of a hundred or so who is maybe at first a bit lost, certainly puzzled; who may well start out a Good Timer, an Egghead, a Performer, a Jock, a Medal Hound, a Gymnast, a Worker Ant; who may indeed have trouble settling on a major, who will be distressed by what sometimes passes for education, who might even be a temporary dropout; but who has a vital capacity for growth and is able to fall in love with learning, who acquires a taste for intellectual pleasure, who becomes in the finest sense of the word a Student.

20 This is the one who keeps the most jaded of us going back to class after class, and he or she must be oh-so-carefully cultivated. He or she must be artfully awakened, given the tools needed to continue learning for a lifetime, and let grow at whatever pace and in whatever direction nature dictates.

21 For I try always to remember that this student is me, my continuing self, my immortality. This person is my only hope that my own search for Truth will continue after me, on and on, forever.

BUILDING VOCABULARY

1. Explain these *colloquialisms* (see Glossary) in Baker's essay.
   - **a.** someone suffering from battle fatigue (par. 3)
   - **b.** I am scratching a severe case of the seven-year itch (par. 3)
   - **c.** worked his face into a case of terminal acne (par. 5)
   - **d.** burns himself out physically and mentally (par. 5)
   - **e.** loudly sniffing out pinko professors (par. 6)
   - **f.** working up an act (par. 8)
   - **g.** gives barely a nod (par. 8)
   - **h.** the walking personification of he-manism (par. 9)
   - **i.** to spend the weekend cruising the local Dairee-Freeze (par. 14)
   - **j.** he or she must be oh-so-carefully cultivated (par. 20)
2. Identify these references.
   - **a.** R.O.T.C. (par. 6)
   - **b.** C.I.A. (par. 7)
   - **c.** Brut (par. 9)
   - **d.** Dairee-Freeze (par. 14)
   - **e.** Gospel freak (par. 15)
   - **f.** Agents of Satan (par. 15)
   - **g.** Gulag Archipelago (par. 15)

THINKING CRITICALLY ABOUT THE ESSAY

Understanding the Writer's Ideas

1. In common language, describe the various categories of college students that Baker names.
2. Who is Anatole France? What process is described in the quotation from him? Why does Baker cite it at the beginning of the essay? What is his attitude toward France's idea?
3. For how long has Baker been teaching? What is his attitude toward his work?
4. About what age do you think Baker is? Why? Explain the meaning of the sentence: "In fact, as the rest of me declines, my eye seems to grow more acute" (par. 3).
5. Choose three of Baker's categories and paraphrase each description and meaning in a serious way.

6. What does Baker feel, overall, is the contemporary college student's attitude toward studying and receiving an education? How does it differ from Baker's own attitude toward these things?
7. Although Baker's classification may seem a bit pessimistic, he refuses to "throw up . . . [his] hands in despair" (par. 18). Why?
8. Describe the characteristics that are embodied in the category of *Student.* To whom does Baker compare the "true" Student? Why?

Understanding the Writer's Techniques

1. What is Baker's thesis in this essay? Does he state it directly or not? What, in your own words, is his purpose?
2. In this essay Baker deliberately creates, rather than avoids, stereotypes. He does so to establish exaggerated representatives of types. Why?

   For paragraphs 5 to 16, prepare a paragraph-by-paragraph outline of the main groups of students classified. For each, include the following information:
   a. type represented by the stereotype
   b. motivation of type for being a student
   c. main activity as a student
   d. condition in which the type ends up
3. This article was published in *The Chronicle of Higher Education,* a weekly newspaper for college and university educators and administrators. How do you think this audience influenced Baker's analysis of types of students? His tone and language?
4. What is Baker's tone in the essay? Give specific examples. In general, how would you characterize his attitude toward the contemporary college student? Why? Does his attitude or tone undergo any shifts in the essay? Explain.
5. Why does Baker use the term "personhoods" in paragraph 4? What attitude, about what subject, does he convey in his use of that word?
6. Why does the author capitalize the names he gives to the various categories of students? Why does he capitalize the word "Truth" in the last sentence?
7. How does Baker use definition in this essay? What purpose does it serve?

8. How does Baker use description to enhance his analysis in this essay?
9. In this essay, what is the role of *process analysis?* (Process analysis, discussed in the next chapter, is telling how something is done or proceeds; see pages 310–312). Look especially at Baker's descriptions of each type of student. How does process analysis figure into the title of the essay?
10. What is the purpose of the one-sentence paragraph 13? Why does Baker set it aside from paragraph 12, since it is a logical conclusion to that paragraph? Why does he use a two-word sentence as the complete paragraph 17? In what ways do these words signal the beginning of the essay's conclusion?

Exploring the Writer's Ideas

1. Do you think Baker's classifications in this essay are fair? Are they representative of the whole spectrum of students? How closely do they mirror the student population at your school? The article was written in 1982: How well have Baker's classifications held up to the present conditions?
2. Into which category (or categories) would you place yourself? Why?
3. Based on your reaction to and understanding of this article, would you like to have Baker as your professor? Why or why not?

IDEAS FOR WRITING

Prewriting

Freewrite for fifteen minutes about the different types of students who are common to your campus. What are the traits or characteristics of each group? What do representatives of each group do? Where do they congregate? How many of these types can you recognize in this classroom?

Guided Writing

Write a classification of at least three "types" in a situation with which you are familiar, other than school—a certain job, social event, sport, or some such situation.

1. Begin your essay with a reference, direct or indirect, to what some well-known writer or expert said about this situation.
2. Identify your role in relation to the situation described.
3. Write about your attitude toward the particular situation and why you are less than thrilled about it at present.
4. Make sure you involve the reader as someone who would be familiar with the situation and activities described.
5. Divide your essay into exaggerated or stereotyped categories which you feel represent almost the complete range of types in these situations. In your categorization, be sure to include motivations, activities, and results for each type.
6. Use description to make your categories vivid.
7. Use satire and a bit of gentle cynicism as part of your description.
8. Select a lively title.
9. In the conclusion, identify another type that you consider the "purest" or "most truthful" representative of persons in this situation. Either by comparison with yourself or by some other means, explain why you like this type best.

Thinking and Writing Collaboratively

In groups of four to five class members, draft an article for your college newspaper in which you outline the types of students on the campus. Try to maintain a consistently lighthearted or humorous tone or point of view as you move from discussion to the drafting of the letter. Revise your paper, paying careful attention to the flow from one category to the next, before submitting the article for possible publication.

More Writing Projects

1. In your journal, write your own classification of three college "types." Your entry can be serious or humorous.
2. In a 250-word paragraph, classify types of college dates.
3. Look in current magazines for advertisements directed at men or women, or both. Write an essay in which you classify current advertisements according to some logical scheme. Limit your essay to three to five categories.

Thinking as a Hobby

William Golding

Novelist William Golding, author of *The Lord of the Flies,* gives an amusing twist to learning how to think, an achievement he classifies into three distinct grades, from the common but lowly grade three to the lofty, truth-seeking grade one.

PREREADING: THINKING ABOUT THE ESSAY IN ADVANCE

What do you associate with the word hobby? What do you associate with the word thinking? If this were an essay simply about hobbies, or if this were an essay strictly about thinking, what would you expect in either case?

Words to Watch

incomprehensible (par. 2) impossible to understand
opaquely (par. 5) without reflecting light, that can't be seen through
contemplated (par. 9) studied
depravity (par. 18) corruption
monologues (par. 24) long speeches delivered by one person
clairvoyance (par. 27) unusual insight
disinterested (par. 28) impartial
proficient (par. 28) skilled
pious (par. 29) devoted to worship
gregarious (par. 29) social, friendly
compulsive (par. 31) irresistible
atheist (par. 31) one who does not believe in God
libertine (par. 33) someone of lax morals
inscrutable (par. 37) impossible to be understood
irreverent (par. 41) without reverence, independent-minded

While I was still a boy, I came to the conclusion that there were three grades of thinking; and since I was later to claim thinking as my hobby, I came to an even stranger conclusion—namely, that I myself could not think at all. 1

2 I must have been an unsatisfactory child for grownups to deal with. I remember how incomprehensible they appeared to me at first, but not, of course, how I appeared to them. It was the headmaster of my grammar school who first brought the subject of thinking before me—though neither in the way, nor with the result he intended. He had some statuettes in his study. They stood on a high cupboard behind his desk. One was a lady wearing nothing but a bath towel. She seemed frozen in an eternal panic lest the bath towel slip down any farther; and since she had no arms, she was in an unfortunate position to pull the towel up again. Next to her, crouched the statuette of a leopard, ready to spring down at the top drawer of a filing cabinet labeled A–AH. My innocence interpreted this as the victim's last, despairing cry. Beyond the leopard was a naked, muscular gentleman, who sat, looking down, with his chin on his fist and his elbow on his knee. He seemed utterly miserable.

3 Some time later, I learned about these statuettes. The headmaster had placed them where they would face delinquent children, because they symbolized to him the whole of life. The naked lady was the Venus of Milo. She was Love. She was not worried about the towel. She was just busy being beautiful. The leopard was Nature, and he was being natural. The naked, muscular gentleman was not miserable. He was Rodin's Thinker, an image of pure thought. It is easy to buy small plaster models of what you think life is like.

4 I had better explain that I was a frequent visitor to the headmaster's study, because of the latest thing I had done or left undone. As we now say, I was not integrated. I was, if anything, disintegrated; and I was puzzled. Grownups never made sense. Whenever I found myself in a penal position before the headmaster's desk, with the statuettes glimmering whitely above him, I would sink my head, clasp my hands behind my back and writhe one shoe over the other.

5 The headmaster would look opaquely at me through flashing spectacles.

6 "What are we going to do with you?"

7 Well, what *were* they going to do with me? I would writhe my shoe some more and stare down at the worn rug.

8 "Look up, boy! Can't you look up?"

9 Then I would look up at the cupboard, where the naked lady was frozen in her panic and the muscular gentleman contemplated thc hindquarters of the leopard in endless gloom. I had

nothing to say to the headmaster. His spectacles caught the light so that you could see nothing human behind them. There was no possibility of communication.

"Don't you ever think at all?" 10

No, I didn't think, wasn't thinking, couldn't think—I was 11
simply waiting in anguish for the interview to stop.

"Then you'd better learn—hadn't you?" 12

On one occasion the headmaster leaped to his feet, reached 13
up and plonked Rodin's masterpiece on the desk before me.

"That's what a man looks like when he's really thinking." 14

I surveyed the gentleman without interest or comprehension. 15

"Go back to your class." 16

Clearly there was something missing in me. Nature had en- 17
dowed the rest of the human race with a sixth sense and left me out. This must be so, I mused, on my way back to the class, since whether I had broken a window, or failed to remember Boyle's Law, or been late for school, my teachers produced me one, adult answer: "Why can't you think?"

As I saw the case, I had broken the window because I had 18
tried to hit Jack Arney with a cricket ball and missed him; I could not remember Boyle's Law because I had never bothered to learn it; and I was late for school because I preferred looking over the bridge into the river. In fact, I was wicked. Were my teachers, perhaps, so good that they could not understand the depths of my depravity? Were they clear, untormented people who could direct their every action by this mysterious business of thinking? The whole thing was incomprehensible. In my earlier years, I found even the statuette of the Thinker confusing. I did not believe any of my teachers were naked, ever. Like someone born deaf, but bitterly determined to find out about sound, I watched my teachers to find out about thought.

There was Mr. Houghton. He was always telling me to 19
think. With a modest satisfaction, he would tell me that he had thought a bit himself. Then why did he spend so much time drinking? Or was there more sense in drinking than there appeared to be? But if not, and if drinking were in fact ruinous to health—and Mr. Houghton was ruined, there was no doubt about that—why was he always talking about the clean life and the virtues of fresh air? He would spread his arms wide with the action of a man who habitually spent his time striding along mountain ridges.

"Open air does me good, boys—I know it!" 20

21 Sometimes, exalted by his own oratory, he would leap from his desk and hustle us outside into a hideous wind.

22 "Now boys! Deep breaths! Feel it right down inside you—huge draughts of God's good air!"

23 He would stand before us, rejoicing in his perfect health, an open-air man. He would put his hands on his waist and take a tremendous breath. You could hear the wind, trapped in the cavern of his chest and struggling with all the unnatural impediments. His body would reel with shock and his ruined face go white at the unaccustomed visitation. He would stagger back to his desk and collapse there, useless for the rest of the morning.

24 Mr. Houghton was given to high-minded monologues about the good life, sexless and full of duty. Yet in the middle of one of these monologues, if a girl passed the window, tapping along on her neat little feet, he would interrupt his discourse, his neck would turn of itself and he would watch her out of sight. In this instance, he seemed to me ruled not by thought but by an invisible and irresistible spring in his nape.

25 His neck was an object of great interest to me. Normally it bulged a bit over his collar. But Mr. Houghton had fought in the First World War alongside both Americans and French, and had come—by who knows what illogic?—to a settled detestation of both countries. If either country happened to be prominent in current affairs, no argument could make Mr. Houghton think well of it. He would bang the desk, his neck would bulge still further and go red. "You can say what you like," he would cry, "but I've thought about this and I know what I think!"

26 Mr. Houghton thought with his neck.

27 There was Miss Parsons. She assured us that her dearest wish was our welfare, but I knew even then, with the mysterious clairvoyance of childhood, that what she wanted most was the husband she never got. There was Mr. Hands—and so on.

28 I have dealt at length with my teachers because this was my introduction to the nature of what is commonly called thought. Through them I discovered that thought is often full of unconscious prejudice, ignorance and hypocrisy. It will lecture on disinterested purity while its neck is being remorselessly twisted toward a skirt. Technically, it is about as proficient as most businessmen's golf, as honest as most politicians' intentions, or—to come near my own preoccupation—as coherent as most books that get written. It is what I came to call grade-three thinking, though more properly, it is feeling, rather than thought.

True, often there is a kind of innocence in prejudices, but in those days I viewed grade-three thinking with an intolerant contempt and an incautious mockery. I delighted to confront a pious lady who hated the Germans with the proposition that we should love our enemies. She taught me a great truth in dealing with grade-three thinkers; because of her, I no longer dismiss lightly a mental process which for nine-tenths of the population is the nearest they will ever get to thought. They have immense solidarity. We had better respect them, for we are outnumbered and surrounded. A crowd of grade-three thinkers, all shouting the same thing, all warming their hands at the fire of their own prejudices, will not thank you for pointing out the contradictions in their beliefs. Man is a gregarious animal, and enjoys agreement as cows will graze all the same way on the side of a hill. 29

Grade two thinking is the detection of contradictions. I reached grade two when I trapped the poor, pious lady. Grade-two thinkers do not stampede easily, though often they fall into the other fault and lag behind. Grade-two thinking is a withdrawal, with eyes and ears open. It became my hobby and brought satisfaction and loneliness in either hand. For grade-two thinking destroys without having the power to create. It set me watching the crowds cheering His Majesty the King and asking myself what all the fuss was about, without giving me anything positive to put in the place of that heady patriotism. But there were compensations. To hear people justify their habit of hunting foxes and tearing them to pieces by claiming that the foxes liked it. To hear our Prime Minister talk about the great benefit we conferred on India by jailing people like Pandit Nehru and Gandhi. To hear American politicians talk about peace in one sentence and refuse to join the League of Nations in the next. Yes, there were moments of delight. 30

But I was growing toward adolescence and had to admit that Mr. Houghton was not the only one with an irresistible spring in his neck. I, too, felt the compulsive hand of nature and began to find that pointing out contradiction could be costly as well as fun. There was Ruth, for example, a serious and attractive girl. I was an atheist at the time. Grade-two thinking is a menace to religion and knocks down sects like skittles. I put myself in a position to be converted by her with an hypocrisy worthy of grade three. She was a Methodist—or at least, her parents were, and Ruth had to follow suit. But, alas, instead of relying on the Holy Spirit to convert me, Ruth was foolish enough to open her 31 pretty mouth in argument. She claimed that the Bible (King James Version) was literally inspired. I countered by saying that the Catholics believed in the literal inspiration of Saint Jerome's *Vulgate,* and the two books were different. Argument flagged.

32 At last she remarked that there were an awful lot of Methodists, and they couldn't be wrong, could they—not all those millions? That was too easy, said I restively (for the nearer you were to Ruth, the nicer she was to be near to) since there were more Roman Catholics than Methodists anyway; and they couldn't be wrong, could they—not all those hundreds of millions? An awful flicker of doubt appeared in her eyes. I slid my arm round her waist and murmured breathlessly that if we were counting heads, the Buddhists were the boys for my money. But Ruth had *really* wanted to do me good, because I was so nice. She fled. The combination of my arm and those countless Buddhists was too much for her.

33 That night her father visited my father and left, red-cheeked and indignant. I was given the third degree to find out what had happened. It was lucky we were both of us only fourteen. I lost Ruth and gained an undeserved reputation as a potential libertine.

34 So grade-two thinking could be dangerous. It was in this knowledge, at the age of fifteen, that I remember making a comment from the heights of grade two, on the limitations of grade three. One evening I found myself alone in the schoolhall, preparing it for a party. The door of the headmaster's study was open. I went in. The headmaster had ceased to thump Rodin's Thinker down on the desk as an example to the young. Perhaps he had not found any more candidates, but the statuettes were still there, glimmering and gathering dust on top of the cupboard. I stood on a chair and rearranged them. I stood Venus in her bath towel on the filing cabinet, so that now the top drawer caught its breath in a gasp of sexy excitement. "A-ah!" The portentous Thinker I placed on the edge of the cupboard so that he looked down at the bath towel and waited for it to slip. Grade-two thinking, though it filled life with fun and excitement, did not make for content. To find out the deficiencies of our elders bolsters the young ego but does not make for personal security. I found that grade two was not only the power to point out contradictions. It took the swimmer some distance from the shore and left him there, out of his depth. I decided that Pontius Pilate was a typical grade-two thinker. "What is truth?" he said, a very common grade-two thought, but one that is used always as the end of an

argument instead of the beginning. There is a still higher grade of thought which says, "What is truth?" and sets out to find it.

But these grade-one thinkers were few and far between. They 35
did not visit my grammar school in the flesh though they were there in books. I aspired to them, partly because I was ambitious and partly because I now saw my hobby as an unsatisfactory thing if it went no further. If you set out to climb a mountain, however high you climb, you have failed if you cannot reach the top.

I *did* meet an undeniably grade-one thinker in my first year 36
at Oxford. I was looking over a small bridge in Magdalen Deer Park, and a tiny mustached and hatted figure came and stood by my side. He was a German who had just fled from the Nazis to Oxford as a temporary refuge. His name was Einstein.

But Professor Einstein knew no English at that time and I 37
knew only two words of German. I beamed at him, trying word lessly to convey by my bearing all the affection and respect that the English felt for him. It is possible—and I have to make the admission—that I felt here were two grade-one thinkers standing side by side; yet I doubt if my face conveyed more than a formless awe. I would have given my Greek and Latin and French and a good slice of my English for enough German to communicate. But we were divided; he was as inscrutable as my headmaster. For perhaps five minutes we stood together on the bridge, undeniable grade-one thinker and breathless aspirant. With true greatness, Professor Einstein realized that any contact was better than none. He pointed to a trout wavering in midstream.

He spoke: "*Fisch.*" 38

My brain reeled. Here I was, mingling with the great, and 39
yet helpless as the veriest grade-three thinker. Desperately I sought for some sign by which I might convey that I, too, revered pure reason. I nodded vehemently. In a brilliant flash I used up half of my German vocabulary. "*Fisch. Ja. Ja.*"

For perhaps another five minutes we stood side by side. 40
Then Professor Einstein, his whole figure still conveying good will and amiability, drifted away out of sight.

I, too, would be a grade-one thinker. I was irreverent at the 41
best of times. Political and religious systems, social customs, loyalties and traditions, they all came tumbling down like so many rotten apples off a tree. This was a fine hobby and a sensible substitute for cricket, since you could play it all the year round. I came up in the end with what must always remain the justification for grade-one thinking, its sign, seal and charter. I devised a

coherent system for living. It was a moral system, which was wholly logical. Of course, as I readily admitted, conversion of the world to my way of thinking might be difficult, since my system did away with a number of trifles, such as big business, centralized government, armies, marriage. . . .

42 It was Ruth all over again. I had some very good friends who stood by me, and still do. But my acquaintances vanished, taking the girls with them. Young women seemed oddly contented with the world as it was. They valued the meaningless ceremony with a ring. Young men, while willing to concede the chaining sordidness of marriage, were hesitant about abandoning the organizations which they hoped would give them a career. A young man on the first rung of the Royal Navy, while perfectly agreeable to doing away with big business and marriage, got as red-necked as Mr. Houghton when I proposed a world without any battleships in it.

43 Had the game gone too far? Was it a game any longer? In those prewar days, I stood to lose a great deal, for the sake of a hobby.

44 Now you are expecting me to describe how I saw the folly of my ways and came back to the warm nest, where prejudices are so often called loyalties, where pointless actions are hallowed into custom by repetitions where we are content to say we think when all we do is feel.

45 But you would be wrong. I dropped my hobby and turned professional.

46 If I were to go back to the headmaster's study and find the dusty statuettes still there, I would arrange them differently. I would dust Venus and put her aside, for I have come to love her and know her for the fair thing she is. But I would put the Thinker, sunk in his desperate thoughts, where there were shadows before him—and at his back, I would put the leopard, crouched and ready to spring.

BUILDING VOCABULARY

1. Identify the following:
   - **a.** Venus of Milo (par. 3)
   - **b.** Rodin (par. 3)
   - **c.** Boyle's Law (par. 17)
   - **d.** Pontius Pilate (par. 34)
   - **e.** Einstein (par. 36)

2. Golding is a novelist. His choice of words or phrases frequently gives a special vividness and punch to his observations, as in this sentence: "On one occasion the headmaster *leaped* to his feet, reached up and *plonked* Rodin's masterpiece on the desk before me" (par. 13). Find six other examples of Golding's use of words or phrases that, like the italicized words above, are especially effective.

THINKING CRITICALLY ABOUT THE ESSAY

Understanding the Writer's Ideas

1. Why did the writer, as a boy, come to the conclusion that he "could not think at all" (par. 1)?
2. How does the writer's boy's eye view of the statuettes behind his headmaster's desk differ from those of the headmaster?
3. Why does the writer not understand what his teachers mean when, say, he has broken a window and they exclaim, "Why can't you think"?
4. What does he learn when he watches his teachers to find out about thought?
5. What are the three grades of thinking that the writer classifies for himself as a boy?
6. What are the delights and the dangers of grade-two thinking?
7. What is the justification for grade-one thinking, and what are its pitfalls?
8. What is the difference between thinking as a hobby and thinking as a profession?
9. What does the writer wish to convey by his imaginary rearrangement of the statuettes in his headmaster's study?

Understanding the Writer's Techniques

1. Golding's opening paragraph immediately introduces the three main threads, or themes, of his essay. What are these?
2. How does Golding develop each of these three themes? To what extent are these themes developed in relation to one another?
3. How do we learn what Golding means by claiming thinking as a hobby?

4. What is the *tone* of this essay? How is the tone established? How does the tone contribute to the essay's argument?
5. How does the allegorical use of the statuettes help to maintain the essay's coherence?

Exploring the Writer's Ideas

1. How did Golding become a thinker? How would his essay have changed had he given credit to others, say his teachers, in his development as a thinker?
2. Are the three grades of thinking as distinct and separate as Golding suggests? Can the three grades of thinking coexist in one individual? Give examples from Golding's essay that show how, even as now a professional thinker, he himself can still exhibit more than one grade of thinking.
3. How do you account for the fact that unlike most of Golding's friends and acquaintances, he was able to resist abandoning grade-two thinking for the security of a good job and a contented family life? What does Golding think of the majority of us who are indeed content with life? What is your view?

IDEAS FOR WRITING

Prewriting

Write two or three short anecdotes illustrating the absurdity or incomprehensibility of the adult world from your vantage point as a child.

Guided Writing

Write an essay that classifies adults into two or three categories, ranging from the preachy and hypocritical to the exemplary. Use a wry and bemused tone for the essay.

1. Begin with a bold but catchy statement of how you concluded as a child that the world of adults is strange and even incomprehensible.
2. Tell one or two anecdotes to illustrate the absurdity of the adult world.
3. Explain directly the qualities of the category of adults who are silly or incomprehensible.

4. Tell an anecdote that illustrates how your realization of the absurdity of these adults nevertheless did not of itself help you grow.
5. Give an example of true maturity.
6. Explain the price to be paid for true maturity.
7. Conclude by indicating your relative progress toward maturity at the point of writing the essay.

Thinking and Writing Collaboratively

In groups of four or five discuss the tension between being accepted by your peers and thinking for yourself. Together, sketch out two essays: one in defense of conformity, and one advocating nonconformity.

More Writing Projects

1. Write a dialogue between a grade-three and a grade-one thinker.
2. Write an essay about your search for small plaster models of what you think life is like.
3. Write an essay classifying professors according to attributes of your choice, such as philosophies of grading or tastes in dress.

SUMMING UP: CHAPTER 8

1. Write an essay that classifies the readings in this book by a method other than *exposition* (detailed explanation). As you discuss each category, be sure to give examples that explain why particular readings fall into that classification.
2. Reread Judith Viorst's "Friends, Good Friends—and Such Good Friends" in this chapter. Then, write down the names of several of your closest friends. Keep a journal for one week in which you list what you did, how you felt, and what you talked about with each of these friends. Then write an essay that classifies these friends into three categories. Use entries from your journal to support your method of classification.
3. With the class divided into four groups, assemble a guide to the city, town, or neighborhood surrounding your campus. Each group should be responsible for one category of information: types of people; types of places; types of entertainment; types of services; and so on. Be sure that each category is covered in detail; you may refer to E. B. White's essay "The Three New Yorks" as a model. After each group has completed its work, choose someone to present findings to the class. Now write your own guide to the areas based on the classifications discussed.
4. Although Viorst's, Baker's, and Golding's essays are classifications, they also present new ways of looking at a group of people. Viorst has an underlying message about how to choose friends, Baker has a warning about how not to be stereotyped, and Golding has a warning to offer about the social price of independent thinking. Write a classification essay entitled "What to Avoid When ___________." Fill in the blank with an activity that would involve a decision-making process on the part of the reader.
5. Many of the essays in this book deal with crucial experiences in the various authors' lives. Among others, Hughes and Wong tell us of coming-of-age experiences; Selzer writes of his special insights into human nature; and Erdrich and Thomas describe their relationships to the world of nature. Try writing an essay that classifies the personal essays that you have read in this anthology.

CHAPTER 9

Process Analysis

WHAT IS PROCESS ANALYSIS?

Process analysis explains to a reader how something is done, how something works, or how something occurs. Like classification, it is a form of analysis, or taking apart a process in order better to understand how it functions. This kind of writing is often called *expository* because it *exposes* or shows us information. If you use cookbooks, you are encountering process analysis each time you read a recipe. If you are setting up a new VCR, you may wish the writer of the manual were more adept at writing process analysis when you find the steps hard to follow. "How to" writing can therefore give the reader steps for carrying out a process. The writer might also analyze the steps someone took already in completing a process, such as explaining how Harriet Tubman organized the Underground Railroad or how women won the right to vote.

Planning a good process analysis requires the writer to include all the essential steps. Be sure you have all the tools or ingredients needed. Arrange the steps in the correct sequence. Like all good writing, a good process essay requires a thesis to tell the reader the *significance* of the process. The writer can tell the reader how to do something, but also should inform the reader about the usefulness or importance of the endeavor.

In this chapter, Russell Baker tells us, tongue in cheek, how to carve a turkey. Henry Louis Gates, Jr., explains how to "de-kink" your hair. Jerrold G. Simon advises us how to write a resume. And, from Ernest Hemingway, we learn how to make our next experience of camping a success. As you read about these processes, watch how each writer uses the same technique to achieve a different result.

HOW DO WE READ PROCESS ANALYSIS?

Identify what process the writer is going to analyze. As you read, make a quick outline of the steps the writer introduces.

Watch the use of transitions as the writer moves from one step to the next.

Assess the audience that the writer has aimed at. Is the writer addressing innocents or experts? If the writer's purpose was to explain how to prepare beef stew, he would give different directions to a college freshman who has never cooked before than he would give to a cooking class at the Culinary Institute of America, where everyone was familiar with the fundamentals of cooking. Ask yourself, then: Is there enough information in the analysis? too much?

How does the writer try to make the piece lively? Does it sound as dry as a technical manual, or is there an engaging tone?

HOW DO WE WRITE PROCESS ANALYSIS?

Decide to analyze a process with which you are very familiar. Unless you can do it well yourself, you won't be able to instruct or inform your readers.

Process begins with a good shopping list. Once you have your topic, make lists of ingredients or tools.

Arrange the essential steps in logical order. Don't assume your reader already knows how to do the process. As you know from those incomprehensible VCR instructions, the reader should be given *every* step.

List the steps to *avoid* when carrying out the procedure.

If possible, actually try out the process, using your list as a guide, if you are presenting a method for a tangible product, like making an omelet. Or imagine that you are explaining the procedure over the telephone.

If your topic is abstract, like telling someone how to become an American citizen, read it aloud to a willing listener to see if he or she can follow the steps clearly.

Use *definition* to explain terms the reader may not know, especially if you are presenting a technical process. At the same time, avoid jargon. Make the language as plain as possible.

Describe the appearance of the product or *compare* an unfamiliar item with a familiar one.

Be sure to think about your audience. Link the audience to the purpose of the process.

Formulate a thesis statement that tells what the process is, and why it is a good process to know.

Sample thesis statement:

> Buying and renovating an old car is a time-consuming process, but the results are worthwhile.

Writing the Draft

Write a rough draft. Turn your list into an essay by developing the steps into sentences, using your thesis to add significance and coherence to the process you are presenting. Don't just list; analyze the procedure as you go along. Keep in mind the techniques of writers like Russell Baker, who doesn't just carve a turkey, but creates an entire dinner scene by the way he selects lively verbs and uses *hyperbole* (see Glossary) to raise his process analysis beyond the ordinary.

Add transitions when necessary to alert the reader that a new step is coming. The most common transition words help a reader to follow steps: *first, second, third; first, next, after, last.*

Proofread, revise, and create a final draft.

A STUDENT PARAGRAPH: PROCESS ANALYSIS

Process analysis lends itself to a variety of approaches, ranging from a methodical step-by-step explanation of a task such as how to prepare a pie, to assessment of a series of related historical events. As you read the following one-paragraph composition, consider the student's success in providing the reader with a flexible approach to a typical problem.

Topic sentence

Phrase "the first step" starts the process

"Next" signals the second step

Finding the right used car can be a real challenge. Unless you are totally open to possibilities, the first step in the process is to focus on one make and model that interests you. Next, you should consult the Blue Book, which lists car makes and models by year, and provides a rough guide to fair prices based on condition. It's a good idea to have the book handy before moving to the next stage in your search; you can probably disqualify a number of cars based on asking price alone. (If the asking price is significantly higher than the Blue Book suggests, the seller is not always trying to hoodwink you. There might be a good reason for the price—exceptionally good condition, or an unusual number of "add-ons," for example. Still, it makes sense to use caution in these cases.) At this point, you are ready to start the actual search, beginning with a scanning of these resources. Don't limit your search to these resources, however; continue your hunt by consulting more local venues, such as campus bulletin-board postings. There are several other promising routes to finding the wheels of your dreams: car rental companies usually sell off their rentals after they've reached a ripe old age—sometimes a venerable 3 to 5 years! Police auctions are another possibility, though the successful bidder is usually required to plunk down cash for the car right away, and the cars come with no warranty—you can find a real bargain here, but it's only really a safe bet if you can take along a mechanic. In fact, consulting a good mechanic should always be the last step in the process: after you have located the car of your dreams, get an inspection before you write that check, just to make sure that your dream machine doesn't explode.

Parenthetical remark qualifies earlier statement

"At this point" moves reader to third step

"Continue your hunt by consulting" advances the process

"Several other promising routes" adds to process

Concluding step cautions, adds humor

How to Write a Resume

Jerrold G. Simon

Few processes provoke more anxiety than presenting yourself as a candidate for a job. Here the psychologist and career development specialist Jerrold G. Simon provides a primer on how to get yourself started that aims to be supportive, lucid, and useful. As you read this selection, look for the methods the writer uses to achieve these ends.

PREREADING: THINKING ABOUT THE ESSAY IN ADVANCE

What thoughts and emotions does searching for a job stir in you? What do you expect from a "How to" book or essay?

Words to Watch

formats (par. 6) general arrangements
chronological (par. 6) in order of occurrence
prospective (par. 8) potential
extracurricular (par. 13) outside of formal instruction
articulate (par. 28) able to speak well

If you are about to launch a search for a job, the suggestions I offer here can help you whether or not you have a high school or college diploma, whether you are just starting out or changing your job or career in midstream. 1

Before you try to find a job opening, you have to answer the hardest question of your working life: "What do I want to do?" Here's a good way. 2

Sit down with a piece of paper and don't get up till you've listed all the things you're proud to have accomplished. Your list might include being head of a fund-raising campaign, or acting a juicy role in the senior play. 3

Study the list. You'll see a pattern emerge of the things you do best and like to do best. You might discover that you're happiest working with people, or maybe with numbers, or words, or well, you'll see it. 4

5 Once you've decided what job area to go after, read more about it in the reference section of your library. "Talk shop" with any people you know in that field. Then start to get your resume together.

6 There are many good books that offer sample resumes and describe widely used formats. The one that is still most popular, the *reverse chronological,* emphasizes where you worked and when, and the jobs and titles you held.

7 Your name and address go at the top. Also phone number.

8 What job do you want? That's what a prospective employer looks at first. If you know exactly, list that next under *Job Objective.* Otherwise, save it for your cover letter (I describe that later), when you're writing for a specific job to a specific person. In any case, make sure your resume focuses on the kind of work you can do and want to do.

9 Now comes *Work Experience.* Here's where you list your qualifications. Lead with your most important credentials. If you've had a distinguished work history in an area related to the job you're seeking, lead off with that. If your education will impress the prospective employer more, start with that.

10 Begin with your most recent experience first and work backwards. Include your titles or positions held. And list the years.

11 The most qualified people always get the job. It goes to the person who presents himself most persuasively in person and on paper.

12 So don't just list where you were and what you did. This is your chance to tell *how well you did.* Were you the best salesman? Did you cut operating costs? Give numbers, statistics, percentages, increases in sales or profits.

13 No job experience? In that case, list your summer jobs, extracurricular school activities, honors, awards. Choose the activities that will enhance your qualifications for the job.

14 Next list your *Education*—unless you chose to start with that. This should also be in reverse chronological order. List your high school only if you didn't go on to college. Include college degree, postgraduate degrees, dates conferred, major and minor courses you took that help qualify you for the job you want.

15 Also, did you pay your own way? Earn scholarships or fellowships? Those are impressive accomplishments.

16 No diplomas or degrees? Then tell about your education: special training programs or courses that can qualify you. Describe

outside activities that reveal your talents and abilities. Did you sell the most tickets to the annual charity musical? Did you take your motorcycle engine apart and put it back together so it works? These can help you.

Next, list any *Military Service.* This could lead off your resume if it is your only work experience. Stress skills learned, promotions earned, leadership shown. 17

Now comes *Personal Data.* This is your chance to let the reader get a glimpse of the personal you, and to further the image you've worked to project in the preceding sections. For example, if you're after a job in computer programming, and you enjoy playing chess, mention it. Chess playing requires the ability to think through a problem. 18

Include foreign languages spoken, extensive travel, particular interests or professional memberships, *if* they advance your cause. 19

Keep your writing style simple. Be brief. Start sentences with impressive action verbs: "Created," "Designed," "Achieved," "Caused." 20

Make sure your grammar and spelling are correct. And no typos! 21

Use 8½" × 11" bond paper—white or off-white for easy reading. Don't cram things together. 22

Make sure your original is clean and readable. Then have it professionally duplicated. No carbons. 23

Now that your resume is ready, start to track down job openings. How? Look up business friends, personal friends, neighbors, your minister, your college alumni association, professional services. Keep up with trade publications, and read help-wanted ads. 24

And start your own "direct mail" campaign. First, find out about the companies you are interested in—their size, location, what they make, their competition, their advertising, their prospects. Get their annual report—and read it. 25

Send your resume, along with a cover letter, to a specific person in the company, not to "Gentlemen" or "Dear Sir." The person should be the top in the area where you want to work. Spell his name properly! The cover letter should appeal to your reader's own needs. What's in it for him? Quickly explain why you are approaching *his* company (their product line, their superior training program) and what you can bring to the party. Back up your claims with facts. Then refer him to your enclosed resume and ask for an interview. 26

27 And now you've got an interview! Be sure to call the day before to confirm it. Meantime, *prepare yourself.* Research the company and the job by reading books and business journals in the library.

28 On the big day, arrive 15 minutes early. Act calm, even though, if you're normal, you're trembling inside at 6.5 on the Richter scale. At every chance, let your interviewer see that your personal skills and qualifications relate to the job at hand. If it's a sales position, for example, go all out to show how articulate and persuasive you are.

29 Afterwards, follow through with a brief thank-you note. This is a fine opportunity to restate your qualifications and add any important points you didn't get a chance to bring up during the interview.

30 Keep a list of prospects. List the dates you contacted them, when they replied, what was said.

31 And remember, someone out there is looking for someone *just like you.* It takes hard work and sometimes luck to find that person. Keep at it and you'll succeed.

BUILDING VOCABULARY

The writer advises that in composing a resume you should keep your writing style simple; be brief; and start sentences with action verbs.

Go through Simon's essay and pick out six to twelve examples of how he follows his own advice.

THINKING CRITICALLY ABOUT THE ESSAY

Understanding the Writer's Ideas

1. Where and how does the writer let you know what to expect from his essay?
2. Before writing a resume, what critical step must you take first?
3. The writer identifies headings that are important to guide your composing of a resume, as well as what kind of information should be emphasized under each heading. What is the consistent theme of the writer's advice about what to emphasize?

4. The writer advises a proactive approach to job hunting once the resume is finished. What are his recommendations for an active job search?
5. How does the writer's advice about how to behave in an interview mirror his advice about what to emphasize in your resume?
6. What follow-up does the writer recommend, even after the job interview?

Understanding the Writer's Techniques

1. This essay is a guide in the form of suggestions about how to do something. What determines the order of the writer's instructions?
2. What audience do you imagine the writer is addressing in this essay? How are the essay's *style* and *tone* appropriate to that audience?
3. Looking for work can be nerve-wracking. What techniques does the writer employ to quiet the reader's fears?
4. Taking a reader through a process requires definite *transitions* (see Glossary) from one step to the next. Make a list of several of the transitional words or phrases that the writer uses, and write a few words about why these transitional words or phrases are well suited to this purpose.

Exploring the Writer's Ideas

1. By advising the reader to follow the "most popular" formats for resumes, does the writer risk recommending something that will simply blend the result into the crowd of other resumes? If so, what steps could be taken to avoid this result? If not, why not?
2. What could you do to make your resume more individual and original? Does an original resume risk being dismissed as eccentric? How could you avoid such a reaction?
3. Does the you-can-do-it! approach of this essay perhaps set the reader up for disappointment? If so, what could the writer do to avoid such a result? If not, why not?

IDEAS FOR WRITING

Prewriting

Write an outline of the steps involved in writing a reference letter, or writing a lesson plan, or writing your will—or a similar process.

Guided Writing

Write an essay on how to write a job application letter.

1. Start by indicating to readers that whatever their age and whatever the job of their choice, what you are going to say will help them.
2. Identify two or three key questions that must be answered before you can start your application letter.
3. Take the reader through the main stages of an application letter, giving each stage a name.
4. Be careful to move from step to step by means of clear but active, even directive transitional words or phrases (e.g. "Next," or "Make sure . . .").
5. Be careful to assure the reader that the letter can be done well, that the reader has the gifts and record to win the job.
6. Indicate how an application letter should end so as to get helpfully to the next stage—the interview.
7. Give one or two tips about how to present yourself at the job interview.
8. Help the reader to adopt an easy method of tracking his or her applications.
9. End with a mild pep talk, encouraging the reader to take a positive attitude, because success will come in the end.

Thinking and Writing Collaboratively

In groups of four or five, share your experiences of applying to college. Compare and contrast the steps you took to decide where to apply and to decide how to apply.

More Writing Projects

1. Discuss how students in the class have found full- or part-time or summer jobs. Then break up into smaller work groups and develop job search guides for each category, remembering to offer full, detailed instructions to the reader.
2. Interview a group of alumni of your college about what they seek in a job applicant for their firm or profession. Write an article for the school paper based on the interviews.
3. Write a humorous essay about the comparisons and contrasts between you as a creation of your resume and you as a real person, in the context of a real or fictional interview for a job.

Slice of Life

Russell Baker

Russell Baker is well known for his columns in the *New York Times,* in which he satirizes contemporary society, writing about trends in food and style, as well as the rigors of surviving in ordinary life. In "Slice of Life," he humorously describes the process of carving a turkey for a holiday dinner, demonstrating how even the most familiar task can lend itself to detailed and appealing analysis.

PREREADING: THINKING ABOUT THE ESSAY IN ADVANCE

Do certain natural or mechanical tasks or processes that seem to be simple actually turn out to be much more difficult to accomplish? Think about two or three of these "simple" tasks. What surprises await the unsuspecting individual who engages in such processes?

Words to Watch

sutures (par. 3) stitches
skewered (par. 5) secured with a long pin
chassis (par. 11) body; frame
stampede (par. 16) run

1 How to carve a turkey:

2 Assemble the following tools—carving knife, stone for sharpening carving knife, hot water, soap, wash cloth, two bath towels, barbells, meat cleaver.

3 If the house lacks a meat cleaver, an ax may be substituted. If it is, add bandages, sutures and iodine to above list.

4 Begin by moving the turkey from roasting pan to a suitable carving area. This is done by inserting the carving knife into the posterior stuffed area of the turkey and the knife-sharpening stone into the stuffed area under the neck.

5 Thus skewered, the turkey may be lifted out of the hot grease with relative safety. Should the turkey drop to the floor,

however, remove the knife and stone, roll the turkey gingerly into the two bath towels, wrap them several times around it and lift the encased fowl to the carving place.

You are now ready to begin carving. Sharpen the knife on the stone and insert it where the thigh joins the torso. If you do this correctly, which is improbable, the knife will almost immediately encounter a barrier of bone and gristle. 6

This may very well be the joint. It could, however, be your thumb. If not, execute a vigorous sawing motion until satisfied that the knife has been defeated. 7

Withdraw the knife and ask someone nearby, in as testy a manner as possible, why the knives at your house are not kept in better carving condition. 8

Exercise the biceps and forearms by lifting barbells until they are strong enough for you to tackle the leg joint with bare hands. 9

Wrapping one hand firmly around the thigh, seize the turkey's torso in the other and scream. Run cold water over hands to relieve pain of burns. 10

Now, take a bath towel in each hand and repeat the above maneuver. The entire leg should snap away from the chassis with a distinct crack, and the rest of the turkey, obedient to Newton's law about equal and opposite reactions, should roll in the opposite direction, which means that if you are carving at the table the turkey will probably come to rest in someone's lap. 11

Get the turkey out of the lap with as little fuss as possible, and concentrate on the leg. Use the meat cleaver to sever the sinewy leather which binds the thigh to the drumstick. 12

If using the alternate, ax method, this operation should be performed on a cement walk outside the house in order to preserve the table. 13

Repeat the above operation on the turkey's uncarved side. You now have two thighs and two drumsticks. Using the wash cloth, soap and hot water, bathe thoroughly and, if possible, go to a movie. 14

Otherwise, look each person in the eye and say, "I don't suppose anyone wants white meat." 15

If compelled to carve the breast anyhow, sharpen the knife on the stone again with sufficient awkwardness to tip over the gravy bowl on the person who started the stampede for white meat. 16

17 While everyone is rushing about to mop the gravy off her slacks, hack at the turkey breast until it starts crumbling off the carcass in ugly chunks.

18 The alternative method for carving white meat is to visit around the neighborhood until you find someone who has a good carving knife and borrow it, if you find one, which is unlikely.

19 This method enables you to watch the football game on neighbors' television sets and also creates the possibility that somebody back at your table will grow tired of waiting and do the carving herself.

20 In this case, upon returning home, cast a pained stare upon the mound of chopped white meat that has been hacked out by the family carving knife and refuse to do any more carving that day. No one who cares about the artistry of carving can be expected to work upon the mutilations of amateurs, and it would be a betrayal of the carver's art to do so.

BUILDING VOCABULARY

One of Baker's most effective techniques in creating humor is to select adjectives and verbs that not only illustrate the process he is analyzing, but exaggerate the steps and the results. *Hyperbole* in writing is the use of extreme exaggeration either to make a particular point or to achieve a special effect. In paragraph 3, for instance, Baker includes among the tools needed for carving a turkey a meat cleaver or an ax. He describes the necessary strength involved in removing a drumstick when he advises the carver to "exercise the biceps and forearms by lifting barbells until they are strong enough for you to tackle the leg joint with bare hands." (par. 9) Reread the essay, and select at least ten verbs or description words that use hyperbole, and then write synonyms for them.

THINKING CRITICALLY ABOUT THE ESSAY

Understanding the Writer's Ideas

1. What does Baker reveal about the situation in which he is carving the turkey while he outlines the steps in the process? Give examples.

2. What is the tone of the essay? What is the author's purpose in satirizing the process of turkey carving? What does the tone imply about the author's attitudes toward chores like turkey carving that conventionally fall to men at holiday dinners?
3. Who is the "you" the author is addressing?

Understanding the Writer's Techniques

1. Where is the thesis? What is unusual about how Baker sets up his main idea?
2. Look at a cookbook page that gives instructions on how to carve a turkey. How does the language in the cookbook differ from Baker's language? In what ways is Baker's process similar to that in the cookbook? Could you actually carve a turkey using the cookbook directions? using Baker's directions?
3. Why does Baker use so many short paragraphs? How would the effect of the essay change if it were written in longer paragraphs?
4. How would you characterize the tone of the essay? Look up the definitions of *irony, cynicism,* and *sarcasm.* Which term do you think most closely describes Baker's tone? Does his tone fit the subject matter? Explain.

   Go back to your list of hyperbolic words from Building Vocabulary and note for each whether you think it is intended to be ironic, cynical, or sarcastic.
5. Think about the title of the essay. What does this *metaphor* (see Glossary) suggest the essay is about besides turkey carving?
6. How does Baker use narration in this essay? description? illustration?
7. Which sentence alerts us that this is a process analysis essay? Write an outline of the process steps discussed.
8. Writing teachers often tell their students: "Show. Don't tell." In other words, use gestures and actions to characterize someone or make a point rather than just give the reader an explanation. How does Baker use "showing" rather than "telling" in this essay? Give five examples.
9. What does the final paragraph reveal about the author's attitude toward "the carver's art"?

Exploring the Writer's Ideas

1. Great satirists like Jonathan Swift, who wrote political and moral satire in *Gulliver's Travels* (1729), and Mark Twain,

who wrote dozens of satirical tales of nineteenth-century American life, felt that satire was a technique for calling attention to weakness or flaws in the society in which they lived. In what way might Baker share this purpose?

2. Do you think Baker has written this essay from personal experience? Why do you think so?
3. Through his process analysis, Baker implies that holiday dinners are not always the cheerful events pictured on greeting cards. In what ways have your experiences of holiday dinners been like Baker's, where nothing goes according to plan and even the simplest chores are disasters?
4. Turkey carving as Baker analyzes it is a ritual. Rituals are actions we repeat periodically that have symbolic value for us. What changes in society in recent years have made rituals often seem outdated or inappropriate?
5. What personal or family rituals are important to you? Has your attitude toward them changed in recent years?

IDEAS FOR WRITING

Prewriting

Think of a simple task—like carving a turkey—which at first appears easy, but actually contains more complicated features. Brainstorm on paper, listing the steps involved, and placing a star or asterisk next to any step that could prove to be difficult.

Guided Writing

Write an essay in which you explain how to do something that is generally thought of as a simple activity. Use process analysis to show that the activity may look simple, but is in reality a mine field of potential embarrassment. You could analyze changing a flat tire for the first time, for instance, or trying to assemble a Christmas present for a child.

1. Decide on a tone for your essay. Use some hyperbole, irony, or sarcasm.
2. Prepare a direct thesis statement.
3. Make a list of the tools needed for this process, and include it in the introduction.
4. Use the body of the essay to give instructions on the process and to describe the dangers hidden behind the apparently

simple activity. Include the reactions of others who may observe you carrying out the process, for instance.

5. Give excuses for why the process won't work, assigning blame to others rather than yourself.
6. Conclude with a solution that will get you out of doing this process in the future.

Thinking and Writing Collaboratively

Discuss the techniques of humor that Baker draws on to amuse his readers. List the techniques and identify which ones he uses most successfully. Place your list on the chalkboard for class discussion. Which might group members use in their own writing? Why?

More Writing Projects

1. In your journal, write about the process you recently used to deal with an extremely embarrassing moment. Make sure you tell what led up to the moment and what happened during and after the incident.
2. Write a paragraph about the process you use when you're out with one person and meet someone else whose name you don't remember.
3. Write a process analysis essay telling how to get satisfaction when you've bought a defective product or gotten bad service in a store.

Camping Out

Ernest Hemingway

In this essay by Ernest Hemingway (1899–1961), the author uses the pattern of process analysis to order his materials on the art of camping. Hemingway wrote this piece for the *Toronto Star* in the early 1920s, before he gained worldwide recognition as a major American writer. In it, we see his lifelong interest in the outdoors and his desire to do things well.

PREREADING: THINKING ABOUT THE ESSAY IN ADVANCE

As you prepare to read Hemingway's essay, take a minute or two to think about your own experiences in nature or any unknown place you once visited. If you have ever camped out or attended summer camp, for example, how did you prepare for, enter into, and survive the experience? What problems did you encounter, and how did you overcome them?

Words to Watch

relief map (par. 2) a map that shows by lines and colors the various heights and forms of the land

Caucasus (par. 2) a mountain range in southeastern Europe

proprietary (par. 7) held under patent or trademark

rhapsodize (par. 9) to speak enthusiastically

browse bed (par. 9) a portable cot

tyro (par. 11) an amateur; a beginner in learning something

dyspepsia (par. 13) indigestion

mulligan (par. 18) a stew made from odds and ends of meats and vegetables

1 Thousands of people will go into the bush this summer to cut the high cost of living. A man who gets his two weeks' salary while he is on vacation should be able to put those two weeks in fishing and camping and be able to save one week's salary clear. He ought to be able to sleep comfortably every night, to eat well every day and to return to the city rested and in good condition.

But if he goes into the woods with a frying pan, an ignorance of black flies and mosquitoes, and a great and abiding lack of knowledge about cookery the chances are that his return will be very different. He will come back with enough mosquito bites to make the back of his neck look like a relief map of the Caucasus. His digestion will be wrecked after a valiant battle to assimilate half-cooked or charred grub. And he won't have had a decent night's sleep while he has been gone. 2

He will solemnly raise his right hand and inform you that he has joined the grand army of never-agains. The call of the wild may be all right, but it's a dog's life. He's heard the call of the tame with both ears. Waiter, bring him an order of milk toast. 3

In the first place he overlooked the insects. Black flies, no-see-ums, deer flies, gnats and mosquitoes were instituted by the devil to force people to live in cities where he could get at them better. If it weren't for them everybody would live in the bush and he would be out of work. It was a rather successful invention. 4

But there are lots of dopes that will counteract the pests. The simplest perhaps is oil of citronella. Two bits' worth of this purchased at any pharmacist's will be enough to last for two weeks in the worst fly and mosquito-ridden country. 5

Rub a little on the back of your neck, your forehead and your wrists before you start fishing, and the blacks and skeeters will shun you. The odor of citronella is not offensive to people. It smells like gun oil. But the bugs do hate it. 6

Oil of pennyroyal and eucalyptol are also much hated by mosquitoes, and with citronella they form the basis for many proprietary preparations. But it is cheaper and better to buy the straight citronella. Put a little on the mosquito netting that covers the front of your pup tent or canoe tent at night, and you won't be bothered. 7

To be really rested and get any benefit out of a vacation a man must get a good night's sleep every night. The first requisite for this is to have plenty of cover. It is twice as cold as you expect it will be in the bush four nights out of five, and a good plan is to take just double the bedding that you think you will need. An old quilt that you can wrap up in is as warm as two blankets. 8

Nearly all outdoor writers rhapsodize over the browse bed. It is all right for the man who knows how to make one and has plenty of time. But in a succession of one-night camps on a 9 canoe trip all you need is level ground for your tent floor and you will sleep all right if you have plenty of covers under you. Take twice as much cover as you think that you will need, and then put two-thirds of it under you. You will sleep warm and get your rest.

10 When it is clear weather you don't need to pitch your tent if you are only stopping for the night. Drive four stakes at the head of your made-up bed and drape your mosquito bar over that, then you can sleep like a log and laugh at the mosquitoes.

11 Outside of insects and bum sleeping the rock that wrecks most camping trips is cooking. The average tyro's idea of cooking is to fry everything and fry it good and plenty. Now, a frying pan is a most necessary thing to any trip, but you also need the old stew kettle and the folding reflector baker.

12 A pan of fried trout can't be bettered and they don't cost any more than ever. But there is a good and bad way of frying them.

13 The beginner puts his trout and his bacon in and over a brightly burning fire the bacon curls up and dries into a dry tasteless cinder and the trout is burned outside while it is still raw inside. He eats them and it is all right if he is only out for the day and going home to a good meal at night. But if he is going to face more trout and bacon the next morning and other equally well-cooked dishes for the remainder of two weeks he is on the pathway to nervous dyspepsia.

14 The proper way is to cook over coals. Have several cans of Crisco or Cotosuet or one of the vegetable shortenings along that are as good as lard and excellent for all kinds of shortening. Put the bacon in and when it is about half cooked lay the trout in the hot grease, dipping them in corn meal first. Then put the bacon on top of the trout and it will baste them as it slowly cooks.

15 The coffee can be boiling at the same time and in a smaller skillet pancakes being made that are satisfying the other campers while they are waiting for the trout.

16 With the prepared pancake flours you take a cupful of pancake flour and add a cup of water. Mix the water and flour and as soon as the lumps are out it is ready for cooking. Have the skillet hot and keep it well greased. Drop the batter in and as soon as it is done on one side loosen it in the skillet and flip it over. Apple butter, syrup or cinnamon and sugar go well with the cakes.

17 While the crowd have taken the edge from their appetites with flapjacks the trout have been cooked and they and the bacon

are ready to serve. The trout are crisp outside and firm and pink inside and the bacon is well done—but not too done. If there is anything better than that combination the writer has yet to taste it in a lifetime devoted largely and studiously to eating.

The stew kettle will cook you dried apricots when they have resumed their predried plumpness after a night of soaking, it will serve to concoct a mulligan in, and it will cook macaroni. When you are not using it, it should be boiling water for the dishes. 18

In the baker, mere man comes into his own, for he can make a pie that to his bush appetite will have it all over the product that mother used to make, like a tent. Men have always believed that there was something mysterious and difficult about making a pie. Here is a great secret. There is nothing to it. We've been kidded for years. Any man of average office intelligence can make at least as good a pie as his wife. 19

All there is to a pie is a cup and a half of flour, one-half teaspoonful of salt, one-half cup of lard and cold water. That will make pie crust that will bring tears of joy into your camping partner's eyes. 20

Mix the salt with the flour, work the lard into the flour, make it up into a good workmanlike dough with cold water. Spread some flour on the back of a box or something flat, and pat the dough around a while. Then roll it out with whatever kind of round bottle you prefer. Put a little more lard on the surface of the sheet of dough and then slosh a little flour on and roll it up and then roll it out again with the bottle. 21

Cut out a piece of the rolled out dough big enough to line a pie tin. I like the kind with holes in the bottom. Then put in your dried apples that have soaked all night and been sweetened, or your apricots, or your blueberries, and then take another sheet of the dough and drape it gracefully over the top, soldering it down at the edges with your fingers. Cut a couple of slits in the top dough sheet and prick it a few times with a fork in an artistic manner. 22

Put it in the baker with a good slow fire for forty-five minutes and then take it out and if your pals are Frenchmen they will kiss you. The penalty for knowing how to cook is that the others will make you do all the cooking. 23

It is all right to talk about roughing it in the woods. But the real woodsman is the man who can be really comfortable in the bush. 24

BUILDING VOCABULARY

For each word below write your own definition, based on how the word is used in the selection. Check back to the appropriate paragraph in the essay for more help, if necessary.

a. abiding (par. 2)
b. valiant (par. 2)
c. assimilate (par. 2)
d. charred (par. 2)
e. solemnly (par. 3)
f. requisite (par. 8)
g. succession (par. 9)
h. studiously (par. 17)
i. concoct (par. 18)
j. soldering (par. 22)

THINKING CRITICALLY ABOUT THE ESSAY

Understanding the Writer's Ideas

1. What is Hemingway's main purpose in this essay? Does he simply want to explain how to set up camp and how to cook outdoors?
2. What, according to the writer, are the two possible results of camping out on your vacation?
3. Why is oil of citronella the one insecticide that Hemingway recommends over all others?
4. Is it always necessary to pitch a tent when camping out? What are alternatives to it? How can you sleep warmly and comfortably?
5. Explain the author's process for cooking trout. Also explain his process for baking a pie.
6. Is it enough for Hemingway simply to enjoy "roughing it" while camping out?

Understanding the Writer's Techniques

1. Does the author have a stated thesis? Explain.
2. Identify those paragraphs in the essay that involve process analysis, and explain how Hemingway develops his subject in each.

3. What is the main writing pattern in paragraphs 1 and 2? How does this method serve as an organizing principle throughout the essay?
4. How would you characterize the author's style of writing? Is it appropriate to a newspaper audience? Is it more apt for professional fishermen?
5. In what way does Hemingway employ classification in this essay?
6. Analyze the tone of Hemingway's essay.
7. The concluding paragraph is short. Is it effective, nevertheless, and why? How does it reinforce the opening paragraph?

Exploring the Writer's Ideas

1. Camping out was popular in the 1920s, as it is today. What are some of the reasons that it remains so attractive today?
2. Hemingway's essay describes many basic strategies for successful camping. He does not rely on "gadgets" or modern inventions to make camping easier. Do such gadgets make camping more fun today than it might have been in the 1920s?
3. The author suggests that there is a right way and a wrong way to do things. Does it matter if you perform a recreational activity correctly as long as you enjoy doing it? Why?

IDEAS FOR WRITING

Prewriting

Freewrite for fifteen minutes about your favorite pastime, activity, or hobby. How do you approach this activity? What steps must be observed in order to be successful at it? How might other people fail at it whereas you are successful?

Guided Writing

Write an essay on how to do something wrong, and how to do it right—going on vacation, looking for a job, fishing, or whatever.

1. Reexamine the author's first three paragraphs and imitate his method of introducing the right and wrong ways about the subject, and the possible results.

2. Adopt a simple, informal, "chatty" style. Feel free to use a few well-placed clichés and other forms of spoken English. Use several similes.
3. Divide your subject into useful categories. Just as Hemingway treated insects, sleeping, and cooking, try to cover the main aspects of your subject.
4. Explain the process involved for each aspect of your subject. Make certain that you compare and contrast the right and wrong ways of your activity.
5. Write a short, crisp conclusion that reinforces your longer introduction.

Thinking and Writing Collaboratively

As a class, choose a process—for example, applying to college—which clearly involves a "right way" and "wrong way" of accomplishing the activity. Then divide the class into two groups, with one group outlining the correct steps and the other the incorrect or incomplete steps to completing the process. List both approaches on the chalkboard for comparative discussion.

More Writing Projects

1. How do you explain the fascination that camping out holds for many people? Reflect on this question in your journal.
2. In a paragraph, describe how to get to your favorite vacation spot, and what to do when you get there.
3. If you have ever camped out, write a process paper explaining one important feature of setting up camp.

In the Kitchen

Henry Louis Gates, Jr.

Henry Louis Gates, Jr., is the author of several books, including *Black Literature and Theory* and *The Signifying Monkey,* which won a 1989 National Book Award. In this selection he examines the politics of the hairdo by recalling his experiences as a child in his mother's home beauty parlor.

PREREADING: THINKING ABOUT THE ESSAY IN ADVANCE

Michael Jackson, America's pop icon, was criticized by some in the African-American community for having his hair altered to conform to Anglo features (such as straight hair). Do you think you should have the right to change your looks even if it means trying to conform to the standards of beauty of an ethnic or cultural group other than your own?

Words to Watch

transform (par. 4) to change the appearance or form of

southpaw (par. 4) a left-handed person, especially a left-handed baseball pitcher

refrain (par. 7) repeated phrase or utterance

preposterous (par. 7) absurd

tiara (par. 24) a crown or fine headdress

We always had a gas stove in the kitchen, in our house in Piedmont, West Virginia, where I grew up. Never electric, though using electric became fashionable in Piedmont in the sixties, like using Crest toothpaste rather than Colgate, or watching Huntley and Brinkley rather than Walter Cronkite. But not us: gas, Colgate, and good ole Walter Cronkite, come what may. We used gas partly out of loyalty to Big Mom, Mama's Mama, because she was mostly blind and still loved to cook, and could feel her way more easily with gas than with electric. But the most important thing about our gas-equipped kitchen was that Mama used to do hair there. The "hot comb" was a fine-toothed iron instrument 1 with a long wooden handle and a pair of iron curlers that opened and closed like scissors. Mama would put it in the gas fire until it glowed. You could smell those prongs heating up.

2 I liked that smell. Not the smell so much, I guess, as what the smell meant for the shape of my day. There was an intimate warmth in the women's tones as they talked with my Mama, doing their hair. I knew what the women had been through to get their hair ready to be "done," because I would watch Mama do it to herself. How that kink could be transformed through grease and fire into that magnificent head of wavy hair was a miracle to me, and still is.

3 Mama would wash her hair over the sink, a towel wrapped around her shoulders, wearing just her slip and her white bra. (We had no shower—just a galvanized tub that we stored in the kitchen—until we moved down Rat Tail Road into Doc Wolverton's house, in 1954.) After she dried it, she would grease her scalp thoroughly with blue Bergamot hair grease, which came in a short, fat jar with a picture of a beautiful colored lady on it. It's important to grease your scalp real good, my Mama would explain, to keep from burning yourself. Of course, her hair would return to its natural kink almost as soon as the hot water and shampoo hit it. To me, it was another miracle how hair so "straight" would so quickly become kinky again the second it even approached some water.

4 My Mama had only a few "clients" whose heads she "did"—did, I think, because she enjoyed it, rather than for the few pennies it brought in. They would sit on one of our red plastic kitchen chairs, the kind with the shiny metal legs, and brace themselves for the process. Mama would stroke that red-hot iron—which by this time had been in the gas fire for half an hour or more—slowly but firmly through their hair, from scalp to strand's end. It made a scorching, crinkly sound, the hot iron did, as it burned its way through kink, leaving in its wake straight strands of hair, standing long and tall but drooping over at the ends, their shape like the top of a heavy willow tree. Slowly, steadily, Mama's hands would transform a round mound of Odetta kink into a darkened swamp of everglades. The Bergamot made the hair shiny; the heat of the hot iron gave it a brownish-red cast. Once all the hair was as straight as God allows kink to get, Mama would take the well-heated curling iron and twirl the straightened strands into more or less loosely wrapped curls. She claimed that she owed her skill as a hairdresser to the strength in

her wrists, and as she worked her little finger would poke out, the way it did when she sipped tea. Mama was a southpaw, and wrote upside down and backward to produce the cleanest, roundest letters you've ever seen.

5 The "kitchen" she would all but remove from sight with a handheld pair of shears, bought just for this purpose. Now, the kitchen was the room in which we were sitting—the room where Mama did hair and washed clothes, and where we all took a bath in that galvanized tub. But the word has another meaning, and the kitchen that I'm speaking of is the very kinky bit of hair at the back of your head, where your neck meets your shirt collar. If there was ever a part of our African past that resisted assimilation, it was the kitchen. No matter how hot the iron, no matter how powerful the chemical, no matter how stringent the mashed-potatoes-and-lye formula of a man's "process," neither God nor woman nor Sammy Davis, Jr., could straighten the kitchen. The kitchen was permanent, irredeemable, irresistible kink. Unassimilably African. No matter what you did, no matter how hard you tried, you couldn't de-kink a person's kitchen. So you trimmed it off as best you could.

6 When hair had begun to "turn," as they'd say—to return to its natural kinky glory—it was the kitchen that turned first (the kitchen around the back, and nappy edges at the temples). When the kitchen started creeping up the back of the neck, it was time to get your hair done again.

7 Sometimes, after dark, a man would come to have his hair done. It was Mr. Charlie Carroll. He was very light-complected and had a ruddy nose—it made me think of Edmund Gwenn, who played Kris Kringle in "Miracle on 34th Street." At first, Mama did him after my brother, Rocky, and I had gone to sleep. It was only later that we found out that he had come to our house so Mama could iron his hair—not with a hot comb or a curling iron but with our very own Proctor-Silex steam iron. For some reason I never understood, Mr. Charlie would conceal his Frederick Douglass-like mane under a big white Stetson hat. I never saw him take it off except when he came to our house, at night, to have his hair pressed. (Later, Daddy would tell us about Mr. Charlie's most prized piece of knowledge, something that the man would only confide after his hair had been pressed, as a token of intimacy. "Not many people know this," he'd say, in a tone of circumspection, "but George

Washington was Abraham Lincoln's daddy." Nodding solemnly, he'd add the clincher: "A white man told me." Though he was in dead earnest, this became a humorous refrain around our house—"a white man told me"—which wc used to punctuate especially preposterous assertions.)

8 My mother examined my daughters' kitchens whenever we went home to visit, in the early eighties. It became a game between us. I had told her not to do it, because I didn't like the politics it suggested—the notion of "good" and "bad" hair. "Good" hair was "straight," "bad" hair kinky. Even in the late sixties, at the height of Black Power, almost nobody could bring themselves to say "bad" for good and "good" for bad. People still said that hair like white people's hair was "good," even if they encapsulated it in a disclaimer, like "what we used to call 'good.' "

9 Maggie would be seated in her high chair, throwing food this way and that, and Mama would be cooing about how cute it all was, how I used to do just like Maggie was doing, and wondering whether her flinging her food with her left hand meant that she was going to be left-handed like Mama. When my daughter was just about covered with Chef Boyardee Spaghetti-O's, Mama would seize the opportunity: wiping her clean, she would tilt Maggie's head to one side and reach down the back of her neck. Sometimes Mama would even rub a curl between her fingers, just to make sure that her bifocals had not deceived her. Then she'd sigh with satisfaction and relief: No kink . . . yet. Mama! I'd shout, pretending to be angry. Every once in a while, if no one was looking, I'd peek, too.

10 I say "yet" because most black babies are born with soft, silken hair. But after a few months it begins to turn, as inevitably as do the seasons or the leaves on a tree. People once thought baby oil would stop it. They were wrong.

11 Everybody I knew as a child wanted to have good hair. You could be as ugly as homemade sin dipped in misery and still be thought attractive if you had good hair. "Jesus moss," the girls at Camp Lee, Virginia, had called Daddy's naturally "good" hair during the war. I know that he played that thick head of hair for all it was worth, too.

12 My own hair was "not a bad grade," as barbers would tell me when they cut it for the first time. It was like a doctor reporting the results of the first full physical he has given you. Like "You're in good shape" or "Blood pressure's kind of high—better cut down on salt."

I spent most of my childhood and adolescence messing with my hair. I definitely wanted straight hair. Like Pop's. When I was about three, I tried to stick a wad of Bazooka bubble gum to that straight hair of his. I suppose what fixed that memory for me is the spanking I got for doing so: he turned me upside down, holding me by my feet, the better to paddle my behind. Little *nigger,* he had shouted, walloping away. I started to laugh about it two days later, when my behind stopped hurting. 13

When black people say "straight," of course, they don't usually mean literally straight—they're not describing hair like, say, Peggy Lipton's (she was the white girl on "The Mod Squad"), or like Mary's of Peter, Paul & Mary fame; black people call that "stringy" hair. No, "straight" just means not kinky, no matter what contours the curl may take. I would have done *anything* to have straight hair—and I used to try everything, short of getting a process. 14

Of the wide variety of techniques and methods I came to master in the challenging prestidigitation of the follicle, almost all had two things in common: a heavy grease and the application of pressure. It's not an accident that some of the biggest black-owned companies in the fifties and sixties made hair products. And I tried them all, in search of that certain silken touch, the one that would leave neither the hand nor the pillow sullied by grease. 15

I always wondered what Frederick Douglass put on *his* hair, or what Phillis Wheatley put on hers. Or why Wheatley has that rag on her head in the little engraving in the frontispiece of her book. One thing is for sure: you can bet that when Phillis Wheatley went to England and saw the Countess of Huntingdon she did not stop by the Queen's coiffeur on her way there. So many black people still get their hair straightened that it's a wonder we don't have a national holiday for Madame C. J. Walker, the woman who invented the process of straightening kinky hair. Call it Jheri-Kurled or call it "relaxed," it's still fried hair. 16

I used all the greases, from sea-blue Bergamot and creamy vanilla Duke (in its clear jar with the orange-white-and-green label) to the godfather of grease, the formidable Murray's. Now, Murray's was some *serious* grease. Whereas Bergamot was like oily jello, and Duke was viscous and sickly sweet, Murray's was light brown and *hard.* Hard as lard and twice as greasy, Daddy used to say. Murray's came in an orange can with a press-on top. It was so hard that some people would put a match to the can, just to soften the stuff and make it more manageable. Then, in the late sixties, when Afros 17 came into style, I used Afro Sheen. From Murray's to Duke to Afro Sheen: that was my progression in black consciousness.

18 We used to put hot towels or washrags over our Murray-coated heads, in order to melt the wax into the scalp and the follicles. Unfortunately, the wax also had the habit of running down your neck, ears, and forehead. Not to mention your pillowcase. Another problem was that if you put two palmfuls of Murray's on your head your hair turned white. (Duke did the same thing.) The challenge was to get rid of that white color. Because if you got rid of the white stuff you had a magnificent head of wavy hair. That was the beauty of it: Murray's was so hard that it froze your hair into the wavy style you brushed it into. It looked really good if you wore a part. A lot of guys had parts *cut* into their hair by a barber, either with the clippers or with a straightedge razor. Especially if you had kinky hair—then you'd generally wear a short razor cut, or what we called a Quo Vadis.

19 We tried to be as innovative as possible. Everyone knew about using a stocking cap, because your father or your uncle wore one whenever something really big was about to happen, whether sacred or secular: a funeral or a dance, a wedding or a trip in which you confronted official white people. Any time you were trying to look really sharp, you wore a stocking cap in preparation. And if the event was really a big one, you made a new cap. You asked your mother for a pair of her hose, and cut it with scissors about six inches or so from the open end—the end with the elastic that goes up to the top of the thigh. Then you knotted the cut end, and it became a beehive-shaped hat, with an elastic band that you pulled down low on your forehead and down around your neck in the back. To work well, the cap had to fit tightly and snugly, like a press. And it had to fit that tightly because it *was* a press: it pressed your hair with the force of the hose's elastic. If you greased your hair down real good, and left the stocking cap on long enough, voilà: you got a head of pressed-against-the-scalp waves. (You also got a ring around your forehead when you woke up, but it went away.) And then you could enjoy your concrete do. Swore we were bad, too, with all that grease and those flat heads. My brother and I would brush it out a bit in the mornings, so that it looked—well, "natural." Grown men still wear stocking caps—especially older men, who generally keep their stocking caps in their top drawers, along with their cufflinks and their see-through silk socks, their "Maverick" ties, their silk handkerchiefs, and whatever else they prize the most.

A Murrayed-down stocking cap was the respectable version of the process, which, by contrast, was most definitely not a cool thing to have unless you were an entertainer by trade. Zeke and Keith and Poochie and a few other stars of the high-school basketball team all used to get a process once or twice a year. It was expensive, and you had to go somewhere like Pittsburgh or D.C. or Uniontown—somewhere where there were enough colored people to support a trade. The guys would disappear, then reappear a day or two later, strutting like peacocks, their hair burned slightly red from the lye base. They'd also wear "rags"—cloths or handkerchiefs—around their heads when they slept or played basketball. Do-rags, they were called. But the result was straight hair, with just a hint of wave. No curl. Do-it-yourselfers took their chances at home with a concoction of mashed potatoes and lye. 20

The most famous process of all, however, outside of the process Malcolm X describes in his "Autobiography," and maybe the process of Sammy Davis, Jr., was Nat King Cole's process. Nat King Cole had patent-leather hair. That man's got the finest process money can buy, or so Daddy said the night we saw Cole's TV show on NBC. It was November 5, 1956. I remember the date because everyone came to our house to watch it and to celebrate one of Daddy's buddies' birthdays. Yeah, Uncle Joe chimed in, they can do shit to his hair that the average Negro can't even *think* about—secret shit. 21

Nat King Cole was *clean.* I've had an ongoing argument with a Nigerian friend about Nat King Cole for twenty years now. Not about whether he could sing—any fool knows that he could—but about whether or not he was a handkerchief head for wearing that patent-leather process. 22

Sammy Davis, Jr.'s process was the one I detested. It didn't look good on him. Worse still, he liked to have a fried strand dangling down the middle of his forehead, so he could shake it out from the crown when he sang. But Nat King Cole's hair was a thing unto itself, a beautifully sculpted work of art that he and he alone had the right to wear. The only difference between a process and a stocking cap, really, was taste; but Nat King Cole, unlike, say, Michael Jackson, looked *good* in his. His head looked like Valentino's head in the twenties, and some say it was Valentino the process was imitating. But Nat King Cole wore a process because it suited his face, his demeanor, his name, his style. He was as clean as he wanted to be. 23

24 I had forgotten all about that patent-leather look until one day in 1971, when I was sitting in an Arab restaurant on the island of Zanzibar surrounded by men in fezzes and white caftans, trying to learn how to eat curried goat and rice with the fingers of my right hand and feeling two million miles from home. All of a sudden, an old transistor radio sitting on top of a china cupboard stopped blaring out its Swahili music and started playing "Fly Me to the Moon," by Nat King Cole. The restaurant's din was not affected at all, but in my mind's eye I saw it: the King's magnificent sleek black tiara. I managed, barely, to blink back the tears.

BUILDING VOCABULARY

For each word below write your own definition based on how the word is used in the selection. Check back to the appropriate paragraph in the essay for more help, if necessary.

a. galvanized (par. 5)
b. assertions (par. 7)
c. prestidigitation (par. 15)
d. follicle (par. 15)
e. din (par. 24)

THINKING CRITICALLY ABOUT THE ESSAY

Understanding the Writer's Ideas

1. The word "Kitchen" in the title takes on two meanings in the essay. What are they?
2. Gas was used in this writer's kitchen even though people had turned to electricity in the 1960s. Why?
3. What does the writer mean when he states that his mother "did hair"?
4. What does the word "turn" (par. 6) describe?
5. What is the history behind "good" and "bad" hair?
6. As a child, how did the writer worry about his hair? Explain.
7. Describe the two things all hair-straightening techniques have in common.
8. What was it about Nat King Cole's hair that impressed this writer so much?

9. How were the hot irons used to straighten hair?
10. Hearing a Nat King Cole song while in Zanzibar, the writer says he had to "blink back the tears." What is going on?

Understanding the Writer's Techniques

1. Find the thesis and paraphrase it.
2. What process is described in paragraph 3? Give examples of the process described in paragraph 3.
3. Given the detailed descriptions of de-kinking hair, what audience does this writer have in mind in employing this strategy?
4. Where in the essay does the writer make a transition to describe two of the most common processes of hair straightening? How are these processes detailed?
5. Though the other de-kinking processes mentioned in the essay are detailed, the most famous one (Nat King Cole's) is not described at all. What might this suggest about the writer's attitude toward this subject?
6. The essay's entire structure is not focused entirely on process. What other rhetorical mode does the writer use? Identify the places where this occurs.
7. What makes Gates's concluding paragraph different from others more common in essays?

Exploring the Writer's Ideas

1. Gates claims the "kitchen," those hairs on the back of the neck, are "unassimilably" African. Yet, his mother specialized in getting rid of the kitchen. Do you think this writer approves or disapproves of his mother's activity? Explain.
2. Gates tells of jokes about the "white man." Gates says he found the jokes funny even though he also admits he wanted good hair, like that of whites. How would you explain this writer's contradictory feelings about white people?
3. How do you feel about this writer's claims that most everyone he knew thought kinky hair was "bad"? Do you think this is an exaggeration? Why or why not?
4. Are there still examples today of people who remake themselves to look "white" or like those who are held up as role models, like Madonna or other rock stars? Is this impulse positive or negative? Why?

5. The author suggests that the de-kinking was physically painful. Does anything in the essay suggest all the pain was worth it? Explain.
6. By calling Nat King Cole's straightened hair a "black tiara" is this author concluding that straight hair (looking white) is indeed admirable? How do you feel?

IDEAS FOR WRITING

Prewriting

Use your journal to recall times when you felt good or bad about the way you look.

Guided Writing

Write an essay on how you once may have tried to make yourself look the "right" or "wrong" way. Remember the time you dressed for a date or to go to church or to get a job.

1. Examine Gates's first paragraph and imitate his method of introducing the thesis.
2. Divide your process into its important parts, like Gates who divides de-kinking into its steps: hot comb, the kitchen, the clients, the grease, and the pressure.
3. Make sure that your process is detailed in a way that keeps a general audience in mind (or people who don't know your process).
4. Try to use definition paragraphs to explain terms that describe your process which are unknown to your general audience.
5. Write a conclusion that tells a story, like Gates on Nat King Cole. Remember that this story should reflect an overall feeling you have about your topic.

Thinking and Writing Collaboratively

Your group has been assigned the task of creating a behavior code pamphlet for your school. Use process technique to make clear how students should act in different situations. Explain what happens (the process) if someone's behavior challenges the guidelines.

More Writing Projects

1. In your journal, make notes on the ways that you have seen people change their looks to please others.
2. In a paragraph, describe the process by which people learn who looks the right way or the wrong way.
3. Write a process essay on something your parents or caregiver taught you as a child. Tell of learning to swim or to ride a bike.

SUMMING UP: CHAPTER 9

1. Divide the class into groups and choose one Guided Writing essay per group using the Gates, Baker, or Hemingway selection. Collaboratively discuss, evaluate, correct, edit, and rewrite the Guided Writing process essay. By consensus, establish grades for the original and the revised essay. Present your findings to the class.
2. On the basis of your experience reading the four essays in the section, write about the types of processes the authors deal with (you may want to read the introduction to the previous chapter on classification) and how they manage these processes. Clarify the main steps that you consider to be important in the writing of any process analysis.
3. Jerrold G. Simon in his essay provides a kind of recipe for brewing a resume. To continue the metaphor, everyone has a favorite food. For this exercise, contribute a recipe for your favorite food to be included in a class cookbook. In addition to describing the step-by-step process for preparing the food, you should also tell something about the tradition behind the food, special occasions for eating it, the first time you ate it, and so forth. The goal should be to make the process clear and reassuring, to emphasize how following these simple steps can make anyone a great cook!
4. All four of the essays in this chapter tell us how to do things that can have direct and immediate effects on our lives—straightening hair, carving a turkey, camping, getting a job. Try to write an essay that describes a process with much less immediate effect.
5. Interview a classmate about something that he or she does very well. Make sure the questions you ask don't omit any important steps or materials used in the process. Take careful notes during the interview, then try to replicate the process on your own. If there are any difficulties in accomplishing the process, reinterview your classmate. After you are satisfied that no steps or materials have been left out, write up the procedure in such a way that someone else could easily follow it.

CHAPTER 10

Cause-and-Effect Analysis

WHAT IS CAUSE-AND-EFFECT ANALYSIS?

Cause-and-effect analysis answers the basic human question: *Why?* Why do events occur, like hurricanes or the election of a new president? Why does one student do better in math than another? In addition, this form of analysis looks at the *expected* consequences of a chain of happenings. If we raise the minimum wage, what will the likely consequences be?

Basically, cause-and-effect analysis (also called causal analysis) looks for *causes* or conditions, and suggests or examines *results* or consequences (the effects).

Like most of the writing strategies you have been studying, causal analysis parallels a kind of thinking we do in everyday life. If you are a student who has returned to school after being away for several years, someone might ask you why you decided to come back. In answering, you would give causes: You needed a better job to support your children; you wanted to learn a new skill; your intellectual curiosity drove you back; and so on. These would be *causes.* Once you were attending school, a classmate might ask you what changes coming back to school have made in your life. You might consider the pride your children feel in your achievement, or the fact that you have less time to prepare meals, or that you sleep only four hours a night. Those are the *consequences* or results of your decision. In a few years' time, after graduation, the effects might be very different: a better job or a scholarship to graduate school might be one of the long-term results.

Thinking about causes can go beyond everyday life to help us understand social and political change: What were the causes of the Amcrican Civil War? What were the consequences for the nation? What caused the Great Depression? Why were women denied the vote until 1920? Why did so many Irish immigrants come to America around 1900, and what were the consequences for the growth of American industry?

In looking at such large questions, you will realize that there are different kinds of causes. First, there is the *immediate* cause that gives rise to a situation. This is the cause (or causes) most directly related, the one closest at hand. But as you can see from the historical questions in the previous paragraph, we also need to go beyond the immediate cause to the *ultimate* cause, the basic conditions that stimulated the more obvious or immediate ones.

For example, although we might identify the immediate cause of the Los Angeles riots of 1992 as the Rodney King trial, the ultimate causes for racial unrest grow from the social and economic conditions of the poor in America. To find the "real" causes, we have to think critically, to examine the situation deeply.

Often, a writer has to consider many causes and rank them in order of importance. Depending on the length of the essay, a writer may have to select from among many causes. If a small town begins to lose businesses to a large mall, the chamber of commerce may ask why businesses and customers prefer the mall to shopping in town. Convenience, parking, competitive pricing, and entertainment may be identified as causes: Since the town cannot solve all these problems at once, it may focus on one, and try to lure shoppers back downtown by building a larger municipal parking lot. The result, perhaps, will be that shoppers will return to Main Street.

One difficulty in working with causal analysis is that we cannot always prove that a cause or an effect is absolute. We can only do our best to offer as much evidence as possible to help the reader see the relation we wish to establish. Therefore, we have to support our causes and effects with specific details and evidence drawn from personal experience, from statistics, or from experts' statements in newspapers or books. A writer can interview people, for instance, and collect data about local shopping habits or visit the library to read articles on the Los Angeles riots.

In the essays in this chapter, you will find a variety of uses for causal analysis. Stephen King analyzes why we crave horror movies. Anne Roiphe looks at the causes for the failure of half the marriages in America. Nancy Shute explains what science knows about the causes of aging. Finally, Susan Jacoby combines both process analysis and narrative with causal analysis techniques to examine the reasons women opt out of courses in math and science. As you read each piece, keep in mind the kinds of causes the writers present and the ways in which they add support to their analysis.

HOW DO WE READ CAUSAL ANALYSIS?

Reading causal analysis requires us to ask ourselves these questions:

- What are the writer's topic and the main cause? Make an outline of the causes as you read.
- Are immediate causes or ultimate causes presented? How do you know?
- Does the author show the consequences of the event? Why or why not?
- How does the author develop the analysis? Identify the writing strategies used: narrative, description, illustration, process analysis, and so on. Which is most effective in supporting the causal analysis and why?
- What is the tone of the essay?

HOW DO WE WRITE CAUSAL ANALYSIS?

Select a topic you can manage. If you try to find the causes of psychological depression, you may need to study a great deal of Freud before you can write the essay. If, on the other hand, you decide to write about causes of suicide among college freshmen, you would narrow the scope of the essay and thus control it more easily.

Write a working thesis that tells the cause and effect you are analyzing. Why is it important?

Sample thesis statement:

> Many causes lie behind Americans' return to more healthful eating habits, but the most important are fear of disease, desire to lose weight, and curiosity about new types of food.

Make a list of the major causes and under each cause, add at least one specific example to support it.

Plan whether you want to concentrate on either causes or effects, or on a balance of the two.

Be sure that you have included all the necessary links in the chain of reasoning that you began in the thesis.

Avoid oversimplification.

Include both major and minor causes and effects.

Writing the Draft

Write an introduction that presents the thesis and your statement of the significance of the thesis.

Use transitions as you move from one cause to the next.

Use narrative, description, process analysis, and other techniques to support your causes.

Conclude by reminding your reader of the importance of understanding this chain of events.

Proofread your draft carefully. Ask a classmate to read it to see if your causes seem logical.

Make corrections and prepare a final copy.

A STUDENT PARAGRAPH: CAUSE-AND-EFFECT ANALYSIS

The student who wrote the following paragraph concentrated on one aspect of the thesis sentence provided earlier in this chapter introduction to focus her causal analysis. Examine the way she weaves examples as her support for an analysis of American's changing eating habits.

The arrival of ethnic restaurants and groceries in what used to be called "white-bread" neighborhoods has transformed the eating habits of mainstream American culture—in most cases, for the better.	Topic sentence
While <u>chicharron de pollo</u> (fried chicken cracklings) and jerk pork might not be much better for you nutritionally than what you can get at McDonald's, much of the newly arrived	Contrasting examples
"exotic" food is far less fatty than typical fast-food fare. <u>Phô</u> (a Vietnamese noodle soup), rice and beans, hummus, <u>chana saag</u> (Indian chickpeas and spinach), and similar dishes provide leaner, more healthful fuel for the body than a Philly cheese steak and fries.	Supporting examples, with definitions

Transition "too" signals shift to related topic; examples follow

Many people are beginning to think they taste better, too. The positive influence of these cuisines doesn't stop at the restaurant door, either. Many Americans are beginning to bring the culinary habits of other cultures into their own kitchens, imitating their techniques (stir frying, for example), adopting their principles (using meat as a flavoring, instead of the centerpiece of the meal), and borrowing their more healthful ingredients (yogurt instead of sour cream, olive oil instead of butter, a wider range of fresh vegetables and spices). In the process, the traditions of newly arrived immigrants receive appropriate recognition, and native habits evolve in a positive direction: the effect is not only better eating, but a broadening of the American cultural horizon.

Concluding sentence establishes main effect of altered eating habits

Why We Crave Horror Movies

Stephen King

Stephen King is America's best-known horror writer. Because he is an acknowledged master of this genre, his thoughts on why people love horror movies offer an unusual insight into this question. King also gives us a unique glimpse into why he himself creates horror.

PREREADING: THINKING ABOUT THE ESSAY IN ADVANCE

Do you think that we all have a dark side to our personalities that we rarely reveal? Explain.

Words to Watch

innately (par. 4) by essential characteristic; by birth

voyeur (par. 6) a person who derives sexual gratification from observing the acts of others

penchant (par. 7) a definite liking; a strong inclination

remonstrance (par. 10) an expression of protest

anarchistic (par. 11) active resistance and terrorism against the state

subterranean (par. 12) hidden; secret

1 I think that we're all mentally ill; those of us outside the asylums only hide it a little better—and maybe not all that much better, after all. We've all known people who talk to themselves, people who sometimes squinch their faces into horrible grimaces when they believe no one is watching, people who have some hysterical fear—of snakes, the dark, the tight place, the long drop . . . and, of course, those final worms and grubs that are waiting so patiently underground.

2 When we pay our four or five bucks and seat ourselves at tenth-row center in a theater showing a horror movie, we are daring the nightmare.

3 Why? Some of the reasons are simple and obvious. To show that we can, that we are not afraid, that we can ride this roller

coaster. Which is not to say that a really good horror movie may not surprise a scream out of us at some point, the way we may scream when the roller coaster twists through a complete 360 or plows through a lake at the bottom of the drop. And horror movies, like roller coasters, have always been the special province of the young; by the time one turns 40 or 50, one's appetite for double twists or 360-degree loops may be considerably depleted.

We also go to re-establish our feelings of essential normality; the horror movie is innately conservative, even reactionary. Freda Jackson as the horrible melting woman in *Die, Monster, Die!* confirms for us that no matter how far we may be removed from the beauty of a Robert Redford or a Diana Ross, we are still light-years from true ugliness. 4

And we go to have fun. 5

Ah, but this is where the ground starts to slope away, isn't it? Because this is a very peculiar sort of fun indeed. The fun comes from seeing others menaced—sometimes killed. One critic has suggested that if pro football has become the voyeur's version of combat, then the horror film has become the modern version of the public lynching. 6

It is true that the mythic, "fairytale" horror film intends to take away the shades of gray. . . . It urges us to put away our more civilized and adult penchant for analysis and to become children again, seeing things in pure blacks and whites. It may be that horror movies provide psychic relief on this level because this invitation to lapse into simplicity, irrationality and even outright madness is extended so rarely. We are told we may allow our emotions a free rein . . . or no rein at all. 7

If we are all insane, then sanity becomes a matter of degree. If your insanity leads you to carve up women like Jack the Ripper or the Cleveland Torso Murderer, we clap you away in the funny farm (but neither of those two amateur-night surgeons was ever caught, heh-heh-heh); if, on the other hand your insanity leads you only to talk to yourself when you're under stress or to pick your nose on the morning bus, then you are left alone to go about your business . . . though it is doubtful that you will ever be invited to the best parties. 8

The potential lyncher is in almost all of us (excluding saints, past and present; but then, most saints have been crazy in their own ways), and every now and then, he has to be let loose to scream and roll around in the grass. Our emotions and our fears form their own body, and we recognize that it demands its own 9 exercise to maintain proper muscle tone. Certain of these emotional muscles are accepted—even exalted—in civilized society; they are, of course, the emotions that tend to maintain the status quo of civilization itself. Love, friendship, loyalty, kindness—these are all the emotions that we applaud, emotions that have been immortalized in the couplets of Hallmark cards and in the verses (I don't dare call it poetry) of Leonard Nimoy.

10 When we exhibit these emotions, society showers us with positive reinforcement; we learn this even before we get out of diapers. When, as children, we hug our rotten little puke of a sister and give her a kiss, all the aunts and uncles smile and twit and cry, "Isn't he the sweetest little thing?" Such coveted treats as chocolate-covered graham crackers often follow. But if we deliberately slam the rotten little puke of a sister's fingers in the door, sanctions follow—angry remonstrance from parents, aunts and uncles; instead of a chocolate-covered graham cracker, a spanking.

11 But anticivilization emotions don't go away, and they demand periodic exercise. We have such "sick" jokes as, "What's the difference between a truckload of bowling balls and a truckload of dead babies?" (You can't unload a truckload of bowling balls with a pitchfork . . . a joke, by the way, that I heard originally from a ten-year-old.) Such a joke may surprise a laugh or a grin out of us even as we recoil, a possibility that confirms the thesis: If we share a brotherhood of man, then we also share an insanity of man. None of which is intended as a defense of either the sick joke or insanity but merely as an explanation of why the best horror films, like the best fairy tales, manage to be reactionary, anarchistic, and revolutionary all at the same time.

12 The mythic horror movie, like the sick joke, has a dirty job to do. It deliberately appeals to all that is worst in us. It is morbidity unchained, our most base instincts let free, our nastiest fantasies realized . . . and it all happens, fittingly enough, in the dark. For those reasons, good liberals often shy away from horror films. For myself, I like to see the most aggressive of them—*Dawn of the Dead,* for instance—as lifting a trap door in the civilized forebrain and throwing a basket of raw meat to the hungry alligators swimming around in that subterranean river beneath.

13 Why bother? Because it keeps them from getting out, man. It keeps them down there and me up here. It was Lennon and McCartney who said that all you need is love, and I would agree with that.

14 As long as you keep the gators fed.

BUILDING VOCABULARY

King uses descriptive language in this essay to re-create some of the scary images from horror stories, such as snakes and grubs (par. 1). Make a list of his scary words (at least five). Then find a synonym for each word and use each in a sentence.

THINKING CRITICALLY ABOUT THE ESSAY

Understanding the Writer's Ideas

1. King uses the cause-and-effect method to explore why people crave horror. He says we share an "insanity of man" (par. 11). What does he mean by *insanity?*
2. Due to what three reasons does the writer think we dare the nightmare?
3. What does King mean when he says the "'fairytale'" horror films "take away the shades of gray" (par. 7)?
4. How does King explain his view on anticivilization emotions?
5. King uses the image of alligators (the gator) to make a final point. How do you interpret this?

Understanding the Writer's Techniques

1. What is the thesis? Where is it? How does the essay's title reflect the writer's thesis?
2. King uses first person narration in this essay. What other rhetorical modes does he use to develop his essay?
3. In this cause-and-effect essay, what is the cause and what is the effect?
4. King says we are all insane. What tone does this create for the reader? Is he accusing? humorous? serious?
5. King uses both specific and broad generalizations to develop his thesis. Give an example of something specific and something generalized. Which better supports the thesis and why?
6. Notice how the last and concluding sentence of the essay suddenly addresses the reader ("you"). Why? What purpose does this shift to the second person serve in this essay's conclusion?

Exploring the Writer's Ideas

1. How do you feel about the writer's bold opening statement that we are all mentally ill? Does this statement make you want to stop reading? How do you feel about his assumption?
2. Do you go to horror movies or do you avoid them? Why do you or don't you go? Explain.
3. Why do you think King chose to write out his ideas rather than discuss them with a friend? In what way is the process of writing out our ideas different from the process of thinking out loud in conversation?
4. This writer claims he isn't defending anticivilization emotions (par. 11), but he tells us that we need to "scream and roll around in the grass" (par. 9). Which side is this writer on? Which side are you on? Why?
5. Is it true that in horror tales the villains are always destroyed and good always triumphs? Should this be the case? Why or why not?

IDEAS FOR WRITING

Prewriting

Make a scratch outline of your strongest feelings for or against horror stories.

Guided Writing

Write an essay wherein you analyze your reactions to horror books or movies.

1. Begin the essay by stating your feelings on why you personally like or dislike horror. Use some examples to bring to life for the reader your experience with horror.
2. Describe two or more causes for the way you react to horror.
3. Analyze some of the effects you think horror movies may have on you or others who crave them.
4. Respond to the issue of horror allowing anticivilization emotions to be exercised so they don't "get out," as King says.
5. Conclude by addressing readers, telling them why they should embrace or avoid the horror genre.

Thinking and Writing Collaboratively

Working in a group of four to five students, research what experts say about the causes and effects of television violence on children. Then write an essay that makes these causes and effects clear to an audience of parents.

More Writing Projects

1. In your journal, write about something that scares you.
2. Write a paragraph that explains what causes you to fear something.
3. In an essay, examine the causes and effects of something in your life that frightens you (for example, stage fright, test anxiety, fear of flying, and so forth).

Why Marriages Fail

Anne Roiphe

Anne Roiphe is the author of the well-known novel about relationships, *Up the Sandbox!,* which was later made into a popular film. In this essay, notice how she presents a series of interconnected reasons for the currently high divorce rate.

PREREADING: THINKING ABOUT THE ESSAY IN ADVANCE

What experiences or assumptions do you bring to an essay about failed marriages? Do you know of marriages that have failed? If so, what were the causes?

Words to Watch

obsolete (par. 1) out-of-date; no longer in use
perils (par. 2) dangers
infertility (par. 2) the lack of ability to have children
turbulent (par. 2) very chaotic or uneasy
stupefying (par. 2) bewildering
obese (par. 3) very fat; overweight
entrapment (par. 4) the act of trapping, sometimes by devious methods
yearning (par. 4) a strong desire
euphoric (par. 7) characterized by a feeling of well-being
infidelity (par. 13) sexual unfaithfulness
proverbial (par. 13) relating to a proverb or accepted truth

1 These days so many marriages end in divorce that our most sacred vows no longer ring with truth. "Happily ever after" and "Till death do us part" are expressions that seem on the way to becoming obsolete. Why has it become so hard for couples to stay together? What goes wrong? What has happened to us that close to one-half of all marriages are destined for the divorce courts? How could we have created a society in which 42 percent of our children will grow up in single-parent homes? If

statistics could only measure loneliness, regret, pain, loss of self-confidence and fear of the future, the numbers would be beyond quantifying.

Even though each broken marriage is unique, we can still find the common perils, the common causes for marital despair. Each marriage has crisis points and each marriage tests endurance, the capacity for both intimacy and change. Outside pressures such as job loss, illness, infertility, trouble with a child, care of aging parents and all the other plagues of life hit marriage the way hurricanes blast our shores. Some marriages survive these storms and others don't. Marriages fail, however, not simply because of the outside weather but because the inner climate becomes too hot or too cold, too turbulent or too stupefying. 2

When we look at how we choose our partners and what expectations exist at the tender beginnings of romance, some of the reasons for disaster become quite clear. We all select with unconscious accuracy a mate who will recreate with us the emotional patterns of our first homes. Dr. Carl A. Whitaker, a marital therapist and emeritus professor of psychiatry at the University of Wisconsin, explains, "From early childhood on, each of us carried models for marriage, femininity, masculinity, motherhood, fatherhood and all the other family roles." Each of us falls in love with a mate who has qualities of our parents, who will help us rediscover both the psychological happiness and miseries of our past lives. We may think we have found a man unlike Dad, but then he turns to drink or drugs, or loses his job over and over again or sits silently in front of the T.V. just the way Dad did. A man may choose a woman who doesn't like kids just like his mother or who gambles away the family savings just like his mother. Or he may choose a slender wife who seems unlike his obese mother but then turns out to have other addictions that destroy their mutual happiness. 3

A man and a woman bring to their marriage bed a blended concoction of conscious and unconscious memories of their parents' lives together. The human way is to compulsively repeat and recreate the patterns of the past. Sigmund Freud so well described the unhappy design that many of us get trapped in: the unmet needs of childhood, the angry feelings left over from frustrations of long ago, the limits of trust and the recurrence of old fears. Once an individual senses this entrapment, there may follow a yearning to escape, and the result could be a broken, splintered marriage. 4

5 Of course people can overcome the habits and attitudes that developed in childhood. We all have hidden strengths and amazing capacities for growth and creative change. Change, however, requires work—observing your part in a rotten pattern, bringing difficulties out into the open—and work runs counter to the basic myth of marriage: "When I wed this person all my problems will be over. I will have achieved success and I will become the center of life for this other person and this person will be my center, and we will mean everything to each other forever." This myth, which every marriage relies on, is soon exposed. The coming of children, the pulls and tugs of their demands on affection and time, place a considerable strain on that basic myth of meaning everything to each other, of merging together and solving all of life's problems.

6 Concern and tension about money take each partner away from the other. Obligations to demanding parents or still-depended-upon parents create further strain. Couples today must also deal with all the cultural changes brought on in recent years by the women's movement and the sexual revolution. The altering of roles and the shifting of responsibilities have been extremely trying for many marriages.

7 These and other realities of life erode the visions of marital bliss the way sandstorms eat at rock and the ocean nibbles away at the dunes. Those euphoric, grand feelings that accompany romantic love are really self-delusions, self-hypnotic dreams that enable us to forge a relationship. Real life, failure at work, disappointments, exhaustion, bad smells, bad colds and hard times all puncture the dream and leave us stranded with our mate, with our childhood patterns pushing us this way and that, with our unfulfilled expectations.

8 The struggle to survive in marriage requires adaptability, flexibility, genuine love and kindness and an imagination strong enough to feel what the other is feeling. Many marriages fall apart because either partner cannot imagine what the other wants or cannot communicate what he or she needs or feels. Anger builds until it erupts into a volcanic burst that buries the marriage in ash.

9 It is not hard to see, therefore, how essential communication is for a good marriage. A man and a woman must be able to tell each other how they feel and why they feel the way they do; otherwise they will impose on each other roles and actions that lead to further unhappiness. In some cases, the communication patterns of childhood—of not talking, of talking too much, of not listening, of distrust and anger, of withdrawal—spill into the

marriage and prevent a healthy exchange of thoughts and feelings. The answer is to set up new patterns of communication and intimacy.

At the same time, however, we must see each other as individuals. "To achieve a balance between separateness and closeness is one of the major psychological tasks of all human beings at every stage of life," says Dr. Stuart Bartle, a psychiatrist at the New York University Medical Center. 10

If we sense from our mate a need for too much intimacy, we tend to push him or her away, fearing that we may lose our identities in the merging of marriage. One partner may suffocate the other partner in a childlike dependency. 11

A good marriage means growing as a couple but also growing as individuals. This isn't easy. Richard gives up his interest in carpentry because his wife, Helen, is jealous of the time he spends away from her. Karen quits her choir group because her husband dislikes the friends she makes there. Each pair clings to each other and are angry with each other as life closes in on them. This kind of marital balance is easily thrown as one or the other pulls away and divorce follows. 12

Sometimes people pretend that a new partner will solve the old problems. Most often extramarital sex destroys a marriage because it allows an artificial split between the good and the bad—the good is projected on the new partner and the bad is dumped on the head of the old. Dishonesty, hiding and cheating create walls between men and women. Infidelity is just a symptom of trouble. It is a symbolic complaint, a weapon of revenge, as well as an unraveler of closeness. Infidelity is often that proverbial last straw that sinks the camel to the ground. 13

All right—marriage has always been difficult. Why then are we seeing so many divorces at this time? Yes, our modern social fabric is thin, and yes the permissiveness of society has created unrealistic expectations and thrown the family into chaos. But divorce is so common because people today are unwilling to exercise the self-discipline that marriage requires. They expect easy joy, like the entertainment on TV, the thrill of a good party. 14

Marriage takes some kind of sacrifice, not dreadful self-sacrifice of the soul, but some level of compromise. Some of one's fantasies, some of one's legitimate desires have to be given up for the value of the marriage itself. "While all marital partners feel shackled at times, it is they who really choose to make the marital ties into confining chains or supporting bonds," says Dr. 15

Whitaker. Marriage requires sexual, financial and emotional discipline. A man and a woman cannot follow every impulse, cannot allow themselves to stop growing or changing.

16 Divorce is not an evil act. Sometimes it provides salvation for people who have grown hopelessly apart or were frozen in patterns of pain or mutual unhappiness. Divorce can be, despite its initial devastation, like the first cut of the surgeon's knife, a step toward new health and a good life. On the other hand, if the partners can stay past the breaking up of the romantic myths into the development of real love and intimacy, they have achieved a work as amazing as the greatest cathedrals of the world. Marriages that do not fail but improve, that persist despite imperfections, are not only rare these days but offer a wondrous shelter in which the face of our mutual humanity can safely show itself.

BUILDING VOCABULARY

1. Roiphe loads her essay with some very common expressions to make the discussion more easily understandable to the reader. Below is a list of ten such expressions. Use each in a sentence of your own.
   a. ring with truth (par. 1)
   b. crisis points (par. 2)
   c. tender beginnings (par. 3)
   d. mutual happiness (par. 3)
   e. marriage bed (par. 4)
   f. hidden strengths (par. 5)
   g. marital bliss (par. 7)
   h. healthy exchange (par. 9)
   i. childlike dependency (par. 11)
   j. social fabric (par. 14)
2. Locate and explain five terms that the author draws from psychology.

THINKING CRITICALLY ABOUT THE ESSAY

Understanding the Writer's Ideas

1. What are the "sacred vows" the author mentions in paragraph 1? Identify the source of the expressions "happily ever

after" and "till death do us part." What does she mean when she says that these expressions "seem on the way to becoming obsolete"?
2. What is a "single-parent home"?
3. How does Roiphe define "endurance" in a marriage? What does she mean by "outside pressures" in paragraph 2? What are some of these pressures? Does Roiphe feel they are the primary causes for marriages failing? Why?
4. According to the essay, how do we choose husbands and wives? What is the meaning of "our first home" in paragraph 3? According to Roiphe, for what reason is the way we choose mates a possible cause for marriages failing?
5. What is the "basic myth" of marriage? How does it create a possibly bad marriage?
6. How have the women's movement and the sexual revolution created strains on modern marriages?
7. Explain what the writer means by "Real life, failure at work, disappointments, exhaustion, bad smells, bad colds, and hard times" in paragraph 7. How do they affect marriages?
8. What is the role of communication between husband and wife in a marriage? What are the results of poor communication? What solutions to this problem does Roiphe suggest?
9. What two types of "growth" does Roiphe suggest as necessary to a good marriage? Who are Richard, Helen, and Karen, named in paragraph 12?
10. According to Roiphe, what is the common cause of extramarital sexual affairs? What are her projected results of infidelity?
11. What does Roiphe identify as the primary cause of divorce? What does she propose as a solution to this problem?
12. According to the last paragraph, do you think Roiphe is in favor of divorce? Why? In this paragraph, she presents both the positive and negative effects of divorce. What are the positive effects? the negative effects?

Understanding the Writer's Techniques

1. Where does the author place her thesis?
2. How does the title almost predict for the reader that the writer's main technique of development will be cause-and-effect analysis?
3. One strategy for developing an introductory paragraph is to ask a question. What is the purpose of the questions that the

author asks in the opening paragraph? What is the relationship among the questions? How do the questions themselves dictate a cause-and-effect pattern of development? How do they immediately involve the reader in the topic?

4. In which paragraph does Roiphe list the immediate or common causes of marital failure? Why is this placement effective?
5. The use of clear *topic sentences* for each paragraph can often be an important technique in writing a clear causal analysis because topic sentences usually identify main causes for the effect under discussion. Identify the topic sentences for paragraphs 3, 4, and 6. What causes for marriage failure does each identify?
6. What causal chain of behavior does Roiphe build in paragraphs 8 to 13?
7. Why does Roiphe begin paragraph 14 with the words "All right"? Whom is she addressing? How does this address compare with the technique used in her introduction?
8. What two authorities does Roiphe quote in this essay? How are their citations useful? How are they identified? In what ways do their identifications add to their credibility as sources of opinions or information on Roiphe's topic?
9. Where does Roiphe use statistics in this essay? Why is it especially important to the development of the article?
10. Roiphe makes use of *definition* (see pages 233–237) in a number of places in this essay. What are her definitions of the following?
    - **a.** work [in a marriage] (par. 5)
    - **b.** A good marriage (par. 12)
    - **c.** Divorce (par. 16)
    - **d.** Marriages that do not fail but improve (par. 16)

    Locate other places where she uses definition.
11. In some essays, the introduction and conclusion are each simply the first and last paragraphs. In this essay, the writer uses more than one paragraph for each. Which paragraphs make up her introduction? Which make up the conclusion? Why might she have structured her introduction and conclusion in this way? How does the structure affect the essay?
12. You have learned that two of the most common types of comparisons used by writers to enliven their essays are *similes* and *metaphors*. Look up the definition of these terms in the Glossary to refresh your memory. In addition, writers

may use *extended metaphors.* This technique relies upon a number of metaphoric comparisons that revolve around a main idea rather than a single comparison. Roiphe uses comparisons in a number of paragraphs in this essay. In each of the following cases identify and explain the comparisons indicated:

a. extended metaphor (par. 2)
b. metaphor (par. 7)
c. metaphor (par. 8)
d. metaphor (par. 9)
e. simile (par. 14)
f. metaphor (par. 15)
g. similes, metaphors (par. 16)

How does Roiphe's frequent use of metaphors and similes affect the tone of the essay?

13. Why does Roiphe end her essay with references to successful marriages? Would you consider that as being off the topic? Why or why not?

Exploring the Writer's Ideas

1. Roiphe discusses quite a few causes for marriages failing. Discuss with the class some additional causes. Why are they also important?

2. Paragraph 6 states, "Couples today must also deal with all the cultural changes brought on in recent years by the women's movement and the sexual revolution." Identify these two social phenomena. Among the people you know, have these cultural changes affected their marriages? How? If you are not married, and plan to marry, do you feel that the changes will present any foreseeable problems? If you are not married, and do not plan to marry, have they influenced your decision in any ways? What other effects have these two movements had in American society? Do you think these influences have been positive or negative? Why?

3. If you are married or in a close relationship, how did you choose your mate? If you are not married or in a relationship, what qualities would you look for in a mate? Why?

4. In paragraphs 6 and 7, Roiphe mentions "realities of life" that destroy romantic notions of "marital bliss." What other realities can you add to her list?

5. Paragraph 15 discusses the idea of self-sacrifice in marriage. Roiphe writes, "Some of one's fantasies, some of one's legitimate desires have to be given up for the value of the marriage itself." However, some people insist that for a marriage to survive, each partner must maintain complete integrity, that is, must not be forced into major sacrifices of values or life-styles. What is your opinion of these two opposing viewpoints?
6. Judy Brady in "I Want a Wife" (pages 395–397) provides some insights into marriage that complement Roiphe's. How does Brady's position compare with Roiphe's?

IDEAS FOR WRITING

Prewriting

Free-associate on a sheet of paper about the reasons or causes for *successful* marriages. In other words, which marriages survive despite the high rate of divorce in the United States?

Guided Writing

Using cause-and-effect analysis, write an essay in which you explain *why marriages succeed.*

1. Limit your topic sufficiently so that you can concentrate your discussion on closely interrelated cause-and-effect patterns.
2. In the introduction, involve your reader with a series of pertinent questions.
3. Identify what many people think are common or immediate causes of successful marriages; then show how other causes are perhaps even more important.
4. In the course of your essay, cite at least one relevant statistic that will add extra importance to your topic.
5. Try to use at least one quotation from a reputable authority. Consult your library for books and articles that deal with marriage. Be sure to include full identification of your source.
6. Use clear topic sentences in each paragraph as you present analyses of the various causes for successful marriages.
7. Make use of metaphors, similes, and extended metaphors.

8. In your essay, offer necessary definitions of terms that are especially important to your topic. Try for at least one definition by negation.
9. Write a conclusion in which you make some commentary upon divorce. Make your comment as an outgrowth of your discussion of a successful marriage.

Thinking and Writing Collaboratively

Divide the class into four equal groups. Have members of each group read their essays out loud. Next, select your group's strongest essay and list the reasons your group has selected it. Present your findings to the class, and if time permits, ask the writer of the best essay to read it to the class.

More Writing Projects

1. What is the "ideal marriage"? In your journal, speculate on those qualities that you think would make a perfect marriage. Share observations with others in the class.
2. In a paragraph, explain some of your reasons for ending a relationship (a marriage, a close friendship, a relationship with a girlfriend or boyfriend).
3. Write an essay in which you explain the effects of divorce on the lives of the couple involved. Here, do not concern yourself with causes; look only at the results of the failed marriage.

Why Do We Age?

Nancy Shute

Aging rouses the fascinated and perhaps tearful interest of both young and old Americans. Nancy Shute aims to demystify the subject by telling the reader what science knows about the causes, and possible "remedies," for aging.

PREREADING: THINKING ABOUT THE ESSAY IN ADVANCE

What are your preconceptions about aging? Is your knowledge of aging based on personal experience? Books? Newspapers? Gossip? How could you extend your knowledge? What is your attitude toward your elders?

Words to Watch

ailment (par. 2) illness

Gerontological (par. 2) having to do with aging

hormone (par. 4) a body chemical, associated with vital functioning of the body

immune system (par. 4) disease-fighting organization of the body

nematodes (par. 5) worms with long, cylindrical, unsegmented bodies

enzymes (par. 6) organic substances that cause changes in other substances when they interact

tantalizing (par. 7) teasing, intriguing

proliferating (par. 7) spreading

senescent (par. 8) to grow old

neurobiologist (par. 10) someone who studies the biology of the nervous system

nostrums (par. 11) pet scheme for solving a problem

metabolic (par. 11) the process of breakdown of food in the body and its use as fuel for energy

spartan (par. 14) severe

intrinsic (par. 16) belonging to the nature of a thing, internal to a thing

Check out the nearest bookstore and you'll discover a remarkable thing: Aging has been cured. Titles like *The Anti-Aging Hormones, Younger at Last,* and *Brain Longevity* all promise, if not immortality, at least a few leaps back toward high school. 1

There's just one problem: No one yet knows what causes aging and its inevitable consequence, death. And applying a cure to the ailment when you don't know the cause is haphazard at best. "All these magic bullets have turned out to be blanks," says Gene Cohen, president of the Gerontological Society of America. 2

Scientists didn't start seriously examining aging processes until the 1960s. The task is huge, for aging affects all of the body's organs, tissues, and cells. Most theories of aging fall into two camps: the program camp, which holds that some internal clock primes us to self-destruct; and the error camp, which argues that genetic missteps and the assaults of life eventually damage the body to the point where it can no longer repair itself. 3

Both concepts—preprogrammed life span and ravages of wear and tear—match commonplace experience. Almost all living organisms, from butterflies (12 weeks) to dogs (20 years) to humans (122), do indeed appear to have a maximum lifespan, set by their genes. After age 30, hormone levels drop, the immune system begins to lose its punch, and muscles shrink. At the same time, it is undeniable that we do wear out with age; joints stiffen, teeth loosen, skin sags. 4

At the cellular and molecular level, there is also ample evidence for both notions. Studies of skin proteins show they naturally break down over time (programmed self-destruction) but are also damaged by sunlight (wear and tear). The clock-of-doom idea gets its strongest support from studies showing that life span can be affected by genes. Researchers have doubled the life span of fruit flies to a Methuselan 70 days through selective breeding. Specific genes that appear to control aging are now being identified in simple animals such as nematodes. 5

Some hints of exactly *how* a gene might set the cell's aging clock are also starting to emerge. In 1961, cell biologist Leonard Hayflick launched the modern era of aging research when he discovered that human cells divide 80 or 90 times, then stop. Although they can live for years, these aged cells no longer do their job properly and create enzymes that can damage proteins such as skin collagen. And the fact that the cells are no longer dividing and renewing tissue may play a role in osteoporosis and aging of the skin, or in slower wound healing and susceptibility to disease. 6

7 But researchers found a tantalizing clue in the fact that some cells evade the Hayflick limit and keep dividing. These wildly proliferating cells may eventually become cancerous tumors. Discovering why cancer cells never stop dividing could explain why normal cells do. Much recent speculation centers on telomeres—seemingly useless little bits on the ends of chromosomes, the parts of the cell that carry its DNA. Since the 1970s, scientists have known that when cells divide, unzipping their chromosomes and copying each half into two new wholes, the chromosomes don't copy all the way to the tip. But they didn't know how the chromosomes avoided losing DNA in the process. It turns out that the telomeres, which are made of repeating bits of nonsense DNA, act as protective end caps, allowing all the vital DNA to be copied. With each cell division, a little bit of the telomere breaks off.

8 It's easy to imagine that telomeres act as cellular calendars: When there's no more telomere left, the DNA doesn't copy fully, and the cell becomes senescent.

9 Cancer cells cheat time by exuding telomerase, an enzyme that rebuilds the telomeres and lets the cells proliferate indefinitely. Molecular biologists Carol Greider and Elizabeth Blackburn first discovered telomerase in a single-celled pond organism in 1984. By 1994, Calvin Harley and colleagues had identified telomerase in 90 percent of 101 human tumor samples and in none of 50 normal tissue samples. Harley is now working for a California biotechnology firm that aims to create an antitelomerase anticancer drug.

10 Some have even grander schemes for putting telomerase to practical use. Michael Fossel, a neurobiologist, claims in his 1996 book *Reversing Human Aging* that telomeres are the regulators of aging we've been looking for, and that within 20 years we'll be able to manipulate them enough to end aging. Most researchers are highly skeptical, though. Hayflick, now a professor at the University of California–San Francisco medical school, says that telomeres may tell us a lot about the ultimate limits of life span but little about the aging process. "Telomeres don't cause the aging of the organism," agrees Greider, a senior staff scientist at Cold Spring Harbor Laboratory. "It's gibberish." She also warns against presuming so soon that an antitelomerase drug would be an anticancer drug. "Telomerase is required for cancer cells to divide, but is it required for tumor growth? The answer is not yet known." Telomerase might well grant eternal life—but only to cancers, not to their hosts.

Scientists and hucksters of antiaging nostrums also share, not comfortably, an intense interest in oxygen free radicals. To those who believe that aging is an accumulation of damage and errors, these free radicals are the chief culprits. Forty-three years ago, Denham Harman, a University of Nebraska biochemist, recognized that cells, as part of their metabolic processes, generate oxygen and hydrogen-oxygen molecules that have an extra "free" electron. Unbalanced by the extra electron, these molecules are the juvenile delinquents of the cell, short-lived but dangerous, careening around and demolishing vital fats, proteins, and DNA—particularly DNA in the cell's mitochondria, its power plant. In the past 10 years, free radicals have been implicated in hypertension, atherosclerosis, cataracts, and some cancers, and may also be involved in degenerative neurological diseases, including Lou Gehrig's disease, Parkinson's, and Alzheimer's. 11

Evolution long ago tagged free radicals for the marauders they are and countered them with protective antioxidant molecules. Longer-lived species have higher levels of these protective molecules, which include the enzyme superoxide dismutase and vitamin E and beta carotene. (Superoxide dismutase enjoyed a brief craze in the late 1980s among healthfood enthusiasts until spoilsport researchers pointed out that taking a pill couldn't possibly do any good: the enzyme is broken down in the stomach before it can reach the body's cells.) 12

Telomeres and oxygen free radicals may be the two leading aging theories, but there are plenty more: Researchers are pursuing dozens of different angles on aging, including the influence of hormones (estrogen may be a factor in preventing Alzheimer's), the effect of basal metabolism on life span, and the role played by defects in systems that repair damaged DNA. 13

Amid all the theories, there is one, and just one, antiaging remedy that's proven. It's safe, it's cheap, and it's simple. And no one's buying it. It's caloric restriction, reducing daily food intake by 40 percent. Rats fed this spare repast lived 30 percent longer than their pudgy peers and suffered fewer chronic diseases. Researchers suspect that by lowering the body's temperature by about 1 degree Celsius, the low-calorie diet slows metabolism and reduces the number of free radicals created in the process. Studies are underway testing this spartan diet on primates, but no one expects humans to embrace it. 14

15 Although every gerontologist has a favored theory of aging, you don't have to press very hard to get them to admit that probably all the theories being batted around are partly right—which means that none of them is a complete explanation. Aging is not just one but dozens of intricately intertwined processes, involving genes, hormones, molecules, immune system responses, environmental insults, and ordinary mistakes. Given all that, it's remarkable that we live as long as we do, particularly since humans need to make it until only age 30 to reproduce and raise young. At the turn of the century, the average life span in the United States was around 47 years. Since then, we've extended it to almost 79, thanks largely to better public-health measures such as clean water and vaccines.

16 Despite the proliferation of "life extension" books and potions, research scientists are much more interested in improving the quality of the life we have than in trying to extend it. Aging, they point out, is not a disease; it's a process intrinsic to life itself. "Everything in the universe ages, including the universe," says Leonard Hayflick.

17 But figuring out aging processes, whether it's through telomeres, free radicals, or one of the many other hypotheses under investigation, should help us to understand why, as we age, we become more susceptible to diseases such as cancer, atherosclerosis, and Alzheimer's, and to learn how to stay healthy and independent as we age.

BUILDING VOCABULARY

By its nature, this essay uses technical or scientific words. Look up the meanings for

a. skin collagen (par. 6)
b. osteoporosis (par. 6)
c. chromosomes (par. 7)
d. DNA (par. 7)
e. telomeres (par. 7)
f. mitochondria (par. 11)
g. atherosclerosis (par. 11)
h. antioxidant (par. 12)
i. beta carotene (par. 12)
j. estrogen (par. 13)
k. basal metabolism (par. 13)

THINKING CRITICALLY ABOUT THE ESSAY

Understanding the Writer's Ideas

1. What are the two major theories about aging?
2. What evidence supports either notion?
3. What do we know about how a gene might set the body's aging clock?
4. What is the role of telomerase in cancer? What uses are scientists planning for telomerase?
5. If telomerase is the key substance of interest to those who believe we are "programmed" to age, what is the equivalent in the eyes of those seeking to understand the damage that life inflicts on the body? How do these substances work?
6. What are the nostrums urged to counteract the wear and tear of cells?
7. What is the one proven antiaging remedy?
8. According to the writer, what can we conclude about the current understanding of aging among scientists?

Understanding the Writer's Techniques

1. What is the writer's thesis statement? Where is it located in the essay?
2. How would you compare and contrast the writer's purpose in writing, and her thesis statement?
3. In the language of our everyday conversation we assume "getting old" to be an obvious phenomenon. But the writer shows both that aging is multifaceted, and that its causes are many. Identify four aspects of aging and the theories about the causes of these aspects of aging that the writer discusses.
4. Why does the writer save her thesis statement for the end?
5. Why does the writer take three paragraphs to conclude her essay?

Exploring the Writer's Ideas

1. Would you be pleased to learn that, as the writer says in her opening paragraph, "Aging has been cured"? Or are you comfortable with the idea that aging "is intrinsic to life itself" (par. 16)? Explain.

2. What features of American society do you think support the idea that we fear and want to stop aging? What features of American society support the idea that aging is intrinsic to life?
3. Although the essay opens with the bold observation that popular books have proclaimed the end of aging, it is focused on the state of scientific knowledge about aging. Why? How would the essay have been different had it used other evidence for its discussion of the subject?
4. Having read this essay, do you believe we shall ever "cure" aging? Explain.

IDEAS FOR WRITING

Prewriting

Write two lists. In one put down all the good things you can think of about the fact that we age and die. In the other put down all the things about aging and dying that you prefer to avert.

Guided Writing

Write an essay that shows how certain beliefs about aging and death lead to certain lifestyle decisions. For example, the desire to stay young may lead to a regular exercise regime.

1. Begin your essay by identifying common views of aging and dying that you intend to discuss. You may want to take one large topic ("Americans live in fear of death") or two or three narrower topics. You will want to decide if you are going to be more or less serious in your approach, or ironic and humorous.
2. Now describe the general results in behavior of this (or these) common attitude(s).
3. Offer telling examples (at least two).
4. Provide an analysis of the effectiveness of the behavior as a "cure."
5. Conclude by a reflection on the issue in light of the effectiveness or ineffectiveness of the behavior(s) you have discussed.

Thinking and Writing Collaboratively

Working in groups of four or five, discuss the habits and attitudes of the members of the group toward exercise. Consider exercise the effect, and through discussion uncover the cause(s). Chart the attitudes and habits of the group.

More Writing Projects

1. Write an essay about one of your grandparents, illustrating the beauties and horrors of old age.
2. Survey opinions in your class about old people. Write a brief analysis of these opinions, speculating about their causes, and also about what they tell you about young people in your town or in the nation.
3. Research the state of knowledge about one major illness associated with age, such as Alzheimer's, and report your findings in a cause-and-effect essay.

When Bright Girls Decide That Math Is "a Waste of Time"

Susan Jacoby

In this article, Susan Jacoby explains how cultural expectations and societal stereotyping are overshadowed by women's own decisions to keep themselves away from scientific and technological studies. Notice how she uses narrative and process analysis to reinforce the causes and effects she is exploring here.

PREREADING: THINKING ABOUT THE ESSAY IN ADVANCE

This article focuses on the reasons why women perform poorly in one academic subject, mathematics. How would you explain this phenomenon? What causes might you identify? Are there academic subjects or professional areas where women are less able or more able to succeed than men? Why or why not?

Words to Watch

sanguine (par. 3) cheerful, hopeful
vulnerable (par. 6) open to attack or suggestion
syndrome (par. 7) a group of symptoms that characterize a condition
akin to (par. 7) similar to
phobia (par. 7) an excessive fear of something
constitute (par. 7) to make up; compose
epitomize (par. 8) to be a prime example of
prone to (par. 15) disposed to; susceptible to
accede to (par. 16) give in to

1 Susannah, a 16-year-old who has always been an A student in every subject from algebra to English, recently informed her parents that she intended to drop physics and calculus in her senior year of high school and replace them with a drama seminar and a work-study program. She expects to major in art or history in college, she explained, and "any more science or math will just be a waste of my time."

Her parents were neither concerned by nor opposed to her decision. "Fine, dear," they said. Their daughter is, after all, an outstanding student. What does it matter if, at age 16, she has taken a step that may limit her understanding of both machines and the natural world for the rest of her life? 2

This kind of decision, in which girls turn away from studies that would give them a sure footing in the world of science and technology, is a self-inflicted female disability that is, regrettably, almost as common today as it was when I was in high school. If Susannah had announced that she had decided to stop taking English in her senior year, her mother and father would have been horrified. I also think they would have been a good deal less sanguine about her decision if she were a boy. 3

In saying that scientific and mathematical ignorance is a self-inflicted female wound, I do not, obviously, mean that cultural expectations play no role in the process. But the world does not conspire to deprive modern women of access to science as it did in the 1930's, when Rosalyn S. Yalow, the Nobel Prize-winning physicist, graduated from Hunter College and was advised to go to work as a secretary because no graduate school would admit her to its physics department. The current generation of adolescent girls—and their parents, bred on old expectations about women's interests—are active conspirators in limiting their own intellectual development. 4

It is true that the proportion of young women in science-related graduate and professional schools, most notably medical schools, has increased significantly in the past decade. It is also true that so few women were studying advanced science and mathematics before the early 1970's that the percentage increase in female enrollment does not yet translate into large numbers of women actually working in science. 5

The real problem is that so many girls eliminate themselves from any serious possibility of studying science as a result of decisions made during the vulnerable period of midadolescence, when they are most likely to be influenced—on both conscious and subconscious levels—by the traditional belief that math and science are "masculine" subjects. 6

During the teen-age years the well-documented phenomenon of "math anxiety" strikes girls who never had any problem handling numbers during earlier schooling. Some men, too, experience this syndrome—a form of panic, akin to a phobia, at any task involving numbers—but women constitute the overwhelming 7 majority of sufferers. The onset of acute math anxiety during the teen-age years is, as Stalin was fond of saying, "not by accident."

8 In adolescence girls begin to fear that they will be unattractive to boys if they are typed as "brains." Science and math epitomize unfeminine braininess in a way that, say, foreign languages do not. High-school girls who pursue an advanced interest in science and math (unless they are students at special institutions like the Bronx High School of Science where everyone is a brain) usually find that they are greatly outnumbered by boys in their classes. They are, therefore, intruding on male turf at a time when their sexual confidence, as well as that of the boys, is most fragile.

9 A 1981 assessment of female achievement in mathematics, based on research conducted under a National Institute for Education grant, found significant differences in the mathematical achievements of 9th and 12th graders. At age 13 girls were equal to or slightly better than boys in tests involving algebra, problem solving and spatial ability; four years later the boys had outstripped the girls.

10 It is not mysterious that some very bright high-school girls suddenly decide that math is "too hard" and "a waste of time." In my experience, self-sabotage of mathematical and scientific ability is often a conscious process. I remember deliberately pretending to be puzzled by geometry problems in my sophomore year in high school. A male teacher called me in after class and said, in a baffled tone, "I don't see how you can be having so much trouble when you got straight A's last year in my algebra class."

11 The decision to avoid advanced biology, chemistry, physics and calculus in high school automatically restricts academic and professional choices that ought to be wide open to anyone beginning college. At all coeducational universities women are overwhelmingly concentrated in the fine arts, social sciences and traditionally female departments like education. Courses leading to degrees in science- and technology-related fields are filled mainly by men.

12 In my generation, the practical consequences of mathematical and scientific illiteracy are visible in the large number of special programs to help professional women overcome the anxiety they feel when they are promoted into jobs that require them to handle statistics.

13 The consequences of this syndrome should not, however, be viewed in narrowly professional terms. Competence in science

and math does not mean one is going to become a scientist or mathematician any more than competence in writing English means one is going to become a professional writer. Scientific and mathematical illiteracy—which has been cited in several recent critiques by panels studying American education from kindergarten through college—produces an incalculably impoverished vision of human experience.

Scientific illiteracy is not, of course, the exclusive province of women. In certain intellectual circles it has become fashionable to proclaim a willed, aggressive ignorance about science and technology. Some female writers specialize in ominous, uninformed diatribes against genetic research as a plot to remove control of childbearing from women, while some well-known men of letters proudly announce that they understand absolutely nothing about computers, or, for that matter, about electricity. This lack of understanding is nothing in which women or men ought to take pride. 14

Failure to comprehend either computers or chromosomes leads to a terrible sense of helplessness, because the profound impact of science on everyday life is evident even to those who insist they don't, won't, can't understand why the changes are taking place. At this stage of history women are more prone to such feelings of helplessness than men because the culture judges their ignorance less harshly and because women themselves acquiesce in that indulgence. 15

Since there is ample evidence of such feelings in adolescence, it is up to parents to see that their daughters do not accede to the old stereotypes about "masculine" and "feminine" knowledge. Unless we want our daughters to share our intellectual handicaps, we had better tell them no, they can't stop taking mathematics and science at the ripe old age of 16. 16

BUILDING VOCABULARY

1. Use a dictionary to look up any unfamiliar words in the phrases below from Jacoby's essay. Then, write a short explanation of each expression.
   a. sure footing (par. 3)
   b. cultural expectations (par. 4)
   c. overwhelming majority (par. 7)
   d. male turf (par. 8)

e. spatial ability (par. 9)
f. the exclusive province (par. 14)
g. ominous, uninformed diatribes (par. 14)
h. acquiesce in that indulgence (par. 15)
i. ample evidence (par. 16)
j. our intellectual handicaps (par. 16)

2. Explain the *connotations* (see Glossary) that the following words have for you. Use each word correctly in a sentence of your own.
   a. disability (par. 3)
   b. conspire (par. 4)
   c. adolescent (par. 4)
   d. vulnerable (par. 6)
   e. acute (par. 7)

THINKING CRITICALLY ABOUT THE ESSAY

Understanding the Writer's Ideas

1. What condition is Jacoby trying to analyze? Is the main *effect* analyzed in this cause-and-effect analysis? On what primary cause does she blame women's "scientific and mathematical ignorance"? What exactly does she mean by that term? How is society to blame? What is the "process" mentioned in paragraph 4? What point does the example of Rosalyn S. Yalow illustrate?
2. Why does Jacoby think that the greater proportion of women students now in science and medical graduate and professional schools does not really mean that there are many women working in these areas?
3. According to Jacoby, when do most girls decide not to study the sciences? Why does this happen?
4. What is "math anxiety"? Who suffers more from it—boys or girls? Why? What does the author mean by "brains" (par. 8)?
5. Who was Joseph Stalin (par. 7)?
6. What subjects does Jacoby identify as "feminine"? Which are "unfeminine"?
7. According to the research evidence discussed in paragraph 9, how do the math abilities of girls and boys change between ninth and tenth grades? What does Jacoby say is the *cause* of this change? What are the *results?*

8. Explain what Jacoby means by the expression "self-inflicted female wound" (par. 4) and "self-sabotage" (par. 10). How are these expressions similar? How are they different?
9. What is the difference between what men and women study at coeducational universities?
10. What does Jacoby mean by "mathematical and scientific illiteracy" (par. 12)? Do only women suffer from this syndrome? According to Jacoby, why does it lead to "an incalculably impoverished vision of human experience"? What does she mean by this phrase? What examples of scientific illiteracy does Jacoby offer?
11. Why does the author think women feel more helpless than men do about scientific changes?
12. What suggestion does Jacoby offer in her conclusion?

Understanding the Writer's Techniques

1. What is the thesis statement of this essay? Why is it placed where it is? Find another statement before it that expresses a similar cause-and-effect relation. How are the two different?
2. Which paragraphs make up the introductory section of this essay? What cause-and-effect relation does Jacoby establish and how does she present it? How does Jacoby use narration in her introduction? How does she use illustration?
3. Both sentences of paragraph 5 begin with the phrase "It is true," yet the sentences contradict each other. How and why does the author set up this contradiction? What is the effect on Jacoby's analysis of beginning paragraph 6 with the words "The real problem is . . ."?
4. How does she use *process analysis* (see pages 376–377) from paragraph 6 to paragraph 8?
5. Where does the author use definition in this essay?
6. Trace the cause-and-effect developments in paragraphs 7 and 8.
7. In paragraph 9, Jacoby mentions a study conducted under "a National Institute for Education grant." How does the evidence she presents support her position in the essay?
8. What is the effect of the phrase "in my experience" in paragraph 10? What expository technique does she use there?
9. Trace the cause-and-effect patterns in paragraphs 11 through 13. Be sure to show the interrelation between the causes and the effects (that is, how the effect of something can also be the cause of something else).

10. How is the first sentence of paragraph 15 ("Failure to comprehend. . . .") a good example in itself of cause-and-effect development?

11. Why does Jacoby use quotation marks around the words "masculine" and "feminine" in the phrase " 'masculine' and 'feminine' knowledge" (par. 16)?

12. What is the overall tone of this essay? At three points, Jacoby switches tone and uses *irony* (see Glossary). Explain the irony in the following sentences.

   a. What does it matter if, at age 16, she has taken a step that may limit her understanding of both machines and the natural world for the rest of her life? (par. 2)

   b. The onset of acute math anxiety during the teenage years is, as Stalin was fond of saying, "not by accident." (par. 7)

   c. Unless we want our daughters to share our intellectual handicaps, we had better tell them no, they can't stop taking mathematics and science at the ripe old age of 16. (par. 16)

   Compare the irony in paragraph 16 with that in paragraph 2. How is the impact the same or different?

13. Who do you think is the intended audience for this essay? Cite evidence for your answer.

14. Jacoby uses a variety of transitional devices to connect smoothly the ideas expressed in the various paragraphs of this essay. Look especially at paragraphs 1 to 4. How does the writer achieve coherence between paragraphs? What transitional elements do you find in the opening sentences of each of those paragraphs? What other transitions do you find throughout the essay?

Exploring the Writer's Ideas

1. One of the underlying suggestions in this essay is that society has long considered there to be "masculine" and "feminine" subjects to study. What is your opinion on this issue? Do you feel that any subjects are particularly more suited to men or women? Which? Why? Are there any other school activities that you feel are exclusively masculine or feminine? Why? Are there any jobs that are more suited to men or women?

2. In paragraph 4, Jacoby mentions the "old expectations about women's interests." What do you think these expectations are? What do you consider *new* expectations for women?

3. A *stereotype* is an opinion of a category of people that is unoriginal and often based on strong prejudices. For example, some prejudicial stereotypes include "All immigrants are lazy"; "All Republicans are rich"; "All women are terrible drivers." What other stereotypes do you know? Where do you think they originate?
4. The general implication of paragraph 8 is that people minimize their skills in order to be socially acceptable. In your experience, where have you seen this principle operating? Do you agree that people sometimes pretend to be unable to achieve something? What motivates them, do you think?
5. A recent study shows that among major nations in the world America's students—boys and girls—are the worst mathematics students. How do you account for the poor showing of Americans as mathematicians? How would you remedy this situation?

IDEAS FOR WRITING

Prewriting

Think about an activity that seems either male-friendly or female-friendly. Take complete notes on the reasons or causes that explain the situations.

Guided Writing

Select a job or profession that is usually male-dominated. Write a cause-and-effect analysis explaining how and why women both have been excluded from this profession and (or) have self-selected themselves from the job. (Some examples may include fire fighters, physicians, marines, bank executives, and carpenters.)

1. Begin with an anecdote to illustrate the condition that you are analyzing.
2. Present and analyze the partial causes of this condition that arise from society's expectations and norms.
3. State your main point clearly in a thesis statement.
4. Clearly identify what you consider "the real problem."
5. If you believe that women have deliberately excluded themselves, explain when and how the process of self-selection begins for women.

6. Analyze the consequences of this process of self-selection and give examples of the results of it.
7. Provide evidence that supports your analysis.
8. Link paragraphs with appropriate transitions.
9. In your conclusion offer a suggestion to change or improve this situation.

Thinking and Writing Collaboratively

Exchange a draft version of your Guided Writing assignment with a classmate. Review your partner's essay for its success in following the recommended guidelines. Is the thesis stated clearly? Are both the main causes and minor causes presented, and with sufficient evidence to support the analysis? Write a brief evaluation of the essay, with recommendations for revision, before returning it.

More Writing Projects

1. In your journal, make a list of everything that comes into your mind about the word "mathematics." Do not edit your writing. When you are finished, share your list with other people in the class. How do your impressions compare? contrast?
2. In a paragraph, analyze why you think boys and men exclude themselves from a certain field or profession—nursing, cooking, grammar-school teaching, and so on.
3. Margaret Mead, the famous anthropologist, once wrote, "Women in our society complain of the lack of stimulation, of the loneliness, of the dullness of staying at home." In an essay write a causal analysis of this situation.

SUMMING UP: CHAPTER 10

1. In her essay, Susan Jacoby analyzes a kind of "self-destructive behavior" on the part of many young women. Write an essay about a friend, relative, or someone else close to you who is doing something that you feel will have a very negative effect on him or her. Analyze *why* he or she is doing this and what effects, both short- and long-term, these actions are likely to have.
2. In this chapter, we hear female voices analyzing some of the experiences of women in American life today. Using their approaches to causal analysis, examine these experiences and the impact that they have had on your own thinking and activities. Clarify the connections between what you have read and how your sense of self has deepened or been sharpened.
3. Working in small groups, develop a questionnaire focusing on male and female roles in our society. After the questionnaire has been prepared, each group member should interview at least three people. When all the interviews have been completed, each group should write a collective analysis of the results and present the analysis to the class.
4. In her essay on aging, Nancy Shute dismisses the popular recipes for long life as unscientific, and goes on to tell us what science has learned about aging. Amplify her points by writing an essay that compares two modes of knowing—such as, for example, myth and science—and their implications for a cause-and-effect analysis of sensitive or highly charged subjects.
5. For the next week, keep a journal about something that is currently causing you to have mixed emotions. (Note: This should not be the same issues you've written about in the Guided Writing exercise following the essay by Stephen King; it should be a *current* issue.) Try to write five reasons each day (or expand upon previous ones). At the end of the week, write an essay that analyzes how the issue is affecting your life or how you plan to deal with it in the future.

CHAPTER 11

Argumentation and Persuasion

WHAT ARE ARGUMENTATION AND PERSUASION?

When we use *argumentation,* we aim to convince someone to join our side of an issue. Often, we want the readers or listeners to change their views and adopt ours. We also use *persuasion* when we want a person to take action in a way that will advance our cause. In everyday life we hear the word "argument" used as a synonym for "fight." In writing, however, an argument is not a brawl but a kind of debate that requires subtle reasoning and careful use of the writers' tools you have learned so far. For this reason, we have put argumentation at the end of the writing course. In preparing your persuasive essay, you will be able to rehearse and refine the skills you have learned to this point.

The first step in arguing successfully is to state your position clearly. This means that a good thesis is crucial to your essay. For argumentative or persuasive essays, the thesis is sometimes called a *major proposition.* This is an idea that can be debated or disputed, and the writer must take a definite side. Taking a strong position gives your essay its argumentative edge. Your readers must know what your position is, and must see that you have supported your main idea with convincing minor points. The weakest arguments are those in which the writer tries to take both sides, and as a result persuades no one. As you will see in the reading selections, writers often concede or yield a point to the opposition, but they do so only to strengthen the one side that they favor.

Writing arguments should make you even more aware of the need to think about audience. Since you already are convinced of the point you are presenting, your essay should focus on the people who will make up their minds on the basis of your evidence. Readers are not usually persuaded by assertion; you can't just tell them that something is true. You need to show them through well-organized support of main and minor points.

Evidence or support can come from many sources. Statistics, personal experience, historical events, news reports, and interviews can all serve to back up an argument. At the same time, a writer can use narrative, description, comparison and contrast, illustration, analysis, and definition to persuade.

Because we use argument in everyday life, we may think it is easy to argue in writing—but just the opposite is true. If we are arguing with someone in person, we can *see* our opponent's response, and quickly change our direction. In writing, we can only imagine the opponent and so must carefully prepare evidence for all possible responses. When we watch an argument on the evening news about abortion clinics, increasing the minimum wage, or accusations of sexual harassment, we often see only what media experts call "sound bites," tiny fragments of information. We may see just a slogan as a picket sign passes a camera. We may hear only a few sentences out of hours of testimony. We seldom see or hear the entire argument. When we turn to writing arguments ourselves, we need to remember to develop a complete and detailed and *rational* argument.

This does not mean that written arguments lack emotion. Rather, written argument channels that emotion into a powerful eloquence that can endure much longer than a shouting match.

In written arguments, the writer states the major proposition, or point he or she wants to make, and keeps it firmly in front of the reader. For example, a writer may want to argue that the U.S. government should grant amnesty to illegal aliens who have been in the country for at least two years. He may be writing to his member of Congress to persuade her to take action on a proposed bill. Once he knows his purpose and his audience, he is ready to plan an argument. Or the writer may want to convince readers that something is true—that single fathers make excellent parents, for example, or that wife abuse is an increasingly serious crime in our society. In this chapter, Molly Ivins uses a sharp wit to lash out at "gun nuts." Judy Brady offers a tongue-in-cheek plea for a wife. Mortimer B. Zuckerman tries to persuade us that we need more police. Finally, Jonathan Kozol advocates a more humane approach to the nation's homeless.

Whatever the writer's topic, the keys to a good argument are

- a clear and effective major proposition
- a logical tone
- an abundance of evidence
- an avoidance of personal attacks

HOW DO WE READ ARGUMENTS?

Try to find out something about the background and credentials of the writer. In what way is he or she an expert on the topic?

Is the proposition presented in a rational and logical way? Is it credible?

Has the writer presented ample reliable evidence to back up the proposition? (If you look at the headlines on supermarket tabloid newspapers that try to persuade us that aliens have been keeping Elvis Presley alive on Mars, you will see why it is important to be able to evaluate a writer's evidence before accepting the proposition!)

Does the writer focus on the main idea, or does the essay distract us with unrelated information?

HOW DO WE WRITE ARGUMENTS?

State a clear major proposition, and stick to it.

Convince readers of the validity of your thesis by making an essay plan that introduces *minor propositions.* These are assertions that help clarify the reasons you offer to support your main idea.

Use *refutation.* This is a technique to anticipate what an opponent will say, and answer the objection ahead of time. Another technique is *concession.* You yield a small point to your opponent, but at the same time claim a larger point on your own side. Using these techniques makes your argument seem fairer. You acknowledge that there *are* at least two sides to the issue. Moreover, these devices help you make your own point more effectively.

Be aware of these pitfalls:

- Avoid personal attacks on your opponent, and don't let excessive appeals to emotion damage the tone of your argument.

- Avoid hasty generalization—that is, using main ideas without properly supporting them.
- Avoid drawing a conclusion that does not follow from the evidence in your argument.
- Avoid faulty analogies—that is, unequal comparisons.

Writing the Draft

Begin the rough draft. State your thesis boldly.

Back up all minor propositions with

statistics
facts
testimony from authorities
personal experience

Find a reliable listener and read your essay aloud. Encourage your listener to refute your points as strongly as possible.

Revise the essay, taking into account your listener's refutations. Find better support for your weakest points. Write a new draft.

Revise the essay carefully. Read it aloud again if possible. Prepare a final copy.

A STUDENT PARAGRAPH: ARGUMENTATION AND PERSUASION

In the following paragraph, the student begins quite forcibly by stating his position on custody battles during divorce cases—in other words, in an argumentative mode. Examine the simple but effective way he provides evidence for his position.

Main proposition; "outrageous" a cue for sympathy	The outcomes of custody battles during divorce proceedings exemplify the outrageous prejudice against fathers in our culture.
Cites authority to support main proposition	Recently, the <u>Houston Chronicle</u> reported on the outcome of a child custody case the paper had followed for nearly six months.
Case study provides evidence	In the case, both father and mother wanted sole custody of their only child. The mother, a defense attorney at a high-flying Houston firm, worked 60–70 hours a week; she had maintained this schedule from the time the

child, now six, was two-months-old. She frequently spent at least one weekend day at the office; she traveled on business as many as 10 weeks out of the year. The father, a freelance writer who worked at home, was acknowledged by both spouses to be the child's primary caretaker, and to have filled this role from the time the child was two-months-old and the wife returned to work. He typically woke the child, prepared breakfast, helped her choose clothing to wear, packed her a lunch, and walked her to school. He picked her up from school, accompanied her on playdates or took her to play in the park, made dinner for them both, helped the child with her homework, bathed her, read her a story, and put her to sleep. The mother ordinarily arrived home from work after the child was already asleep, and often left for work before the child was awake. Guess who got custody? The mother, of course. Sadly, judges persist in assuming that mothers are always the better—the more "natural"—caretaker. This assumption leads them all too often to award custody to the mother, despite evidence in many cases that the child has been raised primarily by the father, and would be better off continuing in his care.

Identification of opposition: conservative judges

Refutation and conclusion that reinforces main proposition

Get a Knife, Get a Dog, but Get Rid of Guns

Molly Ivins

The columnist Molly Ivins, a native and long-time resident of Texas, attacks "gun nuts" in a spirited, wry, and sometimes angry essay. As a professional writer for popular audiences, Ivins is alert to the need to be both persuasive and entertaining. Keep an eye out for how she manages to achieve these goals.

PREREADING: THINKING ABOUT THE ESSAY IN ADVANCE

Stop a moment to explore your attitudes about guns. Can you say *why* you think what you do? Are your opinions based on reliable evidence? Are your opinions well-reasoned?

Words to Watch

ricochet (par. 3) bounce off a surface
civil libertarian (par. 4) a person who believes strongly in freedom of speech and action
infringed (par. 5) violated
perforating (par. 6) making holes in
lethal (par. 8) deadly
wreak . . . carnage (par. 8) cause great bloodshed
martial (par. 12) warlike
literally (par. 13) actually
psychosexual (par. 13) having to do with the emotional aspects of sexuality
psyches (par. 14) emotional make-up

Guns. Everywhere guns. 1

Let me start this discussion by pointing out that I am not antigun. I'm pro-knife. Consider the merits of the knife. 2

In the first place, you have to catch up with someone in order to stab him. A general substitution of knives for guns would promote physical fitness. We'd turn into a whole nation of great 3 runners. Plus, knives don't ricochet. And people are seldom killed while cleaning their knives.

4 As a civil libertarian, I, of course, support the Second Amendment. And I believe it means exactly what it says:

5 *A well-regulated militia being necessary to the security of a free state, the right of the people to keep and bear arms shall not be infringed.* Fourteen-year-old boys are not part of a well-regulated militia. Members of wacky religious cults are not part of a well-regulated militia. Permitting unregulated citizens to have guns is destroying the security of this free state.

6 I am intrigued by the arguments of those who claim to follow the judicial doctrine of original intent. How do they know it was the dearest wish of Thomas Jefferson's heart that teenage drug dealers should cruise the cities of this nation perforating their fellow citizens with assault rifles? Channeling?

7 There is more hooey spread about the Second Amendment. It says quite clearly that guns are for those who form part of a well-regulated militia, that is, the armed forces, including the National Guard. Their reasons for keeping them away from everyone else get clearer by the day.

8 The comparison most often used is that of the automobile, another lethal object that is regularly used to wreak great carnage. Obviously, this society is full of people who haven't enough common sense to use an automobile properly. But we haven't outlawed cars yet.

9 We do, however, license them and their owners, restrict their use to presumably sane and sober adults, and keep track of who sells them to whom. At a minimum, we should do the same with guns.

10 In truth, there is no rational argument for guns in this society. This is no longer a frontier nation in which people hunt their own food. It is a crowded, overwhelmingly urban country in which letting people have access to guns is a continuing disaster. Those who want guns—whether for target shooting, hunting, or potting rattlesnakes (get a hoe)—should be subject to the same restrictions placed on gun owners in England, a nation in which liberty has survived nicely without an armed populace.

11 The argument that "guns don't kill people" is patent nonsense. Anyone who has ever worked in a cop shop knows how many family arguments end in murder because there was a gun in the house. Did the gun kill someone? No. But if there had been no gun, no one would have died. At least not without a good foot race first. Guns do kill. Unlike cars, that is all they do.

Michael Crichton makes an interesting argument about technology in his thriller *Jurassic Park.* He points out that power without discipline is making this society into a wreckage. By the time someone who studies the martial arts becomes a master—literally able to kill with bare hands—that person has also undergone years of training and discipline. But any fool can pick up a gun and kill with it. 12

"A well-regulated militia" surely implies both long training and long discipline. That is the least, the very least, that should be required of those who are permitted to have guns, because a gun is literally the power to kill. For years I used to enjoy taunting my gun-nut friends about their psychosexual hang-ups—always in a spirit of good cheer, you understand. But letting the noisy minority in the NRA force us to allow this carnage to continue is just plain insane. 13

I do think gun nuts have a power hang-up. I don't know what is missing in their psyches that they need to feel they have the power to kill. But no sane society would allow this to continue. 14

Ban the damn things. Ban them all. 15

You want protection? Get a dog. 16

BUILDING VOCABULARY

1. Identify the following:
   a. the Second Amendment (par. 4)
   b. the judicial doctrine of original intent (par. 6)
   c. Michael Crichton's *Jurassic Park* (par. 12)
   d. NRA (par. 13)
2. This is an essay that argues a certain point of view. It therefore wishes to undermine opposing ideas. List five words or phrases in this essay that aim to strengthen the writer's position by making fun of or otherwise undermining the opposition.

THINKING CRITICALLY ABOUT THE ESSAY

Understanding the Writer's Ideas

1. Why does the writer devote her first three paragraphs to the knife?

2. In your own words, state the writer's interpretation of the Second Amendment.
3. What is the point of comparing guns and cars?
4. In the view of the writer, was there ever an argument for the unlimited access to firearms?
5. What is the writer's response to the argument that "guns don't kill people," it is people using guns who do?
6. Why does the writer allude to *Jurassic Park?*

Understanding the Writer's Techniques

1. What is the *tone* (see Glossary) of this essay? How does the tone support the writer's argument?
2. What is the rhetorical effect of beginning the essay by a discussion of knives?
3. This essay lists and responds to the main arguments in *favor* of unlimited sale and possession of guns. Identify these positive arguments in the order they are presented.
4. Why does the writer present the arguments for guns in the order she does?
5. In addition to responding to arguments by the opposition, the writer puts forward her own arguments against guns. Identify these in the order that they are presented.
6. How does the concluding paragraph reinforce the writer's argument?

Exploring the Writer's Ideas

1. Is the writer too "argumentative"? That is, does she overstep credibility by mocking those who oppose her views? Explain your view.
2. Meddling with amendments to the Constitution is a serious matter, for these provisions have governed the nation well for hundreds of years. Does the writer do justice to the gravity of the documents whose meaning she is interpreting? Could she advance her argument in a less provocative way? Explain.
3. Are you persuaded by the writer's arguments regarding militias? If so, explain why. If not, explain why not.
4. Write a response to the writer's taunt that progun advocates must have something "missing in their psyches."

IDEAS FOR WRITING

Prewriting

Using the same tone as the writer, write a few sentences in support of guns.

Guided Writing

Write an essay which allows you to mock a well-established but controversial position, such as the advocacy of unlimited access to pornography on the grounds of free speech.

1. Begin the essay with a bold mocking statement that puts those opposed to your view on the defensive. Make sure you can usefully return to the example or tactic of your opening at other points in your essay.
2. State the main argument for the opposition point of view, preferably one referring to its basis in law.
3. Refute this argument by short, dismissive sentences and examples.
4. State two or three other arguments for the opposing point of view, again using short, pointed, and mocking retorts.
5. End your essay by a return, in the form of a pithy summary, to the ploy of your opening paragraph.

Thinking and Writing Collaboratively

Divide the class arbitrarily in two. Assign one group the progun position, and the other the antigun position. Have each group take the writer's main points and amplify or refute them.

More Writing Projects

1. Visit a firing range and interview some people there about their views on guns. Write an outline for an essay about your visit.
2. Read the debates that led to the original adoption of the Second Amendment. Write an essay that reflects on the relevance or irrelevance of the arguments of that time to our own.
3. Write an essay that argues for a favored solution of your own to the problem of violence in our society.

I Want a Wife

Judy Brady

Judy Brady, a wife and mother of two children, argues in this essay for a wife of her own. Although her argument might seem strange, her position will become apparent once you move into the essay. She presents many points to support her position, so you want to keep in mind those you think are the strongest.

PREREADING: THINKING ABOUT THE ESSAY IN ADVANCE

As you prepare to read this satirical essay, consider the traditional roles that men and women play in their mutual relationships. What is expected conventionally of a husband? of a wife? Do you accept these roles? Why or why not?

Words to Watch

nurturant (par. 3) giving affectionate care and attention

hors d'oeuvres (par. 6) food served before the regular courses of the meal

monogamy (par. 8) the habit of having only one mate; the practice of marrying only once during life

1 I belong to that classification of people known as wives. I am A Wife. And, not altogether incidentally, I am a mother.

2 Not too long ago a male friend of mine appeared on the scene fresh from a recent divorce. He had one child, who is, of course, with his ex-wife. He is obviously looking for another wife. As I thought about him while I was ironing one evening, it suddenly occurred to me that I, too, would like to have a wife. Why do I want a wife?

3 I would like to go back to school so that I can become economically independent, support myself, and, if need be, support those dependent upon me. I want a wife who will work and send me to school. And while I am going to school I want a wife to keep track of the children's doctor and dentist appointments. And to keep track of mine, too. I want a wife to make sure my

children eat properly and are kept clean. I want a wife who will wash the children's clothes and keep them mended. I want a wife who is a good nurturant attendant to my children, who arranges for their schooling, makes sure that they have an adequate social life with their peers, takes them to the park, the zoo, etc. I want a wife who takes care of the children when they are sick, a wife who arranges to be around when the children need special care, because, of course, I cannot miss classes at school. My wife must arrange to lose time at work and not lose the job. It may mean a small cut in my wife's income from time to time, but I guess I can tolerate that. Needless to say, my wife will arrange and pay for the care of the children while my wife is working.

I want a wife who will take care of *my* physical needs. I 4
want a wife who will keep my house clean. A wife who will pick up after me. I want a wife who will keep my clothes clean, ironed, mended, replaced when need be, and who will see to it that my personal things are kept in their proper place so that I can find what I need the minute I need it. I want a wife who cooks the meals, a wife who is a *good* cook. I want a wife who will plan the menus, do the necessary grocery shopping, prepare the meals, serve them pleasantly, and then do the cleaning up while I do my studying. I want a wife who will care for me when I am sick and sympathize with my pain and loss of time from school. I want a wife to go along when our family takes a vacation so that someone can continue to care for me and my children when I need a rest and change of scene.

I want a wife who will not bother me with rambling com- 5
plaints about a wife's duties. But I want a wife who will listen to me when I feel the need to explain a rather difficult point I have come across in my course of studies. And I want a wife who will type my papers for me when I have written them.

I want a wife who will take care of the details of my social 6
life. When my wife and I are invited out by my friends, I want a wife who will take care of the babysitting arrangements. When I meet people at school that I like and want to entertain, I want a wife who will have the house clean, will prepare a special meal, serve it to me and my friends, and not interrupt when I talk about the things that interest me and my friends. I want a wife who will have arranged that the children are fed and ready for bed before my guests arrive so that the children do not bother us. I want a

wife who takes care of the needs of my guests so that they feel comfortable, who makes sure that they have an ashtray, that they are passed the hors d'oeuvres, that they are offered a second helping of the food, that their wine glasses are replenished when necessary, that their coffee is served to them as they like it.

7 And I want a wife who knows that sometimes I need a night out by myself.

8 I want a wife who is sensitive to my sexual needs, a wife who makes love passionately and eagerly when I feel like it, a wife who makes sure that I am satisfied. And, of course, I want a wife who will not demand sexual attention when I am not in the mood for it. I want a wife who assumes the complete responsibility for birth control, because I do not want more children. I want a wife who will remain sexually faithful to me so that I do not have to clutter up my intellectual life with jealousies. And I want a wife who understands that *my* sexual needs may entail more than strict adherence to monogamy. I must, after all, be able to relate to people as fully as possible.

9 If, by chance, I find another person more suitable as a wife than the wife I already have, I want the liberty to replace my present wife with another one. Naturally, I will expect a fresh, new life; my wife will take the children and be solely responsible for them so that I am left free.

10 When I am through with school and have a job, I want my wife to quit working and remain at home so that my wife can more fully and completely take care of a wife's duties.

11 My God, who *wouldn't* want a wife?

BUILDING VOCABULARY

1. After checking a dictionary, write definitions of each of these words.
   a. attendant (par. 3)
   b. adequate (par. 3)
   c. peers (par. 3)
   d. tolerate (par. 3)
   e. rambling (par. 5)
   f. replenished (par. 6)
   g. adherence (par. 8)
2. Write an original sentence for each word above.

THINKING CRITICALLY ABOUT THE ESSAY

Understanding the Writer's Ideas

1. What incident made Brady think about wanting a wife?
2. How would a wife help the writer achieve economic independence?
3. In what ways would a wife take care of the writer's children? Why would the writer like someone to assume those responsibilities?
4. What physical needs would Brady's "wife" take care of?
5. How would a wife deal with the writer's social life? Her sex life?

Understanding the Writer's Techniques

1. In formal argumentation, we often call the writer's main point the *major* or *main proposition.* What is Brady's major proposition? Is it simply what she says in paragraph 2, or is the proposition more complex than that? State it in your own words.
2. What is the value of the question Brady asks in paragraph 2? Where else does she ask a question? What value does this other question have in its place in the essay? What impact does it have on the reader?
3. The points a writer offers to support the major proposition are called *minor propositions.* What minor propositions does Brady present to show why she wants a wife? In which instances do they serve as topic sentences within paragraphs? What details does she offer to illustrate those minor propositions?
4. In what order has the writer chosen to arrange the minor propositions? Why has she chosen such an order? Do you think she builds from the least to the most important reasons for having a wife? What changes would you urge in the order of the minor propositions?
5. Most of the paragraphs here develop through illustration. Where has Brady used a simple listing of details? Why has she chosen that format?
6. Brady's style is obviously straightforward, her sentences for the most part simple and often brief. Why has she chosen such a style? What is the effect of the repetition of "I

want" at the start of so many sentences? Why has Brady used several short paragraphs (1, 7, 10, 11) in addition to longer ones?

7. What is the author's *tone* (see Glossary)? Point out the uses of *irony* (see Glossary) in the essay. How does irony contribute to Brady's main intent in this essay? How does the fact that Brady is a woman contribute to this sense of irony?

Exploring the Writer's Ideas

1. By claiming that she wants a wife, Brady is showing us all the duties and responsibilities of the woman in a contemporary household. Has Brady represented these duties fairly? Do husbands generally expect their wives to do all these things?
2. To what degree do wives today fit Brady's description? How could a wife avoid many of the responsibilities spelled out in the essay? How does the "modern husband" figure in the way many couples meet household responsibilities now?
3. Brady has characterized all the traditional and stereotyped roles usually assigned to wives. What "wifely responsibilities" has she left out?
4. Has Brady presented a balanced picture of the issues or is her argument one-sided? Support your opinion with specific references to the essay. Could the author have dealt effectively with opposing arguments? Why or why not? What might these opposing arguments be?
5. Answer the question in the last line of the essay.
6. Read the essays "Night Walker" by Brent Staples (pages 167–170) and "How Do We Find the Student in a World of Academic Gymnasts and Worker Ants?" by James T. Baker (pages 290–293). Compare the use of stereotyping in these essays. How is it different from Brady's stereotypes?

IDEAS FOR WRITING

Prewriting

Freewrite for fifteen minutes about why you want a husband or wife, trying to poke fun at or ridicule (as Brady does) the traditional expectations that we bring to this issue.

Guided Writing

Write an essay of 750 to 1,000 words titled, "I Want a Husband."

1. Write the essay from the point of view of a *man*. As Brady wrote as a woman who wanted a wife, you write this essay as a man who wants a husband.
2. Start your essay with a brief personal story as in paragraph 2 of "I Want a Wife."
3. Support your main point with a number of minor points. Expand each minor point with details that explain your premises.
4. Arrange your minor premises carefully so that you build to the most convincing point at the end.
5. Use a simple and straightforward style. Connect your points with transitions; use repetition as one transitional device.
6. Balance your longer paragraphs with occasional shorter ones.
7. End your essay with a crisp, one-sentence question of your own.

Thinking and Writing Collaboratively

Divide the class into one group consisting entirely of males and the other of females. Working in these groups, have the men list the advantages of having a husband, and the women list the advantages of having a wife. Each group should list its key advantages on the chalkboard for class discussion.

More Writing Projects

1. In your journal, copy any three sentences from Brady's essay that you find particularly provocative, challenging, strange, or unbelievable. Explain why you chose them.
2. Write a paragraph in which you argue *for* or *against* this issue: "A married woman belongs at home."
3. Write an essay in which you argue about whose role you think is harder to play effectively in today's society: the role of the mother or the role of the father.

The Case for More Cops

Mortimer B. Zuckerman

Mortimer B. Zuckerman, editor-in-chief of *U.S. News & World Report,* takes the position that we are not yet fully aware that we are at war in America. But once we realize that we have been invaded, he feels his solution is the one we need to consider if we want to win any battles. The culprit? Crime.

PREREADING: THINKING ABOUT THE ESSAY IN ADVANCE

How can the police provide security to people living in crime-ridden communities? Make a list of steps that you think would be effective.

Words to Watch

probation (par. 1) the act of suspending the sentence of a person convicted of a criminal offense and granting that person provisional freedom on the promise of good behavior

ROTC (par. 4) officer training program

Congress (par. 5) the national legislative body of the United States, consisting of the Senate and the House of Representatives

1 We have crime without punishment in America. The probability that a violent criminal or even a violent repeat offender will go to prison and spend most of his time behind bars is only one fifth of what it was in 1960. Fewer than 10 percent of burglaries result in an arrest, barely 1.2 percent in imprisonment. Convicted criminals serve only about a third of their sentences. It is a staggering fact that we have about 3 million of them on the streets without serious probation or police supervision. A rapist averages five years, a convicted murderer just 10 years. Homicide arrests as a share of all murders have declined from 95 percent a decade ago to 50 percent today.

2 Everyone knows there is a complex of real, not fanciful, causes for all this: Understaffed police forces, soft courts, overcrowded prisons, the epidemic of drugs and the breakdown of the

family. But not many people realize just how thin the "thin blue line" has become. Forty years ago, there were 3.2 police officers for every violent felony reported. Today there are 3.2 times the number of violent felonies for every serving officer. In big cities the ratios are worse. In New York it is 6.5 violent felonies per cop, in Boston 6.9; in Los Angeles, Newark and Atlanta it is 10. This calculation does not include the much greater number of unreported felonies or the smaller fraction of police who are on the streets at any one time. Here is a stunning fact: Eighty-three percent of Americans can expect to be victims of a crime at least once in their lifetime.

How would you like to return to the police–violent-crime ratios of 40 years ago, when there was a wholly different sense of security? Given the 544,000 cops that we have today, we would have to increase the number of cops to about 5 million. That is the breathtaking measure of the hold crime has on our society. The wealthy are driven to hire private police; the ordinary public is driven only to despair. There are now 1.5 million private security guards in America. We spend almost twice as much on private police as we do on public police. According to Princeton University's John J. DiIulio, we spend seven times more on transportation and 12 times more on public welfare than we do on criminal justice activities—cops, courts and corrections. 3

We need more police to police America. Five million is beyond what we can hope to do, but we can build much bigger and better forces. Two generations ago, most police officers got their first training in the military, where they served before joining the force. Not so today. Given the downsizing of our military, we should find a way to hire these trained, disciplined military personnel as cops. We should also support the notion of a Police Corps as a supplement to the regular police. These are young people who would be recruited on the ROTC principle, receiving four-year scholarships and repaying the country for this benefit with four years of service as local police officers. 4

To this we must add at least the 100,000 police called for in the Senate version of the crime bill before Congress, rather than the 50,000 in the House version. This number may be just a down payment on the police we will need to regain control of high-crime streets, communities and classrooms, and to prevent violence and disorder from seeping into those neighborhoods that are now relatively peaceful. Congress, which is demanding 5 that local communities pay a portion of the cost of this program, should be careful not to overburden communities with the cost of matching requirements. It is important that there be wide national participation and that it last beyond the first city budget.

6 We are at war today. The enemy is the criminal. Were we to be invaded by a foreign enemy this lethal, we would not be debating if we could afford the soldiers and weapons to defend ourselves. We would spend what is necessary to win the war. Restoring public order and individual security would be the first national priority—not in the future, but today. So must it be with the fight against crime. Only more police and an enhanced certainty of punishment can have the immediate impact we need. Only then can social programs contribute to longer-term solutions. Government must do the one thing people cannot do on their own—provide real security and protection.

BUILDING VOCABULARY

Write sentences in which you use the following words correctly.

a. fanciful (par. 2)
b. epidemic (par. 2)
c. supplement (par. 4)
d. lethal (par. 6)

THINKING CRITICALLY ABOUT THE ESSAY

Understanding the Writer's Ideas

1. Are criminals being punished in ways that will keep them from repeating their offenses?
2. Despite all the political talk on reducing crime, have police forces grown in strength or effectiveness?
3. What kind of response have the wealthy had to the lack of public security?
4. What solution does the writer offer to increase the police force without much cost to a community?
5. What does the writer mean when he states, "We are at war"? Is the writer serious? Why or why not?

Understanding the Writer's Techniques

1. What is the thesis? Would you consider it the major proposition? Explain.
2. What statistics does the writer use? How do these contribute to the effectiveness of the argument?
3. What is the tone of the selection? Would you call it serious or relaxed? Defend your choice.
4. Do you think the writer had an audience of police in mind when he wrote this essay? Keep in mind the magazine where the essay appeared (*U.S. News & World Report*).
5. Comment on the word "Case" in the title. This has a legal meaning, too. Why did the writer choose this word?

Exploring the Writer's Ideas

1. The essay's first sentence makes the bold statement that we "have crime without punishment." Yet statistics also show that prisons are overcrowded. Is the writer wrong? Explain.
2. Is it fair that the wealthy pay for their own security but people who depend on public security must do with less? How do you feel?
3. While a police corps sounds like a good idea, many police officers fear that unpaid workers will create unemployment. Also, a police corps will limit well-paying jobs for those young people interested in a career in law enforcement. Take a position and support it.
4. This writer seems to think that social programs (e.g., job training) won't lessen crime as much as a war on crime. But some argue that crime grows out of the lack of social programs. Are more police the answer? Which side are you on? Why?

IDEAS FOR WRITING

Prewriting

Who do you think has been undervalued in this society? Freewrite in your journal.

Guided Writing

Write an essay called "The Case for ________." Fill in the blank with a word or term that names a group you feel has been ignored, overlooked, or undervalued in our society. You might want to use a term like "jocks," "loners," or "teachers."

1. Write an introduction to set the stage for your argument. Develop a major proposition and state it in your thesis. Place your thesis in a key position in the essay.
2. Use specific examples to support your major proposition.
3. Develop a clear sense of whom your audience is and direct your argument to that group.
4. Draw on other rhetorical strategies as needed: comparison, causal analysis, process, and so forth.
5. Develop a conclusion that clearly warns the reader of the consequences that will follow if he or she doesn't accept the major premise of your argument.

Thinking and Writing Collaboratively

Form groups of three to four class members. As a group, take a position for or against an issue important to your school or community. Then argue the opposite view of the position most people in the group favor. Write an essay that ultimately reflects both views. Conclude your essay by establishing which argument is the strongest.

More Writing Projects

1. In your journal, make a list of everything that comes to mind with the word *rich.*
2. Using the above journal entry, write one paragraph that argues for or against making rich people pay more for social services than others.
3. Choose a topic that focuses on a headline issue in the news and write an essay that argues for a position you feel strongly about. Consider environmental issues or the abortion debate.

Are the Homeless Crazy?

Jonathan Kozol

Jonathan Kozol is an educator and writer on social issues who, until recently, was perhaps best known for his book-length study *Why Children Fail.* In the past few years, he has turned his attention to America's ever-increasing problem of homelessness. In 1988, he published the book *Rachel and Her Children* on the subject, along with this essay, which derives from "Distancing the Homeless," published in the *Yale Review.* In this essay, Kozol examines the idea that much of today's homelessness has resulted from the release of patients from mental hospitals in the 1970s.

PREREADING: THINKING ABOUT THE ESSAY IN ADVANCE

What are your views of the homeless in American society? Should we classify the homeless as crazy, lazy, unfortunate, or abject failures? Why or why not?

Words to Watch

deinstitutionalized (par. 1) let inmates out of hospitals, prisons, and so forth
conceding (par. 2) acknowledging; admitting to
arson (par. 4) the crime of deliberately setting a fire
subsidized (par. 5) aided with public money
destitute (par. 6) very poor
afflictions (par. 7) ills; problems
stigma (par. 7) a mark of shame or discredit
complacence (par. 7) self-satisfaction
bulk (par. 10) the main part
de facto (par. 11) actually; in reality
resilience (par. 12) ability to recover easily from misfortune
paranoids (par. 13) psychotic people who believe everyone is persecuting them
vengeance (par. 14) retribution; retaliation

1 It is commonly believed by many journalists and politicians that the homeless of America are, in large part, former patients of large mental hospitals who were deinstitutionalized in the 1970s—the consequence, it is sometimes said, of misguided liberal opinion that favored the treatment of such persons in community-based centers. It is argued that this policy, and the subsequent failure of society to build such centers or to provide them in sufficient number, is the primary cause of homelessness in the United States.

2 Those who work among the homeless do not find that explanation satisfactory. While conceding that a certain number of the homeless are or have been mentally unwell, they believe that, in the case of most unsheltered people, the primary reason is economic rather than clinical. The cause of homelessness, they say with disarming logic, is the lack of homes and of income with which to rent or acquire them.

3 They point to the loss of traditional jobs in industry (2 million every year since 1980) and to the fact that half of those who are laid off end up in work that pays a poverty-level wage. They point out that since 1968 the number of children living in poverty has grown by 3 million, while welfare benefits to families with children have declined by 35 percent.

4 And they note, too, that these developments have occurred during a time in which the shortage of low-income housing has intensified as the gentrification of our major cities has accelerated. Half a million units of low-income housing are lost each year to condominium conversion as well as to arson, demolition, or abandonment. Between 1978 and 1980, median rents climbed 30 percent for people in the lowest income sector, driving many of these families into the streets. Since 1980, rents have risen at even faster rates.

5 Hard numbers, in this instance, would appear to be of greater help than psychiatric labels in telling us why so many people become homeless. Eight million American families now use half or more of their income to pay their rent or mortgage. At the same time, federal support for low-income housing dropped from $30 billion (1980) to $7.5 billion (1988). Under Presidents Ford and Carter, 500,000 subsidized private housing units were constructed. By President Reagan's second term, the number had dropped to 25,000.

6 In our rush to explain the homeless as a psychiatric problem even the words of medical practitioners who care for homeless

people have been curiously ignored. A study published by the Massachusetts Medical Society, for instance, has noted that, with the exceptions of alcohol and drug use, the most frequent illnesses among a sample of the homeless population were trauma (31 percent), upper-respiratory disorders (28 percent), limb disorders (19 percent), mental illness (16 percent), skin diseases (15 percent), hypertension (14 percent), and neurological illnesses (12 percent). Why, we may ask, of all these calamities, does mental illness command so much political and press attention? The answer may be that the label of mental illness places the destitute outside the sphere of ordinary life. It personalizes an anguish that is public in its genesis; it individualizes a misery that is both general in cause and general in application.

There is another reason to assign labels to the destitute and single out mental illness from among their many afflictions. All these other problems—tuberculosis, asthma, scabies, diarrhea, bleeding gums, impacted teeth, etc.—bear no stigma, and mental illness does. It conveys a stigma in the United States. It conveys a stigma in the Soviet Union as well. In both nations the label is used, whether as a matter of deliberate policy or not, to isolate and treat as special cases those who, by deed or word or by sheer presence, represent a threat to national complacence. The two situations are obviously not identical, but they are enough alike to give Americans reason for concern. 7

The notion that the homeless are largely psychotics who belong in institutions, rather than victims of displacement at the hands of enterprising realtors, spares us from the need to offer realistic solutions to the deep and widening extremes of wealth and poverty in the United States. It also enables us to tell ourselves that the despair of homeless people bears no intimate connection to the privileged existence we enjoy—when, for example, we rent or purchase one of those restored town houses that once provided shelter for people now huddled in the street. 8

What is to be made, then, of the supposition that the homeless are primarily the former residents of mental hospitals, persons who were carelessly released during the 1970s? Many of them are, to be sure. Among the older men and women in the streets and shelters, as many as one-third (some believe as many as one-half) may be chronically disturbed, and a number of these people were deinstitutionalized during the 1970s. But to operate on that assumption in a city such as New York—where nearly half the homeless are small children 9 whose average age is six—makes no sense. Their parents, with an average age of twenty-seven, are not likely to have been hospitalized in the 1970s, either.

10 A frequently cited set of figures tells us that in 1955 the average daily census of non-federal psychiatric institutions was 677,000, and that by 1984 the number had dropped to 151,000. But these people didn't go directly from a hospital room to the street. The bulk of those who had been psychiatric patients and were released from hospitals during the 1960s and early 1970s had been living in low-income housing, many in skid-row hotels or boardinghouses. Such housing—commonly known as SRO (single-room occupancy) units—was drastically diminished by the gentrification of our cities that began in the early '70s. Almost 50 percent of SRO housing was replaced by luxury apartments or office buildings between 1970 and 1980, and the remaining units have been disappearing even more rapidly.

11 Even for those persons who are ill and were deinstitutionalized during the decades before 1980, the precipitating cause of homelessness in 1987 is not illness but loss of housing. SRO housing offered low-cost sanctuaries for the homeless, providing a degree of safety and mutual support for those who lived within them. They were a demeaning version of the community health centers that society had promised; they were the de facto "halfway houses" of the 1970s. For these people too—at most half of the homeless single persons in America—the cause of homelessness is lack of housing.

12 Even in those cases where mental instability is apparent, homelessness itself is often the precipitating factor. For example, many pregnant women without homes are denied prenatal care because they constantly travel from one shelter to another. Many are anemic. Many are denied essential dietary supplements by recent federal cuts. As a consequence, some of their children do not live to see their second year of life. Do these mothers sometimes show signs of stress? Do they appear disorganized, depressed, disordered? Frequently. They are immobilized by pain, traumatized by fear. So it is no surprise that when researchers enter the scene to ask them how they "feel," the resulting reports tell us that the homeless are emotionally unwell. The reports do not tell us that we have *made* these people ill. They do not tell us that illness is a natural response to intolerable conditions. Nor do they tell us of the strength and the resilience that so many of these people retain despite the miseries they must endure.

A writer in the *New York Times* describes a homeless woman standing on a traffic island in Manhattan. "She was evicted from her small room in the hotel just across the street," and she is determined to get revenge. Until she does, "nothing will move her from that spot. . . . Her argumentativeness and her angry fixation on revenge, along with the apparent absence of hallucinations, mark her as a paranoid." Most physicians, I imagine, would be more reserved in passing judgment with so little evidence, but this reporter makes his diagnosis without hesitation. "The paranoids of the street," he says, "are among the most difficult to help." 13

Perhaps so. But does it depend on who is offering the help? Is anyone offering to help this woman get back her home? Is it crazy to seek vengeance for being thrown into the street? The absence of anger, some psychiatrists believe, might indicate much greater illness. 14

"No one will be turned away," says the mayor of New York City, as hundreds of young mothers with their infants are turned from the doors of shelters season after season. That may sound to some like a denial of reality. "Now you're hearing all kinds of horror stories," says the President of the United States as he denies that anyone is cold or hungry or unhoused. On another occasion he says that the unsheltered "are homeless, you might say, by choice." That sounds every bit as self-deceiving. 15

The woman standing on the traffic island screaming for revenge until her room has been restored to her sounds relatively healthy by comparison. If 3 million homeless people did the same, and all at the same time, we might finally be forced to listen. 16

BUILDING VOCABULARY

1. Throughout this essay, Kozol uses medical and psychiatric *jargon* (see Glossary). List the medical or psychiatric terms or references that you find here. Then look up any five in the dictionary and write definitions for them.
2. Explain in your own words the meanings of the following phrases. Use clues from the surrounding text to help you understand.
   - **a.** sufficient number (par. 1)
   - **b.** primary cause (par. 1)
   - **c.** poverty-level wage (par. 3)

d. median rents (par. 4)
e. low-income housing (par. 5)
f. sheer presence (par. 7)
g. intimate connection (par. 8)
h. chronically disturbed (par. 9)
i. skid-row hotels (par. 10)
j. precipitating cause (par. 11)
k. low-cost sanctuaries (par. 11)
l. mutual support (par. 11)
m. demeaning version (par. 11)
n. natural response (par. 12)
o. intolerable conditions (par. 12)
p. angry fixation (par. 13)

THINKING CRITICALLY ABOUT THE ESSAY

Understanding the Writer's Ideas

1. According to Kozol, who has suggested that the deinstitutionalizing of mental-hospital patients is the major cause of homelessness? Does he agree? If not, what does he identify as the major causes?
2. In the opening paragraph, what two groups does Kozol link together? Why? What relation between them does he suggest?
3. In New York City today, what percentage of the homeless are children? What is the average age of their parents? In the past twenty years, has the number of children living in poverty increased or decreased? What about welfare payments to families with children? How has this affected the homelessness situation?
4. What are "gentrification" and "condominium conversion" (par. 4)? How have they affected homelessness?
5. Explain the meaning of the statement: "Hard numbers, in this instance, would appear to be of greater help than psychiatric labels in telling us why so many people become homeless" (par. 5).
6. List in descending order the most common illnesses among the homeless. From what does Kozol draw these statistics? What is his conclusion about them?
7. In your own words, summarize why Kozol feels that journalists and politicians concentrate so heavily on the problems of mental illness among the homeless.

8. What are SROs? Explain how they figure in the homeless situation.
9. What is meant by the "press" (par. 6)? What are "halfway houses" (par. 11)?
10. What is Kozol's attitude toward former President Reagan? toward former New York City Mayor Ed Koch? Explain your answers with specific references to the beginning and ending of the essay.
11. Summarize in your own words the *New York Times* story to which Kozol refers. According to the *Times* reporter, why did the homeless woman mentioned refuse to move from the traffic island? Does Kozol agree with the reporter's interpretation? Explain.
12. In one sentence, state in your own words the opinion Kozol expresses in the last paragraph.

Understanding the Writer's Techniques

1. Which sentence states the *major proposition* of the essay?
2. Describe Kozol's argumentative purpose in this essay. Is it primarily to *convince* or to *persuade?* Explain.
3. In paragraph 1, the author uses a particular verbal construction that he doesn't repeat elsewhere in the essay. He writes: "It is commonly believed . . ."; "it is sometimes said . . ."; and "It is argued. . . ." Why does he use the "it is" construction? What effect does it have? How does he change that pattern in paragraph 2? Why?
4. In paragraph 2, Kozol uses the phrase "mentally unwell" instead of the more common "mentally ill," and he uses "unsheltered people" instead of "homeless people." Why does he use these less-expected phrases? Does he use them again in the essay? Why?
5. *Cynicism* adds an edge of pessimism or anger to a statement that might otherwise be perceived as *irony* (see Glossary). In the sentence, "The cause of homelessness, they say with disarming logic, is the lack of homes and of income with which to rent or acquire them" (par. 2), the clause set off by commas might be considered cynical. Why? Find and explain several other examples of cynicism in this essay. Are they effective? Are they justified?
6. Identify the *minor proposition* statements in this essay. How do they add *coherence* (see Glossary) to the essay?

7. How important is Kozol's use of *statistics* in this essay? Which are the most effective? Why?
8. What is the difference between *refutation* (see Glossary) and *negation*? Kozol uses refutation as a major technique in this essay. Analyze his use of refutation in paragraphs 1 and 2. List and discuss at least three other instances where he uses refutation. Where in the essay does he specifically use negation?
9. Evaluate Kozol's use of *cause-and-effect analysis* in paragraphs 1 through 6. In paragraph 12, how does Kozol revise the more commonly cited causal relationship between homelessness and mental illness?
10. Discuss Kozol's use of *comparison* in paragraph 7. In what ways does he use *illustration?* How is his use of illustration in the last paragraph different from his other uses of it?
11. Characterize the overall *tone* of the essay. How and why does Kozol develop this tone? Who is the intended *audience* for this essay? What is the *level of diction?* How are the two connected? What assumption about the audience is implied in the last sentence of paragraph 8?
12. Writers often use *rhetorical questions* in order to prompt the reader to pay special attention to an issue, but rhetorical questions are usually not meant to be answered. Evaluate Kozol's use of rhetorical questions in paragraph 12. What is the effect of the one-word answer, "Frequently"? Where else does he use rhetorical questions? What message does he attempt to convey with them?
13. Returning to the thesis in the course of an essay is often an effective technique to refocus the reader's attention before beginning a new analysis or a conclusion. Explain how Kozol uses this technique in paragraph 11 to make it a key turning point in the essay.
14. Although Kozol cites various studies and authorities, he makes little use of *direct quotations.* Why? Identify and analyze the three instances where he *does* use direct quotations. How does it help to convey his attitude toward the material he's quoting?
15. Evaluate Kozol's conclusion. How does he establish an aura of unreality in paragraphs 15 and 16? Why does he do so? Does he effectively answer the title question? Explain.

Exploring the Writer's Ideas

1. In small groups, discuss your own experiences, both positive and negative, with homeless people.
2. If possible, conduct an interview with one or more homeless people. Try to find out:
   a. how they became homeless
   b. how long they've been homeless
   c. what they do to survive
   d. whether they feel there may be an end to their homelessness

   Write a report based on your interviews and share it with your classmates.
3. This essay is an excerpt from a much longer essay entitled "Distancing the Homeless," published in the *Yale Review.* How is the theme of that title expressed in this essay?
4. Kozol presents an impressive array of statistics. Working in small groups, compile as many other statistics about homelessness as possible. Each group should then draw a subjective conclusion from the data and be prepared to present and defend it to the class as a whole.
5. Read the following description of New York City's Bowery district:

   > Walk under the El at night and all you feel is a sort of cold guilt. Touched for a dime, you try to drop the coin and not touch the hand, because the hand is dirty; you try to avoid the glance, because the glance accuses. This is not so much personal menace as universal—the cold menace of unresolved human suffering and poverty and the advanced stages of the disease alcoholism. On a summer night the drunks sleep in the open. The sidewalk is a free bed, and there are no lice. Pedestrians step along and over and around the still forms as though walking on a battlefield among the dead. In doorways, on the steps of the savings bank, the bums lie sleeping it off. Standing sentinel at each sleeper's head is the empty bottle from which he drained his release. Wedged in the crook of his arm is the paper bag containing his things.

   This description is from E. B. White's 1949 essay "Here Is New York," the same essay from which the selection "The Three New Yorks" (pages 283–285) is drawn. It is but one small indication that the current problem of homelessness is nothing new. Try to find other examples, either written or visual, that indicate that homelessness is a long-standing social issue. (You may want to contact such organizations as the Coalition for the Homeless and the Salvation Army.)

In your own experience, how have the conditions of homelessness changed in your own environment over the past five years? The past one year?

IDEAS FOR WRITING

Prewriting

Draft a brief outline arguing for or against a specific issue of campus concern—for example, date rape, political correctness, drugs, or AIDS counseling. In your outline, list at least three main reasons that support the position you are advocating.

Guided Writing

Choose a controversial local issue about which you hold a strong opinion that is not the generally accepted one. (For example, you might write about a decision by the town council to build a new shopping mall on an old vacant lot; the limiting of public library hours in order to save money; a decision to open a halfway house in your neighborhood; and so forth.) Write an essay that will convince the reader of the validity of your stance on the issue.

1. Begin your essay with a discussion of the commonly held opinion on this issue. Use the verbal construction "it is" to help distance you from that opinion.
2. In the next section, strongly refute the commonly held opinion by stating your major proposition clearly and directly.
3. Develop your opinion by the use of comparative statistics.
4. While trying to remain as objective as possible, establish a slightly cynical edge to your tone.
5. If appropriate, include some jargon related to the issue.
6. Explain and refute the causal logic (cause-and-effect analysis) of the common opinion.
7. About midway through the essay, return to the thesis in a paragraph that serves as a "pivot" for your essay.
8. Link ideas, statistics, and opinions by means of well-placed minor proposition statements.

9. Continue to refute the common opinion by
   a. using rhetorical questions
   b. citing and showing the invalidity of a recent media item on the issue
   c. lightly ridiculing some of the "big names" associated with the common opinion on the issue
10. Conclude your essay with a somewhat unrealistic, exaggerated image that both reinforces your opinion and invokes the reader to reexamine the issue more closely.

Thinking and Writing Collaboratively

In groups of four to five, discuss the alternatives or the opposition viewpoint to the arguments presented in your Guided Writing essay. Jot down notes, and then incorporate the opposition viewpoint—and your refutation or answer to it—in your final draft.

More Writing Projects

1. In your journal, freewrite about this topic: the homeless. Do not edit your writing. Write nonstop for at least fifteen minutes. When you finish, exchange journal entries with another student in the class. How do your responses compare? contrast?
2. Do you think it is correct to give money to panhandlers? Write a paragraph in which you state and defend your opinion.
3. Write an essay in the form of a letter to your local chief executive (mayor, town supervisor, and so forth) in which you express your opinion about the local homeless situation. Include some specific measures that you feel need to be enacted. Draw freely on your journal entry in question 1 of this exercise.

SUMMING UP: CHAPTER 11

1. Keep a journal in which you record your thoughts on, and observations of, homelessness in your part of the country. Try to gather specific data from reading, television viewing, or observation. Ask such questions as:

   How many are male? female?
   How many are children?
   How many are elderly?
   How many appear to be mentally ill?
   What symptoms or signs do they exhibit?

   Use the data, along with your observations, to present your position on homelessness in a letter to the editor of your campus or local newspaper.
2. Invite a local expert to class to speak on a current controversial issue. Write an essay of support for, or opposition to, the speaker's opinions.
3. Justify the inclusion of the essays by Kozol, Ivins, Brady, and Zuckerman under the category "Argumentation and Persuasion." Treat the major issues that they raise, their positions on these issues, their minor propositions and use of evidence, and the tone of their language. Finally, establish the degree to which you are persuaded by these arguments.
4. Exchange with a classmate essays that you've each written for a Guided Writing exercise in this chapter. Even if you agree with your partner's opinion, write a strongly worded response opposing it. Be sure you touch on the same, or similar, major and minor propositions.
5. Fill in the blanks in the following essay topic as you please, and use it as the major proposition for a well-developed argumentation-persuasion paper. Draw on the expository writing skills you have studied throughout the book. "I am very concerned about ___________, and I believe it's necessary to ___________."

CHAPTER 12

Prose for Further Reading

SHORT CLASSICS

The Allegory of the Cave

Plato

And now, I said, let me show in a figure how far our nature is enlightened or unenlightened: Behold! human beings living in an underground den, which has a mouth open towards the light and reaching all along the den; here, they have been from their childhood, and have their legs and necks chained so that they cannot move, and can only see before them, being prevented by the chains from turning round their heads. Above and behind them a fire is blazing at a distance, and between the fire and the prisoners there is a raised way; and you will see, if you look, a low wall built along the way, like the screen which marionette players have in front of them, over which they show the puppets. 1

I see. 2

And do you see, I said, men passing along the wall carrying all sorts of vessels, and statues and figures of animals made of wood and stone and various materials, which appear over the wall? Some of them are talking, others silent. 3

You have shown me a strange image, and they are strange prisoners. 4

Like ourselves, I replied; and they see only their own shadows, or the shadows of one another, which the fire throws on the opposite wall of the cave? 5

6 True, he said; how could they see anything but the shadows if they were never allowed to move their heads?

7 And of the objects which are being carried in like manner they would only see the shadows?

8 Yes, he said.

9 And if they were able to converse with one another, would they not suppose that they were naming what was actually before them?

10 Very true.

11 And suppose further that the prison had an echo which came from the other side, would they not be sure to fancy when one of the passers-by spoke that the voice which they heard came from the passing shadow?

12 No question, he replied.

13 To them, I said, the truth would be literally nothing but the shadows of the images.

14 That is certain.

15 And now look again, and see what will naturally follow if the prisoners are released and disabused of their error. At first, when any of them is liberated and compelled suddenly to stand up and turn his neck round and walk and look towards the light, he will suffer sharp pains; the glare will distress him and he will be unable to see the realities of which in his former state he had seen the shadows; and then conceive some one saying to him, that what he saw before was an illusion, but that now, when he is approaching nearer to being and his eye is turned towards more real existence, he has a clearer vision—what will be his reply? And you may further imagine that his instructor is pointing to the objects as they pass and requiring him to name them—will he not be perplexed? Will he not fancy that the shadows which he formerly saw are truer than the objects which are now shown to him?

16 Far truer.

17 And if he is compelled to look straight at the light, will he not have a pain in his eyes which will make him turn away to take refuge in the objects of vision which he can see, and which he will conceive to be in reality clearer than the things which are now being shown to him?

18 True, he said.

19 And suppose once more, that he is reluctantly dragged up a steep and rugged ascent, and held fast until he is forced into the presence of the sun himself, is he not likely to be pained and irritated? When he approaches the light his eyes will be dazzled and

he will not be able to see anything at all of what are now called realities.

20 Not all in a moment, he said.

21 He will require to grow accustomed to the sight of the upper world. And first he will see the shadows best, next the reflections of men and other objects in the water, and then the objects themselves; then he will gaze upon the light of the moon and the stars and the spangled heaven; and he will see the sky and the stars by night better than the sun or the light of the sun by day?

22 Certainly.

23 Last of all he will be able to see the sun, and not mere reflections of him in the water, but he will see him in his own proper place, and not in another; and he will contemplate him as he is.

24 Certainly.

25 He will then proceed to argue that this is he who gives the season and the years, and is the guardian of all that is in the visible world, and in a certain way the cause of all things which he and his fellows have been accustomed to behold?

26 Clearly, he said, he would first see the sun and then reason about him.

27 And when he remembered his old habitation, and the wisdom of the den and his fellow-prisoners, do you not suppose that he would felicitate himself on the change, and pity them?

28 Certainly, he would.

29 And if they were in the habit of conferring honors among themselves on those who were quickest to observe the passing shadows and to remark which of them went before, and which followed after, and which were together; and who were therefore best able to draw conclusions as to the future, do you think that he would care for such honors and glories, or envy the possessors of them? Would he not say with Homer,

> Better to be the poor servant of a poor master,

and to endure anything, rather than think as they do and live after their manner?

30 Yes, he said, I think that he would rather suffer anything than entertain these false notions and live in this miserable manner.

31 Imagine once more, I said, such a one coming suddenly out of the sun to be replaced in his old situation; would he not be certain to have his eyes full of darkness?

32 To be sure, he said.

33 And if there were a contest, and he had to compete in measuring the shadows with the prisoners who had never moved out of the den, while his sight was still weak, and before his eyes had become steady (and the time which would be needed to acquire this new habit of sight might be very considerable) would he not be ridiculous? Men would say of him that up he went and down he came without his eyes; and that it was better not even to think of ascending; and if any one tried to loose another and lead him up to the light, let them only catch the offender, and they would put him to death.

34 No question, he said.

35 This entire allegory, I said, you may now append, dear Glaucon, to the previous argument; the prison-house is the world of sight, the light of fire is the sun, and you will not misapprehend me if you interpret the journey upwards to be the ascent of the soul into the intellectual world according to my poor belief, which, at your desire, I have expressed—whether rightly or wrongly God knows. But, whether true or false, my opinion is that in the world of knowledge the idea of good appears last of all, and is seen only with an effort; and, when seen, is also inferred to be the universal author of all things beautiful and right, parent of light and of the lord of light in this visible world, and the immediate source of reason and truth in the intellectual; and that this is the power upon which he who would act rationally either in public or private life must have his eye fixed.

36 I agree, he said, as far as I am able to understand you.

37 Moreover, I said, you must not wonder that those who attain to this beatific vision are unwilling to descend to human affairs; for their souls are ever hastening into the upper world where they desire to dwell; which desire of theirs is very natural, if our allegory may be trusted.

38 Yes, very natural.

39 And is there anything surprising in one who passes from divine contemplations to the evil state of man, misbehaving himself in a ridiculous manner; if, while his eyes are blinking and before he has become accustomed to the surrounding darkness, he is compelled to fight in courts of law, or in other places, about the images or the shadows of images of justice, and is endeavoring to meet the conceptions of those who have never yet seen absolute justice?

40 Anything but surprising, he replied.

Any one who has common sense will remember that the bewilderments of the eyes are of two kinds, and arise from two causes, either from coming out of the light or from going into the light, which is true of the mind's eye, quite as much as of the bodily eye; and he who remembers this when he sees any one whose vision is perplexed and weak, will not be too ready to laugh; he will first ask whether that soul of man has come out of the brighter light, and is unable to see because unaccustomed to the dark, or having turned from darkness to the day is dazzled by excess of light. And he will count the one happy in his condition and state of being, and he will pity the other; or, if he have a mind to laugh at the soul which comes from below into the light, there will be more reason in this than in the laugh which greets him who returns from above out of the light into the den. 41

That, he said, is a very just distinction. 42

Advice to Youth

Samuel Langhorne Clemens (Mark Twain)

1 Being told I would be expected to talk here, I inquired what sort of a talk I ought to make. They said it should be something suitable to youth in something didactic, instructive, or something in the nature of good advice. Very well. I have a few things in mind which I have often longed to say for the instruction of the young; for it is in one's tender early years that such things will best take root and be most enduring and most valuable. First, then, I will say to you, my young friends—and I say it beseechingly, urgingly—

2 Always obey your parents, when they are present. This is the best policy in the long run, because if you don't they will make you. Most parents think they know better than you do, and you can generally make more by humorizing that superstition than you can by acting on your better judgment.

3 Be respectful to your superiors, if you have any, also to strangers, and sometimes to others. If a person offends you, and you are in doubt as to whether it was intentional or not, do not resort to extreme measures; simply watch your chance and hit him with a brick. That will be sufficient. If you shall find that he had not intended any offense, come out frankly and confess yourself in the wrong when you struck him; acknowledge it like a man and say you didn't mean to. Yes, always avoid violence; in this age of charity and kindliness, the time has gone by for such things. Leave dynamite to the low and unrefined.

4 Go to bed early, get up early—this is wise. Some authorities say get up with the sun; some others say get up with one thing, some with another. But a lark is really the best thing to get up with. It gives you a splendid reputation with everybody to know that you get up with the lark; and if you get the right kind of lark, and work at him right, you can easily train him to get up at half past nine every time—it is no trick at all.

5 Now as to the matter of lying. You want to be very careful about lying; otherwise you are nearly sure to get caught. Once caught, you can never again be, in the eyes of the good and the pure, what you were before. Many a young person has injured himself permanently, through a single clumsy and illfinished lie,

Text of a lecture given by Clemens in 1982.

the result of carelessness born of incomplete training. Some authorities hold that the young ought not to lie at all. That, of course, is putting it rather stronger than necessary; still, while I cannot go quite so far as that, I do maintain, and I believe I am right, that the young ought to be temperate in the use of this great art until practice and experience shall give them that confidence, elegance, and precision which alone can make the accomplishment graceful and profitable. Patience, diligence, painstaking attention to detail—these are the requirements; these, in time, will make the student perfect; upon these, and upon these only, may he rely as the sure foundation for future eminence. Think what tedious years of study, thought, practice, experience, went to the equipment of that peerless old master who was able to impose upon the whole world the lofty and sounding maxim that "truth is mighty and will prevail"—the most majestic compound fracture of fact which any of woman born has yet achieved. For the history of our race, and each individual's experience, are sown thick with evidence that a truth is not hard to kill and that a lie told well is immortal. There is in Boston a monument of the man who discovered anaesthesia; many people are aware, in these latter days, that that man didn't discover it at all, but stole the discovery from another man. Is this truth mighty, and will it prevail? Ah no, my hearers, the monument is made of hardy material, but the lie it tells will outlast it a million years. An awkward, feeble, leaky lie is a thing which you ought to make it your unceasing study to avoid; such a lie as that has no more real permanence than an average truth. Why, you might as well tell the truth at once and be done with it. A feeble, stupid, preposterous lie will not live two years—except it be a slander upon somebody. It is indestructible, then, of course, but that is no merit of yours. A final word: begin your practice of this gracious and beautiful art early—begin now. If I had begun earlier, I could have learned how.

Never handle firearms carelessly. The sorrowing suffering 6
that have been caused through the innocent but heedless handling of firearms by the young! Only four days ago, right in the next farmhouse to the one where I am spending the summer, a grandmother, old and gray and sweet, one of the loveliest spirits in the land, was sitting at her work, when her young grandson crept in and got down an old, battered, rusty gun which had not been touched for many years and was supposed not to be loaded, and pointed it at her, laughing and threatening to shoot. In her fright she ran screaming and pleading toward the door on the other side

of the room; but as she passed him he placed the gun almost against her very breast and pulled the trigger! He had supposed it was not loaded. And he was right—it wasn't. So there wasn't any harm done. It is the only case of that kind I ever heard of. Therefore just the same, don't you meddle with old unloaded firearms; they are the most deadly and unerring things that have ever been created by man. You don't have to take any pains at all with them; you don't have to have a rest, you don't have to have any sights on the gun, you don't have to take aim, even. No, you just pick out a relative and bang away, and you are sure to get him. A youth who can't hit a cathedral at thirty yards with a Gatling gun in three-quarters of an hour, can take up an old empty musket and bag his grandmother every time, at a hundred. Think what Waterloo would have been if one of the armies had been boys armed with old muskets supposed not to be loaded, and the other army had been composed of their female relations. The very thought of it makes one shudder.

7 There are many sorts of books; but good ones are the sort for the young to read. Remember that. They are a great, an inestimable, an unspeakable means of improvement. Therefore be careful in your selection, my young friends; be very careful; confine yourselves exclusively to Robertson's Sermons, Baxter's *Saint's Rest, The Innocents Abroad,* and works of that kind.

8 But I have said enough. I hope you will treasure up the instructions which I have given you, and make them a guide to your feet and a light to your understanding. Build your character thoughtfully and painstakingly upon these precepts, and by and by, when you have got it built, you will be surprised and gratified to see how nicely and sharply it resembles everybody else's.

The Death of the Moth

Virginia Woolf

Moths that fly by day are not properly to be called moths; they 1 do not excite that pleasant sense of dark autumn nights and ivy-blossom which the commonest yellow underwing asleep in the shadow of the curtain never fails to rouse in us. They are hybrid creatures, neither gay like butterflies nor sombre like their own species. Nevertheless the present specimen, with his narrow hay-coloured wings, fringed with a tassel of the same colour, seemed to be content with life. It was a pleasant morning, mid-September, mild, benignant, yet with a keener breath than that of the summer months. The plough was already scoring the field opposite the window, and where the share had been, the earth was pressed flat and gleamed with moisture. Such vigour came rolling in from the fields and the down beyond that it was difficult to keep the eyes strictly turned upon the book. The rooks too were keeping one of their annual festivities; soaring round the tree-tops until it looked as if a vast net with thousands of black knots in it has been cast up into the air; which, after a few moments sank slowly down upon the trees until every twig seemed to have a knot at the end of it. Then, suddenly, the net would be thrown into the air again in a wider circle this time, with the utmost clamour and vociferation, as though to be thrown into the air and settle slowly down upon the tree-tops were a tremendously exciting experience.

The same energy which inspired the rooks, the ploughmen, 2 the horses, and even, it seemed, the lean bare-backed downs, sent the moth fluttering from side to side of his square of the window-pane. One could not help watching him. One was, indeed, conscious of a queer feeling of pity for him. The possibilities of pleasure seemed that morning so enormous and so various that to have only a moth's part in life, and a day moth's at that, appeared a hard fate, and his zest in enjoying his meagre opportunities to the full, pathetic. He flew vigorously to one corner of his compartment, and, after waiting there a second, flew across to the other. What remained for him but to fly to a third corner and then to a fourth? That was all he could do, in spite of the size of the downs, the width of the sky, the far-off smoke of houses, and the romantic voice, now and then, of a steamer out at sea. What he could do he did. Watching him, it seemed as if a fibre, very thin but pure, of the enormous energy of the world had been thrust into his frail and diminutive body. As often as he crossed the pane, I could fancy that a thread of vital light became visible. He was little or nothing but life.

3 Yet, because he was so small, and so simple a form of the energy that was rolling in at the open window and driving its way through so many narrow and intricate corridors in my own brain and in those of other human beings, there was something marvelous as well as pathetic about him. It was as if someone had taken a tiny bead of pure life and decking it as lightly as possible with down and feathers, had set it dancing and zigzagging to show us the true nature of life. Thus displayed one could not get over the strangeness of it. One is apt to forget all about life, seeing it humped and bossed and garnished and cumbered so that it has to move with the greatest circumspection and dignity. Again, the thought of all that life might have been had he been born in any other shape caused one to view his simple activities with a kind of pity.

4 After a time, tired by his dancing apparently, he settled on the window ledge in the sun, and the queer spectacle being at an end, I forgot about him. Then, looking up, my eye was caught by him. He was trying to resume his dancing, but seemed either so stiff or so awkward that he could only flutter to the bottom of the window-pane; and when he tried to fly across it he failed. Being intent on other matters I watched these futile attempts for a time without thinking, unconsciously waiting for him to resume his flight, as one waits for a machine, that has stopped momentarily, to start again without considering the reason for its failure. After perhaps a seventh attempt he slipped from the wooden ledge and fell, fluttering his wings, on to his back on the window-sill. The helplessness of his attitude roused me. It flashed upon me that he was in difficulties; he could no longer raise himself, his legs struggled vainly. But, as I stretched out a pencil, meaning to help him to right himself, it came over me that the failure and awkwardness were the approach of death. I laid the pencil down again.

5 The legs agitated themselves once more. I looked as if for the enemy against which he struggled. I looked out of doors. What had happened there? Presumably it was midday, and work in the fields had stopped. Stillness and quiet had replaced the previous animation. The birds had taken themselves off to feed in the brooks. The horses stood still. Yet the power was there all the same, massed outside indifferent, impersonal, not attending to

anything in particular. Somehow it was opposed to the little hay-coloured moth. It was useless to try to do anything. One could only watch the extraordinary efforts made by those tiny legs against an oncoming doom which could, had it chosen, have submerged an entire city, not merely a city, but masses of human beings; nothing, I knew, had any chance against death. Nevertheless after a pause of exhaustion the legs fluttered again. It was superb this last protest, and so frantic that he succeeded at last in righting himself. One's sympathies, of course, were all on the side of life. Also, when there was nobody to care or to know, this gigantic effort on the part of an insignificant little moth, against a power of such magnitude, to retain what no one else valued or desired to keep, moved one strangely. Again, somehow, one saw life, a pure bead. I lifted the pencil again, useless though I knew it to be. But even as I did so, the unmistakable tokens of death showed themselves. The body relaxed, and instantly grew stiff. The struggle was over. The insignificant little creature now knew death. As I looked at the dead moth, this minute wayside triumph of so great a force over so mean an antagonist filled me with wonder. Just as life had been strange a few minutes before, so death was now as strange. The moth having righted himself now lay most decently and uncomplainingly composed. O yes, he seemed to say, death is stronger than I am.

I Have a Dream

Martin Luther King, Jr.

1 Five score years ago, a great American, in whose symbolic shadow we stand, signed the Emancipation Proclamation. This momentous decree came as a great beacon light of hope to millions of Negro slaves who had been seared in the flames of withering injustice. It came as a joyous daybreak to end the long night of captivity.

2 But one hundred years later, we must face the tragic fact that the Negro is still not free. One hundred years later, the life of the Negro is still sadly crippled by the manacles of segregation and the chains of discrimination. One hundred years later, the Negro lives on a lonely island of poverty in the midst of a vast ocean of material prosperity. One hundred years later, the Negro is still languishing in the corners of American society and finds himself an exile in his own land. So we have come here today to dramatize an appalling condition.

3 In a sense we have come to our nation's capital to cash a check. When the architects of our republic wrote the magnificent words of the Constitution and the Declaration of Independence, they were signing a promissory note to which every American was to fall heir. This note was a promise that all men would be guaranteed the unalienable rights of life, liberty, and the pursuit of happiness.

4 It is obvious today that America has defaulted on this promissory note insofar as her citizens of color are concerned. Instead of honoring this sacred obligation, America has given the Negro people a bad check; a check which has come back marked "insufficient funds." But we refuse to believe that the bank of justice is bankrupt. We refuse to believe that there are insufficient funds in the great vaults of opportunity of this nation. So we have come to cash this check—a check that will give us upon demand the riches of freedom and the security of justice. We have also come to this hallowed spot to remind America of the fierce urgency of *now.* This is no time to engage in the luxury of cooling off or to take the tranquilizing drugs of gradualism. *Now* is the time to make real the promises of Democracy. *Now* is the time to rise from the dark and desolate valley of segregation to the sunlit path of racial justice. *Now* is the time to open the doors of opportunity to all of God's children. *Now* is the time to lift our nation from the quicksands of racial injustice to the solid rock of brotherhood.

It would be fatal for the nation to overlook the urgency of the moment and to underestimate the determination of the Negro. This sweltering summer of the Negro's legitimate discontent will not pass until there is an invigorating autumn of freedom and equality. 1963 is not an end, but a beginning. Those who hope that the Negro needed to blow off steam and will now be content will have a rude awakening if the nation returns to business as usual. There will be neither rest nor tranquility in America until the Negro is granted his citizenship rights. The whirlwinds of revolt will continue to shake the foundations of our nation until the bright day of justice emerges. 5

But there is something that I must say to my people who stand on the warm threshold which leads into the palace of justice. In the process of gaining our rightful place we must not be guilty of wrongful deeds. Let us not seek to satisfy our thirst for freedom by drinking from the cup of bitterness and hatred. We must forever conduct our struggle on the high plane of dignity and discipline. We must not allow our creative protest to degenerate into physical violence. Again and again we must rise to the majestic heights of meeting physical force with soul force. The marvelous new militancy which has engulfed the Negro community must not lead us to a distrust of all white people, for many of our white brothers, as evidenced by their presence here today, have come to realize that their destiny is tied up with our destiny and their freedom is inextricably bound to our freedom. We cannot walk alone. 6

And as we walk, we must make the pledge that we shall march ahead. We cannot turn back. There are those who are asking the devotees of civil rights, "When will you be satisfied?" We can never be satisfied as long as the Negro is the victim of the unspeakable horrors of police brutality. We can never be satisfied as long as our bodies, heavy with the fatigue of travel, cannot gain lodging in the motels of the highways and the hotels of the cities. We cannot be satisfied as long as the Negro's basic mobility is from a smaller ghetto to a larger one. We can never be satisfied as long as a Negro in Mississippi cannot vote and a Negro in New York believes he has nothing for which to vote. No, no, we are not satisfied, and will not be satisfied until justice rolls down like waters and righteousness like a mighty stream. 7

I am not unmindful that some of you have come here out of great trials and tribulations. Some of you have come fresh from narrow jail cells. Some of you have come from areas where your 8 quest for freedom left you battered by the storms of persecution and staggered by the winds of police brutality. You have been the veterans of creative suffering. Continue to work with the faith that unearned suffering is redemptive.

9 Go back to Mississippi, go back to Alabama, go back to South Carolina, go back to Georgia, go back to Louisiana, go back to the slums and ghettos of our northern cities, knowing that somehow this situation can and will be changed. Let us not wallow in the valley of despair.

10 I say to you today, my friends, that in spite of the difficulties and frustrations of the moment I still have a dream. It is a dream deeply rooted in the American dream.

11 I have a dream that one day this nation will rise up and live out the true meaning of its creed: "We hold these truths to be self-evident; that all men are created equal."

12 I have a dream that one day on the red hills of Georgia the sons of former slaves and the sons of former slaveowners will be able to sit down together at the table of brotherhood.

13 I have a dream that one day even the state of Mississippi, a desert state sweltering with the heat of injustice and oppression, will be transformed into an oasis of freedom and justice.

14 I have a dream that my four little children will one day live in a nation where they will not be judged by the color of their skin but by the content of their character.

15 I have a dream today.

16 I have a dream that one day the state of Alabama, whose governor's lips are presently dripping with the words of interposition and nullification, will be transformed into a situation where little black boys and black girls will be able to join hands with little white boys and white girls and walk together as sisters and brothers.

17 I have a dream today.

18 I have a dream that one day every valley shall be exalted, every hill and mountain shall be made low, the rough places will be made plain, and the crooked places will be made straight, and the glory of the Lord shall be revealed, and all flesh shall see it together.

19 This is our hope. This is the faith with which I return to the South. With this faith we will be able to hew out of the mountain of despair a stone of hope. With this faith we will be able to transform the jangling discords of our nation into a beautiful symphony of brotherhood. With this faith we will be able to work

together, to pray together, to struggle together, to go to jail together, to stand up for freedom together, knowing that we will be free one day.

This will be the day when all of God's children will be able to sing with new meaning 20

> My country, 'tis of thee,
> Sweet land of liberty,
>   Of thee I sing:
> Land where my fathers died,
> Land of the pilgrims' pride,
> From every mountain-side
>   Let freedom ring.

And if America is to be a great nation this must become true. So let freedom ring from the prodigious hilltops of New Hampshire. Let freedom ring from the mighty mountains of New York. Let freedom ring from the heightening Alleghenies of Pennsylvania! 21

Let freedom ring from the snowcapped Rockies of Colorado! 22

Let freedom ring from the curvaceous peaks of California! 23

But not only that; let freedom ring from Stone Mountain of Georgia! 24

Let freedom ring from Lookout Mountain of Tennessee! 25

Let freedom ring from every hill and molehill of Mississippi. From every mountainside, let freedom ring. 26

When we let freedom ring, when we let it ring from every village and every hamlet, from every state and every city, we will be able to speed up that day when all of God's children, black men and white men, Jews and Gentiles, Protestants and Catholics, will be able to join hands and sing in the words of the old Negro spiritual, "Free at last! free at last! thank God almighty, we are free at last!" 27

MODERN ESSAYS

An American Childhood

Annie Dillard

1 When everything else has gone from my brain—the President's name, the state capitals, the neighborhoods where I lived, and then my own name and what it was on earth I sought, and then at length the faces of my friends, and finally the faces of my family—when all this has dissolved, what will be left, I believe, is topology: the dreaming memory of land as it lay this way and that.

2 I will see the city poured rolling down the mountain valleys like slag, and see the city lights sprinkled and curved around the hills' curves, rows of bonfires winding. At sunset a red light like housefires shines from the narrow hillside windows; the houses' bricks burn like glowing coals.

3 The three wide rivers divide and cool the mountains. Calm old bridges span the banks and link the hills. The Allegheny River flows in brawling from the north, from near the shore of Lake Erie, and from Lake Chautauqua in New York and eastward. The Monongahela River flows in shallow and slow from the south, from West Virginia. The Allegheny and the Monongahela meet and form the westward-wending Ohio.

4 Where the two rivers join lies an acute point of flat land from which rises the city. The tall buildings rise lighted to their tips. Their lights illumine other buildings' clean sides, and illumine the narrow city canyons below, where people move, and shine reflected red and white at night from the black waters.

5 When the shining city, too, fades, I will see only those forested mountains and hills, and the way the rivers lie flat and moving among them, and the way the low land lies wooded among them, and the blunt mountains rise in darkness from the rivers' banks, steep from the rugged south and rolling from the north, and from farther, from the inclined eastward plateau where the high ridges begin to run so long north and south unbroken that to get around them you practically have to navigate Cape Horn.

6 In those first days, people said, a squirrel could run the long length of Pennsylvania without ever touching the ground. In those first days, the woods were white oak and chestnut, hickory, maple, sycamore, walnut, wild ash, wild plum, and white pine.

The pine grew on the ridgetops where the mountains' lumpy spines stuck up and their skin was thinnest.

The wilderness was uncanny, unknown. Benjamin Franklin had already invented his stove in Philadelphia by 1753, and Thomas Jefferson was a schoolboy in Virginia; French soldiers had been living in forts along Lake Erie for two generations. But west of the Alleghenies in western Pennsylvania, there was not even a settlement, not even a cabin. No Indians lived there, or even near there. 7

Wild grapevines tangled the treetops and shut out the sun. Few songbirds lived in the deep woods. Bright Carolina parakeets—red, green, and yellow—nested in the dark forest. There were ravens then, too. Woodpeckers rattled the big trees' trunks, ruffed grouse whirred their tail feathers in the fall, and every long once in a while a nervous gang of empty-headed turkeys came hustling and kicking through the leaves—but no one heard any of this, no one at all. 8

In 1753, young George Washington surveyed for the English this point of land where rivers met. To see the forest-blurred lay of the land, he rode his horse to a ridgetop and climbed a tree. He judged it would make a good spot for a fort. And an English fort it became, and a depot for Indian traders to the Ohio country, and later a French fort and way station to New Orleans. 9

But it would be another ten years before any settlers lived there on that land where the rivers met, lived to draw in the flowery scent of June rhododendrons with every breath. It would be another ten years before, for the first time on earth, tall men and women lay exhausted in their cabins, sleeping in the sweetness, worn out from planting corn. 10

A Twofer's Lament

Yolanda Cruz

1 I grew up and graduated college in the Philippines; I've spent the last twenty years in the United States. I see a tremendous difference between the perception of education there versus here, then versus now—of whether securing an education is viewed as an opportunity or as a privilege.

2 I received a bachelor of science degree from the University of the Philippines. I was an agricultural science major, but I had just as many courses in engineering as in philosophy, in language as in math, in literature as in physics, in physical education as in the arts. The five-year curriculum was extremely strict: inflexible in terms of course choices, not only rigorous but quite brutal. There was no entrance exam; your freshman year *was* the entrance exam, and it was trial by fire. Anyone who survived the thirty-six-credit requirement was permitted to continue. We took those painful but marvelously edifying years one at a time, savoring and suffering every midterm exam, sweating every horrific term paper, including the dreaded senior thesis. Every student wrote one based on original research—that is, every student who made it to senior year. Many didn't.

3 Courses were taught in English (in a country whose citizens speak approximately 100 non-English languages and dialects) by a faculty that was 40 percent women. These women were not merely technicians or teaching assistants but professors, deans, lecturers and research scientists, with Ph.D.s from American, Canadian, Australian and European universities, just like the men. At the time, our student body was also about 40 percent women, although in recent years, I'm told, this figure has grown to about 50 percent. We enjoyed no financial aid or student loans; we went to university the old-fashioned way—on full scholarship, paying full tuition or working. There was only one criterion for admission: academic excellence. The occasional congressman's son or niece got in, but the brutal freshman year was a great equalizer. It didn't matter that your grandfather had graduated fifty years before either, because that didn't guarantee whether or not you would do well in your courses. It didn't matter how tall you were, what ethnic group you represented, what sport you played or what sex you were; or that you came from a finishing school in Switzerland or a public school in the boonies.

The only criterion for admission—and for success—was that you could do your stuff and do it well.

It struck me as extraordinary, therefore, that when I matriculated at the University of California at Berkeley, I had to identify myself by sex, ethnicity and other criteria such as financial need. I considered my Graduate Record Examination and Test of English as a Foreign Language scores as relevant; after all, I was to be a graduate student in an English-speaking country. But sex? Ethnicity? I wasn't even sure what "ethnicity" meant. (Even today, I'm not sure whether I'm Asian, Filipino or Pacific Islander. I usually end up checking the box marked "other.") Financial need? That was my concern; I intended to work my way through graduate school. I wasn't asking for privileges, only opportunities. 4

Imagine my shock, then, when one of the second-year grad students came up to me, shook my hand and said that he had been looking forward to meeting the "twofer" who had been accepted that year. I discovered later that "twofer" meant I was a double whammy; not only was I a woman in a male-dominated field, but I was also not white. Little did that second-year student know that I was transferring from another department and had been accepted into his department because I had aced all the courses there. I remember feeling diminished by his remark; it was as if I had somehow been accepted because my sex and skin color made up for my lack of smarts. Years later I had a similar jolt. In 1986, shortly after I took my present teaching job, I asked one of my colleagues if my sex and ethnicity had anything to do with my getting hired. He said yes: it was affirmative action. And there I was, assuming I had gotten the job because I was good. 5

Until recently I thought nothing of this. I figured it came with the territory of living a foreigner's life in an alien country. Then a talk with one of my research students, a Hispanic-American woman, brought back a bit of the pain. Last year this student was accepted into Ph.D. programs in molecular biology at Harvard, CalTech and the University of California at San Francisco. After recounting for me the back and forth of her interviews, she asked a poignant question: Did I think she'd been admitted to these universities because she is a twofer? At that moment, I realized my experience at Berkeley had nothing to do with my being foreign. It had to do with the American perception of education as a privilege, deserved or undeserved. My student did not want an unde- 6 served privilege. Like me, all she wanted was an opportunity. How cruel that a person so young, so bright, is made to feel that she is being given a handout, not a hand.

7 More recently I encountered, in an exchange with my daughter, Elsa, the confusion that seems to accompany the delineation between opportunity and privilege. After Elsa came home with a perfect eighth-grade report card, she regaled me with tales of her classmates who, after earning high marks, had received from their parents gifts, allowance increases, shopping sprees, and spring breaks in the Caribbean. "Why can't I get $20 for every A I bring home, Mama?" Elsa asked.

8 Smart kid. She knew she had me cornered. I searched my mind for a fitting response. Without losing my cool, I said, "My dear, I love you very much, but in this household you do not get paid for A's. Instead, you will have to pay me for every grade of B or lower that you bring home." Elsa realized that an A was simply an opportunity to move farther in her coursework; it did not entitle her to an automatic privilege.

9 Being awarded a privilege and given an opportunity are similar in that the odds are stacked in the recipient's favor. With privilege, however, the odds are handed to you; with opportunity, you stack the odds in your own favor. It is hard not to see the dignity in the latter enterprise—the sublime feeling of self-worth, self-respect and pride that it engenders.

Women Are Just Better

Anna Quindlen

My favorite news story so far this year was the one saying that in England scientists are working on a way to allow men to have babies. I'd buy tickets to that. I'd be happy to stand next to any man I know in one of those labor rooms the size of a Volkswagen trunk and whisper "No, dear, you don't really need the Demerol; just relax and do your second-stage breathing." It puts me in mind of an old angry feminist slogan: "If men got pregnant, abortion would be a sacrament." I think this is specious. If men got pregnant, there would be safe, reliable methods of birth control. They'd be inexpensive, too. 1

I can almost hear some of you out there thinking that I do not like men. This isn't true. I have been married for some years to a man and I hope that someday our two sons will grow up to be men. All three of my brothers are men, as is my father. Some of my best friends are men. It is simply that I think women are superior to men. There, I've said it. It is my dirty little secret. We're not supposed to say it because in the old days men used to say that women were superior. What they meant was that we were too wonderful to enter courtrooms, enjoy sex, or worry our minds about money. Obviously, this is not what I mean at all. 2

The other day a very wise friend of mine asked: "Have you ever noticed that what passes as a terrific man would only be an adequate woman?" A Roman candle went off in my head; she was absolutely right. What I expect from my male friends is that they are polite and clean. What I expect from my female friends is unconditional love, the ability to finish my sentences when I am sobbing, a complete and total willingness to pour their hearts out to me, and the ability to tell me why the meat thermometer isn't supposed to touch the bone. 3

The inherent superiority of women came to mind just the other day when I was reading about sanitation workers. New York City has finally hired women to pick up the garbage, which makes sense to me, since, as I discovered, a good bit of being a woman consists of picking up garbage. There was a story about the hiring of these female sanitation workers, and I was struck by the fact that I could have written that story with- 4 out ever leaving my living room—a reflection not upon the quality of the reporting but the predictability of the male sanitation workers' responses.

5 The story started by describing the event, and then the two women, who were just your average working women trying to make a buck and get by. There was something about all the maneuvering that had to take place before they could be hired, and then there were the obligatory quotes from male sanitation workers about how women were incapable of doing this job. They were similar to quotes I have read over the years suggesting that women are not fit to be rabbis, combat soldiers, astronauts, firefighters, judges, ironworkers, and President of the United States. Chief among them was a comment from one sanitation worker, who said it just wasn't our kind of job, that women were cut out to do dishes and men were cut out to do yard work.

6 As a woman who has done dishes, yard work, and tossed a fair number of Hefty bags, I was peeved—more so because I would fight for the right of any laid-off sanitation man to work, for example, at the gift-wrap counter at Macy's, even though any woman knows that men are hormonally incapable of wrapping packages and tying bows.

7 I simply can't think of any jobs any more that women can't do. Come to think of it, I can't think of any job women don't do. I know lots of men who are full-time lawyers, doctors, editors and the like. And I know lots of women who are full-time lawyers and part-time interior decorators, pastry chefs, algebra teachers, and garbage slingers. Women are the glue that holds our day-to-day world together.

8 Maybe the sanitation workers who talk about the sex division of duties are talking about girls just like the girls that married dear old dad. Their day is done. Now lots of women know that if they don't carry the garbage bag to the curb, it's not going to get carried—either because they're single, or their husband is working a second job, or he's staying at the office until midnight, or he just left them.

9 I keep hearing that there's a new breed of men out there who don't talk about helping a woman as though they're doing you a favor and who do seriously consider leaving the office if a child comes down with a fever at school, rather than assuming that you will leave yours. But from what I've seen, there aren't enough of these men to qualify as a breed, only as a subgroup.

This all sounds angry; it is. After a lifetime spent with 10
winds of sexual change buffeting me this way and that, it still makes me angry to read the same dumb quotes with the same dumb stereotypes that I was reading when I was eighteen. It makes me angry to realize that after so much change, very little is different. It makes me angry to think that these two female sanitation workers will spend their days doing a job most of their co-workers think they can't handle, and then they will go home and do another job most of their co-workers don't want.

Death of a Homeless Man

Scott Russell Sanders

1 This past winter, not long after Christmas, a man named John Griffin burned to death in South Boston. He was fifty-five, a veteran of the Korean War, an alcoholic, well-known and liked by his neighbors, who remembered him as a streetwise philosopher, a genial storyteller, gracious and kindly and full of song. His body, from which all the clothing had been burned away except for tatters at ankles and wrists, was found twenty feet from Dorchester Bay. Evidently Griffin had collapsed on his way to the water, for staggery footprints marked a trail back over the sand to his plywood hovel. No one knows what set his clothes alight, whether a cigarette or the fire of twigs and cardboard he'd been using to keep warm

2 So there you have it, the death of a homeless man. At this point a good journalist would tell you how many hundreds of thousands, even how many millions, of souls go to sleep cold and hungry and roomless each night in this rich land. Although I am thankful for those conscientious reporters, I am not any sort of journalist, good or bad; I am a novelist, snagged on particulars. I cannot get beyond that charred body of John Griffin, those wristlets and anklets of cloth, those eloquent footprints in the sand, the quenching waters only a few paces beyond his outstretched arms. Instead of brooding on statistics about poverty, I keep seeing his little shanty cobbled together out of scavenged plywood, the cigarette butts and empty vodka bottles strewn on the ground.

3 As it happens, one of those who passed by John Griffin's homestead almost daily (while jogging) was Boston Mayor Raymond Flynn. Another who saw him regularly was a minister, Leonard Coopenwrath. Both men described Griffin as a friend, and both attended his funeral, along with a cardinal, the police commissioner, the state secretary for human affairs, and other dignitaries. No one could figure out what to do with Griffin alive, but they turned out in force to bury him.

4 Mayor Flynn was quoted in the papers as saying, "It goes to show you that this country is not meeting the needs of people with physical and mental problems." Indeed, indeed. The mayor seems to be a compassionate man, and so I respect his grief as genuine, although it occurs to me that the city of Boston, as the local portion of "this country," ought to shoulder part of the blame for Griffin's suffering.

As if in counterpoint, the Reverend Coopenwrath observed, "I don't think the system failed him. He wanted to live basically apart from shelters and we must respect that." I'm all for respecting a man's desires, but if those include a preference for spending the Boston winter in a plywood lean-to instead of a public shelter, I think I would take a hard look at the shelter. I would ask what sort of help this Korean War veteran received for his alcoholism, where he last worked, what agency last trained him for a job, what doctors last examined him; what relatives or neighbors or church ever thought of taking him in. 5

When I reflect on what my nation is up to, what it is achieving with all its huffing and puffing, I do not think about the Gross National Product or the Dow Jones Industrial Average; I think about John Griffin. The GNP, as everyone knows, or should know, is gross indeed, including the price of Griffin's funeral and vodka while ignoring the value of his stories and songs. The stock market seesaws wildly at news of a polyp on the President's colon, but does not so much as tremble over the incineration of John Griffin, would not tremble even if the suffering of all the jobless, homeless, futureless, people in America could be added together by some calculus into a Gross Misery Product. 6

There is no such calculus, for the simple reason that suffering, like death, is personal. Each of us meets it, or avoids it, inside the arena of his or her own skin. You can tote up dollars or tons or kilowatts or spectators, and arrive thereby at a number that might be cause for boasting or lamenting; but you cannot work arithmetic on pain. So much should be obvious in a country that lights candles at the shrine of individualism. We brag to the would about valuing the sovereignty of self. What we actually value is the right of (selected) individuals to accumulate wealth and power at the expense of community and planet. 7

On the night of his death, John Griffin was cold, abandoned, most likely drunk, and, in the last few minutes, wrapped in flames. He dwelt at the center of an utterly private agony. I can share in it only faintly, through imagination. That is where the drive for change begins, unshielded by statistics or mansions, in empathy with those who suffer. 8

The Ugly Tourist

Jamaica Kincaid

1 The thing you have always suspected about yourself the minute you become a tourist is true: a tourist is an ugly human being. You are not an ugly person all the time; you are not an ugly person ordinarily; you are not an ugly person day to day. From day to day, you are a nice person. From day to day, all the people who are supposed to love you on the whole do. From day to day as you walk down a busy street in the large and modern and prosperous city in which you work and live, dismayed, puzzled (a cliché, but only a cliché can explain you) at how alone you feel in this crowd, how awful it is to go unnoticed, how awful it is to go unloved, even as you are surrounded by more people than you could possibly get to know in a lifetime that lasted for millennia, and then out of the corner of your eye you see someone looking at you and absolute pleasure is written all over that person's face, and then you realize that you are not as revolting a presence as you think you are (for that look just told you so). And so, ordinarily, you are a nice person, an attractive person, a person capable of drawing to yourself the affection of other people (people just like you), a person at home in your own skin (sort of; I mean, in a way; I mean, your dismay and puzzlement are natural to you, because people like you just seem to be like that, and so many of the things people like you find admirable about yourselves—the things you think about, the things you think really define you—seem rooted in these feelings): a person at home in your own house (and all its nice house things), with its nice back yard (and its nice backyard things), at home on your street, your church, in community activities, your job, at home with your family, your relatives, your friends—you are a whole person. But one day, when you are sitting somewhere, alone in that crowd, and that awful feeling of displacedness comes over you, and really, as an ordinary person you are not well equipped to look too far inward and set yourself aright, because being ordinary is already so taxing, and being ordinary takes all you have out of you, and though the words "I must get away" do not actually pass across your lips, you make a leap from being that nice blob just sitting like a boob in your amniotic sac of the modern experience to being a person visiting heaps of death and ruin

and feeling alive and inspired at the sight of it; to being a person lying on some faraway beach, your stilled body stinking and glistening in the sand, looking like something first forgotten, then remembered, then not important enough to go back for; to being a person marveling at the harmony (ordinarily, what you would say is the backwardness) and the union these other people (and they are other people) have with nature. And you look at the things they can do with a piece of ordinary cloth, the things they fashion out of cheap, vulgarly coloured (to you) twine, the way they squat down over a hole they have made in the ground, the hole itself is something to marvel at, and since you are being an ugly person this ugly but joyful thought will swell inside you: their ancestors were not clever in the way yours were and not ruthless in the way yours were, for then would it not be you who would be in harmony with nature and backwards in that charming way? An ugly thing, that is what you are when you become a tourist, an ugly, empty thing, a stupid thing, a piece of rubbish pausing here and there to gaze at this and taste that, and it will never occur to you that the people who inhabit the place in which you have just paused cannot stand you, that behind their closed doors they laugh at your strangeness (you do not look the way they look); the physical sight of you does not please them; you have bad manners (it is their custom to eat their food with their hands; you try eating their way, you look silly; you try eating the way you always eat, you look silly); but they do not like the way you speak (you have an accent); they collapse helpless from laughter, mimicking the way they imagine you must look as you carry out some everyday bodily function. They do not like you. *They do not like me!* That thought never actually occurs to you. Still, you feel a little uneasy. Still, you feel a little foolish. Still, you feel a little out of place. But the banality of your own life is very real to you; it drove you to this extreme, spending your days and your nights in the company of people who despise you, people you do not like really, people you would not want to have as your actual neighbour. And so you must devote yourself to puzzling out how much of what you are told is really, really true (Is ground-up bottle glass in peanut sauce really a delicacy around here, or will it do just what you think ground-up bottle glass will do? Is this rare, multicoloured, snout-mouthed fish really an aphrodisiac, or will it cause you to fall asleep permanently?). Oh, the hard work all of this is, and is it any wonder, then, that on your return home you feel the need of a long rest, so that you can recover from your life as a tourist?

2 That the native does not like the tourist is not hard to explain. For every native of every place is a potential tourist, and every tourist is a native of somewhere. Every native everywhere lives a life of overwhelming and crushing banality and boredom and desperation and depression, and every deed, good and bad, is an attempt to forget this. Every native would like to find a way out, every native would like a rest, every native would like a tour. But some natives—most natives in the world—cannot go anywhere. They are too poor. They are too poor to escape the reality of their lives; and they are too poor to live properly in the place where they live, which is the very place you, the tourist, want to go—so when the natives see you, the tourist, they envy you, they envy your ability to leave your own banality and boredom, they envy your ability to turn their own banality and boredom into a source of pleasure for yourself.

He Rocked, I Reeled

Tama Janowitz

In high school, I took a remedial English class—maybe it wasn't remedial, exactly, but without my knowing it, I had signed up for some kind of English class for juvenile delinquents. 1

Well, it wasn't supposed to be a class for juvenile delinquents, but somehow everybody but me knew that that was who it was for; maybe it was listed in the course catalog as being for those students in the commercial program, the general program, whatever it was called to distinguish it from the academic precollege preparation program. 2

But anyway, on the first day I figured out who this course was directed at: The students were surly and wore leather jackets, and the girls all had shag hair-dos as opposed to straight and ironed, which was how the "nice" girls wore their hair. 3

Knowing me, I must have signed up for that class because it indicated that no work would be involved. And I was prepared for the worst, because somehow, having moved and switched schools so many times, I had been stuck in juvenile delinquent classes before. 4

The juvenile delinquent classes generally meant angry teachers and angry students who never read the books assigned and never spoke in class, which was no wonder because the teacher was generally contemptuous and sneering. 5

But this class ended up being different; the main thing was that the teacher, Mr. Paul Steele, didn't seem to know he was teaching students who weren't supposed to be able to learn. He assigned the books—by Sherwood Anderson, by Hemingway, by Melville—and somehow by the due date everyone had read them and was willing to talk about them. 6

Mr. Steele was a little distracted, a little dreamy, and most excellent. It was one of the few times up until that age I had a teacher who spoke to me—and the rest of the class—with the honesty of one adult talking to others, without pretense or condescension; there was no wrong or right, just discussion. 7

In college, I had another great course—in geology, a subject for which I had no interest. Once again, I had signed up for something that looked easy, a "gut" course to fulfill the science requirement. 8

But this guy—I believe his name was Professor Sand, an apt name for a geology teacher—was so excited and in love with 9 rocks, with everything pertaining to the formation of the earth, that to this day rocks and everything pertaining to the formation of the earth still get me excited.

10 Oolitic limestone, feldspar, gypsum, iron pyrite, Manhattan schist—the names were like descriptions of food, almost edible, and as around that time I was starting to become interested in writing, the enthusiasm that the teacher had for the subject was transferred to me into an enthusiasm for language.

11 And the names of the different periods—the Jurassic, the Pre-Cambrian—even though I can't remember much about them, the words still hold mystery and richness.

12 At the end of the semester, there was a field trip up to the Catskills, to put into practice some of the techniques discussed in class. We were taken to a fossil bed of trilobites where, due to the particular condition of the sedimentary bed, only the trilobite bodies had been preserved over the millennia.

13 After a few minutes of listening to the professor's explanation, I bent over and picked up a piece of rock with a small lump sticking out of it and took it over to him.

14 To me, all I had found was a rock with a lump; but Professor Sand was totally amazed—I was the only one ever to find a fossilized trilobite complete with head.

15 Really, at that point there was little to stop me from becoming a geologist except for the fact that I knew I could never do anything involving numbers, weights or measurements, which I suspected would at some point have some bearing on the subject.

16 I remember another teacher, in graduate school, Francine du Plessix Gray, who taught a course called Religion and Literature—another subject in which I had no interest. But the way she spoke was so beautiful, in an accent slightly French-tinged. And because she was so interested in her topic, the students became interested, and her seminars were alive and full of argument.

17 Of course, I had many other fine teachers along the way, but the ones who stand out in my mind were those who were most enthusiastic about what they were teaching.

18 Many subjects in which I initially thought I was interested were totally destroyed for me by the teacher's dry, aloof, pompous, disengaged way of speaking.

19 But when the teacher was as excited about the topic—as if he or she was still a little kid, rushing in from the yard to tell a story—that was when the subject became alive for me.

Glossary

Abstract and concrete are ways of describing important qualities of language. Abstract words are not associated with real, material objects that are related directly to the five senses. Such words as "love," "wisdom," "patriotism," and "power" are abstract because they refer to ideas rather than to things. Concrete language, on the other hand, names things that can be perceived by the five senses. Words like "table," "smoke," "lemon," and "halfback" are concrete. Generally you should not be too abstract in writing. It is best to employ concrete words naming things that can be seen, touched, smelled, heard, or tasted in order to support your more abstract ideas.

Allusion is a reference to some literary, biographical, or historical event. It is a "figure of speech" (a fresh, useful comparison) used to illuminate an idea. For instance, if you want to state that a certain national ruler is insane, you might refer to him as a "Nero"—an allusion to the emperor who burned Rome.

Alternating method in comparison and contrast involves a point-by-point treatment of the two subjects that you have selected to discuss. Assume that you have chosen five points to examine in a comparison of the Volkswagen Jetta (subject A) and the Honda Accord (subject B): cost, comfort, gas mileage, road handling, and frequency of repair. In applying the alternating method, you would begin by discussing cost in relation to A + B; then comfort in relation to A + B; and so on. The alternating method permits you to isolate points for a balanced discussion.

Ambiguity means uncertainty. A writer is ambiguous when using a word, phrase, or sentence that is not clear. Ambiguity usually results in misunderstanding, and should be avoided in essay writing. Always strive for clarity in your compositions.

Analogy is a form of figurative comparison that uses a clear illustration to explain a difficult idea or function. It is unlike a formal comparison in that its subjects of comparison are from different categories or areas. For example, an analogy likening "division of labor" to the activity of bees in a hive makes the first concept more concrete by showing it to the reader through the figurative comparison with the bees.

Antonym is a word that is opposite in meaning to that of another word: "hot" is an antonym of "cold"; "fat" is an antonym of "thin"; "large" is an antonym of "small."

Argumentation is a type of writing in which you offer reasons in favor of or against something. (See Chapter 11, pp. 385–389.)

Audience refers to the writer's intended readership. Many essays (including most in this book) are designed for a general audience, but a writer may also try to reach a special group. For example, William Zinsser in his essay "Simplicity" (pp. 38–47) might expect to appeal more to potential writers than to the general reading public. Similarly, Elizabeth Wong's "The Struggle to Be an All-American Girl" (pp. 129–136) could mean something particularly special to young Chinese Americans. The intended audience affects many of the writer's choices, including level of diction, range of allusions, types of figurative language, and so on.

Block method in comparison and contrast involves the presentation of all information about the first subject (A), followed by all information about the second subject (B). Thus, using the objects of comparison explained in the discussion of the "alternating method" (see p. 448), you would for the block method first present all five points about the Volkswagen. Then you would present all five points about the Honda. When using the block method, remember to present the same points for each subject, and to provide an effective transition in moving from subject A to subject B.

Causal analysis is a form of writing that examines causes and effects of events or conditions as they relate to a specific subject (see Chapter 10, pp. 346–350).

Characterization is the description of people. As a particular type of description in an essay, characterization attempts to capture as vividly as possible the features, qualities, traits, speech, actions, and personality of individuals.

Chronological order is the arrangement of events in the order that they happened. You might use chronological order to trace the history of the Vietnam War, to explain a scientific process, or to present the biography of a close relative or friend. When you order an essay by chronology, you are moving from one step to the next in time.

Classification is a pattern of writing in which the author divides a subject into categories and then groups elements in each of those categories according to their relation to each other (see Chapter 8, pp. 269–273).

Clichés are expressions that were once fresh and vivid, but have become tired and worn from overuse. "I'm so hungry that I could eat a horse" is a typical cliché. People use clichés in conversation, but writers generally should avoid them.

Closings or "conclusions" are endings for your essay. Without a closing, your essay is incomplete, leaving the reader with the feeling that something important has been left out. There are numerous closing possibilities available to writers: summarizing main points in the essay; restating the main idea; using an effective quotation to bring the essay to an end; offering the reader the climax to a series of events; returning to the introduction and echoing it; offering a solution to a problem; emphasizing the topic's significance; or setting a new frame of reference by generalizing from the main thesis. Whatever type of closing you use, make certain that it ends the essay in a firm and emphatic way.

Coherence is a quality in effective writing that results from the careful ordering of each sentence in a paragraph, and each paragraph in the essay. If an essay is coherent, each part will grow naturally and logically from those parts that come before it. Coherence depends on the writer's ability to organize materials in a logical way, and to order segments so that the reader is carried along easily from start to finish. The main devices used in achieving coherence are transitions, which help to connect one thought with another.

Colloquial language is language used in conversation and in certain types of informal writing, but rarely in essays, business writing, or research papers. There is nothing wrong with colloquialisms like "gross," "scam," or "rap" when used in conversational settings. However, they are often unacceptable in essay writing—except when used sparingly for special effects.

Comparison/contrast is a pattern of essay writing treating similarities and differences between two subjects. (See Chapter 6, pp. 201–205.)

Composition is a term used for an essay or for any piece of writing that reveals a careful plan.

Conclusion (See *Closings*)

Concrete (See *Abstract and concrete*)

Connotation/denotation are terms specifying the way a word has meaning. Connotation refers to the "shades of meaning" that a word might have because of various emotional associations it calls up for writers and readers alike. Words like "American," "physician," "mother," "pig," and "San Francisco" have strong connotative overtones to them. With denotation, however, we are concerned not with the suggestive meaning of a word but with its exact, literal meaning. Denotation refers to the "dictionary definition" of a word—its exact meaning. Writers must understand the connotative and denotative value of words, and must control the shades of meaning that many words possess.

Context clues are hints provided about the meaning of a word by another word or words, or by the sentence or sentences coming before or after it. Thus in the sentence, "Mr. Rome, a true *raconteur,* told a story that thrilled the guests," we should be able to guess at the meaning of the italicized word by the context clues coming both before and after it. (A "raconteur" is a person who tells good stories.)

Definition is a method of explaining a word so that the reader knows what you mean by it. (See Chapter 7, pp. 233–238.)

Denotation (See *Connotation/denotation*)

Derivation is how a word originated and where it came from. Knowing the origin of a word can make you more aware of its meaning, and more able to use it effectively in writing. Your dictionary normally lists abbreviations (for example, O.E. for Old English, G. for Greek) for word origins and sometimes explains fully how they came about.

Description is a type of writing that uses details of sight, color, sound, smell, and touch to create a word picture and to explain or illustrate an idea. (See Chapter 3, pp. 93–97.)

Dialogue is the exact duplication in writing of something people say to each other. Dialogue is the reproduction of speech or conversation; it can add concreteness and vividness to an essay, and can also help to reveal character. When using dialogue, writers must be careful to use correct punctuation. Moreover, to use dialogue effectively in essay writing, you must develop an ear for the way other people talk, and an ability to create it accurately.

Diction refers to the writer's choice or use of words. Good diction reflects the topic of the writing. Malcolm X's diction, for example, is varied, including subtle descriptions in standard diction and conversational sarcasms. Levels of diction refer both to the purpose of the essay and to the writer's audience. Skillful choice of the level of diction keeps the reader intimately involved with the topic.

Division is that aspect of classification (see Chapter 8, pp. 269–273) in which the writer divides some large subject into categories. For example, you might divide "fish" into saltwater and freshwater fish; or "sports" into team and individual sports. Division helps writers to split large and potentially complicated subjects into parts for orderly presentation and discussion.

Effect is a term used in causal analysis (see Chapter 10, pp. 346–350) to indicate the outcome or expected result of a chain of happenings. When dealing with the analysis of effects, writers should determine whether they want to work with immediate or final effects, or both. Thus, a writer analyzing the effects of an accidental nuclear explosion might choose to analyze effects immediately after the blast, as well as effects that still linger.

Emphasis suggests the placement of the most important ideas in key positions in the essay. Writers can emphasize ideas simply by placing important ones at the beginning or at the end of the paragraph or essay. But several other techniques help writers to emphasize important ideas: (1) key words and ideas can be stressed by repetition; (2) ideas can be presented in climactic order, by building from lesser ideas at the beginning to the main idea at the end; (3) figurative language (for instance, a vivid simile) can call attention to a main idea; (4) the relative proportion of detail offered to support an idea can emphasize its importance; (5) comparison and contrast of an idea with other ideas can emphasize its importance; and (6) mechanical devices like underlining, capitalizing, and using exclamation points (all of which should be used sparingly) can stress significance.

Essay is the name given to a short prose work on a limited topic. Essays take many forms, ranging from a familiar narrative account of an event in your life to explanatory, argumentative, or critical investigations of a subject. Normally, in one way or the other, an essay will convey the writer's personal ideas about the subject.

Euphemism is the use of a word or phrase simply because it seems less distasteful or less offensive than another word. For instance, "mortician" is a euphemism for "undertaker"; "sanitation worker" for "garbage collector."

Fable is a narrative with a moral (see Chapter 4, pp. 124–128). The story from which the writer draws the moral can be either true or imaginary. When writing a fable, a writer must clearly present the moral to be derived from the narrative, as Rachel Carson does in "A Fable for Tomorrow."

Figurative language, as opposed to *literal,* is a special approach to writing that departs from what is typically a concrete, straightforward style. It involves a vivid, imaginative comparison that goes beyond plain or ordinary statements. For instance, instead of saying that "Joan is wonderful," you could write that "Joan is like a summer's rose" (a *simile*); "Joan's hair is wheat, pale and soft and yellow" (a *metaphor*); "Joan is my Helen of Troy" (an *allusion*); or use a number of other comparative approaches. Note that Joan is not a rose, her hair is not wheat, nor is she some other person named Helen. Figurative language is not logical; instead, it requires an ability on the part of the writer to create an imaginative comparison in order to make an idea more striking.

Flashback is a narrative technique in which the writer begins at some point in the action and then moves into the past in order to provide necessary background information. Flashback adds variety to the narrative method, enabling writers to approach a story not only in terms of straight chronology, but in terms of a back-

and-forth movement. However, it is at best a very difficult technique and should be used with great care.

General/specific words are necessary in writing, although it is wise to keep your vocabulary as specific as possible. General words refer to broad categories and groups, while specific words capture with more force and clarity the nature of a term. The distinction between general and specific language is always a matter of degree. "A woman walked down the street" is more general than "Mrs. Walker walked down Fifth Avenue," while "Mrs. Webster, elegantly dressed in a muslin suit, strolled down Fifth Avenue" is more specific than the first two examples. Our ability to use specific language depends on the extent of our vocabulary. The more words we know, the more specific we can be in choosing words.

Hyperbole is obvious and intentional exaggeration.

Illustration is the use of several examples to support an idea (see Chapter 5, pp. 162–166).

Imagery is clear, vivid description that appeals to our sense of sight, smell, touch, sound, or taste. Much imagery exists for its own sake, adding descriptive flavor to an essay, as when Richard Selzer in "The Discus Thrower" writes, "I unwrap the bandages from the stumps, and begin to cut away the black scabs and the dead, glazed fat with scissors and forceps. A shard of white bone comes loose." However, imagery can also add meaning to an essay. For example, when Orwell writes at the start of "A Hanging," "It was in Burma, a sodden morning of the rains. A sickly light, like yellow tinfoil, was slanting over the high walls into the jail yard," we see that the author uses imagery to prepare us for the somber and terrifying event to follow. Writers can use imagery to contribute to any type of wording, or they can rely on it to structure an entire essay. It is always difficult to invent fresh, vivid description, but it is an effort that writers must make if they wish to improve the quality of their prose.

Introductions are the beginning or openings of essays. Introductions should perform a number of functions. They should alert the reader to the subject, set the limits of the essay, and indicate what the *thesis* (or main idea) will be. Moreover, they should arouse the reader's interest in the subject, so that the reader will want to continue reading into the essay. There are several devices available to writers that will aid in the development of sound introductions.

1. Simply state the subject and establish the thesis. See the essay by E. B. White (p. 283).
2. Open with a clear, vivid description of a setting that will become important as your essay advances. Save your thesis for a later stage, but indicate what your subject is. See the essay by Erdrich (p. 98).

3. Ask a question or a series of questions, which you might answer in the introduction or in another part of the essay. See the Jordan essay (p. 245).
4. Tell an anecdote (a short, self-contained story of an entertaining nature) that serves to illuminate your subject. See the Staples essay (p. 167).
5. Use comparison or contrast to frame your subject and to present the thesis. See the Goodman essay (p. 217).
6. Establish a definitional context for your subject. See the Johnson essay (p. 261).
7. Begin by stating your personal attitude toward a controversial issue. See the Ivins essay (p. 390).

These are only some of the devices that appear in the introductions to essays in this text. Writers can also ask questions, give definitions, or provide personal accounts—there are many techniques that can be used to develop introductions. The important thing to remember is that you *need* an introduction to an essay. It can be a single sentence or a much longer paragraph, but it must accomplish its purpose—to introduce readers to the subject, and to engage them so that they want to explore the essay further.

Irony is the use of language to suggest the opposite of what is stated. Writers use irony to reveal unpleasant or troublesome realities that exist in life, or to poke fun at human weaknesses and foolish attitudes. For instance, in Orwell's "A Hanging," the men who are in charge of the execution engage in laughter and lighthearted conversation after the event. There is irony in the situation and in their speech because we sense that they are actually very tense—almost unnerved—by the hanging; their laughter is the opposite of what their true emotional state actually is. Many situations and conditions lend themselves to ironic treatment.

Jargon is the use of special words associated with a specific area of knowledge or a specific profession. It is similar to "shop talk" that members of a certain trade might know, but not necessarily people outside it. For example, the medical jargon in Kozol's essay helps him defend his opinion on a nonmedical subject. Use jargon sparingly in your writing, and be certain to define all specialized terms that you think your readers might not know.

Journalese is a level of writing associated with prose types normally found in newspapers and popular magazines. A typical newspaper article tends to present information factually or objectively; to use simple language and simple sentence structure; and to rely on relatively short paragraphs. It also stays close to the level of conversational English without becoming chatty or colloquial.

Metaphor is a type of figurative language in which an item from one category is compared briefly and imaginatively with an item from another area. Writers create metaphors to assign meaning to a word in an original way.

Narration is telling a story in order to illustrate an important idea (see Chapter 4, pp. 124–128).

Objective/subjective writing refers to the attitude that writers take toward their subject. When writers are objective, they try not to report their own personal feelings about their subject. They attempt to control, if not eliminate, their own attitude toward the topic. Thus in the essay by Roiphe (pp. 357–366), we learn about the underlying causes of divorce, but the writer doesn't try to convince us of the rightness or wrongness of it. Many essays, on the other hand, reveal the authors' personal attitudes and emotions. In Frisina's essay (pp. 77–83), the author's personal approach to the process of reading seems clear. She takes a highly subjective approach to the topic. Other essays, such as Kozol's (see pp. 406–416), blend the two approaches to help balance the author's expression of a strong opinion. For some kinds of college writing, such as business or laboratory reports, research papers, or literary analyses, it is best to be as objective as possible. But for many of the essays in composition courses, the subjective touch is fine.

Order is the manner in which you arrange information or materials in an essay. The most common ordering techniques are *chronological order* (involving time sequence); *spatial order* (involving the arrangement of descriptive details); *process order* (involving a step-by-step approach to an activity); *deductive order* (in which you offer a thesis and then the evidence to support it); and *inductive order* (in which you present evidence first and build toward the thesis). Some rhetorical patterns such as comparison and contrast, classification, and argumentation require other ordering techniques. Writers should select those ordering principles that permit them to present materials clearly.

Paradox is a statement that *seems* to be contradictory but actually contains an element of truth. Writers use it in order to call attention to their subject.

Parallelism is a variety of sentence structure in which there is "balance" or coordination in the presentation of elements. "I came, I saw, I conquered" is a good example of parallelism, presenting both pronouns and verbs in a coordinated manner. Parallelism can also be applied to several sentences and to entire paragraphs (see the Brady essay, pp. 395–400). It can be an effective way to emphasize ideas.

Personification is giving an object, thing, or idea lifelike or human qualities. Like all forms of figurative writing, personification adds freshness to description, and makes ideas vivid by setting up striking comparisons.

Point of view is the angle from which a writer tells a story. Many personal or informal essays take the *first-person* (or "I") point of view, as the essays by Malcolm X, Benjamin, Hughes, Orwell, and others reveal. The first-person "I" point of view is natural and fitting for essays when the writer wants to speak in a familiar and intimate way to the reader. On the other hand, the *third-person* point of view ("he," "she," "it," "they") distances the reader somewhat from the writer. The third-person point of view is useful in essays where writers are not talking exclusively about themselves, but about other people, things, and events, as in the essays by Kozol, Carson, and White. Occasionally, the second-person ("you") point of view will appear in essays, notably in essays involving process analysis where the writer directs the reader to do something; part of Ernest Hemingway's essay (which also uses a third-person point of view) uses this strategy. Other point-of-view combinations are possible when a writer wants to achieve a special effect—for example, combining *first-* and *second-person* points of view. The position that you take as a writer depends largely on the type of essay you write.

Prefix is one or more syllables attached to the front of another word in order to influence its meaning or to create a new word. A knowledge of prefixes and their meanings aids in establishing the meanings of words and in increasing the vocabulary that we use in writing. Common prefixes and their meanings include *bi-* (two), *ex-* (out, out of), *per-* (through), *pre-* (before), *re-* (again), *tele-* (distant), and *trans-* (across, beyond).

Process analysis is a pattern of writing that explains in a step-by-step way the methods for doing something or reaching a desired end (see Chapter 9, pp. 310–313).

Proposition is the main point in an argumentative essay. It is like a *thesis,* except that it usually presents an idea that is debatable or can be disputed.

Purpose refers to what a writer hopes to accomplish in a piece of writing. For example, the purpose may be *to convince* the reader to adopt a certain viewpoint (as in Kincaid's essay "The Ugly Tourist," pp. 443–445), *to explain* a process (as in Baker's "Slice of Life," pp. 321–326), or to allow the reader *to feel a dominant impression* (as in Cantwell's "The Burden of a Happy Childhood," pp. 118–122). Purpose helps a writer to determine which expository technique will dominate the essay's form, as well as what kinds of supporting examples will be used. Purpose and *audience* are often closely related.

Refutation is a technique in argumentative writing where you recognize and deal effectively with the arguments of your opponents. Your own argument will be stronger if you can refute—prove false or wrong—all opposing arguments.

Root is the basic part of a word. It sometimes aids us in knowing what the larger word means. Thus if we know that the root *doc-* means "teach" we might be able to figure out a word like "doctrine." *Prefixes* and *suffixes* are attached to roots to create words.

Sarcasm is a sneering or taunting attitude in writing. It is designed to hurt by ridiculing or criticizing. Basically, sarcasm is a heavy-handed form of irony, as when an individual says, "Well, you're exactly on time, aren't you" to someone who is an hour late, and says it with a sharpness in the voice, designed to hurt. Writers should try to avoid sarcastic writing and to use more acceptable varieties of irony and satire to criticize their subject.

Satire is the humorous or critical treatment of a subject in order to expose the subject's vices, follies, stupidities, and so forth. Brady, for instance, satirizes stereotyped notions of wives, hoping to change these attitudes by revealing them as foolish. Satire is a better weapon than sarcasm in the hands of the writer because satire is used to correct, whereas sarcasm merely hurts.

Sentimentality is the excessive display of emotion in writing, whether it is intended or unintended. Because sentimentality can distort the true nature of a situation, writers should use it cautiously, or not at all. They should be especially careful when dealing with certain subjects, for example the death of a loved one, the remembrance of a mother or father, a ruined romance, the loss of something valued, that lend themselves to sentimental treatment. Only the best writers—like Thomas, Paley, Hughes, and others in this text—can avoid the sentimental traps rooted in their subjects.

Simile is an imaginative comparison using "like" or "as." When Orwell writes, "A sickly light, like yellow tinfoil, was slanting over the high walls into the jail yard," he uses a vivid simile in order to reinforce the dull description of the scene.

Slang is a level of language that uses racy and colorful expressions associated more often with speech than with writing. Slang expressions like "Mike's such a dude" or "She's a real fox" should not be used in essay writing, except when the writer is reproducing dialogue or striving for a special effect. Hughes is one writer in this collection who uses slang effectively to convey his message to the reader.

Subjective (See *Objective/subjective*)

Suffix is a syllable or syllables appearing at the end of a word and influencing its meaning. As with prefixes and roots, you can build vocabulary and establish meanings by knowing about suffixes. Some typical suffixes are *-able* (capable of), *-al* (relating to), *-ic* (characteristic of), *-ion* (state of), *-er* (one who), which appear often in standard writing.

Symbol is something that exists in itself but also stands for something else. Thus the "stumps" in paragraph 19 of Selzer's essay "The Discus Thrower" are not just the patient's amputated legs, but they serve as symbols of the man's helplessness and immobility. As a type of figurative language, the symbol can be a strong feature in an essay, operating to add depth of meaning, and even to unify entire essays.

Synonym is a word that means roughly the same as another word. In practice, few words are exactly alike in meaning. Careful writers use synonyms to vary word choice, without ever moving too far from the shade of meaning intended.

Theme is the central idea in an essay; it is also often termed the *thesis.* Everything in an essay should support the theme in one way or another.

Thesis is the main idea in an essay. The *thesis sentence,* appearing early in the essay, and normally somewhere in the first paragraph, serves to convey the main idea to the reader in a clear way. It is always useful to state your central idea as soon as possible, and before you introduce other supporting ideas.

Title for an essay should be a short, simple indication of the contents of your essay. Titles like "The Ugly Tourist" and "I Want a Wife" convey the central subjects of these essays in brief, effective ways. Others, such as "The Blue Jay's Dance" and "Night Walker," also convey the central idea, but more abstractly. Always provide titles for your essays.

Tone is the writer's attitude toward his or her subject or material. An essay writer's tone may be objective ("Death in the Open"), ironic ("I Want a Wife"), comic ("Slice of Life"), nostalgic ("One Writer's Beginnings"), or a reflection of numerous other attitudes. Tone is the "voice" that you give to an essay; every writer should strive to create a "personal voice" or tone that will be distinctive throughout any type of essay under development.

Transition is the linking of one idea to the next in order to achieve essay coherence (see *Coherence*). Transitions are words that connect these ideas. Among the most common techniques to achieve smooth transition are: (1) repeating a key word or phrase; (2) using a pronoun to refer back to a key word or phrase; (3) relying on traditional connectives like "thus," "for example," "moreover," "therefore," "however," "finally," "likewise," "afterward," and "in conclusion"; (4) using parallel structure (see *Parallelism*); and (5) creating a sentence or an entire paragraph that serves as a bridge from one part of your essay to the next. Transition is best achieved when the writer presents ideas and details carefully and in logical order. Try not to lose the reader by failing to provide for adequate transition from idea to idea.

Unity is that feature in an essay where all material relates to a central concept and contributes to the meaning of the whole. To achieve a unified effect in an essay, the writer must design an introduction and conclusion, maintain a consistent tone and point of view, develop middle paragraphs in a coherent manner, and always stick to the subject, never permitting unimportant elements to enter. Thus, unity involves a successful blending of all elements that go into the creation of a sound essay.

Vulgarisms are words that exist below conventional vocabulary, and are not accepted in polite conversation. Always avoid vulgarisms in your own writing, unless they serve an illustrative purpose.

Acknowledgments

Baker, James T. "How Do We Find the Student in a World of Academic Gymnasts and Worker Ants?" by James T. Baker in *Chronicle of Higher Education,* 1982. Reprinted by permission of the author.

Baker, Russell. "Slice of Life" from *There's a Country in My Cellar* by Russell Baker. Copyright © 1990 by Russell Baker. Reprinted by permission of Don Congdon Associates, Inc.

Benjamin, Walter W. "When an 'A' Meant Something" by Walter W. Benjamin, originally appeared in *The Wall Street Journal,* December 3, 1997. Reprinted by permission of the author.

Brady, Judy. "I Want a Wife" by Judy Brady. Copyright © 1970 by Judy Brady. Reprinted by permission of the author.

Cantwell, Mary. "The Burden of a Happy Childhood" by Mary Cantwell, originally published in *The New York Times,* February 1, 1998. Reprinted by permission of the author.

Carson, Rachel. "A Fable for Tomorrow" from *Silent Spring* by Rachel Carson. Copyright © 1962 by Rachel L. Carson. Copyright © renewed 1990 by Roger Christie. Reprinted by permission of Houghton Mifflin Company. All rights reserved.

Castro, Janice. "Spanglish" by Janice Castro, originally published in *Time,* July 11, 1988. Copyright © 1988 Time, Inc. Reprinted by permission.

Clemens, Samuel. "Advice to Youth" by Samuel L. Clemens, a lecture given in 1882 and published in 1923. Public domain.

Cruz, Yolanda. "A Twofer's Lament" by Yolanda Cruz, originally published in *The New Republic,* October 17, 1994. Reprinted by permission of The New Republic. Copyright © 1994 The New Republic, Inc.

Dillard, Annie. Excerpt from *An American Childhood* by Annie Dillard. Copyright © 1987 by Annie Dillard. Reprinted by permission of HarperCollins Publishers, Inc.

Ehrenreich, Barbara. "What I've Learned from Men" by Barbara Ehrenreich. Reprinted by permission of *Ms.* Magazine, © 1985.

Erdrich, Louise. "The Blue Jay's Dance" from *The Blue Jay's Dance* by Louise Erdrich. Copyright © 1995 by Louise Erdrich. Reprinted by permission of HarperCollins Publishers, Inc.

Frisina, Ellen Tashie. "See Spot Run: Teaching My Grandmother to Read" by Ellen Tashic Frisina, © 1988. Reprinted by permission of the author. Ellen Tashie Frisina is a journalism professor at Hofstra University.

Gates, Jr., Henry Louis. "In the Kitchen" by Henry Louis Gates, Jr. Copyright © 1994 by Henry Louis Gates, Jr. Originally published in *The New Yorker.* Reprinted with permission of the author.

Golding, William. "Thinking As a Hobby" by William Golding. Originally appeared in *Holiday,* August 1961. Copyright © 1961 The Curtis Publishing Company.

Goodman, Ellen. "The Tapestry of Friendships," reprinted with the permission of Simon & Schuster, Inc., from *Close to Home* by Ellen Goodman. Copyright © 1979 by Ellen Goodman.

Gornick, Vivian. "My City: Apostles of the Faith That Books Matter" by Vivian Gornick, originally published in *The New York Times,* February 20, 1998. Copyright © 1998 by The New York Times Co. Reprinted by permission.

Hemingway, Ernest. "Camping Out," reprinted with the permission of Scribner, a division of Simon & Schuster, Inc., from *Ernest Hemingway, Dateline:Toronto,* edited by William White. Copyright © 1985 by Mary Hemingway, John Hemingway, Patrick Hemingway, and Gregory Hemingway.

Hughes, Langston. "Salvation" from *The Big Sea* by Langston Hughes. Copyright © 1940 by Langston Hughes. Copyright renewed © 1968 by Arna Bontemps and George Houston Bass. Reprinted by permission of Hill and Wang, a division of Farrar, Straus & Giroux, Inc.

Ingrassia, Michele. "The Body of the Beholder" by Michele Ingrassia, from *Newsweek,* June 24, 1995. © 1995 Newsweek, Inc. All rights reserved. Reprinted by permission.

Ivins, Molly. "Get a Knife, Get a Dog, but Get Rid of Guns" from *Nothin' but Good Times Ahead* by Molly Ivins. Copyright © 1993 by Molly Ivins. Reprinted by permission of Random House, Inc.

Jacoby, Susan. "When Bright Girls Decide that Math Is a Waste of Time" by Susan Jacoby, originally published in *The New York Times,* June 2, 1983. Reprinted by permission of Georges Borchardt, Inc.

Janowitz, Tama. "He Rocked, I Reeled" by Tama Janowitz. First appeared in *Newsday.* Reprinted by permission of International Creative Management, Inc. Copyright © 1989 by Tama Janowitz.

Johnson, Kirk. "Duh, Today's Kids Are, Like, Killing the English Language. Yeah, Right" by Kirk Johnson, originally published in *The New York Times,* August 9, 1998. Copyright © 1998 by The New York Times Co. Reprinted by permission.

Jordan, Suzanne Britt. "Fun, Oh, Boy. Fun. You Could Die from It" by Suzanne Britt Jordan, originally published in *The New York Times,* December 23, 1979. Copyright © 1979 by The New York Times Co. Reprinted by permission.

Kincaid, Jamaica. Excerpt from *A Small Place* by Jamaica Kincaid. Copyright © 1988 by Jamaica Kincaid. Reprinted by permission of Farrar, Straus & Giroux, Inc.

King, Martin Luther, Jr. "I Have a Dream" speech by Martin Luther King, Jr. Copyright © 1963 by Martin Luther King, Jr., copyright renewed 1991 by Coretta Scott King. Reprinted by permission.

King, Stephen. "Why Must We Crave Horror Movies" by Stephen King. Reprinted with permission. © Stephen King. All rights reserved. Originally appeared in *Playboy,* January 1982.

Kingston, Maxine Hong. "Catfish in the Bathtub," from *The Woman Warrior* by Maxine Hong Kingston. Copyright © 1975, 1976 by Maxine Hong Kingston. Reprinted by permission of Alfred A. Knopf, Inc.

Kozol, Jonathon. "Are the Homeless Crazy?" by Jonathon Kozol from "Distancing the Homeless" in *Yale Review,* 1988. Reprinted by permission of the author.

Naylor, Gloria. "A Word's Meaning" by Gloria Naylor, originally appeared in *The New York Times,* February 20, 1986. Reprinted by permission of Sterling Lord Literistic, Inc. Copyright 1986 by Gloria Naylor.

Orwell, George. "A Hanging" from *Shooting an Elephant and Other Essays* by George Orwell, copyright 1950 by Sonia Brownell Orwell and renewed 1978 by Sonia Pitt-Rivers, reprinted by permission of Harcourt, Inc. and the estate of the late Sonia Brownell Orwell and Martin Secker and Warburg Ltd.

Paley, Grace. "Traveling" by Grace Paley, originally published in *The New Yorker,* September 8, 1997, pp. 42–43. Reprinted by permission of the Elaine Markson Literary Agency.

Plato. "The Allegory of the Cave" from *The Republic* by Plato. Translation by F. M. Cornford.

Popkin, James and Katia Hetter. "America's Gambling Craze" by James Popkin and Katia Hetter, originally appeared in *U.S. News & World Report.* Copyright, August 25, 1997, U.S. News & World Report. Visit the Web site at www.usnews.com for additional information. Reprinted by permission.

Quindlen, Anna. "Women Are Just Better" from *Living Out Loud* by Anna Quindlen. Copyright © 1987 by Anna Quindlen. Reprinted by permission of Random House, Inc.

Ritchie, Robert C. "The Coast with the Most" by Robert C. Ritchie, originally published in *The New York Times,* August 1, 1997. Copyright © 1997 by The New York Times Co. Reprinted by permission.

Roiphe, Anne. "Why Marriages Fail" by Anne Roiphe in *Family Weekly,* February 1983. Copyright © 1983 by Anne Roiphe. Reprinted by permission of International Creative Management, Inc.

Sanders, Scott Russell. "Death of a Homeless Man" by Scott Russell Sanders, originally published in *The Progressive,* March 1981.

Selzer, Richard. "The Discus Thrower" from *Confessions of a Knife* by Richard Selzer. (New York: William Morrow, 1979.) Copyright © 1979 by David Goldman and Janet Selzer, Trustees. Reprinted by permission of Georges Borchardt, Inc., for the author.

Shute, Nancy. "Why Do We Age?" by Nancy Shute, originally appeared in *U.S. News & World Report.* Copyright August 25, 1997, U.S. News & World Report. Visit the Web site at www.usnews.com for additional information. Reprinted by permission.

Simon, Jerrold G. "How to Write a Resume" by Jerrold G. Simon, originally published in *Power of the Written Word,* © International Paper Company.

Staples, Brent. "Night Walker" (originally titled "Walk on By: A Black Man Ponders His Power to Alter Public Space") by Brent Staples in *Ms.* Magazine. Reprinted by permission of the author.

Tan, Amy. "Mother Tongue" by Amy Tan. Copyright © 1990 by Amy Tan. Originally appeared in *The Threepenny Review.* Used by permission of the author.

Thomas, Lewis. "Death in the Open" from *The Lives of a Cell* by Lewis Thomas. Copyright © 1973 by The Massachusetts Medical Society. Used by permission of Viking Penguin, a division of Penguin USA.

Viorst, Judith. "Friends, Good Friends—and Such Good Friends" by Judith Viorst. Copyright © 1977 by Judith Viorst. Originally appeared in *Redbook.* Reprinted by permission of Lescher & Lescher, Ltd.

Vonnegut, Kurt, Jr. "How to Write with Style" by Kurt Vonnegut, Jr. Copyright © 1996 International Paper Company. Reprinted with permission.

Welty, Eudora. Excerpt from *One Writer's Beginning* by Eudora Welty. Copyright © 1983, 1984 by Eudora Welty. Reprinted by permission of Harvard University Press, Cambridge, Mass.

White, E. B. "The Three New Yorks" from *Here Is New York* by E. B. White. Copyright © 1949 by E. B. White. Copyright renewed. Reprinted by permission of HarperCollins Publishers, Inc.

Wong, Elizabeth. "The Struggle to Be an All-American Girl" by Elizabeth Wong, originally appeared in the *Los Angeles Times.* Reprinted by permission of Writers & Artists Agency.

Woolf, Virginia. "The Death of the Moth" from *The Death of the Moth and Other Essays* by Virginia Woolf. Copyright © 1942 by Harcourt, Inc., and renewed 1970 by Marjorie T. Parsons, Executrix. Reprinted by permission of the publisher.

X, Malcolm. "Prison Studies" from *The Autobiography of Malcolm X* by Malcolm X with Alex Haley. Copyright © 1964 by Alex Haley and Malcolm X. Copyright © 1965 by Alex Haley and Betty Shabazz. Reprinted by permission of Random House, Inc.

Zinsser, William. "Simplicity" from *On Writing Well* by William Zinsser, 6th ed. Copyright © 1976, 1980, 1985, 1988, 1990, 1994, 1998 by William Zinsser. Reprinted by permission of the author.

Zuckerman, Mortimer B. "The Case for More Cops" by Mortimer B. Zuckerman, originally appeared in *U.S. News & World Report.* Copyright, May 9, 1994, U.S. News & World Report. Visit the Web site at www.usnews.com for additional information. Reprinted by permission.

Index of Authors and Titles